Caponomics: Building Super Bowl Champions

"Be the hero of your own movie." – Joe Rogan

"Then B.I. said, 'HOV remind yourself, nobody built like you, you design yourself.'" – Jay-Z

This book is dedicated to my grandfathers, Frank Malatesta and Alvey Moore, for deciding to get much more out of life than they were given. To my grandmothers, Gwen Malatesta and Dorothy Moore, for supporting them in all of their endeavors and helping to raise our families with the values you've instilled in all of us. And lastly, to my parents, Tim and Kate Moore, for always supporting and believing in me as I chase my dreams.

Table of Contents

Introduction

Upon completing *Moneyball: The Art of Winning an Unfair Game* by Michael Lewis and *The Extra 2%: How Wall Street Strategies Took a Major League Baseball Team from Worst to First* by Jonah Keri in early 2014, I sought out the NFL equivalent to find that nothing similar seemed to exist. At the time, I had begun writing about NFL contracts and the salary cap on my own blog, eventually being brought on at OverTheCap.com in July 2014.

Soon after, Jason Fitzgerald, Over The Cap's founder and lead writer, began writing about how past Super Bowl champions had constructed their salary cap and roster, while also sharing the data used in these articles with me. With the desire I had to find an NFL Moneyball equivalent, I felt this data provided me with an opportunity to create it through analyzing what past champions have done. Also, I came to writing about contracts to help prepare me for a career in the NFL industry, so understanding what NFL teams need to succeed appealed to me in that I might better understand the players I should recruit and sign plus an understanding of player contracts by understanding what NFL teams are looking for. From the salesman standpoint, with a potential career as an NFL agent, I figured by knowing what teams were looking to "buy," I'd know what to "sell" and how to sell players to these teams.

Regarding the need for an explanation of the business side of the NFL, so much of the talk and thought around the NFL centers on how to build each team, the moves and the rosters that teams need to compete for the playoffs and the opportunity for a Super Bowl. The high level of fan interest in these topics is proven by the way the NFL offseason has turned the NFL into a 12-month sport with free agency and the draft process taking over the news cycle. Much of this interest stems from the habit of all fans to consider the moves we would make if we were in charge of our favorite teams. This team building process appeals to us the same way trading cards once did, the same way Madden Franchise mode does, and the way that Fantasy Football appeals to so many of us making it a multi-billion dollar industry. As explained in chapter three, football is simulated "sport war," so I think for many of us it may spark an interest deep in our core and we wonder what we would do as general.

The salary cap principles explained in this book will help fans understand the moves the leaders of their favorite organizations make and the understanding of the salary cap gives fans the base understanding of everything else. When you know how a team is financially set up, when you see what they invest in, you can begin to get a picture for their roster construction and their on field strategy for success.

Through reading this book, readers will understand the organizational processes that each team needs to set up to succeed as well as the principles of valuing NFL players and teams through an understanding of cap costs and production value. This will help readers understand how each team is constructed and the moves the team could make in free agency and the draft to improve. By understanding the principles of value through an understanding of costs and production, readers will understand the thought process that organizations go through when making roster decisions. The reader will understand the decision to let the soon to be expensive receiver walk in free agency because the organization feels they have a rookie contract player or a lower cost veteran they can sign who can take on the departing receiver's role with 80% of the production, but a much smaller percentage of the cost, which then allows the team to become more well rounded in other phases of the game.

Understanding this valuation process in the NFL is one of the business principles from this book that will carry over to a reader's personal and professional lives. This book started with a pile of data and cap figures, but through the process of writing the book, I now have an understanding of how costs can be broken down in a way that helps articulate the value of each player. I had to consider things outside of the cap figures to understand what the cap figures mean in context, things like analytics, traditional stats, strategy, coaching philosophies and more. The future of many businesses is in data analytics and understanding value, and this book will provide an example of that in action in a field that many people enjoy, likely making it easier to digest. After reading this book, the reader will be able to look at data outside of football, combine that with an understanding of the objective that they're trying to accomplish, then create an understanding of how to use and adjust that data to accomplish the objective.

For a business or a person's personal life, the principles of this book can help you consider the aspects of your own life more objectively. It can help a reader question how their life's "inputs" create their "outputs" with diet and exercise being the most obvious example. I've seen a transformation in myself as I got rid of the extra post-football playing weight as I got up to 200 pounds due to a neck injury that restricted my ability to work out and have changed my inputs to get me down to a 165-pound jiu jitsu player who trains five days a week. This process can help a person think, "if I'm trying to accomplish X, then does the stuff I'm doing right now help me get to X?" In business, this same framework can help a business focus their resources toward the outcome they're trying to create.

This book will help the reader become a more intelligent fan; it will provide business insights that will apply elsewhere, and it's a fun, educational practice for understanding value. You'll understand what each kind of player should be worth with an understanding of a player's production and potential. It will help the reader understand how a team's front office and coaching staff should be built as well.

It's my hope that the information in this book can increase the amount of objective analysis seen in football writing, while raising the level of conversation to properly include a financial analysis of each team. With an understanding of team finances through the salary cap, you can really understand what teams are doing in the offseason with each move they make. This information will help writers and fans better explain teams in a more objective manner through understanding the value based decisions that teams make in pursuit of Super Bowl glory. The Super Bowl champion cap data with the offensive and defensive production metrics that are in the back of the book will allow readers to take the information provided by the book, combine it with past team financials, and past champion statistics to understand how their favorite team can be built in a similar manner as something that has worked before. If your team spends 13% of the cap on its quarterback, will it be able to produce on offense at a rate that overcomes a sub-par defense like the 2006 Colts, 2009 Saints, or 2011 Giants did? This process will help the reader understand the production balance that teams need to succeed and how they can use their 100% or 100 units of cap space to build the best roster to accomplish these objectives. It's the kind of stuff that helps a Jaguars fan understand how they've constructed a roster to accomplish these objectives. It's the kind of stuff that helps a Jaguars fan understand how they've constructed a roster that's been able to make up for, and hide, Blake Bortles inefficiencies in 2017. An analysis of this data, plus past Eagles and Chiefs data under Andy Reid, can help Eagles fans see how the roster they've build in 2017 is based on the production needs from past years with the huge benefit of Carson Wentz's low-cost contract.

Caponomics will help cut through much of the clutter in sports media that talks about things outside of the main objective, which is for teams to create sustainable, competitive organizations that can compete for Super Bowls. Readers will learn how the Patriots have stayed on top, you'll understand the various strategies for competing for a playoff spot and a Super Bowl, you'll better understand the moves teams make, and you might learn something that will help you create value in fantasy football if you can apply the lessons of Caponomics there.

I've spent the last three years writing for Over The Cap, researching current markets and various styles of roster construction based on this analysis with a focus and analysis on the strategies that Bill Belichick has used to consistently compete for champions for the last 17 seasons with 14 playoff appearances, 11 AFC Championship appearances, seven Super Bowl appearances, and five championships. With the current increase of information on the NFL salary cap led by Over The Cap as well as an increasing creep of analytics into NFL analysis led by sites like Pro Football Focus and Football Outsiders, fans will need to have a base understanding of both of these as the conversation around football evolves. Writers around the industry have already begun to incorporate analytics into their work and this book will help the reader have a foundation for understanding the future of football and football analysis.

In August 2015, early in the process of writing this book, the Eagles coaching staff under head coach-slash-General Manager Chip Kelly reached out to meet with me after seeing my mentions of this data on Over The Cap during that summer and attempting to re-construct the Super Bowl data themselves to no avail. Since then, even with Kelly leaving, as most of their front office stayed intact, the Eagles have constructed their roster in a manner that agrees with the numbers and beliefs expressed in this book. They also implemented a three quarterback strategy that I had suggested, but with their own improvements on my thoughts as they were able to re-sign Sam Bradford and acquire Chase Daniel and Carson Wentz. It's been fun to watch them construct a roster based around their young quarterback Carson Wentz, as he's a perfect fit for the Andy Reid/Doug Peterson West Coast system that Donovan McNabb ran in Philadelphia and that Alex Smith has run even better in Kansas City as Wentz is at a much lower-cost than Reid had at quarterback at either Philadelphia or Kansas City, and Wentz seems to be even better than the other two. With this roster construction, they had the cap space in 2017 to create a great offensive line, a stable of running backs, and a strong receiving group centered around tight end Zach Ertz with a top wide receiver on a one-year "prove it" deal in Alshon Jeffery, which has helped make Wentz look like an MVP candidate before tearing his ACL for a team that is 11-2 as I write this. The cap space has allowed them to build a formidable defense with a ferocious, penetrating defensive line that goes seven players deep.

The best proof of the information in this book working in practice is the Patriots, though; principles discovered through analyzing how Belichick does things has provided a foundation for understanding the whole salary cap system as he's turned the cap into an advantage through a higher level of understanding of the system than everyone else. Many people looked at Belichick letting players go in the past as a shock that he's willing to part with Player X, but it was because Player Y was coming up behind him and cost far less money, which allowed him to build out the rest of his roster. Now people are more understanding because they know he does it for a reason, which this book helps explain. There's a reason that Tom Brady has seemed to be the only untouchable player on the roster since 2001, while they've also managed his salary cap hits to decrease the overall impact on their team's salary cap to allow Belichick to build out a roster that could compete for a championship every year through value and versatility.

The first four chapters of this book are on the kind of organization a team needs to build to have the processes in place to succeed, then five chapters on the various positional markets through an analysis of current costs and what has worked for Super Bowl teams with an understanding of the various paths to success, plus a final chapter that I hope will create the basis for a better rookie pay structure.

Through analyzing all sides of an NFL organization and the spending markets, the Patriots became a through line for this book because they've not only competed and won Super Bowls, they've created a dynasty that's now lasted almost two decades with a team that's currently 10-3 and was looking like they would collide with that Eagles team on the first Sunday of February 2018 before that Wentz injury. They've constructed various styles of Super Bowl champions: so just within their organization, with the same coach (!), they've showed us various strategies for Super Bowl success. They help show us the various paths of success that NFL teams can take, from the quarterback centric model they've followed for the last decade, back to the rushing offense, defensive juggernaut, and special teams focused champions of the early-2000s. The analysis in this book will help fans understand that there is more to the game of football than just finding a quarterback, there's a wide variety of spending strategies that can create champions and this book will explain it all.

To continue to follow my exploration of Caponomics, you can find my writing at OverTheCap.com as well as at "@ZackMooreNFL" on Twitter. You can also e-mail Caponomics@gmail.com with "E-Mail List" in the subject line to become a part of our e-mail list.

Differences in Accounting of a Player's Cash Salary versus a Team's Salary Cap Charge

Before starting the book, I thought a description of the difference between a player's cash salary, or income, and his salary cap hit. They are not the same thing, one is an account of a player's earnings, while the other is a means of NFL teams accounting for each player's earnings. To start the book off I felt that OverTheCap.com's founder Jason Fitzgerald would be the best person to describe the difference between a player's cash salary versus his salary cap hit:

It is important to understand that a salary cap charge does not necessarily equal a player's actual cash salary is in a given year. The NFL has a unique accounting system in which each team given a budget that they can not exceed. The salary cap accounting system effectively allows a team to purchase "on credit" by deferring salary cap charges to future contract years. To purchase on credit a team can elect to have a portion of salary in any given year be considered a "signing bonus" which, even though paid in full, is prorated in equal installments across the entire remaining length of the contract, up to a maximum of five years.

By keeping cap charges low in a given year a team may be able to increase the amount of more expensive players on the roster in a given year. However by "buying now and paying later" teams run the risk of having excessive salary cap charges for aging players or in some cases cap charges for players no longer playing on the team. The latter scenario occurs when a player is released and has bonus prorations remaining on his contract when he is cut. So while the low cap charges at first give the team the ability to add players to a roster when those charges become excessive the team is hindered from adding to the roster.

To illustrate we can look at two hypothetical players who both receive $6 million in cash upon signing a five year contract. One player receives $1 million as a base salary and $5 million as a roster bonus while the second receives $1 million as a base salary and $5 million as a signing bonus. Both players are earning the identical amount of money but the first player has a $6 million cap charge and the second has just a $2 million cap charge.

The team using the signing bonus will be able to use $4 million more in cap space than the other team in that first contract year, but, assuming all other terms are equal, will have cap charges $1 million higher in each of the remaining years of the contract. If the player was cut after 2 years, the team not using the signing bonus will have no cap charge for the player while the team using the signing bonus will have a $3 million cap charge for a player no longer on the team. This is the manner in which salary cap accounting works allowing the teams to determine how they best see fit to take the charges for the actual cash salary being paid to the player.

Jason Fitzgerald
OverTheCap.com

Chapter 1: Percentages, Process, Quality

Reporting on the state of the Ravens in a news conference after the Baltimore Ravens Super Bowl 47 victory in February 2013, their second in a history that only dates back to 1996, Matt Vensel from *The Baltimore Sun* wrote what we should consider the definition of success for a franchise in the NFL: "General Manager Ozzie Newsome and company made it clear at the State of the Ravens news conference last month that the organization did not plan on going for broke in pursuit of a second straight title in 2013. They said they were more concerned with remaining competitive for the long haul because, if you are in the tourney every year – as the Ravens have been every year from 2008 to today (2012) – you're bound to win one eventually." By "long haul" Newsome meant managing well within their salary cap.[1]

The NFL is structured with a salary cap to promote a more balanced league. This helps bring parity to the sport. Well, other than the Patriots who have hacked the system, which is explained in this book. Creating an organization that can consistently compete for the playoffs every year is no small task. It takes years of researching, experimenting, and creating ideas that can solve the problems presented by your competition while creating an advantage for yourself. Super Bowl seasons are not created by one smart decision, one right move on a big-time free agent. A Super Bowl is the result of three to five-year's worth of decisions that culminate with a roster that can run the team's offensive, defensive and special teams systems well enough to win the Super Bowl against 31 other organizations working toward the same thing. Every football team should be looked at as an ongoing experiment with your roster building off of the lessons learned from each play, each series, each game and each season, so creating stability is critical as it allows your decision makers to continually learn and improve.

Coming from starting a small business and earning my Masters in Business from Rutgers, I learned that the financials were the most important aspect to understand in any business as they tell the story of whether you will succeed or not. While writing a business plan for a sports management firm in an entrepreneurship class, I began to read IBISWorld Industry Reports and found the cost structure benchmarks in the competitive landscape section of each. Each report had a bar graph with percentages making up the 100% of the costs of the industry with the percentage that each cost consumed. These divided into profit, wages, purchases, depreciation, marketing, rent and utilities, and other, with the costs for the "Celebrity & Sports Agents in the US" and the "Advertising Agencies in the US" Industry Reports displaying differences in how their 100% is generally consumed.

Most importantly, if you're far outside of these cost structure benchmarks, it will be difficult to build success.

The Super Bowl about six weeks after that entrepreneurship class concluded was the 43-8 assassination attempt on Peyton Manning's career by a ferocious Seahawks defense. The thing that stuck out to me with this new perspective was that Manning had a cap hit of $17.5 million, 14.2% of the NFL's $123 million salary cap that year, while Russell Wilson's second year of his contract, after being chosen in the third round of the 2012 NFL Draft, cost just 0.55% of the Seahawks salary cap. Both players seemed to have statistically good games as Manning completed 34 of 49 passes (69.4%) for 280 yards with one touchdown and two interceptions, while Wilson went 18 of 25 (72.0%) for 206 yards and two touchdowns, but most of Manning's production came towards the end of the game after the game was already decided. While Manning threw for just 5.7 yards per pass attempt, Wilson recorded a much more efficient 8.2 per attempt.

The Seahawks won by creating a more balanced team with a strong running game to control the tempo of the game for the young quarterback and a defense with the talent in pass rush and coverage to keep any passing attack off its rhythm all afternoon. Denver had a historic offense that was first in the NFL in scoring, yards and passing yards, but their defense was ranked 22nd in points allowed and 19th in yards allowed. Seattle was ranked eighth in scoring offense and first in scoring defense. The Seahawks accomplished this in a league where everyone seemed to have become entirely quarterback focused and the market showed with how high quarterback contracts had been driven by the outrageous rookie contracts at the end of the last CBA and a perceived lack of scarcity that was beginning to force more quarterbacks over 10% of the cap, into the market's first tier, than previously seen in the NFL. A team with the sixth quarterback drafted in the year prior took down, arguably, the greatest of all time; Wilson was even drafted after the Broncos back-up at the time, second-round pick Brock Osweiler.

Peyton Manning was obviously someone you'd want on your team during his record setting 2013 season, but taking up nearly 15% of the cap doesn't come without consequence. When a team can get comparable production out of a quarterback (or any player) for far less money than its opponents, they gain a huge hidden value advantage that helps the team build a more complete roster than their competitors.

The success of the Seahawks with Wilson inspired me to begin to develop data on team player spending allocation for 2013 by using the information provided by Jason Fitzgerald at OverTheCap.com, and in this I began to see patterns and generate some ideas about what I thought the data meant. During the summer of 2014, Jason brought me on at Over The Cap and he also released a few articles dissecting the top cap charges for the Super Bowl champions of the salary cap era. Once Jason sent me the salary cap data on the then twenty Super Bowl champions of the salary cap era, I knew that organizing the data would teach me what teams need to do to win Super Bowls. After running into *Sports Illustrated's* Andy Benoit at the 2015 NFL Combine and being inspired by a conversation we had, I realized traveling back to New Jersey that I could write a book on the data Jason had given me.

The concept of looking at a team's roster and salary cap situation through the lens of percentages of the salary cap is what makes this book and this field of analytics possible. The dollar figures that players make don't mean anything to us outside of the fact that the highest paid player of your favorite team is wealthy enough to hang out with the Sultan of Brunei and his gold underwear for a weekend. The dollar figures they consume of the salary cap don't matter to us because they don't tell us anything about what the contract means in terms of how it affects the team financially. What matters are the percentages; they tell us a story about each NFL team. The percentages give us a context for value and they allow us to cross-reference and compare across years as the salary cap changes every year, thus providing us with years of data to learn from.

Viewing this from the percentages of salary cap perspective, an organization can begin to construct the formula or framework of what you're trying to create, giving you guidelines that help you stay within certain parameters that work for what you're trying to build. This formula or guideline, with accurate salary cap projections, keeps the goal of competing for the playoffs every year in sight because it allows you to plan for the future and make sound, principled decisions that build toward your definition of Quality, which we'll discuss shortly.

Say you have a top of the market quarterback talent like Russell Wilson who, now that he's off his rookie contract, costs around 11 to 12 percent of the salary cap on his second contract. Once you factor in his spending, then you factor in a few of your other top cap hits like cornerback Richard Sherman between eight and nine and a half percent of the salary cap, then figure out how the rest of your roster is going to fit in around them. Once you see where most of your salary cap is invested, once you lock in your core veterans like the Seahawks did, then you can begin to construct strategies for how you're going to create value at the positions where you can't invest a high percentage of your salary cap, and you can do that either through the draft or by signing mid- to low-tier free agents.

In later chapters, we'll discuss what has worked for past champions as well as where current positional markets sit today. Together, these provide context for the value you're placing on a player. Signing a player to a top of market contract is okay, but he has to be a Wilson or Sherman type of player, one who you know has a high probability of providing your team with the value of that contract. To win a Super Bowl with two or three players making top of market rates those players almost have to be Hall of Fame level players who are playing at that level during that season.

Analyzing the Super Bowl champion data helps us develop a cost ceiling guideline for each NFL positional market. As a general rule, no player is worth more than 13% and that should only be for a Peyton Manning or Aaron Rodgers type of player. A pass rusher or cornerback can cost around 12%, but should be done almost exclusively if your quarterback is at a low cost on his rookie deal. And if teams do spend these kinds of rates, or exceed them, they're going to need to find value elsewhere.

Under the old CBA, rookie quarterbacks were forced to play early due to their cost and they were typically in a near impossible situation. Quarterbacks like Sam Bradford were drafted to teams that were bad enough to draft first overall that year and a rookie quarterback contract near the cost of the top of the veteran market over 10% of the cap doesn't help the situation. Bradford's cap hit in 2012, year three of his career, was 12.93%, which is where the top of the quarterback market should be, not where rookie contract players should be.[2] With the current CBA that was agreed to before the 2011 season, even number one overall picks like Jameis Winston are on contracts that cost about four and a half percent of the cap in their fourth season. The issue now may have swung too far in the opposite direction with top picked players who should be starters at quarterback or another position making such low rates even in year four.

The 2013 Seahawks highlighted how a team with a low-cost quarterback, even if that team has a first round pick under the current contract structure, can use that money elsewhere to build a more complete roster. This book is about increasing a team's probability of success based on Ozzie Newsome's definition of making the playoffs on an annual basis; creating cost-managing strategies are critical. Everyone can't just wait around for a Peyton Manning or Andrew Luck to fall into their lap.

Every position has its own cost structure benchmarks, but above all else, the value that a player provides to a team and that team's salary cap situation must be taken into account. What works for one team might not make sense for another, but that doesn't make it wrong. Caponomics isn't a hard science, but cap costs outside of what the data says works must be well and deliberately thought out. If you're trying to make the playoffs every year, then these rules are important and they become more important if you're trying to take that next step towards building a dynasty. Winning a Super Bowl is difficult enough, so clearly overpaying a market or overestimating a player's value is going to have negative consequences in a league with a salary cap.

The Patriots have been dominant because they developed a formula that creates a competitive advantage for them by saving money across multiple positional markets. Bill Belichick has been the Patriots head coach and general manager since he got there in 2000, the Seahawks have been dominant since Pete Carroll and John Schneider became business partners, the Broncos had Gary Kubiak and John Elway running the same system they ran to Super Bowl glory during the 1990s, the Ravens have had the same General Manager in Ozzie Newsome since their inception in 1996 with Brian Billick and John Harbaugh serving as the only head coaches since 1999. Almost all of the most consistent organizations in the NFL have a great head coach and general manager team. These two have to have a complete understanding of their own specialty along with what their partner is trying to accomplish and how he and his specialty fits together. A great working relationship is a requirement for maximizing the value an organization creates with their 100% or 100 units of cap space.

Thinking of the salary cap in terms of percentages of the salary cap makes everything fall in line; it standardizes and simplifies the entire process for your front office and coaching staff, which allows them to focus on their own process for building the team they need to succeed. Having a stable structure for constructing your roster frees the front office and coaches from worrying how they're going to build the team they need to succeed year in and year out; it provides them with an ongoing framework for how their team is going to be constructed and what they'll need to do to build the entire roster over time. This spending framework simplifies the entire process and allows the coaches to develop strategies for finding consistent production in the lower cost roles for accomplishing their overall objectives.

Coaches like Bill Belichick break down larger objectives like production in the passing game into the basic principles of moving the chains efficiently through a high-percentage passing system with the ability to score touchdowns in the red zone rather than settle for field goals. Although he makes sure to have a kicker who can consistently give him three as long as the offense reaches somewhere around the opponent's 35-yard line, he doesn't want to lose the opportunity for four more by not being able to score once they enter the red zone. Most coaches of the passing era we are in have tended to try to accomplish this by finding one of the freak athletes that are in low supply, thus at a high-cost. Belichick's been able to build a historically consistent and prolific passing attack by avoiding reliance on the obvious physical freak at wide receiver, unless Randy Moss is available at a steep discount for reasons outside of his athleticism or production potential, but by instead focusing on players who move the chains and score in the red zone. Scoring in the redzone is a lot about having a power running back who can score on the goal line, a big target at tight end, an outside receiver who can make plays in traffic, and short, quick pass catchers who can get open in small spaces.

The chain movers end up being the Wes Welker, Julian Edelman and Danny Amendola types—guys who get open on the short to intermediate routes and provide the team with between about seven and nine yards per target and a catch rate around 70% or better. Say a player catches 70% of the passes thrown his way and he averages eight yards per target, that means the offense moves 80 yards for every 10 balls thrown his way even if he only caught seven of them. This means the offense moves the ball very efficiently when they throw to him and they're getting a better yard per play output than they could ever receive from even the best rushing attack. A solid, efficient pass-catching running back might catch 70% of balls and give you six yards per target, while the offense is still moving 60 yards in those ten plays his way, which the Patriots always have on their roster.

Belichick broke the running back position down into two distinct roles to create the production of one more expensive, complete running back. One role is the power rusher role that LeGarrette Blount held from 2014 to 2016 with a league leading 18 rushing touchdowns in 2016 and that Corey Dillon excelled in with 37 rushing touchdowns in 43 games from 2004 to 2006. They pair this with a pass-catching tailback in the role that Kevin Faulk made famous and that Dion Lewis and James White have played since the 2015 season, replacing Shane Vereen who left for the Giants. We'll discuss this more in later chapters, but they basically broke down what the complete running back accomplishes from a production standpoint, then re-created it through two running back roles and, typically, three to five players on the roster who can provide some production in those roles. This set up provides them with the production that they need from their rushing attack to balance out the system and some insurance against injury by giving them a few players who can contribute in a pinch. The solid yards-per-target contributions of their pass-catching running backs and their slot receivers also allows them the insurance of having a way to move the football if their rushing offense gets shut down.

By creating a passing offense that can move the ball like this, they give themselves a way to consistently move the football with efficiency and paired with an above average rushing attack, this gives them a versatility that creates a whole new set of problems for opposing defenses. Being efficient moving the chains is the most important thing an offense can do as that means they'll sustain drives, which gives them a better chance of scoring consistently and wears out the opponent's defense, further increasing their chances of scoring as the game goes on.

For red zone scoring, the Patriots have traditionally relied on big-bodied tight ends who were great run blockers first, but had the ability to score in the red zone, plus power rushing running backs like Blount. Before Rob Gronkowski came along, they had players like Daniel Graham and Christian Fauria who combined for nine receiving touchdowns on their 2004 Super Bowl team and Ben Watson from 2004 to 2009 just prior to the drafting of Aaron Hernandez and Gronk. In Gronkowski now, they have the perfect player for what this system requires with his 6'6", 265-pound frame that can post up in the red zone or tower over a safety in between the hashes and pancake defenders in the running game--and he's about half the salary cap cost of the top of the wide receiver market. He also provides them with big play potential at 9.8 yards per target in 2015, which tied A.J. Green near the top of the NFL. In 2016, Gronkowski led the league with 14.2 yards per target and 540 yards on just 38 targets before going down with a back injury halfway through the year.

The Patriots deconstructed what the great Julio Jones type receiver does into the basic principles of what he provides a team. This is one of the ways the best coaches create cost-saving solutions. A player like Jones represents what every team wants in a receiver, so Belichick takes his high catch rate, his ability to move the chains and provide the occasional big play, the ability to take the top of the coverage, score in the red zone and block in the running game, and then finds these qualities in the multiple players who make up his pass catching group. He'll find a lower cost receiver who can play the role that a player like Jones fulfills on the outside with less production, but still the body type and ability to score touchdowns in the redzone. The added benefit of this is that it also gives him an offense filled with potential mismatches to exploit defenses. A Julio Jones-type is certainly an incredible difference maker, but with the top of the WR market at twice the cost of Gronkowski at the top of the tight end market, you can see the intelligence of this strategy. This is a recurring theme with the Patriots, which is why Belichick will be mentioned throughout this book.

Belichick has provided the NFL with the next evolution of the game past where Bill Walsh brought us with his West Coast offense and his 49ers dynasty; Belichick has done it in the salary cap era, having to construct an off-field financial strategy in an industry where all 32 teams have the same amount of money to spend. What Belichick has created in New England is the definition of Ozzie Newsome's success with 11 AFC Championship appearances, seven Super Bowl appearances and five Super Bowl victories in the 15-playoff appearances in the 17 years that Belichick has been at the helm.

In *Zen and the Art of Motorcycle Maintenance*, Robert Pirsig writes, "a real understanding of Quality doesn't just serve the System, or even beat it or even escape it. A real understanding of Quality captures the System, tames it, and puts it to work for one's own personal use, while leaving one completely free to fulfill his inner destiny."[3] This is the perfect description for what Belichick has done.

Belichick's father, Steve, was a respected scout and coach at Navy who helped Bill develop an understanding of the objective of the game—to think in first principles, rather than the on-field formulas that other teams use, the conventional wisdom. As a result, over time, Belichick developed strategies for turning the salary cap into an advantage. For instance, the average starting offensive line for Super Bowl champions costs 11.03% of the salary cap, but the starting offensive line for the Patriots five Super Bowl champions consumed a mere 7.38% of the cap. His ability to identify what he needs to succeed in his system at technical and subjective positions, like offensive line that has very little objective data, is a testament to decades of watching more film than anyone else in the sport and working with offensive line coaching legend Dante Scarnecchia. His film watching is so renowned that Ryan Holiday included him in a chapter of his book, *Ego is the Enemy*, as proof of Belichick's attention to detail and his lack of ego that helped him focus on the seemingly small stuff from an early stage in his career.[4] He also uses objective metrics to find value at other positions.

Belichick has earned his cost savings through a mastery of subjective analysis, but we're in the middle of an analytics revolution that will compel NFL teams to use a combination of subjective and objective data to define exactly what they're looking for at each position. Belichick embraces both the subjective and objective understanding of the sport and saves money on offense, while still acquiring the pieces needed for his on-field strategy. This further allows him to use the money saved to create a defense that can defend against all potential mismatches. As a defensive focused coach coming up the ranks, Belichick learned what schemes and match-ups were difficult to defend, and created his offense to expose these holes and inefficiencies in opposing defenses. Conversely, his defense is filled with players who can defend against mismatches and keep the offense off balance through its ability to disrupt the quarterback with pass rush and pass coverage along with a strong rushing defense.

Belichick spends more than the average on special team specialists, another beneficiary of the offensive cost-savings as he understands that spending an extra one or two percent of the salary cap on a kicker might be the difference between winning a couple of close games or not each year especially come playoff time. His ability to secure top-notch kickers is a huge reason why the Patriots have led the NFL with a winning percentage of .704 and playoff record of 25-9 from 2001 through 2016. They've led the NFL with a .709 winning percentage in games decided by three points or less as well during that time. Four of the five highest paid of the 23 salary cap era Super Bowl champion kickers were Patriots; two of their five Super Bowl victories were decided by last second field goals. Clearly the strategy of spending a little extra for consistency in the kicking game has paid off for them. He knows that investing in punters and athletes on special teams as well helps win the field position battle as well.

The objective of football is to score more points than your opponent and you do this through creating an efficient, versatile and consistent roster. An important x-factor for all three of those principles is risk mitigation. By constructing a roster filled with mismatch creators at low cap hits, who are often below market rates and almost always less expensive than the typical cost of their production for the Patriots, Belichick creates a strategic advantage in the salary cap and insurance for when players do get injured. With Tom Brady as the only offensive skill player to play all 16 games in 2015, the Patriots still went 12-4 and made the AFC Championship.

Since Belichick has been in New England, he's been building his definition of Quality through his subjective experience, but also with objective measurables for each position, metrics for what he's looking for in each role and statistics for the production needed to succeed. In the past, a coach's definition of Quality was almost entirely defined by subjective measures, like his experience—it lacked objective measurements. With technological advancements like RFID chips inside shoulder pads that will track every player's movements and Pro Football Focus working to objectively measure everything that happens on the field, football is creating the kind of one-on-one scenarios that allow for data collection that baseball has had all along. With these match-ups isolated, NFL coaches are gaining the ability to quantify what's needed for everything on the field. In the past, basic statistics like yardage and basic metrics for speed like 40-yard dash times were all that existed, but RFID chips, along with other technological advances, are going to allow coaches to pinpoint exactly what they need. Once you create the outline of what you're looking for, as with the salary cap framework, it becomes much easier to find what you need.

In *The Extra 2%: How Wall Street Strategies Took a Major League Baseball Team from Worst to First*, Jonah Keri explains how the Tampa Bay Rays used new defensive analytics to go from a team that finished last in the American League East for the ninth time in their then ten years of existence to the American League Champion the next season.[5] They did this by looking at information no one else was paying attention to at the time. After seeing what the Oakland Athletics accomplished by focusing on high on-base percentages, everyone else was focused on offense for cost savings. As new defensive analytics become available in football, we'll see someone do the NFL equivalent of what the Rays did.

While the Tampa Bay Rays and Oakland Athletics looked at different sets of new data, they married together old school scouting with new school analytics to create vastly different definitions of Quality. Paul DePodesta, who was with Oakland during the time that *Moneyball* chronicled, is now with the Cleveland Browns painting the same concepts on a different canvas. In a DePodesta profile for the April 2016 edition of *ESPN Magazine*, David Fleming writes that, while most NFL teams "begrudgingly use analytics," DePodesta and the Browns will differentiate themselves by the extent to which they will use data to influence their decision-making. Fleming writes, "DePodesta would like decisions to be informed by 60 percent data, 40 percent scouting. Present-day NFL is more 70 percent scouting and 30 percent data."[6]

The Houston Astros just earned the first World Series in their history during this 2017 postseason. A *Sports Illustrated* article from June 2014 titled "Astro-Matic Baseball" by Ben Reiter inspired an *SI* cover headline that predicted this 2017 World Series win.[7] In it, Reiter talks about the origin of the process that led to this victory and he wrote it after the Astros had lost 106, 107, and 111 games in the 2011 through 2013 seasons, after they had begun the process of building up their roster through the draft. The Browns are currently in a similar team building cycle through the draft. George Springer, the 2017 World Series MVP, was one of these players as the #11 pick in the 2011 MLB Amateur Draft. Sig Mejdal, the Astros sabermetrics analyst and a former NASA engineer who earned a degree in mechanical engineering and aeronautical engineering at the University of California-Davis, is one of the main characters of the piece using a story about how he would go to Lake Tahoe during his summers off from school to work as a blackjack dealer.

Reiter uses blackjack to make an analogy to baseball writing: "Blackjack is an exercise in hard probabilities. Evaluating baseball players is something else. Some information you can gather about a baseball player is hard: how fast he can throw a fastball, how quickly he can reach first base. But much of it is soft: how diligently he will work, how his power stroke might develop, how likely he is to become injured. 'How do you combine the soft information with the hard information in a way that allows you to make the best decisions?' asks Luhnow. 'That is the crux of what we're trying to do here.'" Reiter goes on to write, "they are trying to do it in a way that synthesized quantitative and qualitative information about players," this is another aspect of the sort of analytics and scouting split that must be address.

The mental side of a prospect won't be covered in this book, but a player's mental make up is certainly a part of the whole team building process that can't be ignored. Sure, Deshaun Watson is a great player, but when you add his ability to overcome adversity throughout his personal life with a kid who everyone says is a terrific person, you get a prospect that has a high likelihood of success due to his ability and his personal traits. These are traits that football analytics can't necessarily explain; it takes scouts, and even sports psychologists like Dr. Kevin Elko who spent the time before the 2016 NFL Draft interviewing quarterback prospects for the Eagles before they drafted Carson Wentz.[8] This all factors into that 60/40 split we're talking about with DePodesta.

We're in the middle of an analytics revolution that will allow NFL teams to use a combination of subjective and objective data to make decisions on roster building. In Pirsig's *Zen and the Art of Motorcycle Maintenance,* he defines Classic Quality as an understanding of the world that seeks to "bring order out of the chaos and make the unknown known." The other side of this is Romantic Quality. The classic side is all about facts and reason, while the romantic side "proceeds by feeling, intuition, and esthetic conscience" and "feelings rather than facts dominate."[9] The romantic side is the surface level; it sees the world primarily in terms of immediate appearance. A classical understanding sees the world in terms of underlying form, its logic and structure. The romantic loves watching the NFL for the beauty and excitement of it, while the classic is reading this book to understand how it all works and the strategies that teams implement.

To reframe what DePodesta is suggesting, he's trying to define Classic Quality, which we'll refer to as Quality in this book, for the Browns just like he did for the Athletics. DePodesta is going to utilize a 60% objective data to 40% subjective scouting split. To put it simply, this just means he's going to use data to bring more reasoning to the sport, which is something more organizations are already doing. With information and analysis like what we see from Pro Football Focus and technology like RFID chips, the timing couldn't be better for someone like DePodesta as successful teams around the league are already in the process of figuring out this objective and subjective split.

The Quality that we're talking about cannot exist without a balance of the objective and the subjective, the analytics and the scouting. His 20 years of experience in Major League Baseball attempting to find this balance with the Cleveland Indians, Athletics, Los Angeles Dodgers, San Diego Padres and New York Mets is what makes DePodesta's move to the NFL such an exciting case study.

With so many variables in the NFL, even more potential solutions or definitions of Quality exist. This Quality will be influenced by the subject, which is the coaching staff, the front office, and the organization with their history of using whatever systems and strategies they intend to employ. But as generations of coaches start to grow their careers alongside a growing analytics field, the objective side will more heavily influence these definitions of Quality. There will be less of a focus on the subjective analysis of scouts and more of a focus on players who can quantifiably accomplish objectives. Both the objective and subjective will continue to work together in the kind of split DePodesta is working on toward the objective of winning a Super Bowl. Over time, the objective and subjective split will continue to slide toward the objective side as more objective measurements come available.

Teams will build rosters using the core principles that create on field efficiency and off field efficiency via strategic use of salary cap spending. This book will give an outline of what has worked for Super Bowl champions and provide an analysis of what that data means in conjunction with an analysis of where current markets stand. Each organization needs to choose how to use the objective data provided in this book to mold their champion. When a team understands the principles of Caponomics, it can use the salary cap as a strategic lever and achieve the sustained, consistent success that Ozzie Newsome defined for us. As Belichick has shown the league, an understanding of Quality captures the salary cap system and puts it to use for one's use.

Chapter 2: The NFL Hiring Process

The goal of all 32 NFL franchises should be to build a staff of creative problem solvers who understand the principles of success for NFL football: to create consistent efficiency on offense and create a defense that can disrupt their opponent's attempts at generating efficiency on offense.

Offensive efficiency is illustrated through a high yard per play average, which is best achieved through some kind of run-pass balance with a high-percentage passing system. This helps an offense move the chains with consistency, protect the football to ensure you have more opportunities than your opponent to score, and have an offense that can score in the red zone. Efficiency also relies on having a great kicker who can act as a consistent "three-point shooter" if your offense stalls out around your opponent's 35-yard line.

Defensive efficiency is illustrated through disrupting an offense's attempts at these things. An efficient defense forces turnovers through a pass rush that shrinks the amount of time a quarterback has to make a decision. It uses a pass coverage unit of safeties and linebackers and scheme to shrink the window a quarterback has to throw into, while forcing coverage sacks or quarterback hurries and turnovers. The 2015 Broncos had all that, plus sideline-to-sideline demons at linebacker in Brandon Marshall and Danny Trevathan to lead their rush defense. As seen in Super Bowl 50 with Broncos' punter Britton Colquitt shifting the field position against the Panthers multiple times, a punter who can help you win the hidden yardage battle and force your opponent's offense to have to cover more of the field is a weapon for defensive, and overall, efficiency as well.

Winning the hidden-yardage battle with a punter who can pin your opponent deep or a returner who can provide you with better than average field position is a critical, but often overlooked aspect. Your offense, defense, and special teams are their own units, but they all work together to create the end result. Every play that each unit makes affects the other units by either increasing or decreasing their probability of success as a team. With special teams, a big play for either side can swing field position for an entire half.

On both sides of the ball you have to have match-ups on your mind. You're looking for offensive skill players that create mismatches for the NFL defenses that you're going to face, plus a strong offensive line whose skill sets fit your system needs. Defenses are looking for players in the pass rush who give them a match-up advantage against NFL offensive lines with players in pass coverage who can handle every NFL offense's attempt to create mismatches.

To build a coaching and front office staff of creative problem solvers, you have to build your entire organization as an efficient organism that can create dynamic advances in Quality to create efficient systems on the field. In his second book, *Lila,* Robert Pirsig dissects the Metaphysics of Quality, which he breaks into static and Dynamic Quality. The static is the current state of Quality, the definitions you can choose from, while Dynamic Quality is created through either building your own definition of Quality entirely or building off a current framework with Dynamic advances—in football, these are advances that increase your ability to accomplish efficiency on one or both sides of the ball.[1] Many of the best players in the NFL are referred to as dynamic athletes as they're often unlike players seen before becoming a new potential prototype for their position.

In *Zero to One,* a book that stemmed from a course he taught on start-ups at Stanford two years earlier, Silicon Valley Super Investor and co-founder of PayPal Peter Thiel described the lessons of his book on entrepreneurship as being "about how to build companies that create new things."[2] When you enter an industry with an entrepreneurial venture, it has to be because you're either creating something new or you're providing a better way of doing things. To succeed as a business, the entrepreneurial ethos must stick with your company long past the start-up stage. If a company is not growing and improving on itself, then the slow death has already begun as other companies are growing and improving. Others are using the principles of success in your industry to "build a better mousetrap," as the old saying goes. Eventually, any competitive advantage that you did have will cease to exist and your business will become as extinct as the ideas you're still using to run your organization. Old advantages eventually become disadvantages in a different climate. Just like a polar bear can't live in the desert, the Wing-T offense can't live in the 2017 NFL. The game has become so much more dynamic with the need for various strategies for offensive success each week that has phased out styles of offenses like the Wing-T's almost entirely rushing based system. Thiel writes, "today's 'best practices' lead to dead ends; the best paths are new and untried."

The paradox that anyone who is teaching entrepreneurship faces is that a formula for success cannot exist "because every innovation is new and unique, no authority can prescribe in concrete terms how to be innovative." Thiel notes that "every moment in business happens only once," which is the same in football. The next Bill Gates or Bill Walsh isn't going to create the operating system or the West Coast offense, they're going to have to create a new solution, one more applicable to the problem they're trying to solve at their moment in history; if you're copying one of these guys, then you're not learning from them. I believe that if you haven't actually created anything unique yourself, you don't learn the skills that Gates or Walsh earned through their creation process and, because of that, you can't completely understand the system on their level; the NFL is filled with creators at that higher level. You need to think at a high enough level to learn principles from past innovation and then make your own product. His ability to continually create new solutions around Tom Brady to accomplish the objective is why Belichick has remained competitive for almost two decades now. Andy Reid's knowledge of his offensive system is why he's continuously been able to find value on offense and has typically competed at a high level across the roster.

Thiel believes that "a new company's most important strength is new thinking" and *Zero to One* was not written as "a manual or record of knowledge but an exercise in thinking because that is what a start-up has to do: question received ideas and rethink business from scratch." The "single most powerful pattern" that he's noticed is that successful people tend to find value in unexpected places by thinking about business from first principles instead of formulas. An innovator like Walsh or Belichick uses his own deep understanding of the first principles of football mentioned at the beginning of the chapter to generate their own formula. Success in entrepreneurship, or mastery in any field for that matter, has no formula as the creator has to provide it. A coach like Belichick is able to use the salary cap system to his advantage, for instance, which is what has created the Patriots long-running dynasty. Yes, Tom Brady is a great quarterback, but the reason for their success is not that simple. The Patriots have been able to create a spending framework that has guided their spending with him at the top of it averaging a manageable 10.44% of the cap from 2005 through 2015. By comparison, Peyton Manning averaged 12.90% of the cap for the Colts and Broncos during that time. Many of the Super Bowl winning quarterbacks who we now see as elite earned those Super Bowls when they were inexpensive. It becomes much more difficult to compete at those higher numbers because they go from being a great, efficient quarterback on a great team to a great, efficient quarterback on a team that might have some holes, which could also decrease their efficiency.

This Belichick formula, which we'll discuss throughout this book, has made their success as reliable as success can be in a league designed to encourage parity. Even the Yankees and Red Sox have had bad seasons during the Patriots run, and they're in a league where they can spend about three times as much money as their in-division rival Tampa Bay Rays, as they did in 2016. The worst season Brady and Belichick have had together was 9-7 in 2002, then 10-6 in 2005 and 2009. The Patriots went 11-5 in 2001 and in the Matt Cassel led 2008 season; the other years have all been 12-4 or better.

The Pirsig quote from Chapter One bears repeating: "a real understanding of Quality doesn't just serve the System, or even beat it or even escape it. A real understanding of Quality captures the System, tames it, and puts it to work for one's own personal use, while leaving one completely free to fulfill his inner destiny." Building Quality requires understanding the parameters in which you're working in. Belichick's understanding of the principles of the game has allowed him to turn the salary cap into a lever, an advantage that has provided him stability, while much of the rest of the league has struggled to piece together rosters on an almost yearly basis. While some teams can't find their formula, Belichick's perfected his to the point where the average fan can see a seemingly small free agent or waiver wire addition and envision how Belichick intends on using his newly acquired chess piece, knowing the player has a strong chance of success.

The principles of this book are intended to help NFL franchises better manage their salary cap and achieve the definition of success defined in the beginning of Chapter One. This chapter is about the principles for how to create the staff to create their own definition of Quality, using the salary cap as a strategic lever, like Belichick does.

Two major traits that the great NFL franchises have in common are stability and alignment throughout their organization. The coaching staff and front office must be in complete alignment regarding what's needed on the field and how that will be accomplished by the front office. Belichick's dual role as Patriots head coach and General Manager makes him the most valuable man in football. Very few can balance both the on field process and the salary cap management process--and he has done it masterfully with the help of trusted advisors like Director of Player Personnel Nick Caserio.

When the head coach and General Manager fall out of alignment, disaster strikes. At its most extreme, right before the salary cap era kicked off in 1994, the Cowboys GM Jerry Jones separated his fruitful marriage of business sense with Jimmy Johnson's football principles and ruined a dynasty that earned their third and last Super Bowl the next season under Barry Switzer. The Cowboys haven't regained consistency since but are primed to now in the Dak Prescott and Ezekiel Elliott era. When they were aligned, Jones and Johnson pulled off 51 trades in five years, most of which involved them receiving or improving draft picks, to find value in a way that no one else was exploiting at the time as they made more trades than the rest of the NFL combined.[3] They wrote the blueprint in the early-1990s that Paul DePodesta's Browns are trying to replicate from 2016 forward.

There have been grumblings during the 2017 season that the Browns front office and coaching staff might not be getting along, which could spell doom for the current staff if their internal issues are not worked out. About a week before releasing this book, Browns owner Jimmy Haslem fired Executive Vice President of football operations Sashi Brown, the man who had helped orchestrate much of this rebuild, but made a smart move in hiring John Dorsey, a well respected general manager who helped construct the Chiefs in recent years. Haslem abruptly fired Brown to beat the Giants to hiring Dorsey, which is understandable. That said, Dorsey is the fifth Browns general manager since Haslem started owning the team in 2011. Let's hope he sticks with the Moneyball thinking as he fired Brown during a year where the Astros and 76ers have proven that focusing on the long-term for a few years to rebuild works. Seeing that Dorsey is someone quoted a few times in this book, as he seems to know the right way to do things, I think the Browns are in good hands under his leadership.

During the earlier days of football, Vince Lombardi gave us a successful representation of a head coach and General Manager who used his autonomy to create success like Belichick. In Dallas, the Cowboys showed us another model when they started up in 1960 as they hired Tom Landry as the head coach with Tex Schramm as GM and legendary scout Gil Brandt as their brain trust. This is the model that most teams will likely need to follow: a trifecta with a head coach, a player personnel, and salary cap guy as their GM, plus a head of analytics and scouting who will establish and oversee the organization's objective and subjective split mentioned in Chapter One. That head of analytics and scouting will hopefully be a Paul DePodesta type of strategist, but with more of a background in football.

These three have to be in complete alignment and this can be created through stability within the organization by creating a staff aligned in their understanding the principles of the sport and how your organization is trying to execute on them. Great organizations seem to hire from within, having members of the family who understand what you stand for and understand your systems stepping up into a role they've been groomed for. Every franchise should have a plan for developing coaches and staff members for bigger roles within their organization. A great way to create stability long-term is the coaching trees we've seen sustain the great franchises for long stretches. Denver, Green Bay, Philadelphia, and San Francisco have had sustained success over the last two to three decades by using coaches from the limbs of the Bill Walsh coaching tree. Alignment is a natural byproduct of stability. And coaching trees are created by the kind of creative teachers that teams should ideally find as head coaches who have the understanding of the principles of the system and thus can pass those principles on to others.

If your organization is in a constant cycle of firing coaches, then you're in a cycle of wasting resources and you'll never be able to create your salary cap formula. You can't get to first principles if you keep changing who is in charge and who is trying to lead the execution of this plan on the field.

If you're the owner of a franchise and you're firing a coach quickly, then why are you investing in people that you clearly must not believe in? If you're not willing to give a coach a few years to work out his plan, then why did you even hire him? And when you do decide the time has come to move on from a coach, what kind of process are you going through to come to your decision? What are the objective standards or metrics that you'll use to determine if you're going to fire a head coach or General Manager?

Ever since firing Super Bowl winning head coach Jon Gruden on the Black Monday following his second straight 9-7 season in 2008, the Buccaneers went through three head coaches in seven seasons with Dirk Koetter being their fourth having started in 2016—and they have had little success on the field. During Belichick's now 18-year reign, the Jets, Bills, and Dolphins have started their seasons with a different head coach 19 times in 54 total seasons; an average of one coach every three seasons for the Patriots' competition. The Dolphins have fired a head coach in the middle of a season three times during this time, which gives them the lead between those three with nine total head coaches. How can they possibly expect to compete with the steady and methodical Patriots with that kind of turmoil? The Browns have struggled for years in the most competitive and deepest division in football because the Steelers, Ravens, and Bengals have each had stability for over a decade. Since coming back into existence in 1999, the Browns haven't only had 26 different starting quarterbacks heading into 2017, but Hue Jackson is their eighth head coach and ninth overall counting Terry Robiskie's interim tag in 2004.

If you're firing coaches this quickly, then the resulting failure is on the decision maker's head, not the carousel of head coaches, a la Dan Snyder in Washington. Every head coach and general manager team should be given at least a cycle of draft picks, which would be at least four or five years, similar to college where you're trying to allow a head coach the time to get his guys in there and execute his plan and his strategies. If you do have to let go of a coach, make sure that you have someone who can run a system similar to his or even better suited for your current roster, so the transition is not a drastic change. Try to stay within similar styles of play. The key point is that every organization should create a system and set of parameters for hiring head coaches.

Likewise, decision makers should have parameters for what they're looking for in their front office. According to Jenny Vrentas from *Sports Illustrated*, headhunting firm Korn Ferry is a part of some of the big head coaching and front office decisions in the NFL.[4] Hiring qualified outsiders to consult on these decisions is probably something teams that don't have an established culture should practice; speaking to someone outside your organization can give you a new perspective. Even if you don't take their advice, it can help you form your principles for what you want in these hires.

If you do have a firm like Korn Ferry come in, they should not be the final decision maker because if they do make the decision for you, then your decision makers won't completely understand why the hire was made, nor do the outsiders have the same understanding of your organization that people inside the organization do. As a result, they will be unqualified to know when a firing should be made. Korn Ferry isn't going to be around when the organization's decision makers have to explain their firing decision to fans.

As someone from an NFL front office that recently went through a coaching change told me regarding the Korn Ferry process, "in theory what you wrote is exactly right. In practice they always lead the team back to their people. I've seen their work and it isn't special. In this business people only trust who they know, so they aren't giving other candidates a fair shake. If the owner isn't hands on in the business and wants to outsource his hire, then he can use a company and live with the person he is given, but if an owner is involved with the team day-to-day, then he should be leading the process and not be biased on the candidates before he gets a chance to meet and evaluate."

The end goal for any NFL franchise should be to be able to hire from within and this front office person agreed. Once a culture is established, then developing a strategy for front office development can begin. The front office must be schooled in every front office process like the head coach should be educating his staff on the principles of his system and all the on field processes. You're trying to build a staff that exemplifies the versatility and efficiency of the product you're trying to put on the field.

In a 2015 Korn Ferry report, former Cleveland Indians' GM and current Toronto Blue Jays President and CEO, Mark Shapiro, shared some of their process in Cleveland.[5] Being a small market team, the success of former staff members, like current Braves President of Baseball Operations John Hart and Shapiro himself, and the success of their organization on the field is a sign they have a history of creating strategic advantages that allow them to compete with the big spenders. When Hart left Cleveland for the Texas Rangers, this process helped him hire current Texas Rangers President of Baseball Operations and GM Jon Daniels.

Shapiro says their process for developing front office talent is two-pronged: first, selection of talent; and, second, developing their understanding of organizational culture. He looks at every hire all the way down to the interns with the intention that these people could eventually become their GM. They hire creative thinkers. They don't hire interns to do busy work, but to contribute to their front office immediately with a skill set that differentiates them and demonstrates initiative. The Indians under Shapiro would find these people through an intensive selection process that starts with looking through resumes, then sending customized questionnaires to the best candidates before whittling it down to a final top two or three who are invited in for "rigorous" face-to-face interviews. Their staff finds critical reading skills, writing facility, and an ability to express oneself as critical tools for success in their organization.

Baseball teams in small markets like Cleveland have obstacles that NFL teams don't have to deal with like being the 19th-largest television market in the country and routinely having poor attendance records. These challenges play a role in creating the organizational structure, as Shapiro says, "the only way that we can overcome those challenges is with incremental efficiencies and contributions across the entire organization." Having a small organization creates a more inclusive and flat hierarchical structure that includes everyone in meetings to try and help solve problems. The Korn Ferry report concludes that this "constant exposure to seasoned professionals in various disciplines coupled with hands-on involvement in critical functions tends to be more potent than finishing an MBA program at a business school."

Former Chiefs GM and brand new Browns GM John Dorsey comes from the Ron Wolf school of management in Green Bay and he has a philosophy to expose the entire front office team to the entire draft process, free agency, negotiations, and the salary cap process. Dorsey says it takes three years to expose someone to the whole process. If it takes three years just to expose a new hire to that process, then how can some NFL teams be firing head coaches after just one or two seasons? At least give them the three years to learn, experiment, and improve their process in the role as the head coach. This carousel of coaches and decision makers leaves many organizations in a constant state of chaos and change.

This process gives Dorsey the confidence that the organization is protected if a member of the front office decides to leave as they have young staff members being developed who he believes would be prepared. Dorsey says he has "tried to expand upon the importance of the cap and how it has played such a dynamic role" in Kansas City. My belief is that an understanding of the salary cap is what ties everything together, which is why I felt this book was necessary. The lack of economic obstacles in the NFL with the salary cap means that all 32 teams can turn their roster spending into an advantage—or fail to do so—unlike MLB teams.

The added benefit of exposing the entire staff to this process is that it causes a process of learning and teaching. As Ryan Holiday details in *Ego is the Enemy*, mixed martial arts pioneer Frank Shamrock has a system for training fighters that he calls plus, minus, and equal. As Holiday writes, "each fighter, to become great, needs to have someone better that they can learn from, someone lesser who they can teach, and someone equal that they can challenge themselves against."[6]

Taking a beginner or student's mindset, and eventually a coaching mindset, like Holiday suggests, gives you new perspectives that create possibilities that you might not have seen otherwise.

According to that Korn Ferry report, former Colts GM Bill Polian had a formal development program in Indianapolis that would take new hires through the various jobs to give them exposure. They'd give their staff projects that were outside of their normal area of responsibility like a college scout researching contracts in the offseason and a pro scout researching trades and the draft. Polian says he doesn't think a lot of teams were doing that. Through my experience of writing this book, I know that it should be a requirement as understanding every discipline helps someone better perform in his or her area of expertise. I had to learn about the draft process, free agency, analytics, scouting, and more to figure out how to write this book on the salary cap, which has given me a better understanding of the salary cap.

A pro scout who understands the value that can be found in the draft or through trades is much less likely to try to get the front office to overspend for some more expensive veteran defensive end or wide receiver. A college scout researching contracts gains a perspective on the kind of huge value that can be created by finding a draft pick who outperforms his rookie contract. In time, these staff members become better employees and it creates a staff as versatile as what you're trying to put on the field.

Polian makes another point: "the main impediment to talent development is a lack of longevity and the increased pressure to win." If a team can't trust their hiring process and create stability, then the entire process of team building can't begin. If a coach and GM are looking over their shoulder, then they can't think long-term, so taking the long-view like the Browns are trying to do under DePodesta is the only way to build a sustainable franchise. Building a unique advantage in the NFL is a creative endeavor, so the creators must be given some room to fail, as failure is a prerequisite to creation. They shouldn't be ousted after one season.

In a stable franchise that trusts its hiring process, your staff will feel comfortable enough to explore and create new solutions. Over time, this allows you to create a sustainable organization through the draft to continuously create those new solutions.

Chapter 3: NFL Draft Process

Upon establishing stability in your front office and coaching staff with alignment between the two, you can use the draft for value creation and by understanding your exact needs. The blueprints, frameworks or formulas established by top coaches and organizations allow these teams to establish their prototypes for each position using the principles of offensive and defensive efficiency explained at the beginning of chapter two. These offensive and defensive formulas mold together with special teams objectives to create a team strategy built on three phases of the game to win on a week-to-week and long-term basis.

Maybe the most important aspect of the efficiency focus is that, by nature, it opens up your system to thinking about the quarterback position as a prototype role that you can fill consistently due to the high supply of quarterbacks who fill the job description of what a West Coast or Belichick-style Erhardt-Perkins system needs. Offenses that focus on efficiency slant toward high-percentage passing systems, which place more of an emphasis on accuracy, and since accuracy is a skill, it can be improved through practice, while arm strength and the body mechanics associated with it can only be improved to a point. Most of the biggest arms in the NFL belong to guys who are 6'4" or taller and over 230 pounds like Cam Newton, Ben Roethlisberger, Joe Flacco and Andrew Luck. Drew Brees and Russell Wilson are smaller exceptions, but few humans possess the size and strength to get to that elite arm strength level.

Teams can seem to get enamored by a player's arm strength, like with 2014 draft pick Tom Savage who hasn't been productive since high school, and miss more efficient prospects. Savage was drafted by the Texans 29 picks before the Bengals selected AJ McCarron, a two-time national championship winning quarterback who played against NFL caliber defenders on a weekly basis in the SEC and seems poised to have an opportunity to be a starter somewhere eventually. McCarron possessed a 67.1% completion percentage over his last three seasons as Alabama's starting quarterback. Savage complete 56.8% of passes at Rutgers and Pittsburgh. The Browns drafting a soon-to-be 29-year old Brandon Weeden's big arm in the first round of a deep 2012 draft for quarterbacks is another example of this.

A lack of supply of big-armed quarterbacks exists, so using a system that requires one is an inefficient way to run an organization. It also makes an organization leverage-able by their quarterback when it comes time to extend or re-sign him as they know his skill set could work almost anywhere else in the NFL, while a system quarterback knows his skills are amplified by your system. The team also knows they could move on from the quarterback and still compete if they've prepared the quarterback group properly for the starting quarterback's departure.

Andrew Luck was able to coax a record setting contract that pays top of market salary cap rates after a season in which he completed 55.3% of passes for 268.7 yards per game with 15 touchdowns to 12 interceptions in seven games because the Colts are completely reliant on having a big-time, big-armed quarterback carry them. He rebounded to have a better year in 2016 with a 63.5% completion percentage and 282.7 yards per game with 31 touchdowns to 13 interceptions, but even then the team only went 8-8 with him playing as their spending is focused so heavily on the offense. This has resulted in the 2017 team looking hapless like the 2011 team without their starting quarterback under center. Meanwhile, their biggest competition in the AFC over the course of the last decade and a half, the team that stymied the Colts' Super Bowl chances time after time, was the Patriots who have benefitted from having Hall of Fame quarterback Tom Brady for typically less money than the Colts' quarterback costs. The Colts have been completely focused on having a top quarterback strategy over the last 20 years that they've often neglected building a complete roster. They'll overinvest resources in the passing game by making moves like drafting wide receiver Phillip Dorsett in the first round of the 2015 draft, then signing wide receiver T.Y. Hilton to an extension that August to a team with a defense that finished 25th in the NFL in points allowed that season. Not only were they both receivers, but their basic skill sets are identical as speedy deep threats that are both listed at 5'10", 183-pounds, so they didn't even add diversity of talents or versatility.

During the 2016 offseason, we watched the Broncos let the unproven Brock Osweiler leave for Houston when the price became too much for their formula and the value they believed he would provide. Instead, they opted for a three person competition between low-cost veteran Mark Sanchez, 2015 seventh-round pick Trevor Siemian and 2016 first-round pick Paxton Lynch, which resulted in Siemian winning the job, while allowing them to develop Lynch. The Broncos can now decide what they want to do with Siemian or Lynch on their roster long-term or they could trade Siemian before the 2018 season or Lynch before the 2019 season when his contract runs out, unless they activate the fifth year team option. If they trade Siemian it could be for a return on their initial investment considering he's increased his own value from unknown seventh-rounder to a competent player in Gary Kubiak and Mike McCoy's West Coast systems, which will translate over to most West Coast systems in the NFL today. Because of their ability to do this, they've built a strong and sustainable defense-focused spending formula they will be able to maintain for the foreseeable future. If they don't like either quarterback long-term, they cold invest another early pick in 2018, which seems to be the deepest quarterback draft in recent memory and they'll maintain a defensive focused cap construction with the stars they have there, plus wide receivers in Demaryius Thomas and Emmanuel Sanders who can elevate quarterback play. Their offensive line play in 2017 was probably the most concerning issue as they were one of the worst pass blocking lines in the NFL, which creates a situation few quarterbacks could succeed behind.

According to Sally Jenkins in *The Real All Americans*, football rose in popularity near the ebbing of the frontier wars in the second half of the 1870s and by the 1890s, with the closing of the frontier. Victorian America focused on football as the "new male proving ground and a remedy for the neurasthenia of the age." As she writes, "the phenomenon was at least in part explained by the fear that a generation of Gilded Age young men was becoming soft and over civilized, with nothing left to conquer, and too much time spent in parlors."[1]

Thinking of football born as a societal replacement for war as the first principle of football, an entirely new understanding of the sport opens. The objective of football is to score more points than your opponent; it doesn't matter what strategy you choose to accomplish this. The premise of the sport is a lot like old school wars, where a defense is defending the higher ground or goal line against the invading offensive. In war, you're trying to accomplish different objectives, but the lessons in strategy deeply resonate, which is why many of the best coaches have a passion for military strategy and history.

Ms. Jenkins' book speaks to one of those first big evolutions in football as Pop Warner was able to build the underfunded, undersized and undermanned Carlisle Indian School into a national contender beating the likes of the bigger, stronger and faster Army team led by future General and President Dwight D. Eisenhower at running back. Warner's creativity over the simple use of brute force represented what was likely one of the first shifts in strategic thinking, which is a shift we're continuing to see as the underlying principle for the evolution of the sport. Coaches like Bill Walsh and Bill Belichick have continued the evolution away from the biggest, strongest and fastest simply winning on talent toward a continually increasing emphasis on a strategy of efficiency through creativity and finding the right mix of players to fill the job descriptions on the roster. The NFL salary cap has helped push this evolution over the last two decades as, with a designated amount of spending available, no team can even attempt to compile the most talented roster. It would cost too much money.

The most expensive positions like quarterback, wide receiver, cornerback and pass rusher can become cap killers if the players aren't providing the proper value, and even sometimes when they do as your opponents may build something much more efficient. And with the overpriced nature of current markets, some top of market deals are higher than the value that even a high performer can provide. Waiting for the Peyton Manning, Julio Jones and Von Miller type players to come along in the first round to provide your team with what you need to succeed at a position and compete as an organization isn't an efficient or realistic way to run a business. A team that does that typically has to acquire a pick at the top draft either through finishing at the bottom of the league or a trade and then they have to bet on the right players for the system to work, which is really hard. They then have to pick the Manning and not the Ryan Leaf or else that organization will be relegated to four years of dumpster fires, which will surely result in the head coach and, likely, the general manager seeing their careers end, or get put on pause, unceremoniously in that city. And, if your team did get a top five draft pick at quarterback through being 2-14, then your roster is likely filled with holes that one quarterback who is just starting his career isn't going to fix, you're still in a jam. You still have to find talent elsewhere. If this is done through free agency, these kinds of players can be very expensive.

If you're caught in a cycle where you're chasing an elite quarterback without an efficient system in place, it can set your organization up for a multi-year cycle of free agents avoiding your city unless they're slightly overpaid because playing a 16-game football season is hard enough; playing for a bad team that consistently loses at this sport of simulated war is significantly less fun. In needing to slightly overpay the, typically, overpriced talent that mismanaged organizations are able to acquire, they set themselves up for a disadvantage in the salary cap. We've seen this situation play out during the last decade and a half in places like Oakland, Washington and Cleveland, three organizations that seem to be stabilizing themselves after years of gross inefficiencies, although Washington is always a Dan Snyder outburst away from chaos, which they've seemed to slide back into during the 2017 offseason. The Browns are still bad in 2017, but they at least now seem to have a plan for the future with the way they've acquired draft picks. Without systems based thinking, these organizations floundered for a long time because they had no concept of what they were trying to build without the right coach and front office combination. They spent years cycling through the wrong guys and the various systems they tried to implement.

Over the years that head coaches and coordinators implement their efficient offensive and defensive systems, they create their own identity through their interpretation of the principles of efficient football. Through this process, the coach ends up developing his unique prototype for each position as an almost quantifiable formula that creates their intended end result. These prototypes are measured in terms of size, skill, and production requirements that help organizations find value in unexpected places as we have seen in the Patriots, Seahawks, Ravens, Broncos, and Steelers. Rather than chasing the obviously talented players you'll likely only find in the first round, teams find value through identifying the characteristics that each position requires and then finding those in players who can be found at a lower cost than the top rounds of the draft or the top of a positional market.

Looking at the variations of the West Coast system, we see the various styles of offensive players needed for recently retired Gary Kubiak's Texans and Broncos, Darrelle Bevell's Seahawks, Mike McCarthey's Packers and the Andy Reid Chiefs. Each system has its own vision for their ideal quarterback and with knowledge of the level of production that your team needs to succeed at quarterback (and elsewhere), teams can build their roster around a lesser quarterback while waiting to find their ideal quarterback, but with the ability to improve around that player and project the improvements that have to be made. The Seahawks did this masterfully transitioning from Tavaris Jackson in 2011 to Russell Wilson in 2012, with Matt Flynn signed that year as a low-cost veteran option, by building up their whole roster rather than drafting a quarterback in the first-round early in the rebuild and trying to have him lead a less talented roster, which seemed to be the prevailing strategy under the NFL Collective Bargaining Agreement that ended after the 2010 season.

During the mid-2000s, a huge overvaluation of the quarterback position, economically and philosophically, drove the price of the entire market through the roof. The high priced contracts that were being given to quarterbacks drafted at the top of the first-round, coupled with what seemed to be a desire from coaches around the league to see how many yards their quarterbacks could throw for, were major contributing factors in the rising costs. The unbalanced passing philosophy might have been due to the increase in costs of the market causing organizations to try to justify these costs. This focus on passing then led to teams investing a lot of money at left tackle and wide receiver as well.

Since the market has stabilized a bit with the new CBA and many organizations are in the process of learning the lessons from the pass heavy focus of the previous decade, we're now in a situation where across the NFL, most teams seem to be looking for a passer who can complete above the 2016 NFL average of 63% of his passes with over 250 passing yards per game without turning the ball over, plus a certain level of mobility that can be dependent on the offensive coordinator's system. Mobility isn't just important for running the football, but also for escaping pressure in the pocket and extending plays, so no matter the system, every team is looking for someone with some of that Aaron Rodgers escape-ability factor. There seems to be a certain yards per pass attempt metric that teams are shooting for, which is a newer concept that football people should be studying over the next few years to determine the balance of completion percentage and yards per attempt that is best for each team as well as NFL football in general. While teams want a high completion percentage, they also want to have a passing offense that can move the ball in the seven and a half to eight and a half yards per attempt range, which requires taking a certain number of passes further down the field.

Some systems, like Andy Reid's, prefer a quarterback with the potential to also run for 300 to 400 plus yards over the course of the season as seen by the decade and a half of Donovan McNabb and Alex Smith. That comes out to 19 to 25 rushing yards per game, which could be drive-extending plays that lead to scores. Anyone who knows this knew that Carson Wentz was the ideal system fit for Doug Pederson, a Reid protégé, when they saw him drafted to Philadelphia. Breaking production and skills down into their components makes it much easier to project how a player will fare in his transition to the pro game if a coach asks him to run an offense that fits his strengths.

Quarterback is the best starting point for the conversation on prototypes, but these extend out to every position in unique, self-created systems around the NFL with the Patriots providing the best, most well-known example of this with their pass-catching running back role, their lead power rushing running back, their short, quick slot receivers and big touchdown making tight ends. This extends all the way to the offensive line and then of course defense and special teams as well. They understand the principles of what they're trying to accomplish, so they can mold the system to these principles to accomplish their objective. Once a coach has established his system, he has all of his personalized prototypes for each position, which allows the organization to develop strategies for finding the pieces to build their roster.

Each position and role is basically a job description used to target potential late-round picks, undrafted free agents or low-cost veteran free agents who can contribute to your organization in a way that far exceeds their expectations and salary costs. Over The Cap's Jason Fitzgerald projects that about 75% of an NFL roster turns over every three years, so every organization needs to have a framework for what they're trying to build just to keep the team building process focused enough to consistently fill their roster. As Fitzgerald noted in the middle of the 2017 season, only 22% of the NFL is playing on a contract signed in 2015 or earlier and 52% of NFL rosters are players who signed a contract in 2017. They need to be able to input pieces into a formula rather than create a whole new formula every few years.

The Patriots dynasty of the early-2000s used the framework to turn their roster over between 2001 and 2003 in a way that allowed them to win a second and third Super Bowl. A total of 31 of the Patriots 53-man roster for their Super Bowl 38 victory were added to their roster after the Super Bowl 36 win after the 2001 season: that's 58.5% turnover, and of the 20 Patriots who actually played in both Super Bowls, five were not on the 2004 opening day roster. That high turnover rate was what allowed the Patriots to keep improving yearly as they used the draft and free agency to keep upgrading toward their ideal roster.

Teams should take lessons from the college game, where coaches know they have only three to five years with each player, so they create systems so unique they're usually branded with the coach's name. These systems have very specific prototypes because of their need to continually replenish the roster. If you're looking for the exact same thing as everyone else in your conference, then it becomes more difficult to recruit and even more difficult to create advantages against your opponents.

Alabama is known for "The Process," which is essentially the process of doing things that Saban and his staff have developed over time for managing a college football program that, if followed, will result in a championship caliber team. The premise is simple, like the goal for success for NFL teams explained at the beginning of this book; Saban is trying to create a team that can compete for championships annually by being good enough to be in the mix every year.

In the 2013 book named *The System: The Glory and Scandal of Big-Time College Football*, by Jeff Benedict and Armen Keteyian, former Alabama defensive coordinator and current Georgia head coach Kirby Smart discusses "the blueprint" for success they use to recruit.[2] The authors go on to write, "as detailed by Andy Staples in *Sports Illustrated*, the blueprint targeted high school athletes who fit certain character/attitude/intelligence criteria and position-specific height/weight/speed guidelines tailored to Alabama's offensive and defensive schemes. Cornerbacks, for example, should ideally be between six feet and six feet two inches and about 190 pounds and run a sub-4.5 forty-yard dash; linemen should stand no less than six feet two because, as Smart drily noted, 'big people beat up little people.'" Smart added that they have player descriptions or player profiles, which they might call a job description—and if a really good player doesn't fit those descriptions, they'll pass over them as the player does not fit what they need.

Saban and Belichick are close friends, so I would imagine they've inspired each other in their thinking surrounding their roster building process. With their well-documented obsessions with the game of football, very few coaches have collected as much data as these two have over their careers learning about the sport and looking for new solutions. Those years of experience led to their championships and their championship teams have then provided a proven framework for what has worked before for them to build future champions. Those player descriptions provide the Crimson Tide with a player-based formula for their roster that results in championships.

Having a championship proven blueprint with position and role specific job descriptions turns roster development into something similar to putting ingredients into a recipe that you've already cooked before and know you love. In a conversation on *The Tim Ferriss Show* with Alex Honnold, a rock climber who climbs without a rope, Ferriss said that so much of mitigating risk is figuring out a plan and sticking to it saying, "if I follow these rules, it will likely turn out this way."[3] When you've won championships, your blueprint is no longer just a plan: it has become a formula for success, so Saban doesn't stray far from recruiting players who fit his system and Belichick doesn't spend on expensive pieces in free agency.

The Belichick system is predicated on building a complete roster with strong offensive and defensive lines, a quantity of mismatch creators at the skill positions and a defense that can deal with all the mismatches that offenses can potentially create. He also places a huge emphasis on special teams, identifying the importance of winning the hidden yard battle with your punter and punt returner, having a field goal kicker who can consistently provide you points, and using special teams as a way to gain an advantage when evenly matched otherwise. Understanding the key, simple first principle of football being 11-on-11 simulated team war for sport, NFL teams can use their 53-man roster to put the best 11 players on the field for every situation they could face over the course of a season.

Abiding by the basic principle to build the best roster top to bottom in the NFL means that Belichick, by the law of this principle, must avoid large, risky salary cap expenditures because they can get in the way of building the best, most complete, most versatile roster he can create. During the 2016 offseason, the Patriots traded first-round star defensive end Chandler Jones to the Cardinals because of their successful salary cap framework developed over the Belichick Era. Heavy investment in a small handful of players can become very restrictive, so the Patriots avoid it to keep their cap flexibility. In return, they received a former first-round pick at offensive guard, Jonathan Cooper, who they released early in the 2016 season, and a second-round pick that they traded to New Orleans for 2016 third- and fourth-round picks that they used to select an immediate starter at guard, Joe Thuney, and a contributor at receiver, Malcolm Mitchell, both of whom were key contributors in their 2016 Super Bowl run. They followed the formula, while acquiring two players who will give them tremendous value over the course of their four rookie contract years.

The Patriots Super Bowl salary cap framework has one high cap hit in Tom Brady, who is around 10%, then a second cap hit around five to seven percent, with Jones slated to get a large pay increase in 2018 whether he was given the franchise tag or signed to an extension. Having a defensive end at 7-11% of the cap was not a part of their 2016 formula and, with the extension he received in Arizona, Jones will cost somewhere in that range through 2021. With a handful of less expensive, but key players, hitting free agency during the 2017 offseason for the Patriots, the

Jones trade gave them the flexibility to build their best roster moving forward. They always take the long-view rather than allowing themselves to overpay for a star player who they could replace at a lower cost to build the better overall team.

In *Management Secrets of the New England Patriots*, author James Lavin points out that the 2001 and 2003 Patriots both had just two Pro Bowlers compared to an average of 7.06 Pro Bowlers on the other champions from 1970 to 2003.[4] The conclusion, which I think still holds true today, is that the Patriots "had few great players, but many very good ones." One NFL team's study after 2003 found that the Patriots only had two of the top 60 premier players in Brady and Richard Seymour, but they led the NFL in second tier talent. While that study was probably a more subjective analysis than what we'd approved of today, this notion is supported by how the Patriots salary cap is structured, which they build through the "draft and extend" strategy. Using their formula with a well-developed, and continually improving, analytics and scouting process has allowed the Patriots to draft successfully and then sign key players to extensions before they hit free agency or re-sign them to reasonable contracts in March when they hit free agency, consistently creating value and cap space across the roster. An extension provides the player with more financial security than his mid to late-round rookie contract and the organization with the player at a lower cost than if he were to hit free agency. They combine that with targeting lower tier free agents who they've identified as system fits who will provide value at a lower cost to fill the roles they haven't filled through the draft. Being a well-run organization also makes the Patriots an intriguing destination for free agents, especially older players looking for a chance at a championship with that track record of success also encouraging their homegrown talent to stay home.

Due to Belichick's mastery of the sport and his system, he has a better understanding than anyone else in the NFL of the economic concepts that allow him to continually find value in a way no one else has been able to do and that no one has been close to sustaining for as long as he has. Like that Thiel quote, Lavin points out that the Patriots find value by thinking differently; they have found talent by looking at players who "were overlooked because they were injured, unsuited to the scheme they played in, overshadowed by other great players or simply under appreciated by their team." And since Belichick knows exactly what his system needs, he's able to identify valuable players in later draft rounds as well as in free agency. He also understands where value at certain positions can be found later in the draft. The most consistent, successful organizations in the NFL seem to be able to do this.

The draft process has a supply and demand strategy to it for each position, as do free agent markets, and high levels of production can be found at certain positions in later rounds. Systems can maximize this return on late round investments like we've seen with the way that Mike Shanahan, Gary Kubiak and Andy Reid have found tremendous production from mid- to late-round running backs. Positions like middle linebacker, running back and the interiors of the offensive and defensive lines can consistently be found after the first round, which is what depresses the wages in those positional markets as well. With low-cost talent available, these players have less leverage. Belichick's Super Bowl teams have consistently had low costs at center, guard, running back, slot receiver and even quarterback because his knowledge of his system allows the team to identify the players who can perform in the Patriots system. With Brady out with an injury in 2008 and his DeflateGate suspension in 2016, the Patriots went 13-6 with seventh-round pick Matt Cassel, second-rounder Jimmy Garoppolo and third-round pick Jacoby Brissett. This belies the over simplified conclusion that many fans have that this long-term success is only possible because of Brady, who is a sixth-round pick in his own right.

The systems based approach allows an organization to create a value-based structure for how they build their draft strategy to maximize their return on their draft resources each year. For instance, if a player who fits your system is available in the first round, but another player who has many of the same skills and is available later, a team like the Patriots might use that first-round pick on a need they can't fill with the same confidence later to use the later pick on that lesser hyped player they like. In 2000, Chad Pennington and Tom Brady both had the general label of smart and accurate without superior arm strength. One of them went in the first round to the Jets; the other is a Hall of Famer and might be the greatest quarterback of all-time.

Great organizations can see where the team is now, what they need now and what they need in the future, which allows them to develop an offseason strategy to fulfill those needs. A team like the Patriots uses the lower tiers of free agency to fill their short-term needs and, generally, use the draft for their long-term needs as they've built a roster with few big short term needs that they're forced to solve with a rookie sixth or seventh rounder, an undrafted free agent, or overspending in free agency like lesser organizations are forced to because a need is so large. The best organizations draft before they need to fix an issue so they can develop players. This development process is part of what allows them to confidently let a veteran walk in free agency if his value to the team exceeds his free agent market costs.

Bringing analytics and the increasing access to actionable data into the fold, organizations will be increasingly able to quantify individual and team production goals for success, then project how a new player would likely fit into that equation. Production goals help frame the entire depth chart, providing decision makers with an idea of what kind of players you might add and subtract from your roster to improve your chances of achieving Super Bowl success. It's like the team uses the system as the base for building their own Wins Above Replacement style football stat like the "W.A.R." stat that exists in baseball.

As explained in Chapter One, Paul DePodesta is shifting the Browns toward an estimated 60% analytics and 40% scouting split from the 70% scouting and 30% analytics split that many in the NFL apparently use. Technology will continue to produce more data that will allow that shift to move further toward the analytics split. The blueprint allows a team to input pieces into a system, which increases the impact of the analytics and scouting process, helping match the right players with the right job description. An ability to consistently fill the roles of a blueprint allows an organization to stay ahead of schedule, always prepared for the future and prepared for a player's potential departure because they're almost always able to find one, or more than one, player who will replace a departing player's production for a lower cost. After 2014, Shane Vereen left for the Giants in free agency for a contract worth $4 million a year, then here come James White and Dion Lewis on contracts that had them both near the league minimum. Similarly, Vereen replaced Danny Woodhead who replaced Kevin Faulk. Vereen and Woodhead shared the role in 2012, while Woodhead was signed by New England in 2010 after being released by the Jets as Faulk had torn his ACL. The best systems have an understanding of the supply and demand within positional markets and across the sport to ensure they're not building an expensive system.

Some of these economic concepts are common sense. There are 1,696 players on active NFL rosters, plus 256 practice squad players for a total of 1,952 players. This doesn't count players on IR during the season, but generally speaking roughly 2,000 players are in the NFL. From a supply and demand standpoint, even if every team in the NFL needs a certain type of player, then the 32 teams are looking for 32 starters and 32 back-ups for a total of about 64 total players needed. Of course since every team doesn't have the exact same system, 32 to 64 of the same prototype isn't required as most systems have slightly different requirements.

Belichick's prototypes at slot receiver and pass catching running back are genius because a massive supply of athletes in the 5'9" to 5'11", 190-pound receiver and 5'8", 200-pound pass catching running back molds exist and they have attributes that lend well to moving the chains and even scoring touchdowns. The increased supply comes from there being more humans in these Belichick molds than the 6'4", 225-pound prototype #1 receiver or the 5'11", 215-pound complete running back. There exists a current trend towards athletes in this 5'9" to 6' range who can move in the open field with the ball in their hands and make people miss. A lower center of gravity with elite quickness can make these players very hard to tackle. Looking at the UFC, the weight classes that need athletes between 5'8" and 5'11", like featherweight (145 pounds), lightweight (155) and welterweight (170), are deeper than flyweight (125), light heavyweight (205), and heavyweight (265) as far more athletes are around the average height of American males.

Teams around the league are using these two Belichick inspired prototypes, but even if they were to all follow his example, Belichick would still be able to find these guys. Not only is there a massive supply of humans in that size, but a growing supply of college football players who are in those molds and working towards being that Wes Welker or Kevin Faulk type of player.

As an aside, NFL coaches should be partially influenced by the college supply; taking note of the Dynamic advancements in the sport we're seeing there and taking them into account when working on improving their system. This is part of why we're seeing spread concepts and mobile quarterbacks being incorporated into the league more every year. If the college game is providing more spread players, then NFL teams finding a way to utilize those players to the best of their ability is only natural. Dynamic advances in Quality eventually become static Quality and new Dynamic advances take their place as the trends forming our future static Quality.

Even in developing a more objective process fueled by the continuous increase in actionable data, there will still be misses, but with stability and alignment within the organization, there will be increasingly fewer misses as the process is improved. Fewer misses means fewer negative cap consequences, fewer mistakes that need to be replaced with higher veteran spending to patch over a draft miss, and less dead money through not needing to go to free agency repeatedly for higher cost, higher risk signings. A 2004 *Washington Post* article by Jason La Canfora and Nunyo Demasio cites a league wide computer study "to determine if there was any relationship between aggressive salary cap spending and winning. Joe Banner, the Eagles president and resident salary cap guru at the time, stated, "there was only one thing that really directly correlated with any consistency and that was that the teams with the smallest amount of miscellaneous charges (meaning dead money) made the playoffs and advanced in the playoffs, way more than the teams that had the larger miscellaneous charges."[5]

While subtracting those potential negatives from the process, less misses means more savings. You're acquiring more contributors at a low draft cost whose low contracts provide the opportunity to sign players to extensions at below free agent market costs. This means short-term savings on rookie contracts and long-term savings by being able to always stay ahead of that player hitting the market with reasonable increases in income through signing bonuses and salaries that incentivize him enough to sign on, while keeping him below free market costs. Solid drafting creates win-win situations for a player and his team, which helps build a positive organizational culture. Simple, good decisions make for positive consequences. Having a higher number of productive players on rookie contracts also leaves more cap space to make smart, reasonable free agent acquisitions.

To maximize the return on investment of a systems based strategy backed by the right analytics and scouting mix, NFL teams need to bridge the gap between industry spending on research and development and what other industries spend. The product that NFL teams produce are their football teams, so R&D means the spending that goes into acquiring and developing the talent that makes up their roster. NFL franchises have become billion dollar businesses with league revenues passing $14 billion in 2016 and Roger Goodell projecting that the league will produce $25 billion in revenues by 2027. We can see the growth in revenues over the salary cap era just by looking at the salary cap jump almost 500% from $34,608,000 in 1994 to $167,000,000 in 2017. Yet, with that increase in revenues, the amount of money that NFL teams spend on their scouting departments is remarkably small, at least in 2011 when Jack Bechta breached the subject in an article titles, "Are NFL scouting departments underfunded?"[6]

As he writes, "most large fortune 1000 companies involved in producing consumer goods and services spend anywhere from 15% to 20% of their gross income on R&D in creating new products or improving on current ones. Translating that corporate investment formula to the NFL would mean that each NFL team would spend about 15% of gross revenues on their scouting departments and all related player diligence expenses."

At the time Bechta wrote the article, he estimated that an average NFL team spent somewhere between $2-3 million per year on R&D, which he considered to be college and professional scouting combined. Considering the public doesn't have complete access to the financial reports of NFL teams, I can't get an exact figure on this spending, but since the Packers are a publicly traded company, their financials are public. They had $375 million in revenues in 2014, so $2-3 million obviously isn't anywhere close to 15% of revenues.[7] Without access to financial data, I can't say much more on this spending, but the low success rate in the NFL Draft supports the idea that league-wide inefficiencies exist and they need to be addressed and improved.

The fifth-year option for first-round rookie contracts was introduced in this CBA to provide teams with the ability to control a first-rounder's rights for his first five years if they choose to, while providing the player with a reasonable fair-market value during his fifth-year. Players drafted in the Top 10 see a fifth-year salary equal to the average of the Top 10 highest paid players at their position and picks 11 through 32 see a fifth-year salary that averages the salaries of the third through 25th highest paid players at their position. These are fair rates as a Top 10 pick should become a Top 10 player at his position by his fifth-year and a player drafted a little later in the first-round should certainly become worth what's basically the average for a veteran starter. In theory, the players drafted in the first-round are the top 32 players coming from college football the previous season who project to have the skills to translate to the next level, so teams should be able to draft players they can develop into starters by their fifth season out of this group.

These options are picked up prior to the start of the first-rounder's' fourth year in the NFL. During the 2016 offseason, just 19 of the 32 first-round picks from the 2013 draft saw their teams sign on to retain their rights for their fifth season. Using a team exercising the fifth-year option as a metric for success, that means that only 59.4% of 2013 first-round picks were considered a success. With the amount of effort that goes into the draft, and the expectations of first round picks, a 59.4% rate of triggering a fair market value team option is a staggering lack of success for billion dollar organizations.

Teams spend months, or it may be more accurate to say years, analyzing the players they might draft with their first pick, yet they are still capable of failing at such a high rate. With the ability to objectively quantify more every year through analytics, an increase in spending on R&D combined with the increasing use of frameworks and formulas will allow teams to find and insert key pieces into their system with increasing accuracy.

I can't give an exact analysis of where teams are or where they should be without access to team's books, but using the 15-20% estimate from other industries, I've come up with two estimates for costs based off the 2014 salary cap and the 2014 Packers revenue to use the same years. By the time this book is released, 2014 will be far in the rearview, but the spending metrics of 15-20% will still apply. Using that year's salary cap, this means the range would be between $19.95 to $26.6 million in spending, while basing that 15-20% off the Packers revenue would come to $56.25 to $75 million.

Bechta's article talked about R&D as spending based off of revenue, but considering that the 2014 cap was $133 million, he believed that spending between 43 and 57% of the salary cap on that expense might be a little too high considering the task at hand. Taking those figures with my outsiders point of view, I'd just bring that basic, total scouting spending up towards $20 to $25 million from the $2 to $3 million Bechta mentioned. These expenses can include developmental spending like salary cap analysis, analytics, player development, sports science and other expenses that go into improving the quality of the players already on your roster. Teams need to increase spending on things that help them identify and develop their core product, the team they put on the field each season. The math matters less than the overall message that, generally speaking, current league-wide draft processes are inefficient and teams aren't spending enough money on it, so the spending on the scouting and analytics process that goes into player acquisition must be increased.

Take the fact that, as of this writing, 25 out of 32 NFL teams use a scouting service like BLESTO or National Football Scouting. BLESTO stands for Bears, Lions, Eagles and Steelers Talent Organization and was established back in the 1960s before the NFL expanded into the economic behemoth it is today. These organizations were founded before the technological advancements that make every college football player's game film accessible to an organization from its offices and before teams had access to the financial resources they have today.

The NFL Combine didn't come into existence until 1982 and, according to the NFL's website, "until the 1970s, teams typically didn't give physical exams to their potential draft picks. In 1976, the New York Jets became one of the first to invite college seniors to team headquarters for physicals and interviews."[8] In an April 1983 article for *The New York Times*, the Jets director of player personnel at the time, Mike Hickey, wrote "besides character and intelligence, the other non-football thing we put a premium on is the medical aspect. We attempt to have every player we are interested in have an orthopedic physical by our team physicians."[9]

Hickey credited this process to the seven years of draft success they'd had since then and up to that point, which had resulted in nearly half of the 36 players the team drafted since 1977 becoming starters. Although it took a lot of time and cost far more money than their previous draft process, Hickey believed the time and money were well spent as they "cut down the odds of making a mistake."

With their success, other teams followed their lead. This meant that top prospects were traveling around the country for interviews and physicals from whichever NFL teams were interested in them in a time consuming and expensive process. As more teams adopted this practice, Tex Schramm recommended to the NFL Competition Committee that teams work together to centralize the evaluation process, so the first NFL Combine was conducted in 1982, bringing the top college players to one location to get medical information and scout the players for its 16 member clubs. National Football Scouting ran this, so the other two major scouting services, BLESTO and Quadra Scouting, started their own camps for the teams that didn't partner with NFS. Considering the teams in the league were nowhere near where they are now financially speaking, I would imagine these combines made being a part of these organizations a requirement. In 1985, the three camps were merged to save costs and the NFL chose NFS, which ran the largest camp at the time, to run the NFL Combine. This pooling of resources was extremely valuable and necessary at the time. Teams became far more able to spend time on physical and psychological testing, which gave personnel departments a far better picture of the players they were drafting than they ever had before.

With the NFL Combine being run through the league today, eliminating a big reason teams originally signed up, plus technology allowing more access to information on prospects, teams can drop out of the scouting services and do it on their own. Two of the teams who don't use these scouting services are the Patriots and the Ravens, two of the best-managed organizations in the NFL over the last two decades.

Membership responsibilities aren't costly at only $100,000 in annual dues, so teams don't necessarily need to drop out, but they do need to drastically increase the amount of money they spend on the rest of their analytics and scouting mix. These scouting services work out underclassmen for future draft years and then provide reports that serve organizations as the starting point and outline of future draft classes. This is valuable, so it is likely to be worth the small expense for a billion dollar organization, but I believe franchises could do this for themselves, keep everything they do in house and build the processes required within their organizations.

I think this anecdote from the Missouri Southern State head coach at the time, Daryl Daye, sums up the attention to detail that teams that handle everything in house go to. Speaking to Ryan Mink from Ravens.com, Daye said he had never seen a scout work as hard or be as thorough as Ravens Southwest Area scout Jack Glowick.[10] Daye said he took his time, stayed late after other scouts were gone and his hard work was rewarded by the team drafting Missouri Southern State's Brandon Williams with the 94th pick in the 2013 draft to replace the expensive and aging Haloti Ngata. They then traded Ngata to the Lions with a seventh-round pick before the 2015 draft for a fourth- and fifth-round pick, while Williams has become one of the best interior defenders in the NFL. This saved them $8.5 million in 2015 and they spent the fourth-rounder on defensive end Za'Darius Smith and traded the fifth-rounder with their second-rounder to move up to draft tight end Maxx Williams. These are the kinds of moves teams can make if they have assets and the ability to draft quality consistently; they create the opportunity for value. The Ravens have spent years working on their draft processes under the same management, thus improving those processes. Stability creates the alignment we talked about and teams are able to save money by moving on from players who cost more than they would be worth to them.

Even with the increase in spending on the analytics and scouting process that we're proposing and even with a blueprint to follow, there will still be misses in the draft. The only way to ensure access to a steady flow of low-cost labor that provides your team the value necessary to sustain success is to stockpile draft picks like the Browns new front office started doing during the 2016 offseason to start a cycle that will lead to an ability to trade players for draft picks as well as let their own free agents go, without signing free agents, to receive some of the 32 compensatory draft picks each year. An excess of draft picks helps create the compensatory pick cycle through successful drafting. Building a yearly surplus of draft picks is critical and compensatory picks play a role in creating that surplus.

Maybe the most important rule to remember with compensatory picks is that when a team re-signs a player, that does not count against them in regards to the compensatory pick formula. So teams that draft well get the benefit of re-signing their players, not needing to go to free agency and with the players they decide against re-signing creating a net loss in free agency, they can earn compensatory picks year after year. Compensatory picks have been around since the beginning of the salary cap era and there have generally been as many compensatory picks as there are teams. From 2011 through 2016, there have been 161 compensatory picks, as the NFL misapplied a rule in 2016 that resulted in a 33rd compensatory pick, and the top five in picks reads like a list of yearly playoff teams with the Ravens (16), Packers (11), 49ers (10), Seahawks (9) and Steelers (9), while the five teams with zero compensatory picks in this time is a list of teams who have had on field or salary cap issues in recent years in the Bears, Jaguars, Saints, Bucs and Redskins. With the 32 added compensatory picks of the 2017 draft, the Packers and Steelers added one each, the Seahawks and 49ers added two, while the Saints and Buccaneers had their first compensatory picks of the new CBA that they acquired through trades, not through the compensatory process. Develop the roster from within and benefit from the positive salary cap cycle that results.

The average number of picks per team in the draft each year is now eight, but the cap era average has been slightly skewed down due to forfeited picks and picks used in the supplemental draft. From 1994 through 2015, only eight teams averaged eight or more draft picks per year: the Patriots, Packers, Titans, Rams, Eagles, Steelers, Bills and Bengals. The Patriots, Packers, Steelers and Eagles represent the kind of success that stability and alignment, plus a draft surplus, make possible. Each team has established their style of football and they have continued to fill competitive rosters. Their winning percentages are .543 or better from 1994 through 2016 with the first three winning over 60% of their games. The Titans had a .542 winning percentage under Jeff Fisher, but are on their third head coach since parting ways after the 2010 season, although they seem poised to make a jump in 2017 with head coach Mike Mularkey and quarterback Marcus Mariota. The Rams and Bills have had plenty of draft picks, but a constant cycle of coaches hasn't allowed either of them to build a consistent winner. The Bengals' winning percentage during the cap era is dragged down by the pre-Marvin Lewis era as they've drastically improved their processes since hiring him.

When the 2016 draft is added in, the 49ers, Browns, Ravens, Seahawks, Texans, Dolphins, Cowboys, Bears, and Vikings also breach eight picks per year to bring the total to 17 of 32 teams averaging over eight picks a year. Seven of the 17 teams (41.2%) have winning percentages under .500 with those teams being the Titans, Rams, Bills, Browns, Bengals, Texans, and Bears. Ten of the 15 teams (66.7%) with less than eight picks per year, the Jaguars, Cardinals, Buccaneers, Raiders, Panthers, Lions, Chargers, Jets, Redskins, and Saints are under .500 for the period.

More opportunities to acquire low-cost, high-value labor increases an organization's ability to create the positive team building cycle we're looking for. From 1994 through 2016, the Patriots and Packers lead the salary cap era with winning percentages of .693 and .641; they also lead the NFL with the most draft picks during that time at 210 and 204, which come out to 9.13 and 8.87 per season. These are the two most homegrown organizations in the NFL with both teams rarely needing to dip into free agency for top of the market talent.

To build the Cowboys 1990s dynasty, Jimmy Johnson and Jerry Jones made 51 total trades, which is more than the rest of the NFL combined at the time. Most of these trades involved draft picks and their ability to find value in trading draft picks led to the use of Jimmy Johnson's Draft Value Chart for the last 25 years.[11] This chart was used as a numerical representation of each pick to balance out value of draft picks in trades. For example, if the 16th pick in the first round is worth 1000 points, then it is considered the equivalent of the 31st (600 points) and 18th pick in the second round (400). During the 2016 offseason, Jason Fitzgerald came up with a more dynamic chart that should be the new standard and will be explained further in chapter 10.

Cleveland has been following the same strategy of compiling draft picks over a few drafts to build their roster. The year before the regime change they had 12 draft picks. With General Manager Sashi Brown and DePodesta leading the way, the Browns tied an NFL record of 14 draft picks set by the 1997 Dolphins. In 2017, they had 10 picks, including three first round picks. As of November 2017, the Browns are slated to have 13 picks in the 2018 draft with two first round picks and three in the second round.

Some will, somewhat rightfully, bash the Browns for passing on Carson Wentz with the second pick of the 2016 draft, but that trade created such a draft surplus that they have the picks and the cap space to make a move during the 2018 offseason for a rookie or veteran signal caller. As ESPN's Pat McManamon detailed in April 2017, the trade netted the Browns nine players and picks in the first and second round of 2018 because of the trade of the 2016 #2 pick and a 2017 fourth rounder to the Eagles for the #8 pick that they acquired from the Dolphins, a third and fourth-round pick in 2016, a first round pick in 2017, and a second round pick in 2018. According to McManamon, those nine players were wide receiver Corey Coleman, offensive tackle Shon Coleman, quarterback Cody Kessler, wide receiver Ricardo Louis, safety Derrick Kindred, wide receiver Jordan Payton, offensive guard/tackle Spencer Drango, safety Jabrill Peppers, and quarterback DeShone Kizer.[12]

They seemed to make another mistake by passing on Deshaun Watson and instead trading the #12 pick to the Texans for the #15 pick as well as the 2018 first-round pick mentioned above. Rightfully, many around the league are questioning them after missing on Wentz and Watson, but the organization made a conscious decisions to build the rest of their roster before investing a top pick in a rookie quarterback who would be thrown into a difficult, rebuilding situation.

Jason wrote an October 2017 article titled, "Thoughts on the Cleveland Browns." He included a table that looked at every quarterback drafted from 2002 through 2014 and "did a quick good, passable, miss rating for the quarterbacks drafted," which is included below:

Pick	Good	Passable	Miss
7	0.0%	7.1%	92.9%
6	0.0%	3.4%	96.6%
5	0.0%	0.0%	100.0%
4	5.9%	11.8%	82.4%
3	6.3%	12.5%	81.3%
2	6.7%	13.3%	80.0%
1	23.7%	15.8%	60.5%
Pick 11-32	11.1%	11.1%	77.8%
Top 10	35.0%	20.0%	45.0%

The point Jason was making was that they missed an opportunity to have the highest probability of success in drafted a quarterback with their top 10 picks and even that #12 pick with Watson still on the board. What I see with this table, and what I see with quite a few past top draft picks, especially within the Browns organization, is that top picks on bad rosters are placed in situations that make it difficult to succeed, which can impede their personal progress. Also, the picks acquired by the Browns allowed them to construct a much better roster for whoever they insert in 2018 now that DeShone Kizer, Cody Kessler, and Kevin Hogan don't seem to be a solution.

What I also see with the table is that 65.0% of top 10 picks at quarterback don't grade out as good quarterbacks, so drafting a quarterback in the top 10 still comes with the risk of failure. Add that probability to a bad roster and you're further decreasing that young quarterback's probability of success. While Wentz and Watson would probably both eventually become the quarterbacks they seem capable of becoming in Cleveland, Cleveland has already tried to draft a quarterback to a bad roster without success. As the old cliché goes, "insanity is doing the same thing over and over again and expecting different results." Tim Couch, Brady Quinn, Brandon Weeden, and Johnny Manziel were all highly regarded players coming out of college, for their various reasons they didn't work out. The team never got better with any of the players on the roster. Couch was the only top ten pick there, but the four of them contributed to the 60.5% miss rate for first round quarterbacks from 2002 to 2014.

This is not to say that the Browns current strategy will work out. We can't predict the future, but they decided they were going to build up a roster, hopefully find a quarterback who could protect the football, which their three quarterbacks haven't in 2017 for a team that leads the NFL in turnovers through 12 games, with a strong running game, which they haven't gotten either, and a great defense, which I believe they're in the process of building. They missed on Wentz and Watson, but they could have just as easily missed on them by drafting them considering the rates of success and the situation they would have been placed into. While we don't know the outcome as of now and they're 1-23 in their last 24 games, we're getting to see this experiment in real time and it is based in logic. I believe the draft picks that have built up the Browns roster will pay off once they find the signal caller for the job in 2018, so, while they missed on two great quarterbacks, I can't fault them for this move. They still have two first round picks in 2018, at least one of which may be a top 10 pick, if not a top pick or a top three pick, and the potential for over $110 million in cap space with over $60 million to rollover into 2018, so the moves they've been waiting to make are likely to happen in 2018 with a roster that will have legitimate building blocks because of the moves they made in years prior. They could even use both first round picks on quarterbacks a la the 1989 Dallas Cowboys considering the way they've constructed the rest of the roster during the last couple years. A draft surplus is key to building up a bad roster as the free agency path isn't a viable path to get from bad to good; it takes draft success and a surplus of picks helps increase the probability of success.

With new General Manager Brandon Beane and head coach Sean McDermott taking over the Bills in 2017, they have shown they'll be implementing a similar strategy with their trades of two productive players in wide receiver Sammy Watkins and cornerback Ronald Darby. In sending Watkins to the Rams they received cornerback E.J. Gaines and a 2018 second round pick. By sending Darby to the Eagles, they got back wide receiver Jordan Matthews and a third round pick. They downgraded at two positions in the short-term, but currently have two picks in each of the first three rounds of the 2018 NFL Draft. They also traded inside linebacker Reggie Ragland to the Chiefs for a fourth-round pick in 2019 during the 2017 training camp as the draft pick for Rex Ryan's 3-4 defense no longer fit the 4-3 defense that McDermott will run. Rather than try and beat the Patriots in the now, which they're unlikely to; the Bills are making the moves to compete in the near future and build a favorable cap situation.

The blueprints, the increase in spending on scouting and analytics, and the development of a surplus of draft picks increases an organization's ability to stay ahead of the salary cap and make future plans. Understanding the value they place on their own players and all potential players they acquire is critical for every team. This is why creative coaches who build an understanding of their own systems are able to find value in a way that an average coach can't, they can quantify how productive they believe certain players will be based on their system's needs and how they fit in.

During the 2016 NFL Draft, ESPN displayed a graphic that showed the composition of NFL rosters in 2015 by the rounds that the players were drafted in. First-round picks made up 14% of NFL rosters, second and third-round picks made up 22%, and players drafted in the fourth-round or later made up 64% of rosters. Similarly, according to Elias, before the start of the 2016 season, more undrafted free agents made up NFL rosters than first and second-round picks combined by a margin of 481 to 480. Through finding contributors in the later rounds, a team creates huge savings with players making near the league minimum, while also giving themselves the opportunity to retain players through the draft and extend strategy. If your roster is going to be made up of a high percentage of late round picks, the best course of action is to acquire these players through the draft, so you can take advantage of their low-cost rookie contracts and you can potentially extend or re-sign them at below market rates, rather than pay the higher rates of free agency. This frame of thinking is why the Patriots and Packers have been able to create cap flexibility for years because they've been extremely stable with their established blueprints that have allowed them to capitalize on the surplus of draft picks they've had.

The draft process is perfected through the steps outlined in this chapter with an understanding of the economic concepts and forces that create player costs in the NFL. Combining a strong draft process with a deep understanding of the positional markets and spending concepts that will be outlined in the coming chapters, teams will be able to optimize salary cap spending to maximize their probability of success.

If you don't create organizational stability and sustain your roster through the processes in this chapter, then you will end up with a situation similar to what we have seen with the chaos of the Redskins during the Dan Snyder Era with the second least number of picks from 1994 to 2016 at 164, which is 7.13 per year with eight different head coaches. Let's take a look at the right way to acquire veterans—the opposite of the Snyder way.

Chapter 4: How to Acquire Veterans

Regardless of how well a team does in the draft, every team will have to use free agency in some capacity. Teams that don't solve their hiring process and waste resources in the draft will have to use free agency more than teams who have a coach who has built and understands his own system well enough to create the alignment with the front office necessary to succeed in the draft.

Teams that don't have draft success will find themselves in a cycle of consistently high costs of labor across their roster because of a lack of talent on their roster acquired through the draft. When a team doesn't have many players they can draft and extend or re-sign, they end up spending that money on free agents. Teams in this cycle may end up spending first tier money on multiple free agents in an attempt to build a team that can compete--and considering the short length of NFL careers, this strategy is very risky. Players can fall off the proverbial cliff in one season to leave your roster with holes that year and dead money the next. The short length of career means free agents must be replaced soon, meaning the strategy has a short window of success with a higher risk of drop off immediately after that window closes.

Spending in free agency then leads to a lack of compensatory picks, which lowers the organization's probability of success in the draft and pushes them further into a cycle of negative cap consequences. A team built on older free agents means your roster lacks the young talent to take your organization into the future, then the lack of compensatory picks due to the spending in free agency means you may lack the resources to acquire that young talent. This can quickly become a cycle of spending in free agency if you don't have success with the draft picks you do have. The 89% Rule in this CBA, which means teams must spend at least 89% of their aggregate salary cap in one of two four-year periods of 2013 through 2016 and 2017 through 2020, may increase the need to spend in free agency to ensure compliance if you have few players within your organization worth extending. That said, no one had trouble meeting the 89% threshold from 2013 to 2016, so reaching it isn't much of a concern, which probably speaks to the need for the next CBA to have a better mechanism to force teams to spend more.

The best organizations, teams like the Patriots and Packers in particular, rarely go to free agency for the big piece. The Packers have consistently gone for the big free agent when he fills a big need on a team with a competitive roster like when they signed Reggie White (1993), Charles Woodson (2006), and Julius Peppers (2014), their three big free agent signings of the cap era. White and Woodson earned championships three and four seasons after being signed, while two of the three teams Peppers was on made the conference championship and the third lost in the divisional round. White and Woodson were also signed in year two of the Mike Holmgren Era and year one of the Mike McCarthy Era. The draft process of both organizations allows them to employ a draft and extend strategy, which helps them sign the top talent on their roster at below free market rates by offering them fair value prior to their reaching free agency. This can be appealing to a player and agent if it provides the player value. In this case that means providing financial security a year or two prior to the end of their rookie contract, which is provided by an increase in their income that makes it worth passing on potentially higher free agency dollars down the road balanced against the risk of injury potentially decreasing the player's earnings in free agency. Players also pass up the opportunity to play themselves into more money by accepting an extension, a downside he can accept for the security of a higher income earlier. They also re-sign key players in free agency if they can agree on a price that the team has determined the player is worth to them; they rarely overextend past the positional cost ceilings explained in later chapters of this book.

In his research, Jason Fitzgerald found that bargain contracts are not found after four or five years in the NFL; they're not found after the rookie deal is over. Bargains come after three years, which is the only time teams can extend most rookie draft picks under this CBA as post-sophomore season extensions have been outlawed—a big blow to players. Taking this approach, both sides can actually win as the player can receive closer to market value for his production immediately and the team can have him at a lower cap hit than he would have otherwise earned on the free agent market. The consequence will be higher cap hits earlier, but something worth doing if you're getting discounts later for elite production. Teams save so much on current rookie contracts that they should have the cap space to take the short-term increase in the individual player's cost for the long-term discount.

Two of the most team friendly contracts in the NFL in the last few years were actually signed after two seasons, which is a great time to strike if the player has already proven to be a franchise cornerstone type of player. These two deals also show the value of early extensions to both the organization and the player. Rob Gronkowski and Antonio Brown were drafted in the second and sixth rounds of the 2010 NFL Draft and both were signed to extension prior to the 2012 season, but after 1000-yard seasons from both of them in 2011. Gronkowski had a stat line of 90 catches for 1327 yards, 14.7 yards per catch, and 17 touchdowns with a catch rate of 72.6% and 10.7 yards per target. Considering that his yards per catch and per target totals show he was more of a downfield target, his catch rate is staggering. A plus 70% catch rate is usually reserved for slot receivers and running backs that catch the ball close to the line of scrimmage. Brown had a stat line of 69 catches for 1108 yards, 16.1 yards per catch and two touchdowns. He had the lowest catch rate of his career at 55.6%, but his 8.9 yards per target was still impressive and he's since seen his catch rate increase to an average of 70.3% from 2014 through 2016.

Gronkowski was signed to a six-year extension worth $54 million that was attached to the two remaining years on his contract and Brown signed a five-year deal worth $41.96 million. Gronkowski's contract is projected to average 4.43% of the cap from 2012 through 2019, which is his 30-year old season. The Pats secured one of the best tight ends in NFL history to a contract through his prime that tops out at 6.27% of a projected $193 million cap in 2019.

Brown's contract slowly increased each year from 2012 to 2015 from 1.88% to 2.54% to 3.40% to 4.97% before jumping to 7.65% of the cap in 2016 as the Steelers re-structured his deal prior to the season to move $4 million from 2017 into 2016 to reward him for being, arguably, the best receiver in the NFL. He had 129 catches, 1698 yards and 13 touchdowns in 2014, then 136 catches, 1834 yards, and 10 touchdowns the next year. The Steelers got the league leader in catches in both seasons and the league leader in yards in 2014, but he was edged out by Julio Jones' 1871 yards in 2015. During the years of his extension, the Steelers got a top tier, Hall of Fame level production for cap hits that are less than half of where the current top of the wide receiver market resides: a top of the market that Brown set when he signed a four-year, $68 million contract extension with the Steelers during the 2017 offseason that will pay him an average annual salary of $17,000,000 from 2018 through 2021 after a 2017 season at 8.2% of the cap. Using cap projections, Brown is projected to average 8.47% of the cap through 2021, his 33-year-old season, peaking at 9.85% in 2018.

Contract extensions remind me of Ben Stiller's risk analyst insurance salesman character from *Along Came Polly*; both sides are trying to determine fair value, while weighing potential risks. Extending drafted players means that teams also get to take advantage of the player development resources they've invested into players with the knowledge that they already fit their system well, an assurance you can't really fully guarantee in free agency no matter how well you analyze a player who is not already a part of your system or organization.

As explained in Jonah Keri's book on the Tampa Bay Rays rise from the MLB cellar to the World Series in 2008 titled, *The Extra 2%: How Wall Street Strategies Took a Major League Baseball Team from Worst to First*, he mentions that the Rays were able to sign two of the stars of that team, outfielder Carl Crawford and third baseman Evan Longoria, to low-cost contracts because they signed them to extensions early in their careers, as they were becoming stars and while on very inexpensive contracts that compelled them to make a deal. As Keri writes, "studies done by Bill James and other analysts confirmed that baseball players tend to peak in their mid- to late twenties."[1] Based off of this, the Rays risked losing the players when they hit their prime if they didn't extend them as the Rays likely wouldn't have the money to pay either player if they ever made it to free agency considering their being a low-budget organization in a league with no salary cap. As will be explained in chapter five with Bill Walsh's innovations to offensive football, adversity and necessity help breed innovation.

With Crawford, he had a great 2003 season, but he broke out as an All Star during the 2004 season where he hit .296, while leading the league in stolen bases and triples. Keri wrote: "advanced defensive metrics, while still in their infancy, suggested that Crawford was also an elite defender (an evaluation generally shared by scouts)." Rays GM Andrew Friedman, who came in from Wall Street in 2004 as the teams Director of Player Development and was named the teams President of Baseball Operations and General Manager after the 2005 season, took charge of crafting a contract in April 2005 that ran through 2010 and made Crawford a tremendous value for the team. By the end of the contract, "Crawford produced $108.9 million worth of value for the Rays over the life of his contract, compared with the deal's maximum value of $35 million."

Friedman then made similar moves by signing pitcher James Shields to a four-year deal worth $11.25 million after just 52 starts in the majors and signing third baseman Evan Longoria early in the 2008 season, after just six games as a professional for the kid, to a six-year deal for $17.5 million with "three club options at the end, making the total package a potential nine-year contract worth about $48 million."

One of the best examples of this strategy in the salary cap era comes from the Packers as they were able to keep Aaron Rodgers below eight percent of the cap through 2012, which was his 29-year old season. They extended him in November 2008, halfway through his first season as a starter, to a $66 million contract with $20 million guaranteed that ran through 2014.[2] Rodgers was at 12.02% of the cap in 2008, which was a year they probably didn't foresee Super Bowl glory with the first year starter, then had what amounts to discounts for one of the best quarterbacks in the NFL during that time at 7.85% in 2009, just $6.5 million during the uncapped 2010 season, 6.46% in 2011, and 7.05% in 2012 before they re-structured his contract in 2013 to a reasonable first tier deal for a top quarterback. They earned a Super Bowl in 2010 and Rodgers earned the MVP in 2011 with a 68.3% completion percentage, 45 touchdowns to six interceptions, an astounding 9.2 yards per attempt and 309.5 yards per game to lead the team to a 14-1 record.

These are the kinds of discounts made possible by extending players before they hit, which is an example of how the Kirk Cousins situation was mishandled in

Washington. According to Albert Breer of *Sports Illustrated*, in August 2015, before Cousins was installed as the starter and had a good first season with the team, then-Redskins GM Scot McCloughan first convinced owner Dan Snyder and president Bruce Allen that the time had come to move on from Robert Griffin III and onto Kirk Cousins. Breer wrote "soon thereafter, with Cousins installed as starter, and believing he was in for a big year, McCloughan made a second appeal to the team's top brass. Let's extend Cousins now, he told them, so we're not stuck holding the bag later."[3]

The way that Snyder and Allen botched this eventually led to McCloughan being removed from his role as GM amid unfounded rumors that he'd returned to alcoholism as, according to my research, Snyder seems to be unable to take personal responsibility for anything he does wrong. So instead of having Cousins on a similar deal to Rodgers and a deal that the Redskins could have lived with even if he became a marginal player, he cost the team 12.85% of their 2016 cap, then 14.34% in 2017 and it seems likely he'll end up in another jersey in 2018.

Teams should try to acquire most of their roster through the draft process, especially their key core players. Football has too many variables to predict, and the careers are too short, to use free agency as the main roster building strategy. The average NFL career lasts a little longer than three years due the prevalence of injuries in the most brutal team sport in the world and a very competitive labor market. Even those who make it through three or four years due to talent and an ability to stay healthy don't get out of it unscathed as players around the league routinely schedule offseason surgeries for injuries the fans don't hear about on top of the big injuries we're all aware of.

Thirty years ago, Bill Walsh saw the reality of free agency that some big spenders still haven't figured out yet: "the players who get all the attention are usually the ones on the downside of their careers. Ironically, the organization is often paying the most money to the team members who are on the descending curve as players."[4] Football Outsiders' analysis of the data available shows declines for running backs after the of age 28; tight ends, defensive ends and defensive backs after 29; wide receivers, linebackers and offensive linemen after 30; defensive tackles after 31; and quarterbacks after 32.[5] Every year teams will become more accurate at predicting positional and personal decline for players, but with most players getting to free agency for the first time at 25, 26, 27 years old, the window of production for many top free agents isn't as long as the four to six year contracts that many top tier free agents tend to sign. College players, especially running backs, must be aware of where they stand on draft boards after their junior season to understand how to maximize their earnings by getting to their second contract quicker. The small difference between salaries of rookie contracts after the first two rounds makes it more beneficial to hit free agency a year earlier than to stay in college to try to increase his draft stock further. In a league with built in low earnings for the first four years of a player's career, getting to free agency as soon as possible might be more beneficial for some players than waiting a year to improve draft stock. That is, if the player is lucky enough to make it that far considering the average NFL career length is between three and four years, shorter than the four year rookie contracts these picks sign.

Since every team does have to use free agency to build a complete 53-man roster, teams can't just avoid it either; they have to find their own strategies for acquiring veterans who create value for the system they're implementing. As a general rule, Bill Belichick seems to sign free agents to short contracts in the lower tiers of their positional markets. He rarely pursues players who are signing five or six year contracts with annual rates in the top tier of their market. The Patriots develop their core through the draft, then go after the players who will fit their system and provide the production needed at a reasonable rate.

Belichick earned an economics degree from Wesleyan University after a childhood of learning the intricacies of the game from his father, Steve, one of the most well-respected scouts in NFL history. Steve's 1962 book *Football Scouting Methods* is referred to by many as the best book on NFL scouting ever written and this academic approach likely led to Bill creating his own scouting manual to use for finding players who fit his exact job descriptions for every position. Belichick's background and life experience prepared him for the reality of a salary capped NFL; his knowledge of football and economics prepared him for the league he found himself in as the Patriots new coach in 2000. As Michael Holley writes in *Belichick & Brady*, "the skill wasn't just in acquiring good players anymore. It was an athlete/asset puzzle now. You had to know the players, know their market value, and know precisely when to either commit big dollars or say good-bye for better, and cheaper, options."[6] This knowledge of economics led to an attitude where Belichick never wanted the Patriots "to be the first to run to free agency and set the market; rather, he spoke a new language, referring to players who had 'good value' and 'position versatility.'"

With every team having the same 100 percentage points or units of cap space to spend, Belichick realized that the game was about getting the best return on your investment, getting the most out of how you spend the dollars available to your team. As Holley writes, "decision-makers saw players in terms of production and dollar signs," which is what we'll use as the definition of production value, the ability to define on-field production with a salary cap figure attached to it. I would argue they should see players in terms of production and percentage of the cap consumed as what those dollar signs mean changes every year. When considering players a team can acquire, the cost of each player versus the production each player is likely to provide the team in his role is a key question to consider. For example, you don't want to pay six percent of the cap for 800 receiving yards if you can potentially find a player at three percent who can earn 700.

According to Holley, Belichick and his top personnel man at the time, Mike Lombardi started putting together their first scouting manual in Cleveland, but by the time they had started to figure it out, they had been fired. In 2000, with Lombardi in Oakland, Belichick's writing partners were Scott Pioli, Ernie Adams, and Bucko Kilroy, and "they wrote with clarity and power, accurately describing some of their championship players before they were even in the building." Roman Phifer, who had been in the NFL for ten years before signing with the Patriots in 2001, was amazed at Belichick's ability to condense masses of information into three key points. For games he'd condense the objective into, "do these three things and we should be in a position to win" and with Lombardi, they realized the three traits that needed to be a part of their players' profiles were "intelligence, power, and versatility." He needs players who have the intelligence to understand the system and each week's gameplan, the explosive power to execute the tasks required and the ability to make their team more versatile.

Having a clear picture of the players they were looking for made value finding much easier because the scouting manual directs the organization toward the players they should be signing. They knew what they were looking for, so they knew what they valued. Using Belichick's offensive, defensive and special teams systems as the blueprint, with each position having a job description that needs filling, their staff can project the consequences of each move they make. They create an understanding of where they can find the players to fill each job and then what those players are likely to provide in value. This understanding of value allows them to create their own organizational and system specific Wins Above Replacement style value metric for every player and move they make with analytics providing them the opportunity to continually improve in accuracy of decision making.

Belichick's knowledge of positional and player markets has allowed him to make value-based decisions to continually fill their roster with players who fit their Super Bowl formula on the field and in the salary cap. Being that he is the Head Coach and General Manager, the Patriots have more alignment between the two positions than anyone else in the league and the scouting manual Belichick started creating in Cleveland with Lombardi provided a foundation that continues to helps create alignment. Head Coaches and General Managers can have disagreements, but the alignment between the two of them and the staff underneath them must be established. A scouting manual should provide everyone involved in the player acquisition and development process with a blueprint for what the organization is looking for accompanied with a value finding process based on that blueprint to get the best return on their salary cap.

Belichick combines a strong understanding of the economic concepts and forces that govern position markets and league-wide cap spending with an understanding of the game of football that is unparalleled to become a trend setter in football philosophies, which in turn has allowed him to create value across his roster through avoiding markets that many other buyers pursue.

Since he's been in New England, they have run a short, high-percentage passing system that has resulted in below market costs at every position on his offense. He has been at the forefront, if not the creator, of offensive trends like the slot receiver, running back by committee and the two tight end approach. While Walsh started the trend of high-percentage passing systems, Belichick has perfected it. Even through Tom Brady's more expensive seasons during his athletic prime in the late-2000s, the Patriots have been able to put together defenses that gave them a chance to not only make the playoffs every year, but also compete in the AFC Conference Championship seemingly every year. Chapter six will explore Belichick's savings on offense in depth, but his combination of economics and football created the philosophical foundation for a cap advantage. Seattle has utilized a similar principled strategy over the first half of the 2010s.

With the core of the roster being built through the draft then extended, or re-signed at the beginning of free agency to reasonable contracts, this creates a cycle of positive cap consequences by creating value during a player's career. The draft and extend process allows teams that acquire their core this way to lock in key players at fair market rates, rather than bidding on top talent in free agency, which also creates the opportunity for compensatory picks. Strong drafting creates a cycle of compensatory picks for your organization, as you'll lose more talent in free agency than you'll need to sign in free agency. The players that you've developed reap the rewards of their development in your system through big contracts elsewhere and your organization reaps the rewards of this investment by receiving compensatory draft picks. This draft success also gives you options, flexibility, which might be why the Browns drafted multiple receivers and pass rushers with their record 14 picks during the 2016 draft. They wanted to be able to decide on who would provide them with the most value in these high-cost markets and the hopes that they will trade the other players at those positions for draft picks or let them walk in free agency to be rewarded in those same high-cost markets the Browns are trying to avoid overextending themselves in. They are also just trying to accomplish the most obvious objective for drafting these players: secure low-cost talent at important and expensive positions.

Great organizations use this process, then move to free agency for the supplemental players who will elevate the play of the team and fill the job descriptions that haven't been filled through the draft. Free agency increases the cost of players through a bidding process open to all 32 teams, while decreasing the likelihood of their success as you don't have a history with them; you don't know exactly how they'll fit into your system, your team, or just a new environment—no matter how much research you do on the player. You would much rather take the risks of underperformance on a player entering the league as rookie contracts cost far less.

If your team is in a dire position where they do need a player at a specific position to compete, then heading to free agency becomes more worth the risk. If you've created stability on your roster and don't have many immediate, desperate needs, then using the top three to four rounds of the draft to find players with the potential to be immediate starters is viable. Even in a situation where a team has a desperate need, drafting two players at the position in the top four rounds could be a viable solution.

Generally speaking, in the mid-2010s, the more expensive positional markets are quarterback, wide receiver, left tackle, defensive end, outside linebacker and cornerback, while running back, tight end, the interior of the offensive and defensive lines, inside linebacker and safety are less costly. Safety is one position that may be climbing into the more expensive category over the next few years. The interior of both lines are seeing their costs increase as interior pass rushing increases in value with quick passing systems decreasing the time to throw after the snap. Knowledge of these markets in combination with a firm grasp of the typical length of career for players at that position, teams can create acquisition strategies and contracts that maximize the value they get out of every player they acquire from the draft to trades to free agency. An understanding of just those two things can create small value advantages across the roster, which add up together to create huge advantages. Analytics can even help teams determine which positions in their systems tend to have a higher performance in their second or third contracts and allow them to look for those in free agency, while trying to extend the others through their prime or sign short free agent contracts rather than give a contract to a player who will be in decline at the end of his deal causing you to either have an underperformer or a dead money cap hit. As more teams collect actionable data through this analytics revolution, the markets will begin to correct themselves with more money going to players who are performing.

Like coaches who have developed their own system can find value in late rounds of the draft as well as after the draft, they can find value through cheaper free agent contracts. Without the need to sign top tier free agents, a team can instead spread the cap space they do have across more players, which mitigates the risk of underperformance and injury. This can also improve your team across the roster, rather than improving only one position.

As Belichick has said, "I think that's how you get good, you get good at everything," so the goal is to create a team that is good in every phase of the game, which can give the coach a variety of potential strategies to employ for victory each week.[7] The Pats can typically win games in any way, the low-scoring and the high-scoring, with running backs to run the clock out. Giving a top of the market contract to free agents in the more expensive positional markets can lead to disrupting your roster balance with a player who has a high likelihood of costing more than the production he will provide. As a general rule, teams should spread their money across their roster as much as they possibly can.

The first, or top tier, of a positional market should be reserved for the top veterans at their position, typically players you've extended from within your organization. These are the kinds of players who you want to make up your core to have the players during their development and into their prime, rather than acquiring them at a higher cost closer to the back-end of their career. Through the draft and extend process, teams are able to more accurately project a player's production, while providing the organization with the ability to project future labor costs, their biggest expense, which is a helpful piece of knowledge for any business.

Over six percent of the cap is considered a first tier investment across all positions except for quarterback, where it is a second tier investment as the first tier is over 10% of the cap. Of the 22 Super Bowl champions, not including the uncapped 2010 Packers, there have been 13 free agent acquisitions over this number with nine of those 13 being on the 2013 Seahawks, 2015 Broncos, 2002 Buccaneers, and 1995 Cowboys. Four of these 22 teams had nine free agent signings over six percent of the cap, while the other 18 teams had just four such free agents. While signing an expensive free agent is a strategy that can work, it has become much more accessible due to the rapidly increasing salary cap under the 2011 CBA and the low-cost of all rookie contracts. These economic factors of this CBA have made it more successful strategy. This topic will be covered in depth in chapter ten.

Tiers are specific by position. More expensive markets have four tiers, while the others have three. We'll go over these in the positional market chapters, but the lower tiers each represent a step down from the tier above them. Going by the four-tier system, the second tier of markets refers to above average starters. In a 2016 article, Jason Fitzgerald writes that tier one players are the big name players who break the bank in free agency, while tier two free agents "won't command as much money but often proves to be more of a value."[8] As Jason points out, these are the kinds of players that someone like him would say, "that's a pretty good value compared to…" The third tier refers to average veteran starters, if they're players signed in free agency, they're typically players who have something to prove if they want to earn more on their next deal or players who have been determined to be average starters. The fourth tier is made up of low-level starters, role players, and special teams guys; in free agency, these are guys who may have difficulty finding a place to play. The principles of these four tiers can be condensed into the three-tier structure. These tiers are specific to each position due to the varied costs of each market and will be explained in the next few chapters.

To find value through veteran acquisitions, organizations should be looking for these second and third tier free agents, in expensive markets especially, rather than the first tier because of the reasons already explained. Great organizations consistently find players on the waiver wire similar to how they find undrafted free agents. While another team might be letting a player go because his costs outweigh his value to them, he might fit your system perfectly and be potentially valuable.

Trades have become more common as teams gain a better understanding of player value and a player's potential value on their roster. Teams should be focusing on acquiring players at the trade deadline or during the offseason who have more time on their deals and are no longer fits for where their organization is or where their organization is trying to go. The trade deadline should be used like teams used it during the 2017 season where many teams moved players that weren't performing for them, weren't under contract for 2018, or had contracts that the team didn't want to continue paying them. Teams should be constantly communicating about players they might consider moving as a means to acquire draft picks that would better serve their future and teams that need a piece for a playoff run should be willing to trade draft picks, especially if they believe they can re-sign the player to an extension and if they have a surplus of draft picks.

Finding valuable players in lower tiers is about what former Patriots linebacker Matt Chatham refers to as "winning stat guys."[9] These are not the players who get the high-sack or high-interception total; they're not the receivers who had 1000-yards the season before, they're the guys who accomplish the first principles of their position. An outside linebacker with less sacks, but who can create consistent pressure on the quarterback and dominate the edge with the ability to cover tight ends and receivers can be much more valuable and productive than the 16 sack guy, while also being available at a lower price. Prior to the 2015 season, the Patriots signed an eight sack guy in Jabaal Sheard and during the next offseason, they let go of the potential 16 sack guy in Chandler Jones, while signing a 31-year old defensive end in Chris Long to a third tier one-year contract because of this logic. Sheard and Long provided 96 quarterback pressures in 2016 to Jones' 66, but the move allowed them to gain draft picks for Jones and re-sign the player who may be their most important defender during the 2017 offseason in linebacker Dont'a Hightower, whom they wouldn't have been able to re-sign if they were enamored with the high sack totals over an understanding of pressure production and the importance of a great linebacker in Belichick's system. Sheard and Long are gone in 2017 with New England relying on Trey Flowers, who also helped replace Jones' production in 2016, plus draft picks they hope will become contributors in 2017 third round pick Derek Rivers and fourth rounder Deatrich Wise, Jr.

Everything comes back to focusing on the process, whatever that process may be. So much of success in life is figuring out your objective, then understanding the process that needs to be undertaken to accomplish that objective. Organizations who understand the process for each position, the list of things they need to do to accomplish their objective, will find players who provide value. Organizations run by coaches and staffs who don't understand the process will pay twice the money for eight more sacks. Sure you'll have a great defensive end, but will you be able to afford your safety that might be coming up on free agency? What does this mean for your defense as a whole? What does it mean for your entire team?

Coaches should create their own scouting manual similar to Belichick's and use it to find value through the draft and veteran acquisition processes. It should be written, edited, re-written, and re-edited dozens of times over the course of a coach's career as he makes his way up from being a positional coach all the way up to the head coaching position and as the league evolves along with his career. Same thing for people on the front office side. Everyone in the NFL who has aspirations of being a decision maker should be creating his own manual for what they believe is needed to succeed in the NFL on the field and in the salary cap. These manuals will create the basis of Quality for future NFL teams and new ideas are the best way to create value. Creativity creates value.

The next four chapters take this player acquisition conversation further with an analysis of the quarterback market, the ebb and flow of positional spending and importance at offensive skill positions, the spending trends along the offensive line, then an analysis of defensive spending. Chapter nine provides an analysis of the objectives of special teams and the spending associated with these objectives. An understanding of the micro and macroeconomics of the salary cap makes creating a Quality football team a matter of planning and execution.

Chapter 5: Quarterback Spending

Every opponent you face presents a new set of problems, and, a set of solutions that can solve them. Sometimes only one solution can work, but in a complex sport like football, a variety of different strategies can solve the problems that your opponents create, and, if executed properly, those strategies can lead to your goal of victory. Done over the course of a season, this leads to a team setting itself up for our definition of success: the ability to consistently make the playoffs to give yourself opportunities to win the Super Bowl.

The recent explosion of mixed martial arts through the UFC has provided an example of problem solving with dire physical consequences, even more so than football as MMA is an individual sport and mistakes don't lead to touchdowns, they lead to lights out and a re-configuration of your facial features.

The individual, one-on-one nature of MMA makes it a fun problem solving exercise for spectators. As you gain more of an understanding of the sport, the fighters and the skill sets they each have, you begin to see and understand the strategies, which provides a much deeper viewing experience. Mixed martial arts have three main areas of focus: stand-up, clinch, and ground combat. In the stand-up game, the main martial arts are boxing, kickboxing, muay thai, karate, taekwondo, combat sambo savate, and sanshou. When fighters get in the clinch, muay thai is a great tactic for striking in the clinch, while freestyle wrestling, Greco-Roman wrestling, judo, sambo, and shanshou improve clinching and the takedowns and throws that bring the fight to the ground. While on the ground, the martial arts that help control the fight on the ground and lead to submissions include Brazilian Jiu Jitsu, judo, sambo, catch wrestling, and submission wrestling. Overlap exists between many of these martial arts, so fighters don't have to train all of them; they have to be trained in all three areas of fighting. Each fighter's skill set is made up of a percentage of these skills and the best, most successful UFC champions with the most title defenses tend to be fighters who have mastery or near mastery in the relevant skills, which allows them to take on all challengers to win in a variety of ways.

UFC 125-pound, flyweight Demetrius Johnson now holds the longest championship reign in UFC history with 11 title defenses because of his complete MMA skill set. When a fighter doesn't have a complete skill set, some opponent and his coach eventually find a hole in his game that the challenger can exploit with his skill set. The same thing happens with NFL teams.

If you look at victory as a solution to an equation, then in fighting and football, the fighter or team with the most potential formulas that can achieve victory will be able to create and use the various strategies of attack that they'll need to beat their opponents over the course of their march to a title. Belichick in particular tries to build his team on a versatility that allows the Patriots to attack the weaknesses of each opponent.

At the time of this writing, Conor McGregor holds the UFC's 155-pound belt having beaten Eddie Alvarez at Madison Square Garden in November 2016 to go with the 145-pound belt he earned by knocking out Jose Aldo in 13 seconds, which he had to relinquish as he was no longer fighting in the division. With 17 of his 21 professional wins coming by knockout, he has a main strategy he sticks to because his boxing is much more technical and powerful than almost every opponent he faces. While McGregor is proficient in all three areas of fighting, he sticks to boxing because he's much better in that area than his opponents and he has a left hand that MMA coach Firas Zahabi of TriStar Gym refers to as the touch of death. Very few fighters are competent enough in a single skill set to dominate using only one skill set, but it is possible if you are elite enough, which McGregor may have proven by going 10 rounds with Floyd Mayweather in August 2017.

We've seen the 2006 Colts, 2009 Saints and 2011 Giants win Super Bowls with offenses led by Peyton Manning, Drew Brees and Eli Manning that were good enough to overcome statistically below average defenses, but an NFL team sustaining success with this strategy is a rarity as few quarterbacks are capable of providing performances good enough to consistently compete for championships. From 2014 through 2016, Brees led the NFL in passing yards each year by averaging 5,010 per season, but the Saints haven't been better than 7-9 in part because his large cap hits, which peaked at 16.61% of the 2015 cap, during those years left a defense that ranked 28th, 32nd and 31st in points against. The 2011 Giants are the worst cap era defense to win a Super Bowl, giving up 25.0 points per game; the Saints have given up 28.2 per game over the three seasons.

In war, the United States Military takes this same strategy of being good at everything. They don't build up one branch, they build up a wide variety of branches and special operations teams; they want to win on land, sea and air. They want to win the fight no matter where the fight takes them.

The main components of football include rushing offense, passing offense, rushing defense, passing defense, and special teams. According to Football Outsiders, "the total Quality of an NFL team is four parts offense, three parts defense, and one part special teams." Football writers/researchers Chase Stuart, Neil Paine, and Brian Burke did an analysis that suggests the split between offense and defense is roughly 58-42 without factoring in special teams. Football Outsiders came to their conclusion by adding their own research that suggests that special teams contribute about 13% to total performance, then dividing the other 87% with the 58-42 split to get roughly 4:3:1. Based on that, a football team's Quality is based on 50% offense, 37.5% defense and 12.5% special teams. This means that offense may be a little more important than defense, but great defenses can have a devastating effect on your opponent's offense, so the capability to destroy an offense's effectiveness is very valuable.[1]

You want to develop a level of competence on offense running and passing the ball with the defensive ability to decrease your opponent's competence in those two, plus a special teams unit that can outperform your opponents. This kind of team-wide versatility is made possible through hiring the right head coach, general manager, and front office personnel to develop systems based on the first principles of the sport while using the salary cap to ensure your roster the opportunity to maximize your system's efficiency, versatility, and consistency.

For good reason the idea that quarterback is the most important position on a roster goes without question and with it being the most expensive positional market, it provides a great place to start the conversation regarding the positional markets themselves and salary cap spending across the roster. Not only is quarterback a high-priced market, but positions that help improve passing production on offense and defensive positions that disrupt the passing game are seeing increases in their market value. If quarterback is the most important player, then naturally players who can increase their performance on offense or decrease their performance on defense are very valuable.

Football Outsiders has found that the oft-regurgitated cliché of needing to establish the run on offense is false. Aaron Schatz writes that "there is no correlation whatsoever between giving your running back a lot of carries early in the game and winning the game," but instead, as Ron Jaworski says, "the pass gives you the lead, and the run solidifies it." The goal is to get ahead, then run the ball to control the clock, not establish the run to start the game.

To further support this point, Schatz writes, "a great defense against the run is nothing without a good pass defense." On average, passing will gain more yardage than running, so if you have a great run defense, but a poor pass defense, your opponent is still going to be able to move the ball well. A lack of ability at either of these creates opportunities for the opponent's offense to exploit the weakness. Run defense becomes especially important come playoff time "to keep the other team from icing the clock if they get a lead. You can't mount a comeback if you can't stop the run."

The 2006 Colts had the worst run defense in football that year and the worst of any cap era champion at an astounding 173.0 rush yards per game, 50.8 yards more per game than the 2009 Saints who are the second worst of this cap era. But, their pass defense was the best of any of these champions giving up just 169.1 yards per game, five yards better than the historic 2002 Bucs defense that Football Outsiders' still ranks as the best pass defense of the 30 years they've been creating and adjusting their Defense-adjusted Value Over Average (DVOA) statistic, which is their measure of efficiency. While the Bucs defense was first in points allowed and first in yards allowed, the Colts team was ranked 23rd and 21st respectively. They weren't a great defense, but maybe the pass defense was enough with Peyton Manning leading an offense producing the second most points in the NFL that year at 26.7 per game and the third most yards per game at 379.4. Manning produced an elite 274.8 passing yards per game with a competent rushing offense at 110.1, which meant they had the rushers to burn the clock when needed and a passing offense that was never out of any game with an elite pass defense that forced opponents to try to come back from deficits by running the football, which burns the clock.

As said in chapter one, this book is about increasing a team's probability of success based on Ozzie Newsome's definition of success, which is to build a team that can make the playoffs every year. To do this, cost-managing strategies are critical, so the spending at quarterback has become excessive for players who are not worth the high cost.

During the spring of 2016, my sister and her classmates at The University of Texas' McCombs Business School (Mackenzie Moore, Victoria Piranian, Alison Strealy, and Meryl Thompson), did a statistical analysis that attempted to answer the question: "is a starting quarterback's salary justified by his team's winning percentage, and what other factors should be accounted for to determine this?" They analyzed the last five NFL seasons and statistics related to the starting quarterback from each of the 32 NFL teams, which resulted in 160 data points. To evaluate a team's overall success, they looked at whether a team's winning percentage was over 50% or not, which they used as the standard for a "successful" season. They separated rookie and veteran contracts and found that the maximum that a starting veteran quarterback can receive before his cap hit begins to negatively effect a team's chances of having a winning season is 8.67% and 5.67% for players in their first four seasons of their careers. Players who make higher than these figures can negatively affect their team's chances of having a winning season. The new CBA made first-round rookie quarterbacks contracts a good value if the player performs at even an average level as even #1 overall picks don't get higher than 4.5% of the cap over those first four seasons.

In 2016, 17 of 32 NFL teams paid their quarterback more than 10% of the cap and Tom Brady was #18 at 8.87% of the cap, which helped them field the NFL's third best scoring offense with the number one scoring defense. From 2005 through

2016, Brady has averaged 10.30% of the salary cap and they've continually reworked his contract to lower his cap hit, while still paying him similar dollar totals. According to Spotrac, Brady has received signing bonuses in every year since 2010 except 2012 and 2017 with those bonuses totaling over $81 million. His cap hits have decreased in each year from 2013 through 2017 as it seems they've also taken into account the potential for decline as he heads into his forties. Brady's cap hit in 2017 is 8.38% of the cap, and after 2016's success, the Patriots had people talking about a potential undefeated season like in 2007 when his cap hit was re-structured to 6.74% to allow the team to trade for Randy Moss. His cap hit does increase to 12.26% of the projected 2018 cap, then 11.40% of the 2018 cap, so we could see the Patriots re-work his deal again after the 2017 season. It seems that the Patriots and their head coach/economist realized that the top of the quarterback market should peak between 10 to 13%, but many others haven't caught on to this. Looking at Brady's prime years that didn't break 13%, it seems he understood that 13% was the peak a quarterback should be paid.

According to Greg Bedard in a May 2015 article for *Sports Illustrated*, after losing the AFC Championship to the Ravens in January 2013, Brady and Robert Kraft had a conversation on a shared flight to California. Kraft explained to Brady that if he wanted to get paid what he's worth in a year or two, "it probably wasn't going to be tenable to the team." The Patriots did not want to pay the high cap figures that other teams were investing in their quarterback, even if they had one as great as Brady, especially considering his age. Bedard writes, "Kraft told Brady that he was basically going to have to play at half price," which would "help the team give him the supporting cast to win and enhance his legacy. Brady thought about it, and agreed."[2] He was signed to an extension that was announced in late February 2013, they then worked together every year to re-structure the contract to maximize his earnings, while minimizing his cap impact. This contract structure helped them rank in the middle of the quarterback market from 2015 through 2017. Their idea proved to work as he earned his fifth Super Bowl in 2016, moving him past Joe Montana, and he is working his way toward a sixth in 2017.

The quarterback market adjusting down to 8.67% or 10% is unlikely, but a decrease in the top of the market to a reasonable 12.5% or 13%, as 13.08% is the Super Bowl record for Steve Young in 1994, should be a realistic goal. The second highest Super Bowl cap hit was Peyton Manning in 2015 at 12.21%. Across from Brady in the biggest rivalry of the current century, Manning made more than Brady in every season except one, the 2006 season where he led the Colts to a Super Bowl at 10.36% of the cap, while Brady was at 13.55% for a Patriots team that lost to Manning in the AFC Championship by a score of 38-34. Does Manning have more than one Super Bowl with the Colts if they were able to spread their money around more? Do the Patriots beat the Colts in 2006 if Brady made less and they had a little more to spend on a pass catcher or someone else?

Could two or three percent of the cap given them a better option to lead the 2006 Patriots receiving group than Reche Caldwell?

The top of the quarterback market has always been high, but in recent years more players than ever at the top of the quarterback market are making first tier money over 10% of the cap and many are making more than 13% of the cap. This is partially pushed by the large rookie contracts at the end of the last CBA, but a cap hit of $25 million in 2016 consumed 16.10% of the $155.27 million cap, while $25 million on the projected 2019 cap of $193 million will only be 12.95% of the cap. In 2016, Eli Manning had a cap hit of $24.2 million that consumed 15.59% of the Giants salary cap. In June 2017, Derek Carr signed a market setting contract worth $125,025,000 over six seasons with his highest cap hit being for $25 million of a projected $179.5 million cap in 2018, so 13.93%. From 2017 through 2020, Carr will consume an average of 11.35% of the projected caps, a manageable number for some prime years of the 2016 MVP candidate's career. With the salary cap increases of 109% per year that I propose in the next CBA in chapter 10, or even just current cap rates of 107.5%, Carr's 2021 and 2021 cap hits could be less than 10% of the cap, which will help the Raiders build the rest of the roster around him dependent on how they handle the Khalil Mack and Amari Cooper negotiations.

After the Carr deal I thought the market might stay in a reasonable range, but then in August, Matt Stafford set a new record with a five-year, $135 million extension that has cap hits from 2017 through 2020 that are projected to average 13.79% of the cap. His three cap hits from 2018 to 2020 are all projected to be over 14.76% and the contract sets new benchmarks that Aaron Rodgers and Matt Ryan may soon best with histories of more production and more team success behind them. Stafford's cash flows, which are different than cap hits as this is income for the player versus the accounting mechanism for teams that cap hits represent, are much higher than every previous benchmark according to Jason Fitzgerald at Over The Cap.[3]

New Contract Year	Benchmark	Stafford	Differential
Year 0	$30,160,000	$34,500,000	14.4%
Year 1	$46,522,481	$51,000,000	9.6%
Year 2	$66,522,481	$70,500,000	5.8%
Year 3	$85,522,481	$92,000,000	6.1%
Year 4	$105,147,481	$112,000,000	4.8%

| Year 5 | $125,025,000 | $135,000,000 | 8.0% |

The absurdity of this contract is best captured with the cash flow differential in the first two years: two figures that blow previous cash benchmarks away in those two years and every year being at least 4.8% above previous benchmarks.

To this point, as Jason pointed out at the time of the signing, "if you don't have one of the true best players you need to be able to have resources to make up the gap. You can make up that gap by being able to sign better defensive players, offensive linemen, etc. But when every quarterback makes the same money, it gives teams with the lesser players no different avenue to bridge the gap." Stafford has zero playoff wins in his career, so thinking that things will be much different with him at such a high cost is hard to understand. Some of the best-managed organizations, like New England, Green Bay, and Seattle seem to understanding of the cap of this market being near 13%, while others struggle trying to overcome their lesser quarterbacks making higher cap percentages. The Giants and Steelers seem to understand this as well outside of cap hits over 15% for Eli Manning and Ben Roethlisberger in 2016. Raiders GM Reggie McKenzie, who came from Green Bay, seems to understand the concept with Carr's deal. Lions GM Bob Quinn, who came up through the Patriots organization, surprisingly doesn't seem to get it with Stafford's contract.

The perceived scarcity at the position could, and likely will, still keep a good percentage of the group bunched up toward the top. Data analysis will hopefully force the market to react to the reality that many quarterbacks become risks rather than security at certain costs and teams can be better served using that money to build the rest of the team, while then drafting and signing players to compete at quarterback. A quarterback must prove he can carry a roster during his rookie contract, or prove he has the potential to, before a team can invest the top tier money that will force him to carry the team.

When looking for later round college prospects and NFL back-ups who could develop into starters, Pro Football Focus provides some of their signature statistics at the college and professional level to help analysts cut through the clutter and find potential system fits. Going beyond traditional statistics helps isolate specific, important situations that illustrate the value a quarterback can produce. Pro Football Focus adjusts old stats like their PFF passer rating that offers an alternative to the out-dated standard by taking into account "dropped passes, throw aways, spikes, and yards in the air and further adjusts the old formula so it makes more sense and is a more accurate measure." Their adjusted completion percentage stat divides a players completions plus drops by his attempts minus throw aways, spikes, batted passes and plays where he was hit as he threw.[4]

Their deep passing stat helps identify quarterbacks who excel in the deep passing game by analyzing all passing attempts that are targeted 20 yards or more downfield. Success here allows offenses to stretch the field and open up the underneath routes. The rating for quarterback passing under pressure reflects a quarterback's performance on plays in which pressure was registered. Quarterback performance drops severely under pressure, so the ability to produce with bodies flying around is very valuable. Alternatively, Pro Football Focus also records quarterback performance on plays where they're kept clean in the pocket.

Pro Football Focus covers a quarterback's performance on play action passes compared to the times they don't use play action. They record quarterback time in pocket to help find out which quarterbacks hold onto the ball the most and how it impacts performance. Altogether these signature statistics provide more specific efficiency metrics that NFL organizations can use to find players who could provide the competition that helps them avoid overpaying a quarterback for average performance and finding value in someone who could be a game manager that grows into something more.

Caponomics isn't a hard science. The goal is to increase probability of success through analyzing data to create your organization's definition of Quality. With more than half of the NFL spending over 10% of the cap on their quarterback in 2016, and spending more than the Patriots spent on arguably the greatest quarterback of all-time, the probability of success for these teams decreases. It can also decrease their future probability of success as they've now overinvested in a player who can't compete for a Super Bowl at an inflated cost, while they could have instead taken a less risky investment. As Jason's quote earlier pointed out, if you have a lesser quarterback, you now don't have the cap space to improve your team around him to bridge the gap with the teams with the better quarterbacks making similar costs to your quarterback. An overpriced quarterback signed in one season might put the team in a position where they now don't feel comfortable drafting a quarterback in the first round two seasons later who could better suit a championship roster construction. They could be overpaying someone who then decreases their flexibility and ability to create a better solution. The probability of success for any organization in any business decreases when their labor costs more than their production value. Large cap hits make it hard to build the complete roster we're looking for and very few quarterbacks can carry a roster with glaring weaknesses, or even just an average defense, to a championship.

When paying that much money, a team has to ask themselves, is this the kind of quarterback who can win shootouts? Because you're running a higher risk of being in a lot of shootouts if you're spending too heavily on offense; so if he's going to cost over 10% of the cap, then he better be worth that in steady production value. A 2016 example of high spending and consequences in action resides in Atlanta where Matt Ryan and Julio Jones at a combined 25.54% of the salary cap led one of the best passing and the best scoring offense in the NFL, while a defense led by former Seattle Seahawks defensive coordinator Dan Quinn as the head coach ranked in the bottom third of the NFL in yards and points allowed. With Ryan throwing for 4944 yards at 309.0 per game with 38 touchdowns to seven interceptions and a 69.9% completion percentage at 9.3 yards per attempt, plus Jones' 1409 yards receiving at 100.6 per game, they're one of the only duos in the NFL who could've competed for a Super Bowl at such an outrageous cost. The Patriots took advantage of their defensive inefficiencies on their way to a historic 25-point comeback for the Super Bowl victory as the Falcons defense lacked depth and wore out in the second half of a game with 99 defensive snaps compared to just 49 for the Patriots defense. This helped Brady pick them apart during the comeback against pass rushers too gassed to create pressure and five fatigued defensive backs that all played 90 or more snaps. Positive or negative consequences of financial decisions that consume a high percentage of a team's cap always show up somewhere.

If you compile a few cap hits that are tier one cap hits for their respective positional markets, or you have two players at an extreme price like Atlanta did, your opponents have a good chance to build move value across their roster and are thus more likely to succeed. If you're paying a quarterback a good bit higher than 13% of the cap and others in division or in conference are getting much better value, then you're making it more difficult to succeed. Huge increases in the salary cap that are coming over the next few years, as it will soon exceed $200 million, are going to allow for some slightly higher payments to veterans, but other teams will continue to find value on their roster to outmaneuver teams that overextend themselves.

The coaching staff should be in a constant process of developing the roster they need to succeed in their continually changing chess match of NFL football. They should develop the production value and skills they're looking for in each role, and then find the best solution to fill that role from a caponomics standpoint. Salary cap value based decisions should be made across the roster with all potential solutions in mind. Every decision is made on a case-by-case basis, but, generally speaking, teams should be focused on a balance between being the best team they can be right now and long-term salary cap flexibility. That is largely what the last two chapters have been all about: building a strong draft process, so the veteran acquisition process can be used to find short-term, almost ancillary, solutions rather than attempt to build a roster through free agency.

Quarterback should be treated similar to the way teams should develop every other position in that teams should always be on the lookout to find and develop a potential replacement through the second through seventh rounds of the draft or an inexpensive veteran in a trade or free agency, so the team can have the ability to let a quarterback go if his costs far outweigh his potential production value to your organization.

Even with an elite, prototype franchise quarterback with a big arm and downfield accuracy, every coach should have an offensive system built on Bill Walsh's first principles for the quarterback position of accuracy, protecting the football, and mobility. Building off of these principles, offenses today are attempting to get rid of most passes in less than 2.5 seconds after the snap, which decreases the potential of the great edge rushers of the NFL today earning a sack, a strip sack or forcing the quarterback into a bad throw. With the abilities of pass rushers today, quarterbacks need to be able to perform under pressure, but a system that decreases the likelihood of pressure is equally important. Mobility helps these quarterbacks escape these pass rushers and create opportunities. Strong systems increase the productivity and abilities of the people within them; they're intended to increase the efficiency of the people within it to accomplish their collective objective of earning first downs and touchdowns, so naturally the most important evolution in football would make the quarterback position more efficient. In Walsh's case, a huge strength of the system is that the system was built with supply and demand in mind.

In 1969, the Bengals' first-round prototype rookie gunslinger, the 6'4", 220-pound Greg Cook, tore his rotator cuff at a time before surgically repairing it and getting back on the field was possible. His career looked over and Walsh scoured the landscape for a quarterback who could come in and help them compete, which led him to Virgil Carter and helped him create the offensive system we now see dominating the NFL. He then drafted Ken Anderson in the third round of the 1971 draft, then Joe Montana in the same round in the 1979 draft for the 49ers. During the 1981 season, the year of the first Super Bowl victory for Walsh and the 49ers, Montana led the NFL in completion percentage at 63.7%, while Anderson was in second at 62.6% for the Bengals. Players who fit his system were clearly being undervalued by the rest of the industry because they hadn't come to the same conclusion regarding offensive football that he had.

As Bill Barnwell wrote in a September 2017 article for ESPN.com, "NFL teams often look for one prototypical quarterback archetype at the expense of other styles of play." He writes that while people around the league and media members focus on the idea that there aren't enough starting quarterbacks to go around, Barnwell points out that teams look for the 6'4" passer with incredible arm-strength as the model quarterback "to an almost comical degree. They place a remarkable emphasis on height and a quarterbacks ability to 'make all the throws.'" This is how quarterbacks like Tom Savage get drafted ahead of A.J. McCarron and how teams were able to overlook a Russell Wilson or a Tom Brady. That thought process is why "players who look like the quarterbacks that General Managers dream about late at night also get second and third chances to prove themselves as viable passers."[5]

Rather than taking the creative path like Walsh, organizations will focus on a singular kind of quarterback, which is part of what has driven the market so high as anyone in the prototypical mold who can perform at a reasonable level gets paid top tier money after their rookie contract is up. Rather than look at the supply of quarterbacks and create a strategy with that supply in mind like Walsh did, teams will look for the small supply of players who seem to fit this prototypical passer mold and even overpay for them versus a more creative solution.

The league has changed a lot since Walsh, as has the collective intelligence of the football industry. Accuracy and protecting the football are still a requirement, but mobility is quickly becoming even more so. Robert Klemko wrote an article for MMQB finding that 13 of the 15 quarterbacks taken in the 2016 NFL Draft came from two-parent homes and that same number "grew up in homes that were valued near or above the median home value in their respective state, according to public records and online real estate figures."[6] Point being, the modern NFL quarterback typically has access to individual instruction growing up, so with that, they're being taught the fundamentals for being a great quarterback, but strength and conditioning coaches have also gained the knowledge to help athletes increase their speed. Most high school programs that kids in this kind of socio-economic situation are likely to go to have incorporated strength and conditioning into their football programs as well. With this, quarterbacks are becoming more accurate and all future quarterbacks should have some mobility, which will provide rushing production and the ability to extend plays when defenders get into the offensive backfield. I think that Nick Saban's move toward mobile quarterbacks is another sign it's a trend that every team should follow; there are just too many benefits to quarterback mobility to not have one who can move if you're trying to succeed in the future of the NFL.

There seem to be four kinds of variables in football for offensive plays. The power running game and deep passes have been around since before the West Coast offense, but Walsh's offense introduced a third, more efficient variable which can act as a stand in for the run game if your rushing offense is stymied. The path the 2014 Patriots took to a Super Bowl was proof of this and of their ability to build a roster that was skilled enough everywhere to exploit a potential weakness. They had 177 rushing yards against the Colts in the AFC Championship, just a week after going for just 14 yards against the Ravens as their short, ball control passing system helped them manage to still move the ball with consistency with New

England throwing for 408 passing yards at 7.7 yards per attempt. A high-percentage, ball control system creates versatility, which can be increased through the on field and salary cap decisions made, provide you a gameplan and strategy that can be tailored for each opponent.

The rushing quarterback is the fourth variable and one that the Panthers almost carried themselves to a Super Bowl with in 2015. Cam Newton led the NFL in carries, carries for first downs and rushing yards on third down plays, which allowed the Panthers to use a running quarterback as a big part of their third down conversion strategy. Most teams are employing the high percentage passing system, but the Panthers had Newton as their third down weapon to move the chains and that worked to the tune of a 17-1 record until they met the Broncos in the Super Bowl. The problem the Broncos gave them was a defense that had a combination of slowing down the run enough with a pass rush that overpowered the Panthers offensive line and got to Newton on a lot of those deep dropbacks due to the deep passing system Mike Shula and the Panthers employed, plus elite man-to-man defenders who blanketed an average group of pass catchers. Excluding a 3rd down and 24 late in the fourth quarter, the Panthers average third and distance was 8.4 yards, so they were further forced into deep dropbacks for deeper routes and deeper targets. This helped the Broncos get pressure on Newton and led to their forced fumble that led to Malik Jackson's touchdown return and the forced fumble that T.J. Ward recovered that led to a two-yard touchdown run from C.J. Anderson.

Mobility isn't only valuable when the quarterback is rushing the football. As the new announcer version of Tony Romo has pointed out numerous times early in the 2017 season, mobility creates space to make a play all over the field, but especially so in the redzone where the field shrinks down with 22 players still on it and a need for a quarterback who can create space to either run against a defense that might be out of place or create time for a receiver to get open in a bunched up defensive backfield. This mobility is almost too much of a factor in moving the chains and scoring in the redzone for teams to accept quarterbacks without it. It adds another variable for success between the twenties and allows the offensive coordinator to spread the offense by the goal line to run a quarterback draw or another play with the potential of getting the offense in the endzone with the whole defense bunched up in this small area. It can force a defender covering a pass catcher or playing in his defensive zone to commit to trying to tackle a quarterback who might run for the pylon, which can then allow him to hit the player or zone the defender just vacated. Mobility is an added variable that defenses have a hard time accounting for all over the field.

In the future, there should be a steady stream of well-prepared quarterbacks with the skills to succeed in efficient offensive systems, teams will be looking for quarterbacks who allow the team to be efficient in all four offensive variables. The ability to run the football as an offense; complete the deep ball with some accuracy; run a short, high percentage passing system; and run the ball for a first down if the defense leaves the opportunity available to you. Don Coryell's Air Coryell system was based on the principle of spreading the defense deep, Walsh's system is based on spreading the defense horizontally to attack the holes created and the spread offense is based on spreading the defense in every direction. A mobile quarterback spreads defenses thin by allowing an offense to take advantage of the math of forcing a defense to play 11-on-11 football and take advantage of any holes that are created because of that.

Creating a strong system and developing young quarterbacks provides a team with a quarterback who can help win a game or two should QB1 go down with a short-term injury like a concussion or a sprain. The Patriots have executed this system-quarterback strategy extremely well, seeing their 2008 team go 11-5 with Matt Cassel under center and 3-1 with Jimmy Garoppolo and Jacoby Brissett as Brady served his DeflateGate suspension in 2016. These systems and the ability to develop players who fit them is a form of risk mitigation and provides the ability for a team to maximize its return on investment through making sensible cap decisions due to the leverage of being able to trust their system. In a way, the system becomes the ultimate metaphor for team as no one, as illustrated in New England, is above the system; no one is worthy of taking up more cap space than they're worth.

In the middle of the 2016 season, linebacker Jamie Collins was traded to the Browns because he could net them draft picks to improve the team in the future, while the Patriots and his agent couldn't come to an agreement on renegotiating his contract. With a slew of players coming up for free agency in the 2017 offseason, the Patriots knew the two sides wouldn't come to an agreement. Rather than pay him more than the amount they had determined he was worth and being unable to sign other key players, they traded him, had one of the players they were developing under him step up and traded the third round compensatory pick gained from the Collins trade with their first round pick to acquire wide receiver Brandin Cooks from New Orleans. Meanwhile, everyone wins, the Browns had extra draft picks to trade and the cap space to pay him what he feels he's worth.

According to Nick Korte at Over The Cap, the Browns and their 44 players under rookie contracts heading into opening day 2016 led the NFL.[7] They spent just 56.2% of their 2016 salary cap on players on the actual team with a ton of open cap space for future years along with 10 draft picks in 2017 and 13 in 2018 as of this writing. They have the space to sign quite a few expensive players these next few years because of how they've set up their roster and since Collins is on the roster and was re-signed, he would not cost against the Browns compensatory selection formula.

With the excess of picks and cap space, they seem to be taking the 2013 Seahawks roster construction strategy with a bunch of young draft picks and a few older, expensive veterans. Due to stars on rookie contracts like Russell Wilson (0.55% of the cap), Richard Sherman (0.49%), Bobby Wagner (0.80%), and Earl Thomas (2.36%), the Seahawks were able to win with Zach Miller's Super Bowl record for a tight end at 8.94% and the injured Sidney Rice's Top 3 wide receiver cap hit at 7.89%. The excess of draft picks that the Browns have presents a huge value opportunity, and Collins became one of the beneficiaries of the cap space they have with a four-year deal with $50 million and $26.4 million in guarantees. They might spend some money in free agency these next few years before their draft picks come up for their second contracts as they have enough draft picks to forgo needing compensatory selections and the cap space to deal with it. With so many draft picks, they'll be able to restart the compensatory cycle as some of those draft picks will head elsewhere when their contracts run out, plus the ability to trade players for draft picks prior to that like the Patriots have.

The first tier of the quarterback market should be considered between 10 and 13% of the salary cap, so that means 17 quarterbacks are in, or above, that tier in 2016 with Eli Manning capping the group at 15.59%. Some inefficient quarterbacks in that group were Jay Cutler and Colin Kaepernick. Many teams began to hand out high contracts in an attempt to gain the apparent security of not having to worry about the quarterback position. Rather than actually provide security, this pay and pray strategy is far riskier than NFL teams realize. First-tier quarterbacks should only be quarterbacks that a team would pick very few others, if any, over--they should be exactly what a team is looking for with what they're trying to do on offense and who can elevate the play of the offense around them. The average top cap hit for a Super Bowl team is 9.37% and the average top quarterback cap hit is 7.90%, so spending over 10% on someone who isn't in that elite category isn't sensible and decreases your chances of success. Building a different quarterback solution through multiple draft picks at the position can be a much more sensible solution than overpaying for someone who can't carry a team at over 10%. For a historical example of this, in year one of the Jerry Jones/Jimmy Johnson Era, the Cowboys drafted both Troy Aikman in the first round out of UCLA and Steve Walsh, who had won a National Championship with Jimmy Johnson at Miami two years earlier, in the first round of the NFL Supplemental Draft. In 2012, Washington took Robert Griffin III #2 overall and drafted Kirk Cousins in the fifth round. While RG3 is out of the NFL, Cousins has become the team's starter.

Joe Flacco is a Super Bowl winning quarterback, but not an elite player for the Ravens, but with a 14.52% cap hit in 2016 and more expensive years coming up, this doesn't maximize their chances of success. He went on a historic Super Bowl run during the 2012 playoffs with 11 touchdowns to zero interceptions in four games leading them to their second championship. He cashed in that offseason with a market setting contract, which set him up nicely for the rest of his career, continually providing him leverage for a renegotiation. They can still remain competitive, but they've only made the playoffs once since Flacco has signed the deal. Much of the debate surrounding quarterbacks centers around if they've won a Super Bowl or not, but many of the quarterbacks that we consider elite today, partially for their Super Bowl triumphs, won their rings when they were on less expensive contracts than the ones they've been on since.

The Patriots had Drew Bledsoe at 10.29% of the cap in 2001 with Brady under one percent on his sixth round contract, so that was an expensive year, but in 2003 and 2004 he was just 4.43% and 6.26%, while passing for far less yards than he has thrown for since. In 2003, Brady averaged 226 passing yards a game and 231 in 2004. By comparison, Brady averaged 256.8 yards in 2014 and 296.2 in 2016. Both the 2003 and 2004 teams had great defenses and the 2004 team was seventh in the NFL with 2134 rushing yards, which comes out to 133 per game, and Corey Dillon rumbling to 1635 of them. Even during his fourth championship season in 2014 with a cap hit of 11.13%, the Pats had a defense with some considerable value finds like Darrelle Revis at 5.26% and great players on rookie contracts like Devin McCourty, Chandler Jones, Dont'a Hightower, and Jamie Collins. It takes nothing away from Brady to say these teams were terrific; it just illustrates the slightly inflated perception of the importance of quarterbacks in general. They are important, but so are the other 52 guys on your roster and even the 10 practice squad positions.

The 2005 Steelers had the fifth best rushing offense in the NFL and the third best scoring defense, while the 2008 champions had the 23rd ranked rushing offense, but a historic defense that gave up just 3.9 yards per play, which leads all cap era champions. Their 4.3 net yards per passing attempt allowed beats the brilliant 2015 Broncos defense by 0.8 yards. That Steelers team was stacked on defense, which helped Ben Roethlisberger capture his second Super Bowl title and his salary cap hits of 4.94% and 6.87% helped the front office build the team around him.

Successful organizations build their roster by using their franchise quarterback's rookie contract to build a roster that can overcome the youth and inexperience of the player, while carrying him along to his future of being that franchise guy when he can be the caliber of quarterback who can bring the team to a Conference Championship Game when he's making over 10% of the salary cap or 15.42% like Big Ben made in 2016 when he took Pittsburgh to one. The Seahawks built their roster around Russell Wilson before he was drafted and leading into the 2013 Super Bowl, then made the salary cap adjustments as he, and the other core players, reached his second contract.

While the Ravens and Steelers exceeded the costs we should consider for the quarterback market in 2016, and forward into the foreseeable future with Flacco's bad contract. They're still great organizations, they've both faced the Patriots in the last two Patriot Super Bowl runs, but many other great organizations have seemed to take note of the quarterback market and pay their players in accordance with the value they believe he will provide them. If you're going to spend top tier money on a quarterback, then you have to ask yourself: is this the kind of quarterback who can carry our team if necessary? Is this the kind of quarterback who can throw for 350 to 400 yards if we're left without a running game due to the defense we're playing or injuries at running back or on the offensive line? Considering the importance of the offensive line in the run game, a lot of times that money would serve the team well to spread to the offensive line to protect the quarterback and increase the proficiency of the run game.

Considering quarterback efficiency decreases sharply when quarterbacks are under pressure, is investing in an offensive line that keeps a less talented quarterback upright a better use of funds than investing in a more talented quarterback with less offensive line investment and a quarterback potentially running for his life? Sam Monson of Pro Football Focus found that the league average for NFL quarterbacks in 2016 was a passer rating of 96.7 when protected and just 62.5 when under pressure; the offensive line is a very important factor and might be worthy of a larger investment than spending first tier money on a lesser quarterback.[8] Can he help us win shootouts if our defense gives up 30? If he's not, then you'll have a hard time winning with a quarterback making more than ten percent of the salary cap.

Coming into 2016, five teams were on playoff streaks of four or more years and three of those teams, the Patriots, Packers, and Seahawks, extended it in 2016.
Playoff Streakers and QB1 Cap Hit (2009-2016)

Year	Salary Cap	Patriots	Packers	Broncos	Bengals	Seahawks
2009	123,000,000	11.89%	8.46%	-	-	-
2010	NO CAP	-	-	-	-	-
2011	120,000,000	11.00%	6.43%	1.76%	0.79%	-
2012	120,600,000	6.63%	7.05%	14.93%	0.98%	0.45%
2013	123,000,000	11.22%	9.47%	14.23%	1.16%	0.55%
2014	133,000,000	11.13%	13.20%	13.16%	6.81%	0.61%
2015	143,280,000	9.77%	12.74%	12.21%	6.70%	4.92%
2016	155,270,000	8.87%	11.82%	*1.11%*	*8.44%*	11.94%

Only one team made the playoffs consistently with a quarterback over 13% of the cap and that was Peyton Manning. Is your quarterback as good as him? Only Hall of Fame type quarterbacks consistently compete over 13% of the cap, but New England and Green Bay have been able to keep their franchise quarterbacks in, and below, the top tier in many years. Having Brady and Aaron Rodgers at such reasonable rates has undoubtedly helped them compete. Taking into account the projected salary cap increases through 2019, Seattle is almost certainly keeping Wilson under 12.20% for the entirety of the four-year, $87.6 million contract he's playing under that was signed in 2015. Capping Wilson at that rate is a very reasonable number considering he's the perfect prototype for Darrelle Bevell's offensive system. Their front office seemed to make a conscious decision to manage his cap hit by giving Wilson a $31 million signing bonus with $61,542,000 in total guaranteed money, which is 70.25% of the contract total and led all multi-year player contracts at the time. With a four-year contract, rather than the standard six-year deals that most teams give top players, the Seahawks and Wilson will likely have a similar negotiating relationship to the Patriots and Brady in that they'll work together to provide both sides with fair value, while avoiding market topping cap hits.

Of the 12 salary capped years where the Patriots and Packers made the playoffs, six of them had Tom Brady and Aaron Rodgers in the second tier of quarterback spending between six and ten percent. Andy Dalton might be considered a top of the third tier quarterback in a more realistic quarterback market and the lower cap hits he did have through 2015 definitely helped the Bengals build a good team with a very good defense around him, rather than a more quarterback centric model. Seattle did the same thing leading into Wilson's second contract.

The year after Wilson signed his deal, the Houston Texans signed Brock Osweiler to a four-year, $72 million contract that would have averaged over 10% of the cap over the course of the contract if he finished it: first tier money to a player who had only played seven games and had huge question marks surrounding him. According to Troy Renck of the *Denver Post*, the Broncos had determined that $16 million per year was the highest they would go, so Houston outbid them by $2 million per year for a quarterback who wasn't very likely to create that value and could put them at a disadvantage even within their division.[9] Tennessee has a mobile and accurate quarterback who protects the football in Marcus Mariota and he'll be on a rookie deal throughout the length of Osweiler's original contract, never breaching five percent of the cap until his fifth year in 2019. Instead Osweiler was traded to the Browns in 2017 with a 2018 second round pick as Houston took the dead money cap hit of $9 million in 2019 to clear $10 million in cap space and Cleveland took a quarterback who could've started for them or be cut after the year with no consequence.

Osweiler ended up being cut before the season leaving a $16 million dead money cap hit against the Browns 2017 cap, which in theory doesn't hurt too much with the team's adjusted salary cap at $217.8 million. But the $16 million came in Osweiler's guarantees from Houston, which Cleveland has now had to pay even though they've cut him. They did receive a second round pick in 2018, but that kind of gamble cost them $16 million in real cash and cap space, so it wasn't worth the risk. That is a steep price to pay for a second round pick. Houston ended up trading their 25th overall pick in 2017 and their 2018 first round pick to Cleveland to move up to #12 to draft their quarterback of the future, who thankfully for them, already looks like he'll be a franchise quarterback, Deshaun Watson.

An adjusted salary cap is when a team rolls over past unused salary cap room into their future salary cap. Rolling over cap space is a great mechanism for teams to use while they're building their roster through the draft and know they're not ready to compete. It allows these teams to save their cap space for when they can use it to compete for the playoffs.

There should be a sliding scale teams take into account based on what the quarterback is able to produce for their system and what is necessary around him in terms of the talent needed to achieve our definition of success, the ability to compete for the playoffs yearly. Every system and roster configuration has production needs that are necessary for the team's success, so production requirements aren't static across the league. Even different variations of the West Coast offense can have different production needs dependent on the quarterback and their system.

Generally speaking, the baseline for a top tier quarterback seems to be a completion percentage over 65%, over 7.5 yards per passing attempt, over 260 yards per game (with the ability to go off for a 300 to 400 yard type of game if facing a prolific rush defense and weaker pass defense), and over 30 touchdowns with interception totals that are preferably in the single digits, but at least below 12. Mobility increases his value as it provides the deadly fourth variable for third-down and redzone efficiency, another source of rushing production outside of the running back, and a real problem for opposing defenses, a game breaking quality that both Rodgers and Wilson possess. Each head coach and offensive coordinator should already know what their ideal production looks like at quarterback and across the offense not because they need to hit the production to win a Super Bowl, but because, like a business plan for an entrepreneurial venture, you want to have a plan to help you stay on track in advancing toward your objective. You want to know what your version of success looks like.

In knowing their version of success, they should understand the adjustments that need to be made to achieve sufficient production if they have a lesser QB. A head coach and General Manager should understand the kind of defense they will need to win if they have a lesser quarterback. They should know what kind of defense they need to compete if they have a top quarterback too. Decisions makers should always be aware of the potential production capabilities of their offense and defense with an understanding of how each move they make could improve them to produce at the necessary rate. By knowing the skills and prototypes of players needed for the roles in their systems, they can find the players needed to succeed in the draft or free agency. By understanding the right statistics to analyze, they can build the complete team they need.

The top tier of the market should currently reside between 10% on the low end and 12.5 to 13% on the top end. Ideally it will decrease over time closer to ten as the salary cap grows and teams gain more data on the need for a more manageable quarterback cap hit to compete, especially so if the NFLPA negotiates a new CBA with more realistic value for rookie contracts in 2020 like discussed in chapter ten. First tier contracts should largely be reserved for quarterbacks between the ages of 26 and 33, 34-year-old seasons considering that is where they will probably have the best balance of physical and mental abilities as a quarterback. Football Outsiders' has found that 32 years old is typically the age where quarterbacks begin to see a decline.[9] As of where the NFL stands today, quarterback's prime earning years should come near the end of his first deal, through his second contract and into the beginning of his third contract. With an increasing emphasis on audibles at the line of scrimmage, the mental side is becoming increasingly important, so the elite chess masters at quarterback can carry that value deep into their thirties as their physically decline and their mental skills work to fill that gap, which is why many of the best quarterbacks in the NFL today are older than 32.

Unsurprisingly, Tom Brady's three highest cap hits of his career come in this time frame as he earned 13.55% of the 2006 cap at the age of 29, 12.60% at 31 in 2008, and 11.89% the next year. New England then took advantage of an uncapped 2010 to give Brady his biggest cap hit of his career at $17.42 million, which would have been 14.51% of the next season's cap, and since that year, his cap hit has continued to creep lower and lower. Again, because it bears repeating as quite a few NFL teams haven't figured this out, you can't compete with the best if they're getting far better production value out of the most expensive positions. Like in a product-based business, if what you're selling is more, or as, expensive and lower quality than your competitors, you're going to have a hard time competing.

The second tier of the quarterback market is between about six and ten percent of the salary cap. These should be accurate and potentially mobile system quarterbacks who are deemed replaceable if the right player were to come along— and they need a little more help from pass catchers, which is another reason why you want to have him at a lower cap hit, so you can make the offensive investments to improve his performance. They are average starting level quarterbacks who can also be deemed replaceable if a viable option is available through the draft at a lower price, which is part of why teams want the extra cap space open rather than spending first tier money on a second tier player.

The pass positions of quarterback, the top three wide receivers and tight end should be thought of as an aggregate cap hit. What are you spending on the main components of your pass game? What about when you add running backs in there too? If you're investing a little less in a quarterback, you can invest more in this group to increase the offensive output.

A second tier quarterback should provide a completion percentage of at least 61 to 62%, over 7.0 to 7.2 yards per attempt, over 235 yards per game, and a slightly worst touchdown-to-interception ratio than first tier quarterbacks. A lot of these players should be the types who can be relied on to play smart football and not turn the ball over.

No quarterback in recent years has better embodied this tier than Andy Dalton of the Bengals with a career average completion percentage of 62.8%, 7.3 yards per attempt, 238.2 yards per game, and an average touchdown-to-interception ratio of 22-to13. Since 2014, when he signed an extension, his stats in these metrics have been 64.7%, 7.6 per attempt, 239.6 yards per game, and 18-to-10. He's never been the kind of player who can carry a team, but he has been efficient, making him a good second tier example as these are the kinds of game managers a team should want at these figures.

Dalton's Super Bowl winning equivalent is Brad Johnson of the 2002 Buccaneers at 9.57% of the cap. Johnson provides a great example of something that worked with his 62.3% completion percentage, 235 yards per game, 6.8 pass yards per attempt, 6.2 net yards per attempt and 22 touchdowns to six interceptions. With a slightly lower cap hit, the Bucs were able to fit both Keyshawn Johnson (4.72%) and Keenan McCardell (1.76%) in a salary cap situation with Warren Sapp, Simeon Rice and Derrick Brooks combining for 23.80% of the cap and a maxed out cap.

Before a difficult and injury plagued 2016 season for the Bengals, Dalton provided them with a 22-9-1 record the during the 2014 and 2015 seasons and, while seemingly not supremely physically gifted or talented, he became very efficient and reliable in that time. He averaged 8.4 yards per attempt in 2015 with 250 passing yards per game and a 66.1% completion percentage to go with 25 touchdowns and seven interceptions; in 2016, he averaged 7.5 per attempt for 263 passing yards per game with a 64.7% completion percentage and 18 touchdowns versus eight interceptions. His production is first tier in some ways, like his accuracy and yards per attempt, but overall his game slants toward the game manager type as Dalton isn't the kind of player a team could build a passing based Super Bowl strategy around.

He signed an extension in August 2014, after a 2013 season where he led the Bengals to an 11-5 record with a 61.9% completion percentage, 33 touchdowns, 20 interceptions and 7.3 yards per attempt for 268 yards per game, 4293 yards. A very good season for a third year signal caller, which earned the contract extension and, because of the extension, the Bengals were able to get him slightly below his free market value, which may have been bumped past his true worth by the free agency market bidding process. It worked out for Dalton as he took a step back in 2014 with a great 64.2% completion percentage, but only 19 touchdowns to 17 interceptions and 7.1 yards per attempt for just 212 yards per game, which might have decreased his market value.

Dalton has provided the Bengals with good value in the second tier and he's become the example for what a current second tier quarterback is: a market setter for quarterbacks who are firmly on the outside of the elite conversation, the kind of quarterbacks who need a strong team and offense around them to win. He might not be the kind of player you'd want at 12.50% with a low likelihood that he could carry an average roster to a Super Bowl like the 2006 Colts, 2009 Saints, or 2011 Giants, but he is a quarterback you might take for six to nine percent of the cap to build around him with a hopefully elite defense. How much of Dalton's efficiency is correlated to the talent of the players around him? Does he elevate his pass catchers or do guys like AJ Green and Tyler Eifert elevate him? As many would argue, he's been completely reliant on AJ Green boosting his performance for his entire career.

In that respect, Alex Smith has been someone who should set the top of this market although he's usually been in the first tier with a cap hit of 10.00% in 2017 that sits right on the border. He is third in the NFL in winning percentage behind Brady and Rodgers from 2011 through 2016 with much of that being attributed to being under offensive coordinator Greg Roman in San Francisco in 2011 and 2012, then Andy Reid, Doug Pederson and Brad Childress since then in Kansas City. Smith's most difficult seasons came early in his career when he had six different offensive coordinators in his first eight seasons, but also when he was asked to throw more due to a weak-rushing offense. The term system quarterback means that a certain skill set fits the system, while the term game manager is used to describe quarterbacks who fit a system and can help a team win if he's a part of a completely balanced system that asks him to throw 30 times per game rather than 40. Elite game managers are in this second tier, which is what Smith has been for his entire career before a shocking 2017 that seems driven by his competitive nature after the Chiefs drafting quarterback Patrick Mahomes in the first round of the 2017 draft. These are the system quarterbacks who are replaceable, but who can win a Super Bowl if provided a complete, balanced roster around them.

Smith is the kind of player who should be at the top of this tier with a stat line from 2013 through 2016 that includes a 64.5% completion percentage, 222.4 passing yards per game, 7.0 yards per pass attempt, and a 19-to-7 touchdown to interception ratio per season. Joe Flacco is another player who would ideally be in the second tier with a line from 2012 through 2016 of 62.0%, 254.4 passing yards a game, a less inefficient 6.8 yards per attempt, and a 20-to-14 touchdown to interception ratio per season. While Smith at least has a reasonable cap hit in 2018 of 11.48% with the Chiefs able to decide to either re-sign him or roll with the highly touted Mahomes, Flacco is in the midst of a contract that has a projected average cap hit of 13.97% from 2017 through 2020, which will diminish the Ravens chances of building the roster around him that he needs to have success as a less than elite player.

Only four quarterbacks were in the second tier in 2016: Brady, Dalton, plus Brock Osweiler and Ryan Tannehill on contracts that enter the first tier in 2017. Brady obviously isn't a game manager, but his being in this tier allowed them to build a team like he was in 2016 with their defense ranking first in the NFL in points allowed at 15.6 per game. Sam Bradford had a cap hit of 8.05% with the Eagles before being traded, but due to his trade to the Vikings, his cap hit ends up in the third tier. The rest of the tier was made up of guys like Tyrod Taylor with the Bills, Ryan Fitzpatrick, who ended up being a bust in 2016 after a reasonable 2015 where his play was elevated by Eric Decker and Brandon Marshall, with the Jets, plus Robert Griffin III in Cleveland, Case Keenum for the Rams, and Chase Daniel as the Eagles back-up.

Joe Flacco at 6.63% of the 2012 cap in his fifth season represents a terrific bottom of second tier example for what has worked for a champion. During that season, in the downfield Air Coryell offense they ran before Gary Kubiak introduced the West Coast principles they're still using heading into 2017, Flacco completed 59.1% of his passes, threw for 239 yards per game, averaged 7.2 yards per pass and 6.3 net yards per attempt with 22 touchdowns to 10 interceptions. The Ravens fired offensive coordinator Cam Cameron in early December 2012, replacing him with quarterbacks coach Jim Caldwell, which may have been the catalyst behind his playoff run with a 57.8% completion percentage, 11 touchdowns to zero interceptions at 9.1 yards per pass and 285 per game. He earned a championship that year, but as his regular season stats indicated, he was not in the elite conversation and the huge contract he signed that offseason has severely restricted the Ravens ability to field a championship caliber roster and will continue with cap hits near to above 14% from 2016 through 2020.

Brady was this caliber of player on the 2003 and 2004 teams with a combined completion percentage of 60.4%, averaging 229 passing yards per game, 7.3 yards per attempt with 51 touchdowns to 26 interceptions. His lower cost allowed for the Ty Law cap hits of 11.74% and 12.67% with the many defensive players over one and two percent of the cap that helped build defenses that ranked first and second in points allowed. He had a third tier cost in 2003 at 4.43% and at the bottom of the second tier at 6.28% in 2004.

In 2012, Flacco was a budding young quarterback at a value that allowed the Ravens to invest 25.22% in the three cap hits more expensive than Flacco, which were outside linebacker Terrell Suggs, nose tackle Haloti Ngata and safety Ed Reed. Suggs' cap hit of 9.55% is a Super Bowl record for edge rushers, Ngata's 8.62% is second to Warren Sapp's record of 9.82% in 2002, and Reed's 7.05% cap hit is the most for a Super Bowl safety, 1.17% more than Troy Polamalu in 2008. Ray Lewis' cap hit of 5.68% is a record for inside linebackers. Because of Flacco's reasonable cap hit, the Ravens were able to keep four elite veteran defenders, four leaders, at each of the three levels of the defense.

After Stafford's monster contract was signed in late August 2017, Jason researched the quarterback market's past contracts and wrote an article asking, "Is the Current NFL Quarterback Overpaid?" In his research of these past cap hits, he ranked the top 30 cap hits at the position and established a table with numbers that represent the average percentage of salary cap spent on each sub-group of quarterbacks at the time.[10]

Tier	2005	2009	2013	2017
1-5	17.0%	15.3%	16.1%	16.5%
6-10	9.7%	11.1%	12.9%	13.2%
11-15	8.9%	9.2%	9.7%	12.8%
16-20	7.4%	7.8%	5.5%	10.7%
21-25	5.2%	6.0%	3.1%	6.0%
26-30	1.9%	2.6%	1.6%	3.2%

As explained earlier in the chapter regarding the first tier of this market and detailed in the table, the quarterback market has become bunched up at the top with 17 players in 2016 over 10% of the cap and the second tier has essentially become non-existent as quarterbacks move from rookie contracts into first tier territory if they just do enough to prove they are their team's starting quarterback. Jason echoes the sentiments in this book in the article writing, "the salary cap is supposed to promote some type of competitive balance in the league. Generally, if you spend highly on one position it should mean that you have an area of weakness at another. The most expensive position has always been the quarterback, so if someone has a great quarterback they should have to break the bank for that player. It should create a system in which the team with the so-so quarterback has extra cap dollars (and dollars in their actual cash budget) to spend on other players to try to counteract the great quarterback" they're competing against.

To gather this information, Jason looked at which quarterbacks were projected to start the season for their teams, then took a historical sample of these quarterback salaries through history and was able to rebuild the top contracts at the position at four-year intervals. The spending at the top of the market has continued to be at a bank busting high rate, but the contracts behind them have begun to restrict teams with lesser quarterbacks as better quarterbacks are making the same amount of money, which restricts the potential paths to success for the teams with the lesser quarterbacks.

Jason writes that Stafford's contract is so high that it could push the market and create a more natural spread of salaries, but the real step towards a more balanced market has to come in the form of a few teams making difficult decisions in realizing their fringe quarterbacks can't be paid the same as the best players at the position. While the general public and the average football writer continue to believe the philosophy that a quarterback is so necessary that overpaying is okay, Jason and I have pointed out for years now on Over The Cap that, as Jason says, "paying a player a big salary doesn't somehow make them a better player." Teams will wonder why they can't compete with an average quarterback making elite money, "then after the season is done, the question will be asked how do you get him more weapons or a better defense?" Jason writes, "hint, the answer isn't to pay him more, it's to pay the quarterback less so you can try to get him far better weapons" than the elite quarterbacks have.

As written in this chapter, paying less in the current market typically means going to the draft, which might not be popular with fans, but is quite all right. I'd rather spend two or three draft picks on potential serviceable quarterbacks than invest 12% of my salary cap for the next five years in a mid-level player who produces at a similar level to quarterbacks you could find in the second or third round who could then allow you to build up the rest of your roster to make the team better around the quarterback you have on the rookie contract and, if that quarterback isn't your quarterback of the future, building up the roster makes the team a viable contender for when you do find the right quarterback. Rookie contracts are low enough that a team can draft multiple quarterbacks to compete at the position.

The max for the third tier is just under that Flacco Super Bowl cap hit at six percent and the floor is two percent, which is where below average starters, quarterbacks coming off their rookie deals who still need to prove their worth, bridge quarterbacks who are high-level insurance for a player on his rookie deal, and quarterbacks in the first four seasons of their first round rookie contracts.

Third tier contracts should be short in the one to three year range as these are transients working to earn their way into a bigger contract and/or providing a team with a bridge to the rookie the franchise is grooming behind him. They should either be unproven guys coming off rookie deals looking to improve their earnings or older veterans looking to prove themselves for another deal as they've been established as a less consistent, fringe starting quarterback. Think what Osweiler's 2016 value should have been or where Jay Cutler is at in 2017 at 5.99% after signing with Miami after Ryan Tannehill's knee injury and post-poning his broadcasting career with FOX . With so much of the NFL in the first tier, hits on third tier contracts, like first round rookie contracts, can create massive value advantages for teams. When you have a player like Marcus Mariota, Jameis Winston, or Carson Wentz becoming franchise quarterbacks in years two, three and four of their rookie contracts, they become valuable weapons that allow you to build a strong roster to elevate their, and the team's, level of play.

The fourth tier represents back-up journeymen who should earn between the veteran minimum and two percent of the salary cap, plus rookie contracts starting with quarterbacks drafted in the second half of the first round all the way down. On the veteran side, these are players who have been given opportunities to start and weren't able to prove they were anything more than a back-up. These are players like Nick Foles, Brian Hoyer, Ryan Mallett, Matt Schaub, Drew Stanton, and Matt Moore.

When it comes to the 23 Super Bowl champions, seven had top quarterback cap hits in the first tier, eight were in the second tier, and seven were in the third tier, including Trent Green and Matt Flynn's dead money cap hit. Kurt Warner and Russell Wilson led their teams at 1.32% and 0.55% respectively; add in Brady at 0.47% in 2001 and three fourth tier quarterbacks led their team to championships regardless of how much their more expensive back-ups made. Aaron Rodgers is the 23rd quarterback and he wasn't in any tier because 2010 was an uncapped year, but his $6.5 million cap hit would have had him in the third tier judging off the salary caps in 2009 and 2011. Adding Rodgers cap hit, only 7 of 23 (30%) Super Bowl champion quarterbacks made first tier money, but 17 teams paid their quarterback first tier money in 2016, so 53% of the NFL invested in a spending strategy that has worked 30% of the time.

Regardless of it being an uncapped year, Rodgers' low cap hit, that was made possible by the Packers extending him very early in his playing career, allowed them to have five defensive players making more money than Rodgers, which helped create a defense that was second in the NFL in points allowed at 15.0 per game. Simultaneously, his 65.7% completion percentage with 28 touchdowns to 11 interceptions and 261.5 yards per game far exceeded expectations for third tier production; in many ways Rodgers had first tier production for third tier money.

The narrative around the NFL is that you need a quarterback to win a Super Bowl, but at what cost? What kind of roster are teams giving up by paying these high costs at quarterback? How much more competitive could many teams around the NFL be if they took a different route? Many of the quarterbacks whose Super Bowl victories we reference as proof of them being elite is derived from years where they were on contracts that didn't pay them like they were elite. We've got Flacco, Rodgers, Drew Brees at 8.67% in 2009, and Ben Roethlisberger at 4.94% and 6.87% during his two Super Bowl seasons. Once they're paid like a Super Bowl winning quarterback, their chances of winning again can decrease due to higher costs. Actor, screenwriter and filmmaker Seth Rogen mentioned on the *Nerdist* podcast with Chris Hardwick that great sequels don't happen often because of the high costs of the stars coming off that success; the same can be said for NFL teams. Other teams bid away much of their top talent, forgoing finding players who fit their Super Bowl winning formula through the draft and instead invested in players they've already seen win a Super Bowl and hoping that they will help their team do the same. Any kind of team can be constructed with any sort of cap configuration, but it becomes more difficult the higher cap costs climb. Add in a few more high cap costs, like most teams tend to have, as quarterback isn't the only expensive position where teams want elite players, and cap space begins to dwindle. Great organizations are able to maneuver and plan their way around big cap hits, but this financial juggling act no easy task.

Quarterback, pass rusher, cornerback, wide receiver and left tackle have become the five most expensive markets in the NFL as they're the main positions associated with passing the football. But with trends toward quick passing systems, expenses are being spread across both the offensive and defensive lines. So top players here are becoming pricier as well; outside of the quarterback market are other high priced markets that most teams are going to want to enter, so rather than pay and pray at quarterback, create competition and use the money to spread your talent around these high priced positions like Denver did when they let Osweiler walk and instead emerged with two quarterback options for the future in Trevor Siemian and Paxton Lynch at a far lower cost than Osweiler.

Denver received four compensatory picks in the 2017 draft after letting Osweiler, Malik Jackson and Danny Trevethan leave for free agent contracts. They drafted cornerback Brendan Langley in the third round and quarterback Chad Kelly in the seventh, while trading away their fifth-round compensatory pick with running back Kapri Bibbs to San Francisco for their fourth-round pick in 2018 and they sent a seventh-round compensatory pick with a fourth-round pick to Cleveland for their two fifth-round selections in 2017, numbers 145 and 175. They drafted highly regarded tight end Jake Butt with the 145th pick as he dropped in the draft due to a torn ACL in Michigan's bowl game at the end of 2016, then traded the

175th pick in a package with the 238th pick in the seventh-round to Green Bay to get the 172nd pick and draft wide receiver Isaiah McKenzie from Georgia. This is the kind of stockpiling of draft picks, and hopefully talent, that the compensatory cycle creates.

Between Siemian and Lynch, the thinking was that the quarterback who doesn't win the quarterback competition can either become a serviceable back-up for the team, be traded for a draft pick, or walk in free agency with the Broncos potentially receiving another compensatory pick down the road if one of them earns even a Chase Daniel level deal around 4% of the cap like he signed with Philadelphia in 2016. In 2018, during the last year of Siemian's rookie contract, he and Lynch are projected to cost the Broncos 1.84% of the cap, while Osweiler would've cost the Texans 11.80% of the cap. If neither quarterback works out, the team can draft another quarterback early.

If you don't think you have a top quarterback or if you think you're going to have to pay someone far more than their worth, don't overspend. Instead improve the rest of your roster and restart at quarterback with a competition. Rather than pay and pray, hopefully you already have a rookie contract quarterback you're developing as a back-up. Three 2016 examples of teams without franchise quarterbacks who created a competition between three quarterbacks in the second tier or lower to create a better cap situation moving forward were the Broncos, Eagles, and Browns.

The Broncos had the Siemian, Lynch and Mark Sanchez competition. In Philadelphia, the Eagles had Bradford, Chase Daniel and Carson Wentz before trading Bradford for a 2017 first-round pick and a fourth round pick in 2018, which left them with two quarterbacks in the third tier. Both teams had low-cost rookie contract quarterbacks with a reliable veteran, system back-up who could win a game in a pinch and provide a leadership example for the young player. In Cleveland, RG3 and Josh McCown were in third tier contracts, while third round rookie Cody Kessler cost less than half a percent of the cap. While Cleveland had a horrific 2016, they tried a similar competition in 2017 with Kessler, Kevin Hogan, and 2017 second round pick DeShone Kizer after adding Osweiler to a second tier contract to create a new four man competition in 2017. As mentioned, Osweiler ended up being cut before the season with a $16 million dead money charge, which wasn't worth the cost. Halfway through the 2017 season, it doesn't seem the trio that stayed on will work out, but they have 13 projected picks in 2018 and the potential to draft a quarterback high in 2018 with two first round picks. With 37 picks from 2016 through 2018, they have a high supply of low-cost labor that will also make them a potential buyer of one of the free agent quarterbacks slated to be available in 2018, plus they have the draft picks to trade for one as well. The surplus of draft picks will continue to create cap rollover for when the time to build a competitive roster comes, which is likely during the 2018 offseason with over $110 million in projected cap space. Osweiler is now back on the Broncos as their third quarterback in 2017 at a cap hit of 0.46% after being released by the Browns. If their offensive line could protect the quarterback and create holes for the running game, they may have still had a defense good enough to compete for the playoffs in 2017 like their 2015 team did with a severely diminished Peyton Manning, but it seems they'll fall short.

All three organizations decided to go with a competition, rather than overpay. The Eagles structured the deal so masterfully that quarterback Super Agent Tom Condon didn't realize the Eagles had any intentions of drafting a quarterback in the draft. He had likely seen the two-year, $35 million contract as an opportunity to get his client $22 million guaranteed, which was $2.5 million more than the franchise tag. But a cap hit that was projected to be over 14% of the 2017 cap meant that the contract was never intended to see year two as the Eagles were never going to invest that much of their cap into a player who doesn't have the mobility that Doug Pederson's offense requires. Essentially Bradford's contract was a one-year deal with the Eagles looking to maximize his value as a trade asset. It just so happened that Minnesota's quarterback, Teddy Bridgewater, went down with a dislocated knee that ended his 2016 season before it began and had him starting 2017 on the Physically Unable to Perform (PUP) list, so Bradford's value skyrocketed and the Eagles were able to trade him and only have $5.5 million in dead money in 2016 and again in 2017, rather than $11 million in 2016, due to a flexible guarantee structure that Philly uses often to allow them to decrease their dead money hit through trades.

When a team gets value at quarterback, they're able to build a team around that quarterback. Making cap decisions that emphasize cap flexibility is something that should be followed at all positions; just because quarterback is the most important position doesn't mean a team should stray from this core principle. Quarterback is important, but so are other expensive markets like pass rusher, cornerback, wide receiver, and left tackle. So is every other position on the roster. Even with those main markets, Super Bowl teams don't just have one pass rusher, they have a whole defensive line that can disrupt the other team's offense. One great cornerback isn't enough. You need multiple defensive backs that can handle the mismatches that the offense creates and the offense needs more than just a top WR1. They need to create mismatches with multiple offensive players.

When a team is getting something closer to the true value of a quarterback, they're then able to make the moves necessary to build a complete team around that quarterback in the way that best complements and supplements the quarterback's skill set. Only a few quarterbacks are the equivalent of that Conor McGregor left hand, so stop constructing teams built to knock people out with the passing game, but who lack the punching power to do it.

Chapter 6: Offensive Skill Spending: Understanding Objectives and Finding Value

The premise for Moneyball in baseball, and the strategies that have come after it, have been based on the most basic principle of the sport. Each offense has 27 outs in a game, so you want to maximize what you do with your outs and minimize what the opponent does with his outs. Those nine innings are all that a baseball team has, so as Aaron Schatz wrote in the *Football Outsiders Almanac 2016*, "imagine if there was a new rule in baseball that gave a team a way to earn another three outs in the middle of the inning. That would be pretty useful, right? That's the way football works."[1]

In 2016, NFL offenses averaged 11 drives per game; you could have more or less depending on the flow of the game and what each team did with their drives. With a drive, like baseball, you're only guaranteed three chances with the fourth one typically being a punt as the average NFL offensive drive starts around the 30 to 31-yard line according to Football Outsiders' drive stats.[2] The objective of offensive football is to score touchdowns and scoring touchdowns from an average of 70-yards away is going to have some steps in between. To accomplish the objective of scoring, an offense needs to be able to consistently earn multiple first downs on your way to the end zone. Rather than focus on the quarterback position and a vague pundit philosophy of "you need a quarterback to succeed in the NFL," the conversation should instead be centered around *the objective: moving the football down the field, so you're in a position to score and then, when you're in the redzone, have the ability to score touchdowns rather than settle for field goals.* Along with producing a few big plays per game and not turning the ball over, those are the four main principles of offensive football.

To produce in these four ways, having a high yard per play average is the first of a handful of key offensive statistical metrics to analyze. The 2016 league average was 5.5 yards per play with the Falcons at number one producing 6.7 per play and the Rams at the bottom at 4.4 per play. The 1999 Rams have the highest yard per play production of any champion at 6.5, while the Super Bowl average is 5.5. A high yard per play average is typically driven by a balanced offense, which will be a recurring theme of this chapter. Passing does have the biggest impact on yards per play, so a high yard per pass average is our first concern. The average Super Bowl champion averaged 7.5 yards per pass attempt, while the 1999 Rams led the way at 8.6. The 2013 Seahawks serve as a great example of a team not passing a lot, but using the times they did pass to do so efficiently with the second least pass attempts per game of any champion at 26.3, but averaging 8.4 yards per pass attempt. The goal for a rushing offense in a balanced offense should be to surpass the Super Bowl average of 4.1 yards per carry, while teams with a rushing based offense should look to be up near the 4.8 yards per carry that Marshall Faulk's Rams team produced to lead all champions although that Rams offense was very balanced with Kurt Warner. Rushing based offenses like the Broncos champions of the late-nineties saw their per carry average just below the 1999 Rams average at 4.6 and 4.7 per carry.

Teams want to produce a high yards per pass attempt average, while producing a high completion percentage – which has continued to creep higher since Bill Walsh introduced his West Coast offense. There has been an increase in league-wide yardage production across the NFL since the innovations of Walsh and others over the last few decades. So with everyone producing a lot of yards, zeroing in on the rate of efficiency of those yards is important. Dolphins legend Dan Marino led the league in passing in 1992 with 4,116 yards, which was 834 yards better than Mark Rypien of the Redskins in second place, but would be 12th in the NFL in 2016 between Andy Dalton and Jameis Winston. Many quarterbacks can produce the 4000-yard season now. You want to find the players who can do it efficiently in your system.

The baseline for a top tier quarterback is a completion percentage over 65% and the baseline for a quality quarterback is about the 2016 league average of 63.0%, but the average for champions has been 62.1% because of the various strategies that have won championships and the increase in accuracy league-wide over time. In 1994, the 49ers led the NFL with a 70.3% completion percentage, the Saints were number two at 64.3% and the Bills were the only other team above 63%. In 2016, the league average was 63.0%, up five percentage points from the 1994 average of 58.0% with the Vikings and Saints both over 70%, then 15 others over 63% as well.

Completion percentage numbers have seen a sharp uptick with the champions since 2009 averaging a completion percentage of 63.8% punctuated by the Saints' 69.5% with Drew Brees' 70.6% completion percentage in 2009 to lead all Super Bowl quarterbacks. Teams want a high completion percentage with a high yards per passing attempt because they don't just want to produce pass yards in chunks: they want to produce it consistently because consistency is the key to moving the chains down the field and scoring touchdowns.

There has been an uptick in passing production during that time as well with teams since 2009 averaging 540 more passing yards per season, almost 34 more per game, than the Super Bowl teams from 1994 through 2008. Only the 1994 49ers, 1999 Rams, and 2006 Colts had over 4000 yards before 2009, while since then the average is 4281 with seven of nine over 4000 except the 2012 Ravens at 3996 and the 2013 Seahawks at 3508 with their run-based strategy.

Football Outsiders makes a point about the running back position that rings true for passing as well: "if their overall yards per carry are equal, a running back who consistently gains yardage on every play is more valuable than a boom-and-bust running back who is frequently stuffed at the line but occasionally breaks a long highlight-worthy run." Teams want a running and passing attack that consistently moves the ball because that means they'll consistently be in high-percentage situations, which will produce a high third down conversion rate and create more "innings" for the offense. Consistent ball movement means fewer third and long situations where they have to gain eight or ten yards to gain a first down—which is far less likely to succeed, as well as providing far fewer potential plays to select from for the offensive coordinator—than an offense in a third and three situation. You want to make progress with each play rather than have to bet on the big play that doesn't come very frequently. Per the Ron Jaworski quote from chapter five, "the pass gives you the lead, and the run solidifies it," so consistent rushers also help protect the lead. In the same vein that it can move the chains and keep the clock moving a high percentage of the time with completions, the short passing attack can play a role in protecting the lead in this way as well.

Regarding first down production and third down conversion rates, the goal for first down production should be shoot for better than the 2016 average of 324.3 over the season or 20.3 per game, which is right in line with the Super Bowl average of 326.9, 20.4 per game. To give some perspective, the top five in 2016 were all above 351 total and 21.9 per game, while the Super Bowl champions were also above this total as the 2016 Patriots were ranked fifth for both, so 22 first downs per game is getting into the elite territory. The 2016 teams peaked with the Saints at 395 and 24.7 per game and the Super Bowl record is 376, which is 23.5 per game, for the 2006 Colts.

The bottom five 2016 teams all had below 290 first downs, which was 18.1 or less per game. The bottom five Super Bowl teams all had less than 294 or 18.4 per game; these were teams reliant on their defense like the 2003 and 2001 Patriots, the 2008 Steelers, the 2000 Ravens, and the 2002 Bucs.

Looking at third down conversion percentages, the average for Super Bowl teams is 42.1%, which constitutes a good baseline. The Super Bowl top two of 56.1% for the 2006 Colts and 51.0% for the 1994 49ers blow past the 2016 Saints league leading 48.6% third down conversion rate. If a team is above 45%, they're in the NFL's top five conversation, while the bottom five in the NFL can be as low as 35% or less.

Once a team has made its way inside the twenty to the redzone, the goal is to score touchdowns rather than settle for field goals. In 2016, the top ten teams in the league in touchdown efficiency in the redzone were above 60%, while the top five were above 65%. These represent the markers that teams should be striving for, while having a kicker who can hit field goals when you don't score touchdowns and be relied on to hit a 52-yarder if your offense gets stalled out at the 35-yard line. He's a great "three-point shooter" if you can't penetrate the defense. *Football Outsiders* found that "play in the red zone has a disproportionately high importance to the outcome of games relative to plays on the rest of the field," which makes sense as these plays are the difference between a team scoring a touchdown, field goal or not scoring at all.

While the emphasis is on moving the ball with consistency, teams also need to have big play threats—players who can produce plays over twenty yards to stretch the defense and give your offense some big chunks towards touchdowns. Pete Carroll has a statistic he cites that if an offense has an explosive pass play of 16+ yards or an explosive run play of 12+ yards, they will score over 75% of the time. While not the twenty plus yard total that is statistically tracked as a big play, that illustrates the importance of having explosive players to make these chunk plays. The 1999 Rams led all champions averaging 4.8 big plays over twenty yards per game, while the offensive Super Bowl average is 3.6. Teams create these big plays through deep receiving threats, players who produce yards after catch, and big rushes.

Teams need to save themselves from committing turnovers or penalties as these can end drives completely, end a drive before it starts with a ten yard holding penalty to make it first and twenty, or change the complexion of the game. In the NFC Divisional Round in January 2017, the Cowboys were driving down the field and made a completion to Terrence Williams down at the Packers 15-yard line, but the catch was called back because wide receiver Brice Butler earned an unsportsmanlike penalty for entering the huddle and leaving without being involved in the subsequent play. This unforced error resulted in a loss of 37 field position yards, which led to a punt rather than a field goal that could have made it 7-6 or a touchdown that could have given Dallas a 10-7 lead. Instead, the Packers took the ball 90-yards down the field after the punt to make it 14-3 on the way to a 21-13 halftime lead in a game they won 34-31.

These statistics and the production that coaches try to find with their system and personnel produce the framework for what kind of production you're looking for, which helps an organization determine what players they're looking for. The key to offensive football is to acquire as many potential mismatches for opposing defenses as possible. Even if an offense has an elite performer like a Julio Jones, they can't win with just that. They need to have a multitude of mismatches because Jones can't completely carry an offense through a playoff run to a Super Bowl win. An offense needs various mismatches to create an opportunity for success each week through an opportunity for different advantages each week and strategies that teams haven't seen on film or can't figure out how to stop because they lack the defensive solution whether in their players or scheme. They need various mismatches that force the defense to take attention off the top option. The goal is to find mismatch creators who maximize your offense's ability to produce results in the statistics and objectives mentioned.

Using the overall offensive statistical production of past Super Bowl champions (full stats in the Appendix) and other successful teams, especially those using a similar system, organizations can use the production of these teams to look at their own and their coach's system and figure out how to build a roster that fulfills the production necessary to succeed. To create a variety of mismatches teams can't afford to pay for top tier players at every skill position—they have to find value. Your staff has to come up with solutions that fill the roles that accomplish offensive objectives in the most efficient way on the field and through the cap. Mismatches and versatility allow a coaching staff to create a different game plan each week; like a great champion UFC fighter, a great offense has a variety of players who have skills that can out-maneuver the defense of all comers, while also not leaving themselves open to being exploited by a defense that excels against the run, pass, or both.

The top tier of the running back market resides between three to six percent of the salary cap with seven being a rarity in today's NFL. This tier is reserved for complete running backs who have the power to convert on a third and one with the ability to create a mismatch in the passing game or pass block on third and six plus. These are three down running backs. Even with this kind of back, teams still need more than one running back in case of injury as running back is one of the most oft-injured positions in the NFL, which has been the main driving force in the decrease in cost at the position.

In recent years, the running back market has crashed due to the lack of success that running backs were having on their second, or free agent, contracts, particularly multi-year deals. This is driven by the injury rate along with the wear and tear of playing running back in the NFL that leads players at the position to see their careers decline earlier than any other position.[3] An increase in teams using the running back by committee approach has likely also contributed to the running back market's decline. The loss of a step of quickness might mean they can no longer hit the hole with the same timing or explosive power necessary to succeed. Lamar Miller had a combined 2643 scrimmage yards in his last two seasons in Miami before entering free agency heading into his 25-year old season and without much wear and tear on his body having averaged a reasonable 233 touches in his three seasons as a starter for the Dolphins. Even with a high level of production and the lack of an injury history, Miller signed a four-year contract with the Houston Texans that is projected to never pay him more than four percent of the salary cap. After 1673 scrimmage yards for the Tampa Bay Bucs in 2015, Doug Martin re-signed on a five-year deal heading into his 27-year old season that paid him 5.15% of the 2016 cap and 4.23% in 2017, but had no dead money in the final three years of the deal, making him easy to cut. Teams have become very tentative in their signing of running backs—and for good reason.

Adrian Peterson earned a market setting and market-busting contract before the 2011 season worth $86.28 million over six years with a $12 million signing bonus and $36 million guaranteed. He was restructured prior to the 2015 season and his cap figures from 2011 through 2016 with the Vikings are below:

Year	Age	Cap	Cap Hit	Cap %
2011	26	120,000,000	12,955,000	10.80%
2012	27	120,600,000	12,705,000	10.53%
2013	28	123,000,000	13,900,000	11.30%
2014	29	133,000,000	14,400,000	10.83%
2015	30	143,280,000	15,400,000	10.75%
2016	31	155,270,000	12,000,000	7.73%

During the 2017 offseason, Le'Veon Bell was franchise-tagged by the Steelers and has made it clear he expects a deal that would be a market buster for where the running back market currently is by rejecting a deal worth $12 million a year over five with $30 million in the first two years, and $42 million over the first three. He also didn't sign his franchise tag until training camp was over as a sign of his displeasure with playing on the $12.1 million tag. According to a rap song he released, he is going to "need 15 a year and they know this." Peterson signed a deal with an average salary of $14.38 million six years ago, so Bell is well within his rights to ask for more than $12 million.

In 2016, Bell averaged 157 yards per game, 105.7 on the ground and 51.3 through the air, which is only outpaced by Priest Holmes 2002 season (163.4) and OJ Simpson's 1975 season (160.2) according to Chase Stuart at FiveThirtyEight. Players like Bell, David Johnson, and Ezekiel Elliott who have the potential to provide their team with 2000 yards per season, over 125 per game, could push this market higher in upcoming years. While the initial instinct may be to scoff at Bell passing up the Steelers seemingly fair market value offer, he's a year younger than Peterson was when he signed that deal, so he's betting on not getting hurt going into free agency as well as betting on a great season, which has risks.

It might be unlikely these three players receive the double-digit cap investment that Peterson received considering the injury rate of the running back position with the fears of decline due to the heavy workload and brutality between the tackles.

We could see an increase towards seven to nine percent of the cap for the most dynamic running backs as these backs have almost become a class of their own with many in the media discussing the need to look at some players as position-less players considering their worth supersedes where their market currently is because they're unique, versatile athletes who break the mold and can provide 125 plus scrimmage yards per game. With wide receivers getting near 10% of the cap for 80 to 100 receiving yards per game, paying a similar rate to a top running back is possible. A back like Bell provides the key objectives of moving the ball in short chunks to move the chains, creating big plays, and scoring touchdowns in the redzone.

The second tier of this market is between one and a half and three percent of the cap, so it includes first round rookie contracts, elite pass catching running backs, plus complete running backs on their third contract who are likely on the decline. The top of the fullback market exists in the second tier of the running back market with Mike Alstott's 2.67% for the 2002 Bucs being a better representation of where the top of the market resides in 2016 than Daryl Johnston's 3.78% for the 1995 Cowboys. With an adjusted salary cap of $209 million in 2017, $42 million more than the $167 million cap due to their rolling over cap space from 2016, San Francisco signed PFF's best fullback in 2016 Kyle Juszcyzk from the Ravens to a four-year deal with projected cap charges of between 2.25% and 3.29% escalating each year through 2020. You can acquire a top fullback and your offense still has a role for someone who can be an extra blocker, pass catching mismatch and occasional goal line battering ram. The 49ers overpaid for Juszcyzk considering where the market is, but with the low-cost and success of rookie contract running backs, a fullback can be a place that money saved at running back goes toward further increasing the production of the running back and the value he creates.

Third tier running backs exist below one and a half percent of the cap and they include all rookie contracts after the first half of the first round, power running backs with no receiving ability, pass catching backs with no rushing ability, and more third and fourth contract backs on the decline. This is where most of the veteran fullback market resides.

Pro Football Focus has some new metrics that teams can use to find running backs for the various running back roles. A player's elusive rating boils down a runners success beyond the point of being helped by his blockers, a key stat in illustrating the value a back creates beyond what his line gives him, which can help show if a player over-performs or under-performs blocking expectations. Breakaway percentage "shows which runners earn the highest (and lowest) percentage of their yardage on big plays (any runs of 15 yards or more)," which shows a player's potential for big plays, but also shows which players are the boom-and-bust variety that Football Outsiders' warns of.[4] As they state, if overall yards are equal, a running back who consistently gains yardage on every play is more valuable. For example, in 2016, Isaiah Crowell had 952 rushing yards on 198 attempts with 452 of those yards on 16 runs over 15 yards to lead the league with 47.5% of his yards coming on those 16 runs. This meant that on his 182 rushes that didn't go over 15 yards, he only had 500 yards, which is just 2.75 per carry and not the kind of consistent production a team hopes for to help move the chains. His low yards per carry average on non-big plays shows how big plays can skew stats and understanding of a team's make-up. While someone might look at Crowell's 952 rushing yards at 4.8 yards per carry in 16 games in 2016 as a sign of the Browns having a player who could be a lead running back, the real story is told in 2017 when he doesn't get as many of those big plays and his yards per carry through eight games is just 3.4. Le'Veon Bell was 22nd of 25 rated running backs with 193, or 15.2%, of his 1268 yards coming on eight breakaway runs, but that meant he averaged 4.25 yards per carry on his 253 non-big play rushes, which is the valuable production that moves the chains.

For running backs involved in the passing game, yards per route run provides an account of the number of snaps that a player went into a pattern and his drop rate takes account of the number of catchable balls he dropped, two key new metrics for efficiency. Lastly, pass blocking efficiency provides a measurement of the pressure allowed on a per snap basis with weighting towards sacks allowed, which can help a team find a running back who can protect their quarterback when necessary. These are all new metrics that teams will be using to find even more value at the position.

Outside of cases like Lamar Miller, players who are still young and without an injury history or heavy workload, it seems the only way to acquire a complete running back is through the draft. In fact, with the crashing of its free agency market, the only way for a running back to really get top tier money is through being drafted and extended by his organization. Rather than seeking a high contract in free agency, an extension after a running back's third season can allow the organization to pay a running back top tier money and security during his prime, while waiting for free agency means lower earnings through the rookie contract and hitting a depressed free agent market while taking on the risk of injury that comes with another season of football. This draft and extend process at running back is mutually beneficial with the player getting closer to fair value through his prime, while the team can avoid overpaying him in years past his prime like can happen at the end of a second contract.

With the decreased costs of first round contracts, drafting a complete back in the top ten picks has become a strong strategy for teams that have already established a strong offensive line as run production is heavily dependent on controlling the line of scrimmage. Ezekiel Elliott was drafted with the fourth pick in 2016 and his contract is projected to cap at 4.11% of the cap in 2019. A game breaking running back like Elliott or Leonard Fournette can be worth a top ten pick, but players chosen in the top ten tend to be of the "can't miss prospect" variety, which means an elite player in an expensive position that has less talent in later rounds of the draft could be worth a lot in terms of value if he performs at an elite level. Even if you don't want to re-sign that expensive receiver or cornerback after his rookie contract, the likelihood of that running back providing value far past his rookie deal doesn't seem to be too high either. That said, considering a team's immediate needs should be the main consideration and for the Cowboys and Jaguars, running back was a place that needed an upgrade.

The trend towards a running back by committee during the 2000s has been largely inspired by coaches like Mike Shanahan with systems that have promoted an ability to find productive running backs all the way to the undrafted ranks. Andy Reid's West Coast offense is similar as both variations of the offense have consistently found backs in the middle to late rounds who emerge as lead running backs who can provide four or more yards per carry and the ability to catch the ball out of the backfield. Productivity at the position is very much a function of the system's strong rushing concepts that have been able to create a huge supply of potential system running backs to choose from, which allows for profitable value discovery. Great systems create efficiency through their design; they improve efficiency by finding the right people to input into that design.

Drafting a running back in the first round is a viable solution in the right circumstances, but the ability to find talent elsewhere and the league wide need for two or three or four potentially productive running backs on a roster drives teams toward finding those running backs in the middle and late rounds of the draft. The need for multiple productive backs is a function of their high injury risk.

One of the best backfield building strategies is to draft a running back in the middle rounds one year, then do the same thing the next year as teams deconstruct the running back position into two separate roles in the lead power rushing back role and the pass catcher role. The Patriots have done this better than anyone under Belichick; Sean Payton and the Saints have also done this well, while West Coast coaches in Cincinnati and coming from that coaching tree have done it very well in the 2010s. Using two players with rushing or pass catching skills decreases the cost of the position as players who can do one, but not the other, can be found in the third tier as a free agent or in the mid- to late-rounds of the draft. These players are far easier to find than complete running backs and, together, they can be just as productive, all while mitigating risk of injury and coming at a lower cost.

The average NFL running back is about 5'11", 215-pounds and the running backs in Shanahan and Reid's system have averaged that height and within four pounds of that weight through 2017. Belichick has gone bigger and stronger for the role of the rusher, then smaller and quicker for the pass catcher with his lead running backs during his time in New England averaging out to 6', 225-pounds, while the pass catching backs average out to 5'9", 200-pounds and every pass catching back they've had is within an inch and five pounds of that number. Their handling of the running back position parallels the MMA concept of different sized athletes having different skills and capabilities. Heavyweight fights tend to have more short fights with knockouts in the first round, while 125-pound flyweights have more five round fights that come down to a judge's decision. Using this strategy, teams can find productive backs for what they're asking them to do in the late rounds and at a discount in free agency.

In New England, the lead rushing back role has averaged about 1200 yards rushing from 2000 through 2016, while the Kevin Faulk pass catcher role are players who average around 400 rushing yards and 400 receiving yards per season with the Dion Lewis and James White combination being perhaps the best solution in the role that they've ever had. The production from the primarily pass catching back has traditionally totaled around 50 total offensive yards per game to go with 70 to 80 rushing yards from the lead rushing back.

In 2016, Dion Lewis only played seven games and averaged 53.8 offensive yards per game. James White and LeGarrette Blount played 16 games with White averaging 44.4 offensive yards per game and Blount creating 75.0 yards per game with 72.6 of those coming on the ground. The whole backfield was a versatile and efficient group and the duo of White and Lewis paid off in the Super Bowl producing 168 yards and three touchdowns in the Super Bowl with Blount being held to 31 yards on 11 carries. The Super Bowl champion regular season average for yards per carry is 4.1 and the typical Patriots runner in both roles has averaged 4.3 yards per carry or more. At the power rushing role, LeGarrette Blount led the NFL with 18 touchdowns in 2016, and Corey Dillon had 37 rushing touchdowns from 2004 to 2006. The goal line battering ram is a key role in an offense looking to have a high redzone touchdown percentage.

A running back who can provide 130 offensive yards per game and score touchdowns is a top tier superstar like an Ezekiel Elliott of the Cowboys. Instead the Patriots have typically gotten that production at an efficient yard per carry rate for bottom tier money and with the versatility to create ways to be productive if one of the backs goes down. A strong pass catching running back, like Shane Vereen during the playoffs in early 2015 for the Patriots, with short, quick slot receivers can provide an offense with a way to move the football if the rushing offense is stopped like they were against the Ravens and Seahawks that year: an added benefit of having an elite pass catcher at running back—and it comes at a low price.

New England had just 57 rushing yards on 21 carries (2.7 yards per carry) against the Seahawks in Super Bowl 49, but Brady had a completion percentage of 74.0% going 37 for 50 for 328 yards, which allowed them to move the chains with consistency against the NFL's best defense. Vereen set a Super Bowl record for a running back with 11 catches, which went for 64 yards. Combined with Julian Edelman and Danny Amendola, that trio had 25 catches on 31 targets, an 80.6% catch rate, for 221 yards (7.1 yards per target) and two touchdowns. When the running game isn't working against a great defense, the short passing game can move the chains, even against a #1 ranked pass defense like the 2014 Seahawks, as those quick passes can hit before the defense has a chance to react and cover in zone coverage or as a receiver breaks away from his man defender on a quick route. They result in short chunk yard completions by the time these explosive athletes get tackled. Vereen's Super Bowl record in Super Bowl 49, then White broke the record for all players with 14 catches that went for 110 yards and a touchdown.

Like at quarterback, the expensive wide receiver market means when first tier money is spent, it must be spent on high production, high efficiency players. If they're your main passing option and they're going to get most of your quarterback's targets as the drivers of your passing offense, then you want them to be capable of driving your efficiency. This first tier of the wide receiver market is between six and nine percent of the cap and it should only be reserved for the elite wide receivers who have the potential to consistently provide 85 to 90 plus catches and over 1200 receiving yards with the ability to score touchdowns by providing a target that gets open in the red zone—which typically means they're big, unless you've found an Antonio Brown, whose first top tier season was actually 2016 before signing a market setting four-year extension after the season. Those totals average out to just over 81 yards on six catches per game, so you're setting that as a kind of baseline for these players in per game production. First tier wide receivers are the kinds of receivers that you intend to run an offense through. They have to be elite, efficient, and able to produce on a good chunk of plays per game. These are players who should have a high yards per target rate of 8.5 plus and, unless he's an elite deep threat and a red zone option like a Mike Evans, these are players you want to have catch rates of at least 63%. If the top tier receiver is a Mike Evans type of player, then the offense must have some kind of short to intermediate option to help produce some of the more consistent efficiency than what deep balls can create, although big plays are important. If a team does spend top tier money, then you need some low-cost veterans and rookie contract players to produce around the rest of the offense.

The Super Bowl average for a team's most productive pass catchers for yardage production is a catch rate of 61.0%, while their third, fourth and fifth receivers have catch rates of 63.6%, 64.4%, an 70.4% respectively, which may be a symptom of the short, ball control passing strategy that we're about to get into. While the receivers who excel on catch rates may not average 1131 receiving yards per season (70.7 per game) like top Super Bowl pass catchers, which are wide receivers in all but two instances, have. These typically slot receivers, tight ends, and running backs that have higher catch rates typically produce less overall production, but are what help draw up the quarterback's efficiency metrics. While these top pass catchers provide over almost 1150 yards on 79.4 catches, which is nearly first tier status, only five of 23 champions had wide receivers over six percent including an injured Sidney Rice on Seattle with three of these first tier players coming since the 2011 CBA.

There becomes an issue with so many teams investing heavily in the quarterback already. Another large investment in one wide receiver can lead to a cap investment over 20%, and creeping towards 25%, in two players focused in the passing game, which can create serious holes elsewhere. As the Belichick quote in chapter four said while acknowledging the 32 different ways to do things with 32 teams, "I think that's how you get good, you get good at everything," so the Patriots are trying to get the best player they can at every position to be competitive across the roster. If you're investing heavily in one thing, then the likelihood of you creating an advantage there, but a disadvantage, elsewhere increases.

The two Super Bowl champions with a quarterback and wide receiver as their two highest cap hits were the 1994 49ers with Steve Young and Jerry Rice at 21.64% and then Peyton Manning and Demaryius Thomas at 21.43%. No other two Super Bowl double cap hits breach 20%. Both organizations had great defenses because the 49ers worked around the salary cap system by re-signing 17 veterans in December 1993 to avoid 1994 cap charges and the Broncos' John Elway did a masterful job of managing the cap as they transitioned from a quarterback-centric offensive team that was runner-up after 2013 to a champion with an historic defense in 2015. Manning and Marvin Harrison with the 2006 Colts are the only other team to have both a top tier quarterback and wide receiver, so this isn't a strategy that has worked consistently. With a heavy investment in two players in the passing game, over 20% becomes invested in two players who won't contribute much to the running game, while not contributing to the defense or special teams' performance. When it does work, it seems to only work with Hall of Fame level players.

In 2016, eight teams had first tier quarterbacks and wide receivers: the Cowboys (with the injured Tony Romo), Redskins, Falcons, Bears, Cardinals, Colts, Steelers, Chiefs and Lions with Calvin Johnson's 8.32% dead money cap hit. If you do have an elite quarterback and wide receiver duo, it can help a team compete for a playoff spot yearly, but it hasn't often won championships in the past according to Super Bowl data. The value of these first tier level wide receivers can't be denied though. Scott Barrett of Pro Football Focus found that in 2016 for the Giants, Eli Manning had a passer rating of 105.3 when targeting his tier one talent on his rookie contract, Odell Beckham, Jr., which would have been the third highest quarterback passer rating in the NFL, but had a passer rating of 78.9 when targeting all other Giants receivers. Manning finished the season with an 86.0 rating, which was 22nd in the NFL.

With the average production of top pass catchers on Super Bowl champs being at 1131 yards, teams who do draft these kinds of players can re-sign them even if they have a top tier investment at quarterback. It may come with cap consequences, but every player is an individual case. These decisions are dependent on who is already on the roster, who is available in the upcoming draft or free agency, and the kind of value you could receive in a trade if you did decide to trade a player prior to the end of his contract to gain some draft picks before he left if you didn't plan on re-signing him due to costs.

If a team does go over six percent of the cap with multiple players or go first tier in two of these more expensive positional markets, then they should be stockpiling talent at other expensive positions through the draft and prepared to transition to a different spending formula as those draft picks mature and reach free agency. When a team has one or more sizeable cap hits, they have to consider how they will deal with this high cap hit. They have to consider which markets they'll have to go young and low-cost at. They have to understand which positions they'll have to hit on in the draft and with that, they'll have to have a depth of knowledge of the players who fit their system at these positions across rookie and veteran markets.

The current market and recent success of teams with top tier receiver investments both proves it as a strategy of success in today's NFL, while also illustrating the flaws with the strategy as well as flaws with the current pay structure as explained in chapter five regarding quarterback costs where the value saved on a sizeable percentage of contracts, most notably rookie contracts, is allowing for increasing investments in the most expensive markets.

On the most successful teams we see a strategy of extending or re-signing receivers because there are many variables can affect the performance of a free agent receiver signed to a new city like a new system and a new quarterback. You don't want to put out a large expense for a wide receiver that runs the risk of growing pains and timing issues with a new quarterback. Extending or re-signing these receivers provides a level of stability and, like we know from the previous chapters, stability is a key principle across an organization.

Looking at the Super Bowl examples of first tier spending at quarterback and wide receiver, the quarterback and receiver have been together for a long time. Young and Rice were on the same roster for eight years, back to 1987, before the 1994 Super Bowl with four of those seasons with Young as the starter after taking over for Joe Montana in 1991. Manning and Harrison had nine years together before they earned the 2006 Super Bowl; Reggie Wayne consumed 5.00% of the cap as well in his sixth season with Manning, while inexpensive Dallas Clark cost 1.17% as a tight end in a fourth year with Manning that included two 100-yard performances with 137 against the Patriots in the AFC Championship. On Manning's Super Bowl with the Broncos, he and Demaryius Thomas were in their fourth year together. The expensive leaders of the 2016 NFC Champion Falcons, Matt Ryan and Julio Jones, were in their sixth year together that consumed 25.54% of the cap, which would have smashed the record for a top paid duo set by Young and Rice in 1994 if they won.

Of course, if you draft a Julio Jones or Odell Beckham Jr. type of player, a team will be likely to sign them to a second contract regardless of the high market costs, which is alright; the strategy that can work. Keeping a first tier receiver within the organization is more successful than going to free agency as staying within the organization will help the player have the best opportunity to produce top tier value if the organization has stability from quarterback to head coach and general manager. In 2013, to commemorate the 20th anniversary of NFL's free agency, Yahoo's Jason Cole created a list of the 20 worst free agent signings of all-time and six of the players were wide receivers. Cole's list is a subjective list, but a theme seen countless times with Jeremy Maclin being the most recent example being cut by the Chiefs during the 2017 offseason as they saw little chance he'd perform up to the top tier contract they gave him.

Jones was a top tier level player almost immediately averaging 73.8 receiving yards per game in his rookie campaign of 2011 and has averaged 109.1 receiving yards per game from 2013 through 2016. Heading into 2017 with 96.3 receiving yards per game over his career, Jones is the NFL's all-time leader with Beckham nipping at his heels at 95.9. Antonio Brown has averaged 82.9 yards per game over his career, but 100.2 from 2013 to 2016. The original freak of all freak receivers, Calvin Johnson retired as the number three player all-time at 86.1 yards per game, which shows that the three current receivers might be in a league of their own, non-quarterbacks who might (almost) be worth a double digit cap hit. With head coach Dan Quinn in his second season in 2016 after coming from Seattle where he led the aggressive and young defense they built through the draft to a Super Bowl in 2013, he was the perfect coach to take over in 2015 and remake the Falcons in a similar low-cost defensive cap strategy that allowed for the huge expense on two elite players in the offensive passing game. According to Pro

Football Reference's tracking, of the nine players who started more than nine games on defense for the Falcons in 2016, every player was in his fourth season or less. Linebackers De'Vondre Campbell and Deion Jones were in their rookie seasons with cornerback Brian Poole and safety Keanu Neal. Defensive tackle Grady Jarrett and edge rusher Vic Beasley were in their second seasons and safety Ricardo Allen was in his third season, while cornerbacks Robert Alford and Desmond Trufant were both in their fourth seasons and cost 1.08% and 1.67% of the cap respectively. Trufant tore his pectoral in November and missed the rest of the season, which surely affected the defensive performance in that Super Bowl loss. As first round picks, Beasley was the most expensive of the group at 2.12%, while Neal cost 1.26%. The savings across the defense by the inexpensive rookie contracts of these starters allowed for the Falcons to field a competitive team with such a large outlay and they were able to build their roster with the knowledge of their costs in mind, so they were able to prepare for the big salaries. Another benefit of these top receivers is that they force the defense to focus their attention on them, which can mean double coverage that then creates one-on-one opportunities for other pass catchers. It's critical to have athletes behind these top receivers who can win these match-ups, which can become hard to produce if the receiver's cost is too high, especially considering that quarterback costs are already high for most teams with competent signal callers.

They did have some money spread to others over one percent of the cap. Defensive end Tyson Jackson, whom they signed as a free agent in 2014, cost 4.09%, former Texans linebacker Brooks Reed cost 2.22%, and 2015 free agent signing Adrian Clayborn cost 1.93% with all three of them starting seven games. Long-time Falcons defensive tackle, a 2005 second round pick for the team, Jonathan Babineaux cost 1.72%, 2013 undrafted free agent linebacker, and primarily special teams player, Paul Worrilow re-signed with the team on a one-year deal that paid him 1.64% of the cap, and free agent defensive end Derrick Shelby cost 1.45%. By the end of the season Clayborn and Shelby were both injured, but out of the four healthy players, they played just 118 of the 396 possible defensive snaps in the Super Bowl, which is only 29.8%.

Devonta Freeman and Tevin Coleman led a rushing attack that was fifth in the NFL with 1928 yards, 120.5 per game. They combined for 1599 of those yards on 345 carries at 4.6 per carry with 18 touchdowns on the ground. Their numbers through the air were astounding with 85 catches on 105 targets for 883 yards and five receiving touchdowns, which comes to 10.4 per reception and 8.4 per target with an 81.0% catch rate. They're elite players in Kyle Shanahan's system, which he grew up under with his father as one of the key innovators who produced the low-cost, running back by committee markets we now see today. Mike Shanahan's ability to find value seemingly anywhere at running back in Denver has influenced the strategies employed today that have depressed the market. Freeman and

Coleman produced 2,482 total offensive yards for about one percent of the salary cap, which, along with the defensive savings, allowed for the Falcons to almost win a Super Bowl with over 25% invested in two great players. With Freeman playing all 16 games and Coleman playing 13, they combined for 168.7 offensive yards per game, which puts them in that Le'Veon Bell production value category that could be worth near 10% of the cap, a sign of their extreme value. NFL organizations abilities to find low-cost performers has surpassed where their abilities were a decade ago, so teams can rely on finding younger players through the draft and undrafted free agency who are reaching a high level of performance during rookie contract years, which creates the opportunity to "overspend" in expensive veteran markets. The value lost for rookies is then used to overvalue veterans. Freeman signed an extension prior to the 2017 season that peaks at a projected 4.59% of the 2020 salary cap, an example of the low costs of the market.

The Falcons got immense value from low-cost players because the organization knew the offensive and defensive systems well enough to find the value to surround Ryan and Jones' big cap hits. They had Shanahan and Quinn running systems they knew intimately, but we saw their flaws exposed on the big stage as they were up 28-3 with just 8:31 left in the third quarter before losing 34-28 in overtime. Their defense was 27th in the NFL in points allowed at 25.4 points per game, which would have set a new cap era Super Bowl record beating the 2011 Giants who were 25th in the league at 25.0 per game. Their thin defense was worn out as the Patriots entered the fourth quarter of a game where they had 99 offensive snaps. This is a specific situation, but a broader lesson: heavy investments in singular pursuits create holes elsewhere as it increases the difficulty of creating depth on the rest of the roster, while decreasing the margin for error on any investment.

While the 2013 Seahawks team they tried to mimic was built on draft picks, they had a different strategy and roster construction that allowed for expenses in lower cost markets. While Zach Miller (8.94%) and Sidney Rice (7.89%) were poor values, especially with Rice being hurt, they were made affordable with Russell Wilson consuming 0.55% of the cap with Matt Flynn's 3.25% dead money charge in the expensive quarterback market and the draft success of the organization. They were able to "overspend" a little in free agency as they could afford to until they made the transition into the big second contracts of their core of young, rookie contract players who played a key role in earning that championship. The low quarterback percentage was especially important in allowing the team to build a rushing base to their West Coast offense and defensive model they wanted. They had four defensive linemen over 3% of the cap in Chris Clemons (6.64%), Red Bryant (6.18%), Brandon Mebane (4.23%), Michael Bennett (3.90%), and Cliff Avril (3.05%) to have the most expensive defensive line for a Super Bowl champion at 28.18% paired with their inexpensive quarterback. While Percy

Harvin made some big plays in the Super Bowl, he was out for the entire year at 3.98% of the cap and the Seahawks were able to earn the victory with low-cost receivers on rookie contracts in Golden Tate, Doug Baldwin, and Jermaine Kearse. They spent some of the value they saved on quarterback to create a front seven that created pressure in Peyton Manning's face all game. Marshawn Lynch made 6.91% of the cap, while their starting offensive line was the most expensive of the cap era champions at 18.59% with left tackle Russell Okung's record cap hit of 7.76%. The Falcons almost earned their first Super Bowl with a variation of this strategy, but just like the Seahawks, they should be able to continue to compete up to and through the spending transition as Ryan and Jones will see their cap hits declining in the coming years in preparation for the upcoming extensions of the players on their defense and explosive running back duo.

Wide receiver is a position with a ton of statistics to analyze and, when combined with knowledge of measurables and system needs, with the offensive objectives of moving the chains, scoring in the redzone, and producing a few big plays per game, these stats provide the opportunity to find value at the position for decision makers who can use that info to find players at a low-cost and good value. A great strategy to find value is to create an offensive production standard that provides a framework for what you need to accomplish, which then helps determine what kind of players you need to acquire for your system. Similarly, deconstructing what a top tier wide receiver can do into first principles and the production that he provides can create value. The Patriots do that, which will be explained later.

As with the quarterback and running back positions, top tier players can have no holes in their game--they have to be a football equivalent of the five-tool player in baseball, accomplishing all key objectives for their position. These are players with a high likelihood of fulfilling all of the production requirements of the position if healthy, players who can produce in every relevant way. So while lower tier players might not be considered stars or the most productive player at their position, a team can create a pass catching group that can accomplish the key objectives of consistently moving the chains, helping score touchdowns in the redzone and producing chunk plays as an offense.

Along with the high cap costs of a top tier receiver, a prototypical big bodied top tier receiver typically comes through a first round pick, which is a high price for a position where so many other viable options are available. As with the running back position, the draft and extend process is the best way to acquire and manage the career for a top tier wide receiver, especially considering that top tier receivers tend to make themselves identifiable within their rookie contract. The high risk of first tier free agent wide receivers flopping and the need for familiarity between quarterbacks and top wide receivers also drive the need to extend rather than go to free agency. Considering the regression analysis from the women at McCombs that found that 8.67% of the cap is a tipping point for quarterbacks where their cap hit can begin to affect their team's chances of winning, a team can't afford to pay these top tier figures to a player from another organization who has all the potentially negative variables that come along with changing teams and quarterbacks. Nor can teams really afford to pay two players in the pass game that price. You can consider a top tier free agent wide receiver where a young, rookie contract quarterback is developing at a low-cost like the Seahawks did even though Rice and Harvin were failed investments.

The 2012 Ravens with Joe Flacco in his third year with first tier receiver Anquan Boldin and in the last year of Flacco's rookie contract, was a good example of a lower cost, young quarterback being elevated by a top wide receiver. Boldin was a big part of Flacco's huge post-season with 22 catches for 380 yards on 36 targets for a 61.1% catch rate, 17.3 yards per catch, 10.5 yards per target, and four touchdowns in four games.

With the prevalence of heavy passing offenses in college and all the way down to high school with their 7-on-7 leagues and tournaments in the summers, wide receiver has become a position with a large supply of competent players. It presents what may be the best position market for finding value as the second and third tiers are ripe with players who could provide a team with value and production in an increased role than their role in their previous city, plus fourth tier rookies ready to compete. If you know exactly what you're looking for in a specific role in your offense and you do your scouting homework from college all the way through the pros, then the yearly experiment of your offense helps determine what improvements need to be made individually and across the offense, which makes finding productive pieces for these roles much simpler.

The player who is the best example and might be most responsible for a growing emphasis in short, quick receivers and the slot receiver position came to New England as a veteran in 2007 as Belichick traded a second and a seventh round pick in the draft to a contract that, according to Spotrac, paid him an average of 2.93% of the cap over the course of his five-year deal and a max of 3.73% in 2011, the last year of the contract. Welker cost just 1.56% of the cap during the 2007 season where he had 112 catches for 1175 yards and eight touchdowns with a 77.2% catch rate and 8.1 yards per target. People use the term possession receiver like a pejorative without realizing that possession receiver means you get to continue the possession, which means you extend your opportunity to score, which means having a possession receiver is very important.

The Patriots also signed Randy Moss that offseason to a contract that paid him just 2.75% of the cap in 2007 as he was at a discount as the Raiders had to eat just over $4 million in dead money—so he produced an NFL record 23 touchdowns with 98 catches for 1493 yards at a discount. The 2007 team had two of the most efficient and productive wide receivers in the NFL, providing consistent chain moving and touchdowns in the redzone, on an offense that was historic, a large part of the reason they went on that 18-0 run before losing to the Giants in the Super Bowl.

This 2007 season was also when the Patriots illustrated offensive principles that they still abide by now. As then Dolphins safety Cameron Worrell explains in Kevin Clark's article titled, "The Near-Perfect Football Team," this Patriots team was about three to four wide receiver sets, guys in the slot, being quick at the line, the potential for no huddle and shotgun. While at the time Worrell was thinking, "whoa this is totally different," he now notes that "all this one-on-one match-up stuff—that's all the NFL is now." Creating multiple mismatches with your offensive skill players and putting them in one-on-one match-ups that one of the options can win is a key principle in today's NFL. As Clark quotes Panthers head coach Ron Rivera, "they forced us to where we are today as a league," yet few abide by New England's spending patterns on offense.[5]

Another 2007 free agent acquisition, Donte Stallworth, cost 2.54% of the cap while providing 46 catches for 697 yards and three touchdowns. Jabar Gaffney was signed in 2006 and gave them 36 receptions for 449 yards and five touchdowns at 0.57% of the cap. Stallworth had a very efficient 9.3 yards per target with a 61.3% catch rate, while Gaffney was right behind him at 9.0 and a 72.0% catch rate. Per Clark, "the quarterbacks of the four conference championship teams last season (2016) were the four best at throwing to five wide receivers [pass catchers]—another staple the Patriots are credited with popularizing" with this roster. Clark writes that "the guiding principle for the Patriots offense was this: make defense declare exactly what they were doing as soon as they got to the line. They would do this by spreading out defenses as thin as they'd ever been spread before and then moving players around. There was no hiding." Their mix of scheme and elite talent created this across the offense.

Signing cheap receivers in free agency is a recurring theme with Belichick, players whose production he believes he can increase past their low cost, especially with this match-up focus. Brandon Lafell and Danny Amendola were critical playoff performers during the run at the end of the 2014 season. In 2016, they added Chris Hogan, who was never used correctly in Buffalo, and he then led all NFL receivers in 2016 with 11.7 yards per target, which trailed only Rob Gronkowski's NFL leading 14.2 yards per target in the eight games before his seasons ended with a back injury. According to Eliot Crist's February 2017 Pro Football Focus article on the league's best receivers on each type of route in 2016, Hogan was the best go (or fly) route runner in the NFL. "He caught seven of 13 targets, giving him a 53.84 percent catch rate, tied for the highest rate in the league. He led the league in yards (299) and touchdowns (4), as well as tying for the highest WR rating at

138.6. On four of his incompletions, three were overthrown and one was dropped, showing that Hogan was able consistently to beat the defense deep."

Belichick must've seen something on his film with Buffalo that helped him envision Hogan's potential with Brady. Or it might have also been that Hogan's six catches for 95 yards on seven targets against New England in Week 11 of 2015 may have influenced Belichick as, with a defense built to defend various match-ups, he is interested in players who can beat his defense. They signed Welker in 2007 after having to double-team him in 2006 when he was playing for Miami, according to Kevin Clark. As Rodney Harrison said in Clark's article, "if there is a guy who is causing us problems, Bill is going to try to get him to make sure he causes problems for other people."

New England increased their ability to stretch the field in 2017 with the addition of speed burner Brandin Cooks from New Orleans to pair with Hogan and Gronkowski. This opens up the short passing game for guys like Amendola, James White, and Dion Lewis in particular, an especially important task with Edelman out for the year. As Clark writes, with Moss, teams that left players back in coverage to prevent the deep ball would then leave huge chunks of open space available for Welker to keep moving the sticks by running into the uncovered underneath areas making everything a problem. This is something a first tier wide receiver can add, but using Cooks on his rookie contract and Hogan for this deep threat kind of role is a similarly low-cost, effective strategy to get the principles of what Moss did for the offense. They also run terrific crossing routes in the intermediate 15 to 20 yard area that allows them to use their speed to outrace their cover guys and generate big plays. Deep threats can also force those long defensive pass interferences that we seem to see frequently on fade and post routes.

Cooks has played in all 11 Patriots games to this point with 869 receiving yards on phenomenal rate stats of someone in his role. He has a 63.0% catch rate and 10.0 yards per target with 17.0 yards per catch and 79.0 yards per game. Hogan has played eight of those games as he missed three of those games with a shoulder injury and he has a 61.1% catch rate and 8.1 yards per target with 13.3 per catch and 54.8 per game. They've played a key role in helping Brady lead the NFL in passing yards to this point.

With the quantity of statistics, measurables, and clearly defined roles in Belichick's system, he's able to find valuable pass catchers through free agency to produce maximum versatility and mitigate risk of injury, which allows him to focus draft picks and cap dollars elsewhere. Considering the high cost of most NFL quarterbacks, this is a valuable strategy for avoiding an over investment in one discipline. The increased emphasis of the "Mel Blount Rule," starting in 2014, which disallows defenders from contacting receivers beyond five yards from the line of scrimmage when the quarterback is in the pocket, makes having versatility even more important to take advantage of any weak pass defenders on the defense with a third or fourth option of yours who can beat your opponents defender.

The second tier of the wide receiver market is between three and six percent of the cap. Elite, quick technicians are found here because of their typically lower round draft selection, and because they lack the size of the prototypical number one—plus the second-level of number one receivers can populate this tier and both are the best of what this market offers. At the top of this tier are players who can provide thousand yard seasons consistently, while the slot receiver types out of this group can provide this level of production at a high rate of efficiency, like a Doug Baldwin whose 2020 cap hit of $12.4 million comes the closest to breaking the six percent threshold at 5.99% of a projected $207 million salary cap for that year. Toward the bottom of this market are the kinds of receivers who can provide the role of the number one outside receiver in an offense that has versatility and numerous other options, so he's only relied on for 700+ yards or so, while the rest of the production that goes to the elite WR1 gets spread out around the various mismatches the offense has.

Hogan consumed 3.54% of the Patriots cap in 2016 with 38 catches, 680 yards and four touchdowns with 17 for 332 and two in the three playoff games. They frontloaded his contract with $5.5 million in 2016 so the Bills couldn't re-sign him as a restricted free agent for cap reasons, then his cap hit dropped below two percent of the cap for the next two seasons. From 2014 through the projections for 2019, Julian Edelman's cost is projected to average 2.94% of the cap.

Between one and a half and three percent is what we consider third tier receivers and the best in this market tend to gain 400 to 500 plus receiving yards. This market provides opportunities to find a lot of value in free agents who are being undervalued due to their previous usage whether that be through a coach misusing them, being in a below average passing offense, or not getting many opportunities to perform for other reasons. These may also be players coming off an injury. The third tier is a very good spot to find former first and second tier receivers being released off overpriced contracts. Eric Decker, Jeremy Maclin and Torrey Smith find themselves in this tier in 2017 with the Titans, Ravens and Eagles after being released by the Jets, Chiefs and 49ers. Mike Wallace had a similar path in 2016 signing to a two-year deal with the Ravens that cost 2.3% the first year, which saw a line of 72 catches for 1017 yards and four touchdowns, then bumped to 4.8% in 2017.

The Patriots have found most of their free agent wide receivers in this tier over the years. In 2013, they signed Amendola to a contract they've annually restructured to keep him in the third tier and the next year they signed Lafell to a third tier deal. With Edelman in this three percent range through his contract and just 2.07% in 2014, their top three receivers that year were all third tier players, but provided a lot of production, especially during their playoff run with each of the three performing a critical role on the way to the Super Bowl win. Similar story in 2016 with Hogan inserted for Lafell, plus fourth-round rookie Malcolm Mitchell. In 2014, Gronkowski led the team with 1124 receiving yards on a low-cost contract that may have played a part in depressing the tight end market from 2012 on. Right behind him, Edelman and Lafell went for 972 and 953 yards respectively. For the 2016 Falcons, Mohamed Sanu represented a good value to pair with Jones at 1.55% of the cap producing 653 yards and four touchdowns on 59 catches with a 72.8% catch rate before jumping to the second tier at 4.43% in 2017, year two of his contract.

Tier four wide receivers reside between the league minimums and one and a half percent of the cap. They're usually low-level third or fourth receivers who are likely to provide a couple hundred yards and play special teams or rookie contract players ready to compete like Malcolm Mitchell. Lafell cost just 1.50% of the cap in 2014, so he was at the intersection of the bottom two markets and provided them with a great regular season and two important touchdowns against Baltimore and Seattle. An experienced coach who knows his system like Belichick can project how a player outside the system could produce within the system and thus find a valuable piece that can outperform expectations, whether a low-cost veteran or a mid- to late-round pick.

Pro Football Focus has five metrics of wide receiver performance that can be used to find value. Drop rate plus yards per pass route run have already been mentioned for running back and also apply here. There were 13 receivers in 2016 over two yards per route run; Julio Jones caps the group at 3.12, A.J. Green is second at 2.86, and then there are 11 players between 2.0 and a 2.35. There are the top prototypical number one receivers in this group like Jones and Green, then there are the slot, possession receiver types as well like Jarvis Landry and Cole Beasley, so this stat does a good job of standardizing every kind of receiver's production, from the possession player to the deep threat. Receiving targets requires the talent of getting open, so it's a better metric for judging receivers than yards per target as an inaccurate quarterback who misses targets can penalize the receiver. Although for the purposes of this book, yards per target is a good metric for understanding the sort of production teams are looking for in each role from a yard per play standpoint.

Wide receiver rating shows the "quarterback rating when a receiver is thrown at," which is a great metric for the efficiency a player brings to the offense.[6] In 2016 there were six short, quick receivers in top 12 in Cole Beasley, Doug Baldwin,

Brandin Cooks, Antonio Brown, Jamison Crowder, and Jarvis Landry, which supports the premise that this kind of pass catcher is very efficient. The site also keeps track of wide receiver slot performance by covering the production of players within the slot. Lastly, wide receiver deep passing tracks how players perform on all targets that are 20 yards downfield or more. Tight ends are judged by the same metrics minus wide receiver rating and instead pass blocking efficiency.

For many teams, rather than heading to free agency for a Lafell type value, the right receiver selection in the middle to late rounds of the draft can provide this kind of performance if the teams finds the right fit for their system. The best example of an organization with a steady stream of valuable receivers on rookie contracts is the Steelers with a list of draft picks at receiver since the late 1990s that includes Plaxico Burress, Hines Ward, Antwaan Randle El, Santonio Holmes, Mike Wallace, Emmanuel Sanders, Antonio Brown, Markus Wheaton, Martavis Bryant, and Juju Smith-Schuster. The Seahawks have drafted multiple good, quick slot receiver types from Golden Tate in the second round of 2010, Doug Baldwin as an undrafted free agent in 2011, and Tyler Lockett in the third round of 2015. Their 2014 second round pick Paul Richardson seems to have developed into the deep threat they were hoping for when they drafted him during the 2017 season.

The trio of Gronkowski, Edelman, and Lafell combined to cost just 7.63% of the cap, which is a benefit of having a passing offense centered around an elite tight end as that market is much less expensive than the wide receiver market and can provide the redzone threat of a WR1, the high percentage pass catching and chain moving abilities of a slot receiver, and—in the case of the elite tight ends—some of the big play potential without the cost. While a top tight end won't produce the kind of 1800-yard season that a Julio Jones, Odell Beckham or Antonio Brown can, and they're unlikely to eclipse the 1200-yard threshold that makes first tier wide receivers, he can be a key efficient centerpiece surrounded by lower tier receivers who together produce a weekly match-up problem with their versatility. Combining a tight end with a couple short, quick options in the passing game to move the sticks and a deep threat to provide some of those chunk plays helps keep costs lower with an efficiency that is important. With the size and speed of tight ends, plus the quickness of the short, quick receivers and running backs, these two can also provide their share of twenty yard plays on deep receptions and yards after catch when they get one-on-one opportunities with the ball in their hands in space.

After a 2015 season dealing with injuries to their pass catchers, the Patriots let Lafell go in search of someone more efficient and explosive for the role, then added a few players who went on to be key pieces for their 2016 run, especially when Gronkowski went down after eight games. Since 2014, and with an increased emphasis after 2015, the Patriots have clearly pushed for versatility. Vereen left for the Giants for a second tier running back contract and Belichick replaced him with the duo of James White and Dion Lewis who burst on the scene with 798 receiving yards in that pass catcher role, then 645 in 2016. The Patriots duo has been a bigger threat running the football than Vereen as well. Lewis has dealt with injuries the past two seasons, which is why they have roster and cap space for two of these kinds of players rather than just one. After injuries and ineffectiveness, with his catch rate dropping to 50.0% in 2015 from 62.2% in 2014, Lafell was released and replaced with Hogan, plus Mitchell. Tim Wright was the 2014 attempt at replacing Aaron Hernandez as the TE2, then Scott Chandler was the 2015 attempt and both underwhelmed. In March 2016, they replaced Chandler by trading a 2016 fourth-round pick to the Bears for Martellus Bennett and a 2016 sixth-round pick. At 3.33% of the cap, he was supposed to be the Hernandez partner to Gronk, but he ended up replacing him completely after the injury and he did it well with 55 catches for 701 yards and seven touchdowns. His 75.3% catch rate and 9.6 yards per target were phenomenal. With the production of all these receivers in 2016, the Patriots were third behind the Falcons and Redskins with 8.1 yards per pass attempt with their most productive pass catcher missing half the season. Bennett left in free agency and the Patriots traded a fourth-round pick to the Colts for Dwayne Allen and a sixth-rounder.

In Super Bowl 51 against the Falcons, the Patriots had six receivers with over 57 receiving yards in the game to help Brady complete 43 of 62 passes (69.4%) for 466 yards (7.5 yards per target) on the day. If a player can average over 62.5 yards per game over a 16 game season, then he's a 1000-yard receiver. That should illustrate how impressive the Patriots performance was as a unit. As mentioned, James White had 14 catches for 110 yards and a touchdown, Edelman had five for 87, Amendola had 8 for 78 and a touchdown, Mitchell had 6 for 70, Bennett went for 62 on five and Hogan had four catches for 57 yards. Hogan was the most expensive of the group and that group of six cost 12.44% of the cap with Bennett, Edelman and Amendola all over one percent themselves. Add in the injured Gronkowski's cap hit of 4.25% and the group of seven costs 16.69%. While the Falcons had over ten percent invested in Jones, the Patriots spent for versatility. Rather than one great receiver, they opted for a handful of really good pass catchers with three back-ups who could fill the roles Edelman, Hogan, and Gronkowski start at: a strategy that has served them well in 2017 with Edelman and Malcolm Mitchell on injured reserve.

In 2016, Jimmy Graham represented the top of the tight end market at 5.80% for the Seahawks, which is much lower than the record for a Super Bowl champion in Zach Miller at 8.94% for those same Seahawks in 2013 as Carroll has seemed to settle on many of the same value finding offensive principles that Belichick has in terms of a focus on tight ends and quick receivers powering the offense with

Baldwin and Tyler Lockett. Dwayne Allen in the first year of his contract with the Colts at 5.73% was second, followed by James Cameron at 5.15%, then Julius Thomas and Kyle Rudolph at 4.70%. Gronk doesn't show up until number six at 4.25% of the cap and he presents what is arguably the biggest match-up problem in the NFL at less than half the cost of the top of the wide receiver market. Even in his most expensive season, his 30-year old season in 2019, Gronk will only consume 6.22% of the cap.

The tight end market should top out just above Graham, but far below Miller at six and a half, to maybe even seven, percent of the cap with the bottom being three percent, just slightly higher than the second tier of the wide receiver market for the Gronk level player even though he's not currently at that price—but he did get $5.5 million in potential incentives for 2017. Like the other positions, the top tier represents the prototype for the position, the complete player at the position with elite receiving skills and run blocking ability in a 6'5", 260-pound frame and elite speed for a tight end, which is about 4.6 or better in the 40-yard dash. Top tight ends can be relied on to produce at or just below the 1000-yard season that second tier receivers provide, but as a mismatch and a redzone threat that can help turn threes into sixes.

In Gronkowski's renegotiated contract with incentives, the Patriots will have him at 7.49% of the cap if he hits 90% playing time or 80 catches or 1200 receiving yards or All Pro and earns the full $5.5 million. He'll consume 6.44% of the cap if he hit's 80% playing time or 70 catches or 1000 receiving yards or 12 touchdowns and earn $3.5 million in incentives. He'll earn $1.5 million in incentives and consume 5.24% of the cap if he hits 70% playing time, 60 receptions, 800 receiving yards or 10 touchdowns. If he has another injury-plagued year, he might not hit those levels and he'd make 4.34% of the cap in 2017.

Gronkowski's incentive structure illustrates the way these markets acknowledge likely production. If Gronkowski has over 1200 receiving yards in the season, he'll make first tier wide receiver money with first tier wide receiver production, levels rarely met by a tight end. If he has the levels of production that a top tight end is more likely to produce, his cap hit will hit right near the peak of the market at 6.44% and if he produces a little less, but still respectable first tier production, his cap hit will be 5.24%. If he has a below average year for him, he'll still make the first tier tight end money that he's worth for being Rob Gronkowski.

The best way to acquire players at this position is through the draft as every elite tight end in the NFL in 2016 was drafted after the first round except for Carolina's Greg Olsen who was drafted with the 31st pick of the first round in 2007 by the Bears and traded to the Panthers for a third round pick. The tenth pick in the 2014 draft, Eric Ebron of the Lions, seemed to be on the cusp of becoming a first tier player with 61 catches for 711 yards and a lone touchdown with a 71.8% catch rate and 8.3 yards per target in 2016, but has had a weak 2017 through the first half of the season. Tight ends may not typically be drafted in the first round because of the steep learning curve they've typically faced in the NFL as they need to become pro-level in-line blockers against much bigger defensive linemen and polished enough route runners to get open against NFL defensive backs—plus lower levels of tight end production in college has made the position too difficult to project for teams to feel comfortable spending a first round pick on a player. Considering the relatively low-cost of the market, signing a tight end in free agency is a great option if your team is without a productive one.

Targeting tight ends who have been underutilized, as second tight ends during their rookie contracts behind top tight ends can be a good strategy for finding production value at the position. These players learn the position under an elite player, typically fit the mold of that elite player from organizations that have experience drafting productive tight ends, so they know what they're looking for, and most offenses don't have enough targets going to their right end position to create two productive tight ends, so good players can be undervalued. Delanie Walker who was drafted by the 49ers in the sixth round of the draft where they chose Vernon Davis with their #6 overall pick is one example, while Martellus Bennett, who started his career as a second round pick in 2008 who backed up Jason Witten for four years before having 600+ yard seasons with the Giants, Bears, and Patriots, is another.

Walker averaged just 209 yards per season in seven years in San Francisco, but has since averaged 837 yards per season from 2013 through 2016 in Tennessee. Bennett averaged 212 yards per season with the Cowboys before averaging 688 yards per season for those four teams from 2012 to 2016. Walker's costs with the Titans peaked at 4.04% in 2016, while Bennett's costs peaked at 4.53% in 2014 for the Bears during this time. Jack Doyle became a productive player for the Colts after sitting behind Coby Fleener and Dwayne Allen, so the Colts signed him to an extension that peaks at 4.79% in 2017, but drops below three percent in 2018 and 2019.

With most of the best players at the position coming into the league on rookie contracts from the second round or later to start their careers, teams have made the position another good example of the benefits of the draft and extend strategy. During the 2016 offseason, the Chiefs, Redskins, and Eagles extended Travis Kelce, Jordan Reed, and Zach Ertz to contracts that increased their earnings in the short term and provided the team with an offensive centerpiece to build around at a good value. The highest cap hit in the bunch is Reed's $10.3 million number in 2018, which would be 5.74% of that year's projected $179.5 million cap. The low-cost of the market makes it a viable option in free agency, but the late-round contracts of these tight ends leads to many being extended prior to ever getting there. Ebron could get to free agency after an $8.25 million cap hit with his fifth-year option in 2018, 4.60% of the cap, and boost the market rate. Hunter Henry will probably build off his 478 yard, eight touchdown rookie season and he could make it to free agency for a new market setting contract in 2020. Being drafted 35th overall put him on a contract that will pay him $6.38 million over his first four seasons, which could be enough to help him avoid the temptation of an extension and wait to set a new top of market rate. This market has room for growth with these two players, but if they don't bump the market much, the historically deep 2017 NFL Draft class might, with three first round picks for the first time since 2002, with O.J. Howard to the Bucs, Evan Engram to the Giants and the Browns' David Njoku.

 The success of current NFL tight ends, plus past tight ends like Tony Gonzalez who set a new standard for the position where 900 yards per season was seen as a possibility, may drive an increased emphasis on the position down to the college ranks and may make first round picks at tight end more typical in the future. Belichick has always been willing to invest first round picks in tight ends with the #21 pick in 2002 going to Daniel Graham out of Colorado and the #32 pick in 2004 going to Ben Watson. This was the first time they tried to pair together two young tight ends like they later did with Gronkowski and Aaron Hernandez.

Elite tight ends won't produce the same yardage totals as prototypical number ones, which is probably because they don't have that breakaway speed that produces more big plays or the target totals, but like slot receivers, elite tight ends provide another efficient pass catcher on short to intermediate routes. The top twenty tight ends in receiving yards in 2016 had a catch rate of 68.7% and 8.1 yards per target, which can help power an efficient offense with the right complementary pieces. Both slot wide receivers and tight ends have the ability to create big plays through the air and through yards after catch. Where a slot receiver has the quickness to make people miss in space, the tight end has the size to run over smaller defensive backs and out-maneuver slower linebackers and safeties.

As they're typically the inside receiver on their side of the formation with a body built to make catches in traffic, they run similar routes to slot receivers, so they're efficient with a size and speed combination that allows them to get open in the middle of the field. Calling back to earlier in the chapter, Super Bowl champions produced an average of 3.6 big plays per game during the regular season, so while a team without the prototypical number one can't rely on that kind of big play producer, tight ends create the potential for big plays the same way they create their offensive efficiency through versatility and creating mismatches. Add in a few explosive playmakers in these other roles and you're taking steps towards those big plays.

If a team is going to go with a strategy that doesn't rely on a top tier wide receiver, it should strive to have an elite tight end surrounded by the kind of efficient, explosive, and versatile pass catching group described before. The tight end market has less depth than wide receiver as the position requires athletic freaks simply to be able to perform the general tasks of the position with their blocking and receiving duties, which makes it a bit more difficult to find cheap production here along with the slow growth of rookies. Very few humans alive have the frame with the strength, speed, and skills needed to succeed in the NFL as a tight end, so where wide receiver value can be found in undersized receivers with elite quickness and technique, undersized NFL tight ends don't really exist.

Second tier tight ends cost between one and a half and three percent of the cap, right in with the third tier of receivers, and players in this tier are great as a supplementary piece who can produce a mismatch against some teams, but who can't provide the weekly consistency to build an offense around. Since the position takes time to develop, this tier is where teams will invest in a second contract player they believe could become a bigger contributor than he was previously as teams are willing to make a small risk of overpaying in an inexpensive market for the potential reward of a difficult mismatch. While top tier tight ends are the types that teams can trust to produce 800 to 900-yard plus seasons in a versatile pass catching group, second tier tight ends are the 400-yard plus type of players. In that third and bottom tier, which is everyone less than 1.50% of the cap, are veterans who are primarily blocking tight ends and rookie contract players.

The first three Patriots' Super Bowl teams were built in a defensive first model with a ball control offense that didn't turn the ball over. On those teams, their three highest paid receivers plus top paid tight end cost just 7.83%, 7.62%, and 8.45% of the cap as they'd gone low-cost with their money focused on their defense as their strategy for success. As Brady entered an expensive prime in the late-2000s, they continued to keep costs low considering Brady's costs and Belichick's philosophy of success being a function of being good at everything and having the most good players, rather than the most great players. Randy Moss was a great player, but he came as a value signing in 2007 and earned a new deal in 2008 that had a cap hit of 8.54% in 2009 that may have reconfirmed Belichick's commitment to coming up with more efficient solutions to still create a high-output offense, but without the cost of the pricey wide receiver market that Moss was a part of as he was also 32-years old, so the Patriots drafted Gronkowski and Hernandez in the next year's draft. This was the beginning of a long-term experiment that led to their last two Super Bowl victories, which is a huge benefit of building a salary cap framework that is easy to maintain over time.

As the Patriots emphasis on the passing game increased with Brady's increase in production and costs, the cost spent on receivers increased, as seen by the Moss move, but on their last two championship teams, the increase in spending was spent on the second and third most expensive receivers and tight end, rather than a strategy of increased spending on the top receiver like many teams move towards.

As seen in the chart, the Patriots had a considerable increase in spending on second and third most expensive receivers considering their low cost, the 0.72% increase is almost double the cost of the 2003 and 2004 WR3s. The tight end positions saw the big increase of 3.49% for the top paid tight end on the roster and 2.66% for the TE2 as a means of increasing production with two top-level playmakers at the position, but without the bigger increase that a top tier receiver would require.

Patriots Champions

Year	Team	WR1	WR2	WR3	Total	TE1	TE2	Total
2001	Patriots	3.90%	1.80%	1.23%	6.93%	0.90%	0.45%	7.83%
2003	Patriots	3.27%	1.81%	0.83%	5.91%	1.71%	1.29%	7.62%
2004	Patriots	3.96%	1.86%	0.86%	6.68%	1.77%	1.37%	8.45%
2014	Patriots	3.53%	2.07%	1.50%	7.10%	5.64%	4.06%	12.74%
2016	Patriots	3.54%	2.85%	1.88%	8.27%	4.26%	3.34%	12.53%
		3.64%	2.08%	1.26%	6.98%	2.86%	2.10%	9.83%
A	2001-04	3.71%	1.82%	0.97%	6.51%	1.46%	1.04%	7.97%
B	2014-16	3.54%	2.46%	1.69%	7.69%	4.95%	3.70%	12.64%
B-A	Difference	-0.18%	0.64%	0.72%	1.18%	3.49%	2.66%	4.67%

In the 2010 draft, the Patriots took Gronkowski in the second and Hernandez in the fourth as they embarked on a new two tight end strategy and after four below average games from Moss with just 34.8 receiving yards per game, the Patriots released him and put their trust in the young tight ends with Wes Welker, Deion Branch, Brandon Tate, and Danny Woodhead out of the backfield with the new strategy. They went 14-2 before losing to the Jets in the AFC Divisional Round, but they made it back to the Super Bowl with that core of pass catchers minus Tate the next season.

In both Gronkowski and Hernandez, they drafted complete tight ends who also provided elite run blocking, which has always been a key requirement of Patriots tight ends. Having two tight ends with the potential of 1000-yard production, but who can also stay on the field for a power running game creates near impossible to defend versatility, especially when considering the make up of NFL defenses. If the defense goes big to stop the run, then those big players they've put in won't be able to cover the tight ends. If they go smaller in an attempt to cover those tight ends, then the quarterback can audible to a running play that steamrolls the defense with what amounts to seven offensive lineman quality blockers. Very few defenses have the personnel to naturally match-up with these personnel. As defenses began to adjust with smaller, faster defenders, with an increased emphasis on passing exemplified by the 2007 team, Belichick introduced a strategy that exploited that league wide trend. He's constantly changing strategies once the league catches up to a previous innovation of his. This presents a similar opportunity for teams that creatively integrate fullbacks into their system as they're a problem to tackle in the open field and typically have a catch rate over seventy percent like running backs. If Hernandez could have refrained from shooting people in the face, NFL defenses might still be trying to figure out how to find two defensive players who could cover that duo. As explained in the defensive chapter coming up, NFL defenses have been increasing the amount of nickel defense they play over the last decade in particular seeing an increase in snaps of nickel played between 2008 and 2015 from 43.4% to 63.4%. This is when five defensive backs are on the field, which creates a match-up that favors the two tight end set in the running game.

Both players had signed extensions prior to the 2012 season and their 2014 salary cap hits would have cost 4.06% for Gronkowski and 3.49% for Hernandez to consume 7.55% of the Patriots cap if Hernandez didn't become a dead money charge of 5.64%. If they had stayed at that number, they would have cost almost one percent of the cap less than Moss' 2009 charge, but provided more production, versatility, and two mismatches that couldn't be stopped. Having two great mismatches for the price of one also mitigates the risk of injury.

Tight ends usually take a few years to develop, but this duo combined for 87 catches for 1109 yards, which is a 70.7% catch rate and 9.0 yards per target, with 16 touchdowns as rookies. In 2011, they had 169 catches for 2237 yards, and 24 touchdowns with a 71.3% catch rate and 9.4 yards per target before injuries limited them to 21 of 32 total games in 2012. The sky was the limit for the duo and the Patriots have been trying to re-create it ever since because of the offensive and salary cap efficiency of an offense with two great tight ends. While tight ends and slot receivers won't produce the same statistics as a prototypical WR1, only six receivers had over 1200 yards in 2016, so these bulk producers are fairly rare. These tight ends and slots will produce efficient ball movement, which produces first downs and leads to redzone touchdowns that both roles could play a consistent role in scoring.

Whatever defensive model a team chooses, a focus on creating first downs and touchdowns as the main offensive objectives can create value across the offense in making it more versatile and difficult for opponents to defend. A focus on chain moving and touchdown scoring helps frame how to construct the entire offense and that framework creates roles that provide more targeted ways of breaking down positions, positional spending, and contracts. It helps organizations understand the proper spending principles of each position.

The power lead running back--the LeGarrette Blount type--can produce four yards on first down to consistently create second and sixes to keep the offense ahead of the chains. He can move the chains on third and one and create touchdowns at the goal line. The third down pass catching running back and slot receiver provide offenses with high-percentage pass catchers who typically provide between six and nine yards per target, while catching north of 70% of their targets, which helps keep an offense ahead of the chains and convert on third down. With a strong running game, this creates two high-percentage ways to consistently move the ball and another option for ball movement when facing a top rush defense. With their ability to get open quickly after the snap and in a small space, these players can also sneak open in the redzone.

Instead of looking for the prototypical number one receiver, the Patriots find someone who can stretch the field to open up the rest of the offense, while providing big plays and touchdowns throughout the season. They don't have to draft players in the first round or look to free agency for top of the market receivers; they instead look later in the draft or in the second or third tiers of free agency for players they believe are undervalued who can provide production in the main roles in the offense. For receivers, the main two deconstructed roles based on the offensive principles are the efficient pass catcher for first down production and the viable deep threat who can stretch the defense vertically to produce big plays and create space for underneath routes and rushing running lanes. Big athletic tight ends provide an efficient pass catcher between the twenties and that big target in the redzone. Big receivers similarly provide this redzone target, production that an elite tight end can help replace.

Together, a versatile offensive skill group provides an offense with a bunch of difficult match-ups that a defense has to handle and each week the offensive staff can work to figure out which weapon provides the best mismatch for that week's opponent. As in MMA, become so well rounded that you'll always have a weapon to use. A focus on the key offensive objectives will help any team become more versatile and more capable of withstanding the short-term and long-term injuries that populate a football season.

By using data to create value and versatility on offense, teams can spread money saved on other important roles, especially positions that have less data to analyze and thus are more difficult markets for finding value like the offensive line. The skill players mean nothing to your organization if the offensive line can't open holes for the running back or provide protection for the quarterback. Conversely, a defensive line that can force penetration and chaos in the backfield is a very powerful weapon. The league-wide focus on the quarterback position is warranted, but rather than over invest in the passing game, other alternative strategies exist like investing money in defensive players who can decrease your opponent's production on offense on a weekly basis. This strategy starts with the defensive line and extends to the rest of a defense whose objective is to decrease the offense's efficiency, to decrease their ability to move the chains and score touchdowns in the redzone.

Alternative spending strategies based on what has been discussed so far are in the upcoming chapters. If an organization can figure out how to find value and create an efficient offense, then they open themselves up to being a much more versatile and balanced team. If they can create systems with their own positional and role prototypes across the roster, teams can find value and compete on a yearly basis. Like Belichick's scouting manual, organizations should know what their ideal player for every position is, so they can predict the kind of players they will need.

Chapter 7: Spending on the Offensive Line

Fresh off discussing the variety of ways to find value and versatility at the offensive skill positions, the offensive line is where the cap space and draft resources saved can be put to good use. As former NFL offensive lineman and current media personality Ross Tucker wrote in a 2014 article for *Sports Illustrated's Monday Morning Quarterback*, "most front office executives and scouts typically know less about offensive line play than any other position" and that sentiment rings true across the entire industry.[1] The offensive line is not a sexy position, so it doesn't attract eyeballs to it and those who are attracted to studying the position see a sort of complex team martial art in the chaos of the trenches that includes five or more offensive players depending on the play call. Also, like I mentioned with big, prototypical quarterbacks, a small supply of human beings exist who fit the mold of the athletic 6'4", 315-pound offensive lineman, so naturally this would be a position that may have more need for a large investment as supply may not meet demand.

Unlike offensive skill positions, very few objective metrics exist to judge an individual lineman's performance outside of for negatives like sacks allowed and penalties. Some will judge an offensive line group by yards produced, especially rushing, but yards are not a catchall metric and they don't determine individual performance. New outlets like Football Outsiders' and Pro Football Focus are creating their own attempts at quantifying offensive line performance, but PFF's Sam Monson acknowledges "the only guys who know whether a player screwed up are the guys in that offensive line or offensive meeting room. We try to counter that by only grading what a player attempts to do, rather than guessing what he was supposed to do."

In terms of Pro Football Focus' signature stats, they track all passing plays and the stats they use to judge the offensive line are sacks, the quarterback hits, hurries and total pressures allowed. They will attribute sacks to the quarterback in situation where the sack is not the fault of the offensive line, which is a good change to make sacks a more realistic barometer of offensive line play. These stats come together to create a lineman's, and an offensive line's, pass blocking efficiency, which is a rating that measures pressure allowed on a per-snap basis with weighting toward sacks allowed that can help quantify a player's value as a pass blocker. They don't have a statistic to quantify performance in the running game, which leaves half of their job left to more subjective measurements.

Other sources have pass blocking metrics that help like ESPN Stats & Information's pressure rate, which is how often the quarterback is under duress, including sacks and hurries, so a rate statistic for the stuff Pro Football Focus covers. Aaron Schatz from Football Outsiders writes, in an article about how to judge and quantify an offensive line's performance, that the adjusted sack rate covers "sacks (and intentional groundings) per pass play, adjusted for situation and opponent."[2]

To understand run blocking, we have a good unit in the good blocking rate (GBR), which is compiled and covered by K.C. Joyner of ESPN. GBR is a "metric that measures how often an offense gives its ball carriers quality run blocking."[3] Joyner writes that, "good blocking, in this instance, roughly refers to the times when offenses do not allow defenses to disrupt a rush attempt."[4] Running backs can be judged off of good blocking yards per attempt (GBYPA), which "gauges how well a running back does when his blockers give him a favorable run blocking situation. Since most running backs gain only one yard per carry on plays with poor blocking, doing well in this metric is key to good overall production."[5] Both statistics can say a lot about the offensive line and the running backs, which help a team understand what they have, what they need at the position, and the kinds of players they can find elsewhere who can improve either.

Yards before first contact, for a running back, is another stat that tells us a lot about offensive line play and the opportunities that they provide a running back. Football Outsiders' has an adjusted line yards (ALY) stat that Aaron Schatz writes is a metric that "splits value between the blocking and the back based on the length of the run, adjusted for situation and opponent." A running back's "stuffed rate" is "how often running backs are stuffed for a loss or no gain, the most blocking-dependent part of adjusted line yards." Lastly, penalties are a key metric for judging offensive linemen and Schatz judges them on a per game basis that includes declined and offsetting penalties. These stats can help you find players who are outside your organization who can fit what you're doing if combined with subjective analysis that understands a player fits what your offensive system will ask him to do.

The main manner of judging offensive linemen has traditionally been a grading process that Tucker writes, "is actually an inexact science that can be as subjective as art." So, how teams have to judge an offensive lineman outside of some size and skill related measurables is an inexact data collection process left up to the interpretation of the person who's watching it and this judgment is done at a position that almost no one understands well.

Other than Pro Football Focus' relatively new rating system, which has issues already mentioned, but could eventually become the standard for judging offensive lineman (and all positions as they perfect their process), are three other grading processes that coaches around the NFL use. The first is where a coach provides a plus for completing his assignment and a minus when he fails. This creates a cumulative grade over a game, and then over the season, which can become a lineman's identity as a player for better or worse. Those 16 games become a player's report card for the year. According to Tucker, All-Pros grade between 89-93%, while an average player grades between 85-89%, but if a player dips below 85%, then it might become time to start thinking about a career change. As he writes, the difference between being the kind of player making a few million dollars per year and being out of the NFL can come down to just a few plays per game. That kind of pressure goes for any position in the hyper competitive NFL, but it seems especially nerve-wracking at a position with fewer objective measurements.

Mike Devlin, who was the Jets offensive line coach at the time of Tucker's article, and has been the Texans offensive line coach since 2016, developed a second grading system. He used a zero to four grading system. A zero was an egregious mental error or a penalty; one meant a bad block; two meant that the player blocked his man but his technique left something to be desired; three meant executing an assignment with excellent technique; while a four meant a three and then some, which likely means a pancake block.

Tucker writes that most coaches grade performance and technique, which have a strong correlation, but not always. In this grading system, a lineman may get a plus for blocking his man, but also a minus because he didn't take the right footwork. The goal here is to get as many plus/plus plays as possible, while avoiding minus/minus plays.

With the level of expertise necessary to create this grade, this position group requires the input of the team's position coach more than any other. The offensive line coach, along with the offensive coordinator and any assistants directly involved with the offensive line, should be the main voices involved in the grading process. Similar to the issues that Pro Football Focus faces without the knowledge of a lineman's assignments on each play, the best people to judge linemen outside the organization and the only ones who may have a true idea of what they're trying to do are a team's offensive line coaches. There should also be communication between the team's offensive line coach and college line coaches with players they might be interested in. Since offensive line play is something very few people know about, offensive line coaches can build their own community of likeminded people to learn from, so professional offensive line coaches should have grown their network over their career to include many coaches whose opinions they can trust on potential prospects.

The grades offensive line coaches give should be used in combination with the measurables and attributes they've determined they're looking for in their offensive linemen. This is where the scouting department comes in as the offensive coaches should provide them with the list of measurables, attributes, and skills they're looking for, which should be combined with their favorite version of offensive line grades to help the team determine a list of potential prospects for that offseason who can help them discover value in the later rounds of the draft, after the draft, and at a low cost in free agency or on the waiver wire. Matt Miller, one of the best scouts in media, wrote a 2012 article titled, "A Scout's Guide to Grading Offensive Linemen" that divided the job into about a dozen traits that scouts and teams look for in potential offensive linemen.[6]

The first trait that you'll naturally think about when it comes to the offensive line is size. According to Brian Dalek in a 2013 Men's Health article, "researchers at Grand Valley State University did an analysis of the average height, weight and body fat percentage of college football players from 1942 to 2011. While players at all positions gained weight over time and increased body fat, one of the most striking statistics was that college interior linemen gained about one to two pounds per year over sixty years, and all professional players gained up to one and a half per year over seven decades."[7] As Brandon Thorne wrote for Inside The Pylon, there has been a league wide trend towards "athleticism, explosiveness, and power" as the league has settled into an ideal prototype of players in the 6'3" to 6"6" and 300 to 330 pound range.[8] As a general rule, offensive tackles tend to be taller, longer, and leaner, while some offenses prefer just slightly shorter and squatter players on the interior. As Miller writes, with the varying offensive systems in the NFL today, a strict size requirement league-wide doesn't exist, but as a general rule tackles are at least 6'4", 300 pounds, guards are at least 6'3", 290 and centers at least 6'2", 290.

Agility is a main dividing trait between interior linemen and tackles. Miller points out the key dividing factor in pass protection in that interior linemen can be protected by each other, while a tackle is usually on an island in pass protection, so they need elite agility and footwork to deal with the freaks they can encounter on the edge. Where interior linemen have another lineman helping them out, tackles are getting help from tight ends and running backs that are chip blocking, so the backs are only lending a helping hand. Linemen also need the strength to drive their men off the line of scrimmage in the run game and control his area in pass protection. This duality sees itself in pass blocking, as players have to have the agility to handle a speed rusher with the strength to block a power rush move. When run blocking, linemen need the strength to move the pile and open rushing lanes for the ball carrier and the agility to pull, trap block, and move in space to set up his blocks.

Miller explains that with the increasingly spread-style offenses in the NFL today, pulls and traps have become more important. A pull is when an offensive lineman takes a small step back and then works down the line to block on the edge, while for a trap block, the offense purposely opens a hole for the defender to come through and then blocks him from the side to trap the defender in the backfield away from the ball carrier who has already slipped through. The trend toward the spread, the increase in the pace of the game, and increasing athleticism across the defensive line is pushing the trend toward athleticism, explosiveness, and power.

The final two traits that scouts look at across the line are a player's injury history as well as an attitude that revels "in the violence and physicality of the sport" as NFL writer Danny Kelly puts it. You want a line that leans more toward the psyche of Richie Incognito than Jonathan Martin. Awareness is a trait that every offensive lineman and every player on the field must have, but it is especially important at center, as it is their job to identify defensive alignments and plans before the snap. Quarterbacks determine who the Mike linebacker is, which is the defender whom the offensive line centers the blocking scheme off of to allow them to understand which defender they will be blocking, then the center makes protection calls, diagnoses stunts, twists and blitzes, as he adjusts blocking assignments of the entire line accordingly. With an emphasis on intelligence and strength at center, players at the position can have a high performance into their thirties.

With offenses trending toward efficiency, there has been a move towards quick passes to the kinds of athletes mentioned in the offensive skills chapter. NFL.com's Next Gen Stats' Time to Throw metric measures the time in seconds from the moment the ball is snapped to the moment the ball leaves the passer's hand. Of the fifty quarterbacks measured in 2016, Alex Smith was the quickest passing starter with an average time to throw of 2.38 seconds with Tyrod Taylor of the Bills setting the high end at 3.12. Teams seem to use 2.5 seconds as a target for quick passes. CBS Sports' Jared Dubin wrote an article in September 2015 that displayed the increased efficiency of these quicker passes.[9] Of course, the Patriots are one of the teams leading the way in quick passes with their interest in pass catchers who excel on short to intermediate routes. In 2014, Brady threw 66.23% of his passes in under 2.5 seconds, while the league wide average was at 58.55%; Brady completed 70.7% of these passes, while NFL quarterbacks completed 68.7%. On throws over 2.5 seconds, Brady dropped to a 50.0% completion percentage, while the NFL completion percentage dropped to 54.7% on these same throws. Brady's percentage of passes thrown more than 2.6 seconds after the snap has increased in the first half of 2017 with Edelman out and the deep threats on the roster who we discussed in chapter six. We'll see if this is a continuing trend as Belichick always makes new adjustments as defenses adjust to the trends he creates.

In the 2014 Super Bowl against the Seahawks, Brady threw 74.5% of his 50 passes in under 2.5 seconds. As mentioned before, Brady completed 74.0% of his passes with Julian Edelman, Shane Vereen, and Danny Amendola seeing 31 of those 50 targets, 62% of targets. Those three caught 80.6% of those 31 targets for a line of 25 catches for 221 yards and two touchdowns during a game where the Patriots only had 57 rushing yards on 21 carries. Without a running game, those yards at 7.1 yards per target and 8.8 yards per catch were how they moved the ball and earned the win.

The new offensive trend toward quick passes is being met by defenses spreading their pass rush talent and schemes across the line as they try to find ways to get to the quarterback in this short time frame. As this trend continues, college defensive lines will push an increasing number of talented pass rushers with the right body type to the interior and produce more talent for the professional ranks. Time to throw becomes a math problem that defenses try to create a pass rush solution for. Increased pass rush talent across the line allows teams to create pressure with only four rushers, which creates advantageous math in the defensive backfield with potentially seven players in coverage against five eligible receivers. Colleges respond to NFL trends with their coaches implementing strategies that they have seen work in the NFL, which then leads to an increased supply of players who fit these molds in the NFL.

The 2007 Giants and the 2015 Broncos beat the Patriots by holding them to nearly identical rushing stat lines of 16 carries for 25 yards and a touchdown, then 17 carries, 44 yards, and one touchdown eight years later. They also were able to create consistent pressure with four, which allowed them to have seven in coverage. The 2014 Seahawks were hoping to implement the same path to victory and came up just short at the goal line with the famous play call questioned around the world. The goal of these defenses is to shut the Patriots run offense down and force them to rely almost solely on the pass. In 2016, only 14 sacks occurred in less than 2.5 seconds from the snap, so defenses are being built to create an advantage for themselves with this math. Covering the yardage between where an edge rusher starts and the quarterback in less than 2.5 seconds can be a tough task. Defenses want to get offenses in the third and long situations that force the offense into a deeper pass and thus a deeper drop, to allow their pass rushers time to get to the quarterback and create a sack. This defensive objective is moving talent and investments toward the interior of the offensive lines as a means to stop the run on first down and create pass rush advantages on third down. Offenses become far more predictable in third and long versus third and three or less, with the latter being a goal an offense strives for.

The offensive trend creates a defensive trend, then that trend creates a trend of moving offensive line investments to the interior. Every action has a reaction, every strategy has a response. As with offensive skill players, building an offensive line is about value, versatility, and balance to create a unit with no holes; a unit that can win one-on-one match-ups is vital. There can be no weak links in the chain or else a defense with multiple pass rush mismatches can find a mismatch to exploit all game, like a well-rounded group of pass catchers can on offense. Considering how many teams have built strong pass rushes as a core strategy for success, you're likely to meet one of these teams on the road to the Super Bowl, so a team with holes on the offensive line is highly likely to be exploited and bounced from the playoffs.

These trends led to a 2016 season where the three highest cap hits for offensive linemen were interior linemen in Oakland guard Kelechi Osemele, then centers Ryan Kalil of the Panthers and Pittsburgh's Maurkice Pouncey. The other Pouncey brother in Miami, Mike, comes in at number six to make four of the top six paid linemen interior ones. This is part due to the trend, but also due to the fact that each of the four players were in the years with the most expensive cap hits of their contracts. It is a trend that moves into 2017 with half of the 12 offensive linemen over six percent of the cap being left tackles and the other half being interior offensive linemen. According to Spotrac, Over The Cap's little ugly salary cap step-brother who steals our data and doesn't cite it, 175 veteran linemen made more than the league minimum in 2016 and 47 of those players were in the first tier of the offensive line market between three and seven percent. The market could reach up to seven and a half percent in the right situation. The Super Bowl record for an offensive lineman is Russell Okung of the 2013 Seahawks at 7.76%, then an injured Ryan Clady at 7.40% for the 2015 Broncos and Tarik Glenn of the 2006 Colts at 6.77%. Of the 47 players in the first tier of the market, 20 (42.6%) were left tackles and 8 (17.0%) right tackles to combine to make up 59.6% of the first tier. The left tackle position is still seen as the most important position on the line as it protects your quarterback's backside from edge rushers and right tackle is right behind it due to both tackles typically being on an island in pass protection with a need for elite footwork. The best players at the three interior offensive line positions make up the rest of the first tier.

Another important concept regarding elite offensive tackle play is that having a tackle who sets the edge, takes control of, and dominates his guy provides the rest of the offensive line with the opportunity to have a numbers advantage of four against, typically, three on the rest of the defensive line. This allows the other linemen to double team one of the players if they need to and forces the defensive coordinator to blitz to get pressure.

Higher costs of tackles combined with the vital importance of the positional market is the prime spot to use a couple of those first and second round picks that your team has saved by finding some alternative solutions like those discussed in chapter six. Sixteen of the twenty starting offensive tackles on Pro Football Focus'

Top 10 offensive lines of 2016 were drafted by the team they played for, nine of these players were drafted in the first round with a tenth drafted in the second. In February 2015, Western Chief of Arrowhead Pride did an analysis of the percentage of players at each position drafted between 2005 and 2014 that became starters for more than half of their playing career. This table is in the appendix for chapter 10 in the back of this book. In that analysis, he found that 83% of offensive linemen drafted in the first round became consistent starters, while 70% of offensive linemen drafted in the second round became starters. Add in a 40% rate for 3rd round picks and offensive linemen are the most successful draft picks in the first three rounds. While offensive linemen also succeed at a higher rate than many positions in the last four rounds, this illustrates a high probability of a positive return on a draft pick if a team uses their top picks on this position group.[10]

Out of the 50 starters who made up these Top 10 offensive lines, only six were first tier linemen who were signed as free agents and four of those were on a Raiders team that was able to spend some excess cap space on these players because Derek Carr, Khalil Mack, and Amari Cooper consumed just 7.54% of the cap in markets where three players of their caliber can cost over 30% of the cap together. The other two first tier linemen were left tackle Jason Peters of the Eagles and Washington guard Shawn Lauvao. Peters signed with Philadelphia in 2009 after starting his career in Buffalo as an undrafted free agent in 2004.

Solving the offensive line through the draft has the added benefit of continuity, which is probably more important on the line than anywhere else considering the way it needs to perform as a cohesive unit. The second tier between one and a half and three percent is where the bulk of veteran talent on the interior resides as well as less talented veteran tackles, plus most first round rookie contracts. With most of the interior talent in the market in this tier, interior linemen represent a better opportunity for value in free agency than left tackles. Along with the six first tier free agent linemen, four second tier linemen on PFF's ten best lines signed with their team as a free agent, two centers and two right guards. A draft first strategy continues across the line as interior linemen can be found in later rounds, which creates opportunities to create value, and if a team doesn't hit on a late round guard or center, then the low-cost free agent market, a low-risk draft pick or waiver wire acquisition can potentially provide a serviceable replacement if they're in the right scheme with an experienced offensive line coach. The third tier, between the minimum and one and a half percent, is ripe with rookie contract players, and low-level veteran starters. This is where teams need to find a versatile back up or two who can fill one or more positions if a starter goes down.

As a unit, the offensive line has three tiers that represent the unit's total cost. The top of the first tier is nineteen percent of the cap down to fourteen, the second tier is from fourteen down to nine and the bottom of the third is at five percent. With five starters, costs on the line can be the most expensive of any position group, but while 33 first tier offensive linemen were on these 23 champions, only four teams were in the first tier of this market, meaning almost all of teams were able to find value somewhere on the offensive line. Three of these teams were based on a quarterback centric model with the 2011 Giants at 14.41%, the 1994 49ers at 15.84% and the 2006 Colts at 16.25%, all with quarterbacks in the first tier of the quarterback market as these organizations felt a need to protect that investment. All three of these teams were in the top five of the NFL that year with at least over 272 passing yards per game. If you're going to have a top quarterback, then it pays to protect them although there will be some difficulties fielding a great defense with this kind of investment in the quarterback and offensive line, especially if you want to add a first tier wide receiver too. The other two, the 2005 Steelers at 16.44% of the cap and the 2013 Seahawks at 18.59%, were able to take advantage of low-cost starting quarterbacks to build the rest of their team up. Where the first three were built on passing offenses in the top five, the latter two had great defenses with top five rushing offenses and an efficient, young quarterback.

The Seahawks were able to have such a high cost on their line because of the amount of low-cost starters they had like Bobby Wagner (0.80%), Golden Tate (0.72%), Brandon Browner (0.63%), Russell Wilson (0.55%), KJ Wright (0.55%), Richard Sherman (0.49%), Doug Baldwin (0.46%), and Jermaine Kearse (0.39%). This high first tier offensive line strategy is not one that can be replicated by many to Super Bowl success considering the high costs of positions like quarterback, edge rushers, wide receiver, and cornerback. As the Seahawks transitioned into paying second contracts to this young core of stars, they decreased their offensive line investment in a failed attempt to replicate the third tier offensive line strategy the Patriots implemented in the early 2000s.

The Patriots were so good at saving offensive line money under Belichick and black belt master offensive line coach Dante Scarnecchia in those early years that their three champion offensive lines cost 5.09%, 6.57% and 4.65%. Their 2004 costs were so low they were below our third tier floor, which would seem impossible if they didn't do it and rank seventh in the NFL in offensive yards that year. The 2001 team had only one second tier player in center Damien Woody at 1.76%. He bumped up to the first tier at 3.72% as their left guard in 2003 and then Joe Andruzzi at 1.66% in 2004 was their highest paid lineman that year. Those Patriots teams benefitted from second round left tackle Matt Light on his rookie deal at 0.87%, 0.96%, and 1.48% through those champions. As their second round pick in 2009, right tackle Sebastian Vollmer cost 3.07% on the 2014 Super Bowl team after a rookie contract that ended in 2012 and paid a high of 0.81% of the cap, while first round pick Nate Solder cost just 2.04% of the 2014 cap on the fourth year of his rookie contract. Other than Solder, the 2016 Patriots had third round rookie Joe Thuney at left guard, 2015 undrafted free agent David Andrews, 2015 fourth round pick Shaq Mason at right guard, and 2011 fifth round pick Marcus Cannon at right tackle for an injured Vollmer. These teams, with their low-cost line filled with late round interior linemen, represent what's possible with the best offensive line coach in the NFL. The potential for low-cost value on the interior of the offensive line will continue to keep the interior markets slightly lower than offensive tackle other than for top veterans. The savings for rookie contract players at tackle represent the benefits of an early round drafting strategy at the position.

The next closest line to those Patriots teams was the 2012 Ravens at 7.07% with first round left tackle Michael Oher at 1.69% and right guard Marshall Yanda as the other second tier lineman at 3.03%. The 2009 Saints are next at 7.71% with their center through right tackle with cap hits of 2.59%, 2.27%, and 2.03%. The 2015 Broncos come next at 8.15% although left tackle Ryan Clady was on injured reserve at 7.40%, which would've bumped them all the way up to the first tier—another team investing heavily in their offensive line to protect their first tier quarterback.

While the first tier has just five teams and the third tier has six, the second tier leads the way with twelve teams between nine and fourteen percent of the cap. This is where the bulk of the teams should, and will, be; the starting offensive lines of the 23 champions of the cap era came to an average of 11.03% of the cap. At the bottom of this group are the 1996 Packers at 9.12% with four second tier players, the 2008 Steelers at 9.26% with left tackle Max Starks at 5.95%, then the 2014 Patriots at 9.81% with a first tier left guard and right tackle at 3.07% of the cap in Dan Connolly and Sebastian Vollmer, plus first round pick Nate Solder at left tackle on a rookie deal paying him 2.04%. Next came the 2002 Bucs at 10.06% with center Jeff Christy at 5.00%, then right tackle Kenyatta Walker at 1.88%. The Broncos of the nineties are in this tier twice with four second tier linemen on their 1997 line that cost 10.20% and the 1998 team at 12.84% with first tier left tackle Tony Jones at 4.92%, then three second tier linemen. The 2016 Patriots are next at 10.76% as they've increased their investment to protect Brady over the years with left tackle Nate Solder, then right tackles Marcus Cannon and Sebastian Vollmer. The low-cost interior linemen that the Patriots continually find cost a combined 1.04% of the cap, which is a very helpful mechanism for keeping costs low, but a mismatch of Falcons defensive tackle Grady Jarrett against right guard Shaq Mason in the Super Bowl almost derailed their drive for five and is one of the risks of the low-cost option. The Patriots had three first tier tackles this year with Sebastian Vollmer on the IR at 3.06%, but that was due to the 28-year old Cannon being extended during the season as Vollmer was slated to enter 2017 as a 33-year old in the last year of his contract with no dead money, which led to his release before the season.

Next come the 2007 Giants at 11.16% with right tackle Kareem McKenzie at 4.91%, then three-second tier offensive linemen. The 1995 Cowboys are a pinch higher at 11.18% with right tackle Erik Williams at 3.70% and three second tier linemen as well. The 2000 Ravens had their bookends, left tackle Jonathan Ogden and right tackle Harry Swayne, at 6.47% and 4.02%, plus center Jeff Mitchell at 1.65% to pave the way for a rushing attack of Jamal Lewis and Priest Holmes. Last in this tier are the 1999 Rams right at the top at 13.99% with right guard Adam Timmerman, who also earned a ring with the 1996 Packers, at 6.11%, plus left tackle Orlando Pace at 5.78%, then three guys under one percent. The second tier is where most teams will want to end up with a combination of veterans with rookie contract players; even most first round rookie contracts are low enough to help create this second tier balance. As these Super Bowl teams illustrate, constructing a strong line that can stay in this nine to 14 percent of the cap range has many different acquisition strategies for success. Finding elite bookends and pairing them with lower-cost interior linemen seems to be a successful way to do this. Creating chemistry on the offensive line with multiple players working together for a long time is a good thing, but creating continuity in never having to completely remake the line is also important. Having to find three to five new pieces in a short window can be difficult and one of the main problems I think the New York Giants have been having in the mid-2010s as their Super Bowl linemen retired in quick succession.

There are many different ways to spend on the line and different schemes, so teams will place varying degrees of importance to each position on the line, but generally speaking, the hierarchy according to Super Bowl spending goes left tackle, right tackle, then center very close behind that, then the guard positions with left guard given a slight edge. With offensive line spending broken down, we'll now shift focus towards the defensive side of the ball with the on field and spending principles that create success.

Chapter 8: Defensive Spending

Understanding and creating value on offense enables value creation on defense, which creates the potential for a team to create an offense that can accomplish its objectives and a defense that can stop its opponent's offense from accomplishing their objectives. Super Bowl teams have traditionally spent slightly more on offense versus defense, an average of 49.43% versus 45.07%, because of the quarterback market, the wide receiver group, and offensive line costs in particular. If value can be created on offense, it creates huge potential for investment in defenses that need the money as they become more multiple with a need for more elite, versatile athletes to deal with the increasing versatility of modern NFL offenses.

Defensive positions, especially defensive tackle, linebacker, and safety, lack the more obvious objective measurements that offensive positions have like yardage and the rate stats we discussed. Even metrics like tackles are poorly recorded with different sources having different ways of calculating them. Sometimes the best cornerbacks won't have many interceptions once they become established as one of the league's best as quarterbacks will start to look elsewhere. The defensive side of the ball takes much more subjective analysis from the coaching staff and the front office to determine if a player fits their scheme and what the defensive coordinator will ask them to do. Pro Football Focus provides an example of new metrics with their "signature stats," which will help teams better understand how to find value on defense and will be discussed in this chapter.

Along with issues with finding objective measurements on the defensive side of the ball, before accounting for injuries, offenses need one quarterback, two running backs, three wide receivers, two tight ends and five offensive linemen, which is 13 to 14 players. Offenses are going to have more than just 14 offensive players; they're going to have their back-up quarterback, third running back, their fourth receiver, and preferably two more competent offensive linemen, but defenses need more players as a basic for being prepared for each opposing offense they face and to rotate players through for rest and match-ups. Defenders also tire out due to their need to swarm to the ball on every play without knowing where the ball is going on those plays.

Defenses need five or six defensive linemen, three to five linebackers (these first two are especially dependent on system) and five to six defensive backs, which is 13 to 17 players. Bill Belichick has become more multiple on offense these last few years—as have most good offenses—and will continue to do so, which is the same thing a defense is trying to do, become more multiple in their pass rush and coverage to dictate the pressure they want and be prepared for anything, while also having the tacklers on all three levels of the defense to get ball carriers to the ground. Defenses have transformed from 4-3 or 3-4 base defenses into more of a hybrid configuration. For example, according to Pro Football Reference, the 2013 Seahawks had 17 defensive players playing over 40% of snaps to just 13 players on offense. Even with an offense built on versatility, the 2016 Patriots had 19 defensive players playing over 20% of snaps to 16 on offense, then 14 defensive players over 40% to 11 on offense. Defensive players also tend to help more on special teams with their increased tackling abilities.

The main objective is to create the counter to what's already been discussed in the offensive skill chapter: defenses are trying to stop the offense from producing first downs to "extend the inning" and earn three more outs, then stop them from scoring touchdowns once they're in the redzone. To do this, teams need to get the offense behind the sticks on first and second down through stopping the run and short, quick passing game, plus a pass rush to take advantage of third and long to shrink the quarterback's window to throw with linebackers and defensive backs who can cover the multitude of potential mismatches they will face in man-to-man defense with the ability to make tackles in space. Remember that offenses are attempting to achieve a high yards per play, a high yards per pass attempt to drive the per play average, a high completion percentage, a high third down conversion rate, redzone efficiency, and big play ability while protecting the football. A defense is trying to contain and impede that progress.

Defenses must be prepared for the wide variety of situations and potential match-ups they face over the course of the season and the defensive line can become an expensive position group considering the high-costs and the quantity of players needed. As an example of the money needed for defensive spending, defensive linemen rotate throughout games because of the explosiveness required from the position, so unlike offensive linemen who are expected to play the whole game, five to seven defensive linemen are required to create a rotation. The 2016 Patriots had six defensive linemen who played between 44 and 65% of snaps according to Pro Football Reference. After eight games in 2017, the Eagles, an organization that seems to be following the same logic they see the Patriots implemented in many ways, has seven defensive linemen playing between 45 and 71% of snaps. As Jon Gruden mentioned on Monday Night Football, this is like having a baseball bullpen full of flamethrowers to over power the offensive line. This requires a bit of cash or a lot of successful drafting, which means the need for cash later if you want to keep players through their second contracts or a strong process for identifying defensive talent to acquire new defensive talent.

With many defenses getting creative with defensive fronts, transitioning between the 4-3, 3-4, nickel, dime and other configurations to create advantageous match-ups with their athletes, there become multiple players for the 11 defensive positions creating situational role players and increased playing time for other roles. Many defensive coordinators are responding to offenses spreading the field by increasing the amount of nickel and dime defense they play, which means they need at least five competent defensive backs—especially come playoff time when you're facing great quarterbacks each week. Teams can't solely rely on playing zone defense as elite quarterbacks can pick those apart with the knowledge of where the holes in the defense will be, so defenses need capable man-to-man defenders behind the defensive line.

According to Pro Football Focus, from 2008 to 2015, the percentage of the time NFL defenses played nickel, which is when the defense adds a fifth defensive back and take out a linebacker, went from 43.4% to 63.4% due to the changes in offensive personnel to more one back sets, three wide sets and shotgun each year.[1] This offensive chess move has led to the defensive trend toward nickel defenses, which is creating a new hybrid sort of fifth defensive back-slash-linebacker position teams are using, which may be best represented by the 6'1", 215-pound super-athlete Jabrill Peppers during his time at Michigan. This defensive back sized linebacker athlete is also a position I noticed while going to Big 12 games during the 2015 season as I saw these defenses adjust to their pass heavy league with outside linebackers in this smaller mold. As Doug Farrar wrote in a *Bleacher Report* article on one of the Browns' 2017 first round picks prior to the draft, head coaches believe that "the NFL is now less about positions and more about match-ups. In the modern game, it's better to have a player who can move around the field, shape shifting into different roles, than it is to have a guy who does one thing."[2]

He goes on to write, "this is especially true on the defensive side of the ball, where the more traditional roles of defensive end, defensive tackle, linebacker, cornerback, and safety have changed radically. Teams ask linemen to be multi-gap monsters. Linebackers, playing nickel and dime defenses as base concepts, must be able to run and chase to the sideline and up the seam. Cornerbacks are prized for their abilities to slip from outside to the slot and vice versa." As he says, no positions have been more affected by the NFL's push toward versatility than the safety positions with "big-nickel secondaries with three safeties" like the Patriots ran in 2016 and hybrid safeties who can do everything. In Seattle, they're able to go a more traditional route by using two versatile players at linebacker and two at safety, while Bobby Wagner, KJ Wright, Kam Chancellor, and Earl Thomas stay on the field for nearly every defensive snap.

As on offense, avoiding big cap expenses supports the objective to create a variety of pass rushers and coverage guys with the run defenders to stop both the run and the pass. The freakish athletes that are coming into the draft at safety and linebacker, having been groomed in the spread offensive setting of college and high school football, are allowing defensive coordinators to make huge changes in scheme.

As noted in earlier chapters, Belichick never wants to be the first to run to free agency and set the market. According to Robert Klemko of *Sports Illustrated*, Jonathan Kraft gave a 1994 speech to a prominent Patriots fan group that spelled out a vision for a team that had won 19 of 80 games from 1989 to 1993. The salary cap had just been introduced and the younger Kraft explained that this was one of the biggest reasons they bought the team; he believed inefficiencies existed in the market and he used a hypothetical to illustrate his point. Many teams then, and today, commit to a marginally better player at a much higher price, while the Patriots look for value. If Player A makes $10 million per year and is 10% better than Player B who makes $2.5 million, then the Patriots will take Player B every time. This money saved can then be spread to improve other parts of the roster in a much more impactful way than the slightly better, but much more expensive "Player A" would.

This mindset is important across the roster and is applicable for defenses across the league. With increased costs for top of market edge rushers, elite interior rushers, and cornerbacks, the costs at the top of the roster can get out of hand quickly if teams don't understand how to find value—and the high spending then creates a team with holes. When a defense has a glaring weakness, an offensive coordinator can strategize a way to exploit that weakness, so you're playing a dangerous game come playoff time if you're hoping to not run into a team with a dominant wide receiver, mismatches at tight end, and/or a pass catching running back if you lack the athletes to deal with these, and other, match-ups. A defense with a hole is like a well-rounded, complete MMA fighter facing a boxer with no takedown defense or jiu jitsu and knowing he can drag him to the ground and exploit the boxer's weakness.

The current Patriots find this value on offense as well by currently directing their pass game spending to the tight end position—but especially on the defensive side of the ball, the Patriots create value throughout the unit by spending high draft capital, which tends to lead to top tier contracts, on players in low-cost markets like defensive tackle, linebacker and safety to create value and versatility across the defense. They then go to the more expensive markets of edge rusher and cornerback to find lower cost value players, which creates value savings that can be used to build the middle of the roster. The goal is to create a defense that can defend the run and pass, with versatility in the pass rush and defensive backfield. With a salary cap, looking for the perfect prototypes at each and every position is unaffordable in the short-term through free agency and even in the long-term as even if your organization has draft success those players eventually come due for an increase in salary. The more attainable and productive goal is to strive to create an ideal unit by combining skill sets to build that unit to execute the defensive objectives.

New England is not just spending on low-cost markets; they're spending on really valuable skills that come at manageable costs, which then increases the unit's ability to be versatile. They grab run stopping pieces, great tacklers, along with speed and athleticism for the unit. One of the versatile athletes of the Patriots defense is the 5' 11", 215-pound Patrick Chung, who has the ability to defend a variety of match-ups from tight end to running back. In the belief that pass rushing freaks are the best super-athletes to have, the market has lost sight of the other freaks that can populate and help a defense.

The 2016 Patriots had 11 players over three percent of the cap and 15 between one and three percent, including two dead money charges for retired linebacker Jerod Mayo and first-round defensive tackle Dominique Easley, whom they released prior to the season. A quarterback, inside linebacker, wide receiver, safety, two tight ends, two edge rushers, and three offensive tackles, including the injured Sebastian Vollmer and Marcus Cannon, whom they signed to an extension during the season due to his great performance for them in Vollmer's absence, were in that group of 11. Tom Brady represented the highest cap hit at 8.87% and while most would say that cap hit is artificially low due to his wife's net worth, even with that advantage, the Patriots had $13.4 million in cap space, 8.63% of the 2016 cap, which they rolled forward to help re-sign the defensive players they had hitting free agency in the 2017 offseason.

Of the group of 13 players on the roster between one and three percent of the cap, they had two valuable wide receivers in Julian Edelman and Danny Amendola, then all defensive and special teams players. Kicker Stephen Gostowski, punter Ryan Allen, and special teams maven Matt Slater were in the group, then two safeties in Patrick Chung and Duron Harmon, two defensive tackles in Alan Branch and Malcolm Brown, two linebackers in Shea McClellin and Jonathan Freeny, then one defensive end in Chris Long and one cornerback in Logan Ryan. This ability to spend good money on all these defenders helped create a strong, versatile defense. It goes along with Belichick's philosophy of building a roster full of good players rather than shooting for a few great players.

To the oft-repeated point regarding Gisele's net worth being even more than Mr. Brady's, many people will say that Brady can take a salary that no one else can because of his wife. But coming out of the 2016 season, according to Spotrac, 11 current NFL quarterbacks had made over $150 million in their playing career, and that number doesn't count endorsement income, which quarterbacks see plenty of—nationally and locally. (A retired Peyton Manning, albeit as one of the greatest quarterbacks of all-time, and one of the most marketable, still earned $15 million per year in endorsements in 2016 according to Forbes.) Brady was one of those 11 over $150 million, but more quarterbacks will enter that group as the cap increases and the quarterback market stays at a high rate. The cap will pass $200 million by 2020; by 2023 the cap will likely be past $250 million, which would make the current top of market contract for a quarterback of $25 to $27 million 10-11% of the cap. Thirteen percent of the cap with the 2023 projections would be $32.5 million, so potential for a top of the market to reside around 13% for players in their prime, like Brady did, exists if NFL teams can refrain from driving the market to unwinnable heights through the pressure to win now superseding taking a more reasonable, creative approach to the position. Quarterbacks who get to the point where they make these kinds of contracts have the longest careers in the NFL, so they'll have plenty of time to stack paper with the coming increases in the salary cap, while still maintaining a manageable rate. Higher guarantees in the contracts of top signal callers, which makes sense at a position with lower injury risk than almost all others, can play a role in keeping the market at a manageable rate.

This is in line with the Kraft quote as well: the Patriots would likely take an efficient rookie contract quarterback at 3% or at 1% like a Jimmy Garoppolo over an expensive vet who would cost 15% per year. When Brady says he intends on playing into his mid-forties, he and the Patriots know he's going to stay below 12% or even 10% of the cap if they can accomplish that, so the team can build a quality roster around him. In a Benjamin Button-esque transition, old Tom might be reverting to the kind of role he had as a kid on those first three champions, less focused on him carrying the team, more focused on him being an accurate quarterback who doesn't turn the ball over with a great defense. He may still continue to be the best or one of the best quarterbacks in the NFL into his forties, but he and the Patriots acknowledge the decline is likely and they acknowledge the impact that a lower cap hit can have on their ability to win a championship. They also understand that the less money Brady makes, the more they can spend on the players around him to increase his production and efficiency.

In baseball, while the entire MLB was focused on on-base percentage after the Oakland Athletics' popularized it with *Moneyball* and the Red Sox won their first World Series since 1918 in 2004 while leading the majors reaching base on 36% of all plate appearances, the small market Tampa Bay Rays found a lower-cost way to increase their ability to win. According to Jonah Keri in his book, *The Extra 2%: How Wall Street Strategies Took a Major League Baseball Team from Worst to First*, the Rays General Manager at the time, Andrew Friedman, would later say, "we certainly appreciated how defense and pitching were intertwined," but Keri writes that, in the league-wide "rush to acquire on-base machines," defense had been pushed aside. Teams were even overvaluing on-base percentage producers who were terrible in the field without realizing that the value created at the plate was being given back in the field.[3]

This parallels the New Orleans Saints in recent years. As mentioned previously, it might not matter if Drew Brees leads the league in passing yards like he did from 2014 through 2016 at an average cap hit of 13.85%, peaking at 16.61% in 2015; the Saints have gone 7-9 each year with the offense averaging 26.6 points per game with a defense surrendering 28.2 per game over that time. You can't win just based on your offense if you're incompetent on defense.

In 2007, according to Jonah Keri's *The Extra 2%*, Tampa Bay converted just 65.6% of balls in play into outs, which means that opponents hit a stratospheric .344 when putting the ball in play against the Rays pitching. In 2008, they went from the bottom of these defensive efficiency charts to the very top turning 72.3% of balls in play into outs, which means opponents' average sank to .277. According to the plus/minus system used by John Dewan in The Fielding Bible, he suggests, "the change in the Rays fielding was responsible for an 85-run swing, an improvement worth about eight to nine wins." The 2008 team improved from being the worst defense in the majors the year before, to the fourth best in the American League and they made it to the World Series because of it. Thanks to defense and improved pitching, they allowed 273 fewer runs, leading to a 31-win improvement, while their World Series offense scored eight less runs than the year before.

With the focus on defense, they were able to make a few low-cost acquisitions, which was the only way to compete because of their inability to spend as much money as their competition. According to ESPN, the 2008 Yankees led the MLB with a payroll of just over $209 million, while the Rays were second to last at $43.8 million. The Rays still had some good hitters like Carl Crawford and Evan Longoria, both of whom they signed to lower than market rate deals by extending them early in their career before they became superstars (something NFL teams could do more easily if they make a change in the next CBA), but they focused on small moves on defense to make this huge defensive improvement. They traded outfielder Delmon Young and shortstop Brandon Harris, two poor fielders, plus minor league outfielder Jason Pridie to the Twins for a good young pitcher in Matt Garza, slick-fielding shortstop Jason Bartlett, and minor league pitcher Eduardo Morlan.

The Rays made two small adjustments moving Akinori Iwamura from third base to second, letting Longoria take over the position, and putting Melvin Upton in centerfield full-time. Their entire defense was improved by these moves, from the infield to the outfield, which led to the huge improvement in defensive efficiency. All done with small, intelligent investments, similar to the way smart investments on an NFL defense, while not over investing in the passing game, can lead to a different potential strategy for success. Defense isn't currently being severely undervalued in the NFL to the extent that it had been in the mid-2000s in the MLB, but teams can exploit some low-cost markets and inefficiencies to make similar smaller moves for big improvements. Pro Football Focus' metrics also represent a new wave of statistical analysis like what was happening in baseball, so teams that take advantage of these metrics in their earliest stages will gain the most value like the Rays did.

A good philosophy to take from this is: where can you invest that will still accomplish the objective of victory and cost the least amount of money? What's the offensive and defensive production balance you need? What's the production formula you're shooting for? Then, how can you invest and balance your spending on each side of the ball to accomplish a balance of offensive and defensive production that can still achieve victory?

A key point in this is how defensive pressure can be used to decrease the performance of the opponent's quarterback to a level that their lesser quarterback and their offense can outperform their opponent. This is a big reason why teams need to invest the right amount of money in their quarterback, so they have as much cap space as possible to achieve this balance if they don't have an elite quarterback.

Maybe a team can look at Super Bowl champions who've won with a defense focused championship formula at ask what was their offensive and defensive production? How did they invest to achieve this? What made their defense great? What kind of players did they have? Did they have a great rushing offense? The Super Bowl winner's regular season stats in the appendix provide a small glimpse of the kind of exercise teams could do to look at production on both sides to achieve a balance.

Brady was the Patriots' highest cap charge, but they also avoided the first tier of the defensive end and cornerback market even while producing a defense that was first in the NFL, giving up just 15.6 points per game, breaking the Seahawks four-year run leading the NFL. They instead used those cap hits over three percent on 11 high-quality players at mostly pass-game focused positions on offense and a defensive focus with the 13 more above average NFL players right behind them making over one percent of the cap with those two dead cap hits. Twenty-five players was enough for them to build most of the offense and defense, plus a kicker, punter, and special teams All-Pro before getting into their post first round rookie contract players and low-cost veteran contributors.

The defensive side of the ball has two expensive markets: the pass rusher, which is typically an edge rusher, and the cornerback. But according to Super Bowl data, and including Aaron Smith's 5.98% cap hit in 2005 for Pittsburgh, 15 championship winning pass rushers cost six percent of the cap or more, which denotes the top tier for these expensive defensive markets. Part of the reason for there have been 15 rushers is that the group includes defensive ends, outside linebackers and defensive tackles together with the group having nine, three, and three of each respectively, but the goal is the same for each of these investments: to create quarterback pressure that can have a huge impact on the quarterback's performance, maybe more so than anything else a defense can do.

A great pass rush can decrease your opponent's passing efficiency, which can become especially important if a team decides to use a lower-tier quarterback strategy and attempt to decrease their opponents' efficiency to a level where their quarterback can outperform the other team's top tier star on that day. As Sam Monson wrote for Pro Football Focus in an article ranking the 15 best edge rushers of 2016, "sacks are important, but they represent an extremely small percentage of passing plays. Simply applying pressure to quarterbacks this past season dropped their passer rating from 96.7 to just 62.5 (league-wide averages)—or the equivalent of turning Derek Carr into Jared Goff in 2016. Players that generate a lot of pressure are having a huge impact on the game, whether they get home or not, and those that generate comparatively little pressure won't necessarily be saved by a high sack total."[4] (For those of you reading this in the future if Goff becomes a star under new head coach Sean McVay, which seems like a likely possibility with his substantial improvement in 2017 so far, Carr was an MVP candidate in 2016, while Goff completed 54.6% of his passes for 155.6 yards per game on the way to an 0-7 record as the #1 pick for a Los Angeles Rams offense that ran as smoothly as a Ford Pinto under former head coach Jeff Fisher.) On top of generally bothering the quarterback with a defender in his face, pressure disrupts the timing of the offense and timing is very important in today's NFL. It's the difference between hitting an open receiver in a window or not.

Of the seven Super Bowl winning teams with first tier quarterbacks, five of those teams had first tier rushers as well, with the 2015 Broncos having Von Miller and Demarcus Ware both in the first tier. If teams are going to invest top tier money in two players, it seems like a smart idea to invest in a quarterback and a pass rusher with the duality of having elite quarterback production and someone on the defense with the ability to decrease your opponent's efficiency at the position. While the elite cornerback shuts down a team's number one receiver all game or for a play, a great rush can shut down the opponent at the source by disrupting the quarterback, their passing offense and, in turn, their offense. Disrupting the play at the source may have more of an impact. Elite pass rushers force the offensive line to focus their attention on stopping him, which can result in forcing double teams to create more one-on-one and advantageous match-ups for the other defensive linemen.

The pass rush led by Miller and Ware caused Cam Newton, the NFL's MVP for that season, to complete just 43.9% of his passes and help the Broncos earn the victory with a diminished Peyton Manning under center in the final game of his career passing for just 141 yards himself. Their's was an example of the potential impact of the pass rush to help a team win without great quarterback play: the potential for diminishing your opponent's offensive performance to the point where a team with an average offense and decent rushing attack can control the pace of the game and win a low-scoring game. The Panthers had 121 more offensive yards, but Denver's defense created two more turnovers and had seven sacks. Investing first tier money on quarterbacks and pass rushers can be an effective strategy in diminishing your opponent's quarterback's performance, while maintaining a high level of performance out of your own quarterback.

Monson ranked Philadelphia's Brandon Graham as the second best edge rusher of 2016 despite only having six sacks on the year because he had 83 total pressures over the course of the season, which was the third most in the NFL behind the Raiders' Khalil Mack with 96 and Olivier Vernon with 86 for the Giants. Total pressures include quarterback hurries, hits, knockdowns and sacks.

Atlanta's Vic Beasley had 16 sacks to lead the NFL, but only had 56 pressures, so he was left off the list. Graham generated pressure once every 5.8 pass rushing snaps, which was second in the NFL behind Mack at 6.0, and far better than Beasley's rate of creating pressure once every 10.4 pass-rushing attempts. While Beasley would have a big play, Graham would have big games. Mason writes "you can point to multiple games over the season where his [Graham's] pressure led to poor quarterback performances. In Week 16, Graham didn't get a sack on Giants quarterback Eli Manning, but he knocked him to the ground four times and hurried him another five. Manning's passer rating for the game was just 61.3 and a dismal 10.7 when pressured." Graham affected Manning on nine of 63 passes. With Beasley, Monson notes that he converted pressure into sacks at a rate of 28.6%, which is far above the league average of a 15.1% rate for edge rushers and due to his sacks often being "a result of clean-up players or scenarios where Beasley was unblocked." Beasley is growing as a player and will probably be a star, but many of his best games came against weak tackles. In Super Bowl 51 against Marcus Cannon, Beasley rushed the passer 54 times and only got pressure on Brady twice.

When it comes to top tier defensive investments, a good principle to follow would be to keep the cap allocated to the top two players on your roster between fifteen and eighteen percent of the salary cap. Defensive end seems that it would be the choice, but for Belichick, he's been able to avoid top of market guys by focusing on "winning stat guys" who might produce the same total pressures as a player like Beasley at 56, but for less money due to a lower sack total and a lesser perception of the player league-wide. Over his tenure, the winning stat guys that the Patriots have looked for are players who produce pressure over high sack guys with the knowledge that pressure decreased quarterback performance and was a more cumulative statistic than sacks. Also with the knowledge that consistent pressure becomes sacks due to the consistency of that pressure breaking through for sacks. While other teams might invest in expensive, high sack total guys in free agency or draft them in the first round, thus extending them to similarly expensive contracts, Belichick has been finding pressure producers at a lower cost and is able to afford two, three or four of them for a cap cost of one big name, high sack guy. Like targeting the objective of moving the chains on offense, focusing on pressure and shrinking the quarterback's window to make a decision and throw is the objective to focus on with defense as it produces the desired outcome at a better cost and, if done well, more efficiently.

The early-2000s Patriots teams were built on defense and Belichick stayed pretty true to a top of cap formula that landed in that 15 to 19% percent range. Of the 22 salary capped champions of the salary cap era, 12 were in this range of the salary cap and that seems to be a good target for offensive and defensive balance. Staying in this range is possible to maintain if the quarterback cap hit doesn't fly past ten or eleven percent of the cap and is combined with even an edge rusher or cornerback around a reasonable number like seven to seven and a half percent. Even if you have an Aaron Rodgers type of quarterback at 13 percent, an edge rusher at six percent means you're just at nineteen. A team can go outside of these numbers dependent on the quality of the players they can get at these higher numbers, but the range is a range most teams should be using as a reference to maintain the ability to create balance on the roster.

In 2001, Bledsoe had a cap hit of 10.36% with Ty Law second at 7.74%. This was the most expensive of all Patriots champions at 18.10%. Once Brady became the starter, the next two champions had lower cap hits at quarterback at 4.43% and 6.28%, which then saw Law's cost bump to 11.74% and 12.62% in those two seasons. The Patriots took advantage of having a less expensive quarterback to compensate their best defensive player, which is a strategy teams should be implementing when they have a low-cost quarterback. With Peyton retiring after Super Bowl 50, the Broncos went low-cost at quarterback and Von Miller became their big, expensive cap hit in this same manner.

A 30-year old Willie McGinest cost 6.47% of the 2001 Patriots' cap, while consuming 2.64% and 4.55% during the next two Super Bowl seasons as he was signed to a new contract in 2003 that took into account him being past his prime years and paying for who he is as a player at that age rather than who he was.

Even so, he was released prior to the 2006 season for salary cap reasons. Through Brady's prime years of the late-2000s, the Patriots were able to maintain a nice balance with Richard Seymour providing high production at reasonable cap hits for an All-Pro rusher at 6.86% in 2006, 5.78% in 2007 and 5.89% in 2008 with a dead money hit of 4.88% in 2009 after he was traded to the Raiders for a first-round pick in the 2011 draft, which they turned into long-time starting left tackle Nate Solder. Once Randy Moss reached a high-price, with an uncharacteristically high (for the Patriots) 8.54% in 2009, wide receiver wasn't a place where the team could rely on low-cost value, so the team had to move on from Seymour and actually undergo a slight, small rebuild that wasn't actually a rebuild as they still made the Super Bowl at the end of the 2011 season. They traded Moss back to Minnesota during the 2010 season for a third-round pick that turned into Ryan Mallett. Moss averaged just 24.6 yards per game over the last 28 games of his career. This is something smart organizations do: trade a player before the player's trade value is lost and before the decline. Whenever a player's cost exceeds perceived value, Belichick seems to be able to get rid of them for future value. While they traded a fourth round pick to Oakland for Moss during a 2007 offseason where he turned 30, they traded Moss with a seventh round pick in 2012 to the Vikings for the upcoming 2011 draft during the 2010 season.

A February 2015 article I wrote for Over The Cap that compared Peyton Manning and Tom Brady's cap hits helped confirm the importance of salary cap hits for me as Manning's Colts teams always seemed to have average to below average defenses, while Brady seemed to always be a part of a more complete team. With Brady having four Super Bowls and Manning's one up to that point, the conversation regarding who was better revolved around Super Bowls, but, I feel, didn't properly acknowledge the quality and make-up of Brady's first three Super Bowl teams. My research for Over The Cap to that point showed me three teams with special teams, defensive units and running backs that helped Brady earn those championships, while Manning's teams always seemed to be in high-scoring shootouts. Even during both of their prime years, once Brady was off that sixth round rookie contract and the third tier extension that followed it, Manning's average cap hit from 2005 to 2014 was 12.97%, while Brady's was 10.51%, so that leaves at least enough room to afford a solid player worth two percent of the cap. As an example, the versatile and valuable safety Patrick Chung cost New England 2.05% of the 2016 salary cap. Over the course of Manning's career from 1998 to 2015, his defenses allowed an average of 21.6 points per game with an average points allowed ranking of 15th in the NFL, while Brady's defenses averaged three less points per game from 2001 through 2016 and an average points allowed ranking of 7.7. Coincidentally, the Patriots also lead the league in winning percentage in three point games during this time, which will be discussed in chapter nine.

Brady's cap hits from 2006 through 2011, which was the highest earning block of his career from age 29 through 34, were 13.55%, a low 6.73% during their perfect regular season of 2007, then 12.60% in 2008, 11.89% in 2009, and 11.00% in 2011, the three capped years. During the uncapped 2010 season, he had a cap hit of $17.42 million likely so the Patriots could reward him during a season where it wouldn't affect their ability to field a complete team as that would have been 14.52% of a $120 million cap. Brady cost 6.63% during a restructure year in 2012, then two more years over 11% of the cap before sinking under ten, which they might try to maintain through the rest of his career with a restructure after the 2017 season.

The Patriots still made the Super Bowl in 2011, but their defense was 15th in points allowed and 31st in yards allowed. Those are uncharacteristically bad numbers for the Patriots, but may have a side effect of some of the higher expenses on the offensive side of the ball leading into 2011, which caused them to go with veteran bargain finds at pass rusher for a few years. By 2011, they actually hit on free agent acquisitions Andre Carter and Mark Anderson getting 10 sacks a piece, but in the 2012 draft they selected two players who were the foundation of the 2014 Super Bowl defense and a result of the Seymour trade.

As Tom E. Curran detailed for CSN New England, with Solder drafted with Oakland's first round pick in 2011, which they had acquired by trading Richard Seymour, the Patriots were then able to trade their first rounder, the 28th pick, to the Saints for their first round pick in 2012 and the #56 pick in 2011, a second rounder. The Saints drafted Mark Ingram with the pick they received and the Patriots drafted running back Shane Vereen at 56.[5]

The Saints pick ended up being the 27th overall in the 2012 draft after losing to the 49ers in the 2011 NFC Divisional Round, so New England had #27 and #31 after coming up short in the Super Bowl. The Patriots traded with Cincinnati to move up to #21 by trading the #27 and #93 pick in the third round, which allowed them to draft Chandler Jones. They then packaged #31 with a fourth round pick to move up six spots in the first round and draft Dont'a Hightower at #25 overall. They drafted safety Tavon Wilson with the 48th pick in the second round, then defensive end Jake Bequette with the 90th pick in the third round. Special Teams ace Nate Ebner was drafted in the sixth round of this draft as well.

Belichick was looking to build the defense to complement an offense where they'd reverted back to saving money in the passing game through lower cost receivers, which culminated in the valuable receiver groups that led the 2014 and 2016 teams. With Jones, they saw a player who could contribute at a high level right away at a low-cost with the slotted contract that the #21 pick received. Jones cost just 1.68% of the cap during the Patriots 2014 season and he'd already blossomed into one of the top twenty defensive ends in the league, production that would cost far more on the market. Once it became time for his price to increase to the market costs for the positions, the Patriots traded him away to a Cardinals team that has become heavily loaded with older veteran contracts and very little cap flexibility. Jones signed an extension with the Cardinals that will pay him first tier rates and peak just over 10% of the 2019 salary cap, which will hopefully be supplemented with a low-cost rookie contract quarterback for their organization's sake.

When you feel like you can acquire a game breaking immediate star like Jones through the draft and you need immediate help at the position he plays now, on a team with the potential to compete for a championship, second contract costs don't matter as much. A team can reap the rewards of his high performance in the short term, then deal with trading him or re-signing him to a big money deal later if they decide to do so.

With Hightower, the Patriots got an inside linebacker who they were able to re-sign during the 2017 offseason to a contract that caps around five and a half percent of the cap for a player who's one of the most versatile and vital pieces of the Patriots' nickel base defense as a sideline to sideline tackler who can also cover running backs and tight ends in the passing game.

Being a hugely impactful role on the passing game, the first tier for elite pass rushers at defensive end, 3-4 outside linebacker, and on the interior of the defensive line costs between six and nine percent of the cap. Super Bowl champion data supports spending first tier money with 15 in this group and 15 quarterbacks over six percent themselves. As mentioned earlier, the 2015 Broncos had Miller and Ware both in the first tier at 6.81% and 6.05%, so the strategy can even work with two top tier players performing at the elite level they're being paid.

The Patriots made sure they were prepared to move Jones when the time came as the 2016 Patriots had second tier defensive ends in Jabaal Sheard (4.39%) and Rob Ninkovich (3.06%), Chris Long on a third tier, one-year contract (1.53%), plus 2015 fourth-rounder Trey Flowers (0.43%). According to Scott Barrett at Pro Football Focus, the Patriots were 20th in the NFL in sacks with 33, 1.9 sacks below the league average of 34.9 and 26th in hits with 44, which was 4.3 below the league average, but they were sixth in the NFL with 172 hurries, which was 15 more than the league average. (Pro Football Reference has the 2016 Patriots with 34 sacks as Pro Football Focus accounts some sacks to the quarterback, which accounts for the accounting difference.) They had 249 total pressures on the season, which comes out to 15.5 per game. Quarterbacks dropped back to pass 39.4 times per game against New England, so they generated pressure on just under 40% of their opponent's passing attempts with those 15.5 pressures per game. They've placed importance on the right value stat, rather than the most expensive stat. By comparison, Warren Sapp is the most expensive defensive line cap charge on a champion at 9.82% and Calais Campbell of the Cardinals led the NFL in 2016 at the same number. For edge rushers, Terrell Suggs represents the highest Super Bowl charge at 9.55% in 2012, while Reggie White is the most expensive defensive end at 8.90% in 1996.

The Pro Football Focus' stats for defensive linemen that should be most focused on are pass rush productivity and run stop percentage. Pass rush productivity (PRP) is "how many times a player picks up a sack, hit, or hurry (with hits and hurries valued at three-quarters the worth of sacks) and turns that number into the pass rush productivity rating by dividing by the number of pass rushes and multiplying that by 100," which provides a value finding stat for pass rushers.[6] Looking at pass rush productivity in 2016, 33 edge defenders had a PRP over 10, while only two interior defenders were over ten in Aaron Donald and Geno Atkins, which might be what has driven the cost of the top of the interior of the line up recently. Since less interior defenders can produce elite PRP, then the scarcity can drive up the price of those who can as with the Ndamukong Suh contract, which is excessive with projected cap hits around 14.5% in 2018 and 2019. Khalil Mack led all edge defenders with a PRP of 15, while Donald had a PRP rating of 12.6.

Run stop percentage uses Pro Football Focus' "unique data of how many times a player was in run defense and the percentage of those plays he made a defensive stop," which provides a value finding stat for run stoppers whether on the interior or edge, then also at linebacker and safety as well. In looking at the interior of the Patriots line, we see that Vince Wilfork left after the 2014 season for a second tier contract at nose tackle in Houston and the 2016 team instead had a third tier free agent tackle in Alan Branch at 1.77% and 2015 first-round pick Malcom Brown at 1.11%. Branch and Brown were third and fourth in the NFL in 2016 with run-stop percentages of 11.2% and 11.0%, which illustrates the emphasis Belichick's system puts on a low-cost, valuable role in the run game.

Belichick had three low-cost linebackers whom he used to replace 2014 star defender Jamie Collins, who Belichick traded to the Browns midseason for a future mid-round draft pick, which ended up being a third round compensatory pick they traded with their first round pick to New Orleans for Brandin Cooks. If they have the players to replace them and they find they can't re-sign a player, the Patriots trade them to recoup some value rather than simply letting them walk in free agency. The linebackers who replace Collins were Shea McClellin (1.44%), whom they signed from the Bears, Elandon Roberts (0.31%), whom they drafted in the sixth round of the 2016 draft, and Kyle Van Noy (0.29%), whom they acquired from the Lions in a trade less than a week after dealing Collins, taking over the job. Star inside linebacker Dont'a Hightower (4.99%), who we'll get to later, and 2016 third-round pick at defensive tackle, Vincent Valentine (0.39%), rounded out the front seven. The early-2000s Patriots Super Bowl teams used a similar low-cost approach with free agents like Bobby Hamilton, Anthony Pleasant, and Ted Washington, young draft picks like Richard Seymour, Ty Warren, and Vince Wilfork, plus a more expensive, but manageable edge rusher cap hits for the versatile Willie McGinest.

While an elite pass rusher can be a positive investment, paying players near ten percent of the cap at an explosive and violent position is an issue. Along with the risk of injury, teams need to have a rotation of players to keep their legs fresh for pass rush situations and the fourth quarter, so they need multiple good rushers. Von Miller is undoubtedly one of the most impactful and valuable players in the NFL—he's making almost 12% of the 2017 salary cap of $167 million—but he was only able to play 81.18% of their defensive snaps in 2016 according to Pro Football Reference. The lower-snap total is part of the nature of the position. The Giants big 2016 free agent signing, Olivier Vernon was a bit of an outlier playing 93.69% of their snaps and Monson points out that, while he had a great season as PFF's 13th best edge rusher for 2016, maybe he could have even been more impactful in the passing game on a per snap basis if he got the in-game breathers that most edge rushers get. The position is one explosive movement after another on every snap, one violent collision with your counterpart on the offensive line after another, so playing 1,112 snaps, 69.5 per game, like Vernon did is a large and difficult workload. Alternatively, the best cornerbacks can play over 95% and near 99% of snaps if healthy.

New England doesn't just want to find value because of the high costs of rushers and Belichick's ability to find value in pressure producers, they also do this because they need multiple quality defensive linemen and rushers over having one elite rusher who now has to play 90% of your snaps because he costs 10% of the cap. This is Jonathan Kraft's concept: their organization is looking for the value of a quality defensive line over the course of the game rather than any one player, especially considering that any pass rusher has some likelihood of being hurt. The league should invest in elite pass rushers, but that investment shouldn't get near double digits for players who teams likely want playing seventy-five to eighty percent of snaps. Belichick looks to maximize the unit's performance on those snaps and keep their legs fresh in the fourth quarter against offensive linemen who have played all game. In 2015, Chandler Jones played 78.85% of defensive snaps, while Rob Ninkovich played 81.32%; they decided they wanted to a more balanced spread of snap counts in 2016, which they accomplished. With the six defensive linemen playing between 44.30% and 64.91% of defensive snaps. This strategy can also provide a variety of types of rushers to provide advantages in specific weekly match-ups.

As with teams weighing a small sample size like sacks too heavily, teams are also over-investing in what they believe happens on third down versus what happens on first and second down to create third down and long situations with the highest potential for quarterback pressures that force incompletions and sacks that stop drives. The league may be over investing in the sack statistic, rather than the process that creates higher probabilities of sacks and disrupting the quarterback.

Belichick wants quarterback pressures, but he's recently invested first round picks in positions outside of the norm of what would be considered the most important positions and markets according to how the league spends. The way that defenses work together to create the objective of stopping drives requires the ability to stop the plays that come in every situation. One major way to succeed as a defense in this passing era is to get offenses behind the sticks for third and long situations to force the quarterback into deeper drops. Getting pressure or a sack is a math problem: if a defense can get an offense into a situation where the quarterback has to take more than three seconds to throw on a pass from the pocket, a larger number of NFL rushers can get to him in that time. These things work together as a fresh set of legs may increase the likelihood of winning that math problem.

The other high priced market is a cornerback market that has been driven in recent years by Darrelle Revis' monstrous market setting deals set up by the leverage he and his agent were able to create that started with former New York Jets General Manager Mike Tannenbaum ripping up Revis' first-round rookie deal for a four-year, $46 million contract to end a training camp holdout before the 2010 season. As Bill Barnwell pointed out in an April 2013 Grantland article after the Jets traded Revis to the Buccaneers, this deal made his trade an inevitability as the four-year deal would have also set Revis up for another big deal before he hit 30 years old. After getting traded to Tampa Bay, he signed a six-year, $96 million contract that led to a 2013 cap hit of $16 million for Revis, an even 13% of the cap, which was $1 million more than Cortland Finnegan's $15 million with the Rams during an outlier season between a cap hit of $6 million in 2012 and $10 million in 2014, but $4.75 million higher than Jonathan Joseph's at number three. By 2016, his second season back in New York, his $17 million cap hit was over $2.2 million higher than Richard Sherman's cap hit, which was number two.

Five Super Bowl cornerbacks consumed over six percent of the cap in the first tier of the cornerback market and three of those cap hits were Ty Law with the Patriots with two of those cap hits being the ones over ten percent in the years where Brady was at a low cost. Outside of those two, the three highest cap hits for cornerbacks were Law's 7.47% in 2001, then Corey Webster at 6.54% for the 2011 Giants and Deion Sanders at 5.98% in 1995, which we can round up to six; so the first tier should be lower and less utilized than it is today with Revis at

10.95% and Sherman at 9.51% in 2016.

Every position's first tier should be reserved for the elite, so first tier pass rushers should be the elite pressure producers who produce 60 to 65 plus total pressures over the course of a 16-game season, which comes out to at least four pressures per game. Having one of these kinds of pressure producers with a few more marginal rushers, or creating a group of multiple players with pressure totals of say 25 to 40 plus each, can create a defensive front with the potential to harass quarterbacks all season. According to Pro Football Focus' Signature Stats, edge rushers Chris Long led the 2016 Patriots with 57 pressures, 17th in the NFL for edge rushers, Jabaal Sheard had 39, and Trey Flowers had 35. Interior defender Malcolm Brown had 26 and fellow defensive tackle Alan Branch had 17 while linebacker Dont'a Hightower had 21 himself as these six led a defense that was able to create consistent pressure all season. If a team has 11 or 12 drives per game, then producing pressure on a large chunk of those third down passing situations begins to decrease your opponent's chance on some number of those drives. Elite cornerbacks are the type who can be relied on to shut one side of the field off from your opponent, shutting down their number one receiver. With depth in the defensive back unit, this also allows your defensive coordinator to play man-to-man against anyone he faces with no need to double team or play zone.

To determine if a cornerback is one of those elite players, Pro Football Focus has two statistics worth analyzing in passer rating against and yards per coverage snap. According to NFL.com, in 2016, 32 quarterbacks had over 200 passing attempts and below are the passer rating for this group:

2016 Passer Rating of QBs with Over 200 Attempts

	Team	Player	QB Rating
1	Falcons	Matt Ryan	117.1
2	Patriots	Tom Brady	112.2
3	Cowboys	Dak Prescott	104.9
4	Packers	Aaron Rodgers	104.2
5	Saints	Drew Brees	101.7
6	Vikings	Sam Bradford	99.3
7	Redskins	Kirk Cousins	97.2
8	Raiders	Derek Carr	96.7
9	Colts	Andrew Luck	96.4
10	Titans	Marcus Mariota	95.6
11	Steelers	Ben Roethlisberger	95.4
12	Dolphins	Ryan Tannehill	93.5
13	Lions	Matt Stafford	93.3
14	Seahawks	Russell Wilson	92.6
15	Bengals	Andy Dalton	91.8

16	Chiefs	Alex Smith	91.2
17	49ers	Colin Kaepernick	90.7
18	Bills	Tyrod Taylor	89.7
19	Chargers	Phillip Rivers	87.9
20	Cardinals	Carson Palmer	87.2
21	Buccaneers	Jameis Winston	86.1
22	Giants	Eli Manning	86.0
23	Broncos	Trevor Siemian	84.6
24	Ravens	Joe Flacco	83.5
25	Eagles	Carson Wentz	79.3
26	Jaguars	Blake Bortles	78.8
27	Rams	Case Keenum	76.4
28	Panthers	Cam Newton	75.8
29	Texans	Brock Osweiler	72.2
30	Jets	Ryan Fitzpatrick	69.6
31	Bears	Matt Barkley	68.3
32	Rams	Jared Goff	63.6

Looking at passer rating against, in 2016 22 of 79 qualified cornerbacks held quarterbacks under a rating of 80.7 and 11 kept quarterbacks under 70.6. Using that list, those 22 cornerbacks were able to decrease quarterback performance on passes thrown their way to the bottom eight quarterbacks, while the 11 top corners turned quarterbacks into Ryan Fitzpatrick, Matt Barkley and Jared Goff, a very valuable role that produces that ability to shut down a half of the field. Minnesota's Xavier Rhodes had the best passer rating against with a 47.0, while Stephon Gilmore's, who had that 11th best rating of 70.6, was 20 points better than Logan Ryan's 90.6 might have been what inspired Belichick to spend a little more on Gilmore rather than re-sign Ryan.

Yards per coverage snap takes the total receiving yards given up and divides that number by the amount of coverage snaps a player is engaged in. The ageless 38-year old Terence Newman led the NFL giving up just 0.57 yards per coverage snap, while 12 cornerbacks gave up less than 0.9 yards per coverage snap and 22 who gave up less than 1.0 per coverage snap. The 10 to 20 cornerbacks who reach the peak performance of this position constitute the elite tier of this market, which are players who a team can afford to pay over five or six percent of the cap.

Elite pass rushing and coverage skills are both roles of vital importance, the ability to generate pressure and shut down, or more likely merely contain, a Julio Jones or Antonio Brown level receiver is very important, but it has to be done at the right price. Investing heavily in one top tier cornerback can mean nothing if the rest of the coverage group is weak because of a lack of investment in the other cover guys. With the emphasis on offense to create one-on-one match-ups they can take advantage of, teams need at least three competent cornerbacks to cover wide and slot receivers as well as safeties and linebackers who can cover tight ends and running backs. Shutting down one player with a top cornerback won't be enough against teams with a deep group of pass catchers.

Creating consistent pressure becomes harder if an offense is frequently in third and short situations because you can't stop the run or quick passing attack on first and second down. The need to create advantageous third down situations illustrates the importance of the entire defensive unit. The offense is trying to create high percentage situations and opportunities for themselves, while defenses try to decrease the offense's chances of success with each play. Successful defensive units need great players, but, more importantly, they need to have a complete unit as an offensive coordinator has all offseason and then all game week to create a strategy to exploit any weakness. In baseball, if a batter can't hit off-speed pitches, then a pitcher is going to throw him off-speed pitches. Offensive coordinators can exploit a weakness all game, not just for an at-bat.

Belichick seems to have settled on a strategy of avoiding high expenses in expensive markets and pushing for versatility as he was still able to build a defense that ranked first in points allowed during the 2016 regular season despite trading away two of their biggest playmakers from the 2014 and 2015 season, Jones and Collins, because of the impending high costs of their coming second contracts. During the 2016 offseason, Belichick went to free agency to add former Bills' cornerback Stephon Gilmore to a contract that is projected to pay him almost exactly seven percent of the cap in the final four years of a five-year deal that carries him through his 31-year old season. This move, along with Super Bowl data for the pass rusher and cornerback markets, reaffirmed my belief that these top tiers of the defensive market should cap out at seven to seven and a half percent for teams that have a quarterback in the top tier, while teams relying on quarterbacks on rookie contracts or in the lower three tiers can bump those earnings up near ten percent, or even past if loading money into a single year to take advantage of a low-cost quarterback year, to fortify a defense that presumably isn't relying on one of the league's best quarterbacks.

The 2016 Patriots focused on the right stats to produce value on the edge. They created value at cornerback through hitting on elite rookie contract players in Malcolm Butler and Logan Ryan. So Gilmore replaced a departed Ryan, who earned a three-year, $30 million contract with Tennessee and caps just over six percent in 2018, while Gilmore signed a five-year deal worth $65 million that will pay him around seven percent of the cap from 2018 through 2021. As explained by Mike Rodak of ESPN, the Bills then used the money they would have spent on Gilmore to fortify their entire defensive backfield by signing safeties Micah Hyde and Jordan Poyer, drafting cornerback Tre'Davious White in the first round of the

2017 draft, and trading for E.J. Gaines from the Rams. This was a very Moneyball-esque way of thinking as those four players cost about $10 million against the cap, which is only slightly more than Gilmore's cap hit of $8,568,750 in 2017. Gaines will be a free agent after 2017, but the other three Bills defensive backs will cost an average of $12.84 million compared to Gilmore's average of $13.6 million from 2018 through 2020.[7] While the Patriots get a first tier quarterback averaging 7.04% of the cap during that time, the Bills have three players averaging 6.65%. This is a great example of Kraft's Player A/Player B scenario being played out by the Bills.

Long and Sheard departed and were replaced with another set of players intended to be value finds that was headlined by Kony Ealy, who is best known for three sacks and an interception against Denver in Super Bowl 50 for Carolina, signing for under a million, but he was released prior to the season even after 2017 third round pick Derek Rivers tore his ACL. Their fourth round pick out of Arkansas, Deatrich Wise, Jr. will be someone they rely on who made it easier to release Ealy. They traded fifth and seventh round picks in 2018 to Seattle for defensive end and special teamer Cassius Marsh. Interestingly, the seventh round pick that Seattle received was actually the same seventh round pick they had sent to New England a day earlier for cornerback Justin Coleman.

They created the value in the expensive markets in 2016 and combined them with elite players in low-cost markets like great run defenders and competent pressure producers on the interior of the defensive line. Alan Branch had a 2016 PFF pass rush grade of 50.7, but his run defense rating graded ninth at 83.0 and Brown had a similar season himself as the 15th best interior run defender while both had elite run stop percentages. Where those two were average for their position in producing pressure, linebacker Dont'a Hightower provided PFF's best pass rushing grade for all non-edge defending linebackers at 76.0. He had the highest pass rush percentage in this linebacker group and was third with his 21 total quarterback pressures behind Bobby Wagner and Lawrence Timmons. Brown's 26 pressures had him ranked 31st for interior defenders, while Branch's 17 had him ranked 41st. Interestingly, Hightower likely provides a different kind of pressure than the rushers on the interior of the line like Campbell who can cost near ten percent and with the added athleticism and quickness of a linebacker that can get to quarterbacks very quickly. Combined with the four productive edge rushers, the Patriots had multiple potential pressure producers on the field for every third down and they did it at a reasonable price that allowed them to create value.

Like edge rushers, the first tier of the cornerback market is from six to nine percent with the top half of these tiers being reserved for teams without a first tier quarterback. Certain players can be exceptions to these rules and cost more or duos who could cost more, but generally speaking, teams across the league need to take a more Belichickian approach to spending and stop paying players a value that they can not perform at. Too many alternative-spending strategies could produce better results through more versatility than paying players more than they could likely be worth to your organization on contracts that could diminish your ability to win.

At cornerback, Belichick seems to look for a prototype around 5'11", 190-pounds, which may be done for positional versatility as these athletes have enough height to cover the bigger receivers with the quickness and speed to cover the variety of number one receivers in the league. Across the defensive backfield, an understanding of the body type match-ups needed throughout the season to cover the various mismatches that teams may create is important, so they can create a defense with players who have the skills to play man-to-man defense against their various opponents.

The second tier of the two expensive defensive markets are between three and six percent of the cap with the third tier between one and a half and three. Like at wide receiver, these markets provide value potential to help create the versatility across the defensive unit teams are looking for. The second tier includes high-quality players who just aren't at the same level as those in the first tier and, with the lack of actionable traditional statistics for the cornerback position, organizations with an eye for talent and system needs can find some players who represent that much less expensive, but similar quality of player example Kraft used back in 1994. The lack of actionable statistics is likely one of the factors driving the price of the cornerback market, so it takes a good eye and a lot of film study to find value in the market. With the various defensive and coverage schemes that NFL teams run, organizations must find cornerbacks who fit what they do. A team shouldn't sign a player who excelled in a base Cover 3 defense if they run a base Cover 2.

For second tier rushers, we're looking for pressure producers who don't have the sack totals or recognition for their consistent high level of play. These second tier rushers can be paired with multiple lower tier and rookie contract pressure producers to create consistent pressure. The second tier for defensive tackles and defensive ends is also a really great place to find a great run defender. Damon "Snacks" Harrison was signed by the Giants to a top of market deal for an interior run defender at $46.2 million over five-years, which is $9.24 million per year, and had $24 million in guarantees. His contract caps out at 6.35% of the cap in 2017 and spends the rest of the deal in the second tier; he was PFF's Best Run Defender in 2016, for the second straight year, by a long way with Sam Monson writing that "nobody is closer to making an award their own." He writes that Harrison has, up to this point, led the NFL in run stop percentage for the previous four seasons and his last two seasons have produced the highest run stop percentages they've ever recorded for a defensive tackle in their decade of grading.

Monson writes that Harrison "racked up 49 defensive stops in the run game this season, 10 more than any other defensive tackle. That mark tied the record for the most PFF has ever recorded for a defensive tackle, breaking a record he set himself in the year prior. His 15.8% run-stop percentage was 3.9% higher than Kawann Short at number two, then Branch and Brown were the only other two over 11%. Only eight other defensive tackles could even get within half of Harrison's defensive stops tally over the season, and he played fewer snaps against the run than many of them. In the past 10 years, the number of times a defensive tackle has posted more than 40 run stops in a season reads: rest of the NFL, one; Damon Harrison, two.

"There is simply no more disruptive force against the run than Damon Harrison, who is not only able to hold the point of attack and affect running lanes by moving blockers back, but actually shed those blocks and made stops in the hole himself, rather than simply open up opportunities for others to make the play."[8] As Monson points out, the Giants handed him a big-money contract for a run stopper because they recognized the transformative effect he could have on that defense. The 2016 Giants' rush defense was third in the NFL giving up 88.6 rush yards per game, a year after ranking 24th at 121.4 rush yards per game.

Even as the best run defender in the NFL in 2015, Harrison couldn't get a contract anywhere near what an interior lineman who can rush the passer receives, which is a part of a larger trend on defense: positions that affect the passing game are being inflated, while tackles or defensive stops, and the people who play the biggest part in creating them are being valued at a rate that creates an opportunity for coaches like Belichick who understand this with his investments in Branch and Brown on the interior of his defense, plus investments in tackling positions like linebacker and safety. Baseball teams want to be strong up the middle on defense with their catcher, shortstop, second baseman, and centerfielders being the best fielders on their defense. Belichick seems to use a similar philosophy in ensuring his team is stout up the middle. During the 2017 offseason, he went out and signed Lawrence Guy who had PFF's 24th best run defense rating for an interior defender on the Ravens in 2016 to a four-year deal that will cost them less than two percent of the cap through 2020. Guy has the versatility to play inside and outside, which likely helped make the decisions to release Ealy easier.

While Harrison got a deal that caps out just in the bottom of the top tier, Chandler Jones earned a five-year deal at $82.5 million, $16.5 million per year, in the 2017 offseason. He will earn $7.26 million more per year. Harrison was coming off of a 2015 season with the highest PFF grade against the run among all interior defenders at 97.3, while making a "defensive stop on 18.1 percent of all running plays he was on the field for, which is the best rate PFF has ever seen among defensive tackles, and over 150 percent of the best mark we had seen heading into this [2015] season," according to Monson in January 2016 describing Harrison's last season as a New York Jet.[9]

Jones is an elite edge rusher with a 2016 PFF pass rush grade of 86.5, which tied with Von Miller, 11 sacks and 66 total pressures, but the difference in cost of the two skills is huge. While stopping the pass is very important, Jones has a cap hit of $15.5 million in 2018, year two of his contract, which will cost 8.70% of the projected cap. His third year cap hit of $19.5 million will be over ten percent of that year's projected cap, but he will likely be paired with a low-cost quarterback as Arizona transitions away from the high cost of Carson Palmer to what will likely be a rookie contract play so it'll balance itself out. That said, you can see the example of the difference in cost.

The third tier includes veterans who may have a weakness, guys like Lawrence Guy who are elite against the run, but below average against the pass and have strengths that can be utilized by a defensive coordinator that puts him in situations where the defense as a unit can use his strengths to succeed. These can also be third contract, older players perceived to be on the downswing of their careers or coming off injury, like Chris Long was on both accounts, when New England signed him to a cap hit of 1.61% of the cap in 2016. He signed a deal with the Eagles in 2017, even after producing 57 pressures in 2017, that caps at 1.31% of the cap in 2018, albeit his 33-year old season. Even with his age, it seemed that the market undervalued a player with that many pressures. Relying on third-tier players to be more than they are isn't going to maximize his potential or your defense as a unit, which is another reason why the Patriots have a rotation for their defensive front.

Same with the cornerbacks: you're looking for guys with weaknesses, perception issues or a limited role. A clear number two cornerback, a veteran who can play in the slot on third down, a third contract player nearing the end of his career, or a formerly highly regarded player who needs to prove something coming off his rookie contract. In 2016, about 35 to 45 veterans were in the second and third tiers of each of the four markets we're concerned with here: defensive end, defensive tackle, 3-4 outside linebacker and cornerback. Add in the value potential in the draft and the value available here makes it possible to avoid a high top tier investment.

When a team does invest in a top tier player at one of these positions, they should then look to acquire players through the draft to balance out the costs of the high cost player or find value elsewhere on the roster because of the large investment in the defensive line, cornerback group or both. Looking in the later rounds of the draft is like looking for veterans in the same third and fourth tier, below one and a half percent of the cap, that the later round rookie contracts also populate; you're looking for players who aren't great at everything, who aren't elite pass rushers or might be slot cornerbacks. You try taking advantage of that skill set in hopes that he earns his way into a bigger role by developing into a more complete player, while using his strengths in a smaller role. As with any position, teams should also be looking for players who've dropped in the draft because of injury or some other circumstances that decrease their performance level like a new coach or being on a bad team that decreases their perceived value.

If successful in your draft selection, a first round pick leads to high second contract costs, as we see with Chandler Jones, which teams want to avoid in the long-term. The Patriots have displayed a strategy that they last utilized with Jones of keeping a player in town for as long as his costs are manageable for the cap construction they're trying to create, then trade him. With Jones, they got four cheap years from an elite defensive end, peaking at 1.81% of the cap in 2015, and then received a draft pick that they traded to turn into starting guard Joe Thuney and rotational wide receiver Malcolm Mitchell, two immediate needs. Trey Flowers stepped up with seven sacks, 35 pressures, and a 76.4 pass rushing grade in the 2015 fourth-rounder's first-year playing consistently, so he's helping replace Jones along with the other low-cost players the Patriots have at the position.

Most first round picks, especially those that the Patriots get with their annual drafting position near the end of the first round, exist around one to two percent of the cap throughout their contract with players at the top of the round going from one and a half to three percent of the cap in year one toward three to four percent in the later years. With their drafting near the end of the first round every year, the players they draft have lower contracts through four years and then a fifth-year team option that is the average of the third through 25th-highest salaries at the player's position. Using this as an opportunity since the new CBA, the Patriots have been drafting low-cost markets like linebacker and defensive tackle in the first rounds. Jones was a first rounder in 2011, but with his talent and the defensive end market reaching heights the Patriots were never going to be willing to pay a player, they traded him.

They drafted Devin McCourty as a cornerback and he made the Pro Bowl at the position as a rookie before transitioning to safety in 2012 when the Patriots traded to acquire Aqib Talib from the Buccaneers midway through the year. (Talib cost 0.72% in 2012 and 4.01% in 2013, great value for a top cornerback.) Over these last few years since that time, versatile safeties like McCourty, Earl Thomas, Eric Berry, Tyrann Mathieu and Harrison Smith have proven that an elite safety can be the most important player on the defense. As Robert Mays wrote for The Ringer,

McCourty's draft measurables were great for cornerbacks, but outside of being slightly smaller for safety, his speed, quickness and explosive measurables for the position were elite for safeties with his 4.38 forty-yard dash being in the 97th percentile according to MockDraftable.com. Mays explains that McCourty's speed provides a centerfielder for the defense who has an ability to strangle an opponent's deep passing game as well as a versatility and flexibility to the position that makes him the "answer to a variety of questions that inevitably come up throughout the season. When bouts of injury or ineffectiveness hit the Pats defense, Belichick knows he has a guy in his secondary who can play both corner and safety at an All-Pro level."[10] Yet he gets all of this at a lower rate because McCourty is labeled as a free safety rather than a cornerback. While Revis left for a contract that paid him 11.17% and 10.95% in the first two seasons of a front loaded contract, McCourty is just reaching the peak of his contract he signed that same 2015 offseason and he'll make between six and six and a half percent of the cap from 2017 through 2019 if he stays on this deal.

Mays goes on to explain a further nugget of wisdom that speaks to the cerebral role the free safety position has taken on with the influence of the passing game similar to the way defensive leadership has centered around the middle linebacker in the past and still through to today. He writes, "going beyond identifiable skills, McCourty has earned the top compliment that Belichick and the Pats defensive staff could offer: he has their trust. Belichick has said that when McCourty comes off the field, the input he gives based on his vantage point has a ton of influence on the sort of tweaks New England will employ during the course of a game. McCourty is also responsible for most of the checks the Pats install in a given week." The Patriots are getting a quarterback of the defense at a versatile position that produces a lot of tackles for a rate far below the cost of top tier players in the expensive markets. The safety positions might be the most valuable on the defense considering the cost and the impact a great one can have. An elite athlete who can tackle, cover the deep middle and cover offensive mismatches man-to-man is very valuable. Two or three good safeties on a defense provides dynamic versatility.

Hightower was on his fifth-year player option of 4.99% in 2016 and his second contract was an example of Belichick's strategy of drafting low-cost markets in action. The Patriots let him test the market and, according to Rich Cimini, he was offered a five-year, $55 million contract with a max value of $62.5 million by the Jets, but they pulled the offer after seeing his physical and he re-signed with the Patriots for a four-year deal with similar per year numbers at $43.5 million total. His contract caps between about five and five and a half percent in the final three years of his deal through 2020, so like McCourty, these are two of the best and most versatile players at two important positions that produce many of your team's tackles. Rather than pay for the best cornerback and edge rusher in the NFL, which produces great results in the passing game, the Patriots pay for the best players at positions that produce great results for the entire unit with the right mix of efficient and valuable players at cornerback and rushing the passer. Also, like on offense, the Patriots understand the value of versatility in the pass game. Easley was released, but Brown will likely receive contracts that keep him at numbers that cap in this five to six percent of the cap range we've seen with the other two markets. If Brown becomes one of the best defensive tackles in the NFL like Vince Wilfork did, he'll have a couple years in his prime that could peak near eight percent of the cap, like Wilfork did, but those will be correlated with lower costs at quarterback due to Brady either being in the last years of his career in his mid- to late-forties (feels crazy to write that) or a likely rookie contract replacement. The quarterback cost is a key part of the equation as low-costs there allow for high investment elsewhere, which should be encouraged as the team needs to invest in other skills with low-cost quarterback usually meaning lesser quality.

By drafting and extending top talents into the top tiers of these less expensive markets and finding value through lower cost veterans and later round draft picks in more expensive markets, the Patriots can build a complete and versatile defense, rather than have a reliance on high-cost stars with potential weaknesses elsewhere that can be exposed. I recall the AFC Divisional Round in January 2015 where Tom Brady threw 15 balls at the Ravens undrafted free agent cornerback Rashaan Melvin completing 12 for 196 yards and two touchdowns as a prime example of how badly a great offensive coordinator and quarterback can expose a weakness. The next week, LeGarrette Blount exposed the Colts weak defense with 148 yards on 30 carries and three touchdowns to win 45-7. Versatility takes advantage of an opponent's lack of versatility, wherever it may be. This spending philosophy is in line with the very foundational philosophies of the organization and coaching staff with the Kraft belief in market inefficiencies and Belichick's desire to never be the first to run to setting a market.

NFL coaches have from the time the schedule is released in April and the meat of the rosters are all but confirmed at the end of the draft in May to prepare for each of their 16 regular season opponents as well as those who they might face in the playoffs. Once it becomes game week, the coaches can spend the entire week honing in on their ideal strategy based on what they've seen from both their own team and their opponent over the course of the year. The General Manager and head coach should have the goal to create a roster with too many weapons on offense to stop or be fully prepared for and a defense that teams are unable to exploit. Versatility is a key theme in this book as many paths to victories exist, so a team must have their own weapons to execute various strategies with a defense versatile enough to be prepared for anything—and through value creation, this versatility can be created.

Moving into the less expensive markets, inside linebackers and safeties exist with a first tier that starts at three and peaks at seven, while the second tier of the expensive defensive markets is near these same numbers, this represents the peak for run-stopping defensive tackles. There has never been a Super Bowl champion inside linebacker with a cap hit over six percent with Ray Lewis' 2012 cap hit of 5.68% at number one. While Lawrence Timmons had an outlier cap hit in 2016 of 9.75%, Navarro Bowman at 6.59% at two and Brian Cushing at 5.83% represent the more reasonable cap on the market. All three of those linebackers are on 3-4 defenses, so Hightower's 4.99% was the highest for a non-3-4 inside linebacker. But that was a function of it being his fifth season of his first round rookie deal, which paid him the average salary of the third through 25th highest paid linebackers in the NFL. Hightower's new contract averages 4.79% over four years with three cap hits between five and five and a half percent of the cap from 2018 through 2020 after a 3.20% cap hit in 2017. Bobby Wagner's 2015 deal averages 5.08% from 2015 through 2019, while capping at 7.59% in 2018. The non 3-4 inside linebacker market should cap between five and seven, but will typically skew near five. Knowing the value of having versatile sideline-to-sideline tacklers, along with the versatility of a deep linebacking group, has led Belichick to note the value in the low-cost of a vital position and skill set. An athletic inside linebacker can do everything from rush the passer, like Hightower did on the Matt Ryan sack fumble down 28-12 with 8:41 left that helped facilitate the Super Bowl comeback, to cover running backs or tight ends in the passing game, to spying elite running quarterbacks making it a versatile and valuable defensive piece that can be had at a lower price than the pass game focused positions. Similarly, Belichick drafted Jerod Mayo with the 10th pick in the 2008 draft and he was extended after his second year. Then they re-negotiated after his third year to put him on a contract that kept him in a similar range as Hightower outside of a 2012 season that had Mayo at 7.57%.

When judging the value of non-edge rushing linebackers, the statistics to focus on, according to Mike Renner of Pro Football Focus, are run-stop percentage and total coverage stops to combine the importance of their performance versus the run and pass. Tackling efficiency should be included as well, which shows the number of attempted tackles per miss, an important stat to see how well a linebacker performs at his most important skill. Inside that tackling efficiency is our total coverage stops in the passing game that Renner speaks of, which sees the top 11 of 58 linebackers with 21 to 23 stops in the 2016 season.

Fifty linebackers qualified to be counted in run-stop percentage statistics and 11 of them had run-stop percentages over 10%, 19 were over 9%. As the description for run-stop percentage reads on Pro Football Focus, "a player's impact in the running game is sometimes erroneously based on the total volume of tackles made."[11] They point out that tackles on passing plays sometimes skew the numbers due to them being downfield on bigger plays for the offense, which isn't a part of the linebacker's main objective of stopping the offense from producing yardage, especially in the running game. As one linebacker described to me, the core objective of the position is to play the game within the first three to five yards of the line of scrimmage and keep the ball from passing this range. Pro Football Focus writes that stops constitute a "loss" for the offense so run-stop percentage shows the percent of stops per snap that the offense has a play that "constitutes a 'failure' for the offense." In 2012, Mike Renner gave two examples to understand what constitutes a win or loss for the offense, "a two-yard run on first down would be considered an offensive failure because it doesn't really improve their position," as teams are trying to gain four plus yards on first down to be "ahead of schedule" as coaches say. Meanwhile Mike writes that "a 1-yard run on 4th-and-inches that results in a first down wouldn't be considered a failure because the offense greatly improved their position. Generally speaking, linebackers want to keep the ball in front of them and play downhill against the run.

Of the 52 linebackers who qualified to have their coverage stats calculated by Pro Football Focus, the top 12 held the players they covered to under 0.8 yards per coverage snap as they hold the players they cover to lower yardage totals than cornerbacks due to covering running backs and tight ends rather than receivers, meaning typically shorter air yards per target. Pass rush productivity could be included in these stats, but a linebacker's PRP productivity is a bit skewed due to blitzes, and the smaller percentage of snaps that blitzes represent for linebackers versus rushing on almost every pass play like defensive linemen. There were 13 linebackers with PRPs higher than or equal to the dominant Khalil Mack's 15 as an edge defender. Linebackers also take advantage of the surprise of a blitz and the lanes opened up by rushing defensive linemen.

As teams spread the field more every year, and coaches scheme to get their athletes in space to make defenders miss, there becomes an increased importance in finding elite one-on-one tacklers, which continues to increase the value of safeties. Ed Reed's 7.02% cap hit in 2012 is the max for a champion and becomes very viable with a lower cost quarterback and cornerback spending. Troy Polamalu is number two in 2008 at 5.88% and 13 total Super Bowl safeties were above three percent. By focusing top tier investments and draft picks in these less expensive markets, a team can secure three core defensive players at all three levels of the defense through prime earning years for a better value that allows them to build a more complete defense. In theory, this can provide stability on the defense for over half a decade, which is valuable to the defense as a unit and the defensive coordinator, just like we said in chapter two in that stability is a core principle throughout the organization. A franchise quarterback provides stability on offense, while three core players at the three levels of the defense does the same on the other side. Being a team game, this continuity improves the unit's performance, allows the organization to create roster construction strategies around them and create value. Lower expenses for core players allow a team to make small, incremental moves around them rather than the difficult roster decisions that come with multiple big investments in expensive markets.

The lower costs of these roles create a mass of quality players in between one and a half and three percent, as we already discussed in the third tier of the defensive tackle market and the second tiers of the inside linebacker and safety markets. Only nine inside linebackers were over three percent of the cap in 2016; the position that has always been seen as the quarterback of the defense as well as a versatile and an elite tackler, and can be found at a very reasonable rate. Nineteen safeties were above three percent with Jairus Byrd at 7.02%, so the market has less depth in the second tier, but the market is inexpensive whether for a free safety like Earl Thomas or a strong safety like Kam Chancellor. Safeties can be a team's most versatile and athletic playmakers with the ability to cover tight ends, blitz, contribute in the run game and much more. The 2016 Seahawks had a fantastic defensive line with Michael Bennett, Cliff Avril, and Frank Clark, plus a great cornerback in Richard Sherman because they spent a lot of money on their defense, but their two safeties and linebackers Wagner and KJ Wright were a solid value for four of the best players in these lower cost markets. In 2016, Thomas cost 6.38%, Wright was 4.03% of the cap, Chancellor was 3.93%, and Wagner was just 3.91% as already mentioned. These four versatile chess pieces are prepared to defend the pass and keep the same group on the field in the run game, while costing the team a reasonable 18.25% of the cap for four elite players. The Seahawks had a base defense that was prepared for most offensive personnels.

Great on-field statistical metrics for judging safeties don't exist. Renner pointed out to me that run-stop percentage is a good stat, but for pass coverage, an important task for the position, "there's really no good cover metric for them" due to the different roles safeties can play in today's NFL and there being less targets thrown the way of some safeties versus cornerbacks. For judging coverage skills of safeties, it leans to the subjective side of analysis, rather than the objective.

Ten safeties, of the 50 who qualified to be rated in 2016, had run-stop percentages over five percent and the top 12 had run-stop percentages above 6.9% on plays where they started within eight yards of the line of scrimmage. The Giants Landon Collins was third in total run stop percentage at 6.8%, then second on plays where he starts within eight yards of the line of scrimmage with a run stop percentage of 9.3%, which are both confirmation of the subjective analysis of anyone who has watched the Giants: Collins knows how to play downhill and stop ball carriers as he did often for the team in 2016. Quantifying plays where the safety starts within eight yards of the line of scrimmage helps track the number of times a safety plays in more of a strong safety-slash-linebacker role and how well they do in that role.

The low-costs of markets like inside linebacker and safety make them viable for drafting and free agent acquisitions, making these markets much easier to navigate for top talent. Linebacker has slightly more concerns regarding length of career than safety considering the violence of the position, like running back, but both positions can be found through the draft or free agency. Although, by focusing on these markets through the draft, top talent can be acquired and managed in a way that elite cornerbacks and pass rushers cannot, which makes it a replicable strategy and provides stability on the defense. Linebacker and safety are also positions that provide a lot of value on special teams because of that athleticism and tackling ability, so in their early years they can add versatility as role players on defense and value on special teams.

Having gone through offensive and defensive spending now, we have the last of the three phases of the game and the one that we all have a tendency to overlook, special teams. As stated in chapter five, according to the combined analysis of Stuart, Paine, and Burke, with Football Outsiders' input, a football team's Quality is based on 50% offense, 37.5% defense, and 12.5% special teams, so let's get into the impact of that final piece of a championship caliber roster.

Chapter 9: Special Teams Spending and the Battle for Field Position

In Alex Kirby's *The Big Book of Belichick*, the seven-time Super Bowl champion—two as the Defensive Coordinator of the Giants and the five in his current role—gives us a history lesson: "back when the game was invented and even back into the, let's say the 1930s and 1940s. [Robert] Neyland at Tennessee and a lot of his disciples followed the old rule of thumb on field position: inside your own 10, punt on first down, inside your 20, punt on second down, inside your 30, punt on third down. You didn't punt on fourth down until you got the ball outside the 40-yard line, until you got close to midfield. You played defense, you played field position." The low-scoring nature of the early days of football likely looked a lot like the recent low-scoring battles in the Alabama/LSU rivalry where both teams spend the entire game punting and playing defense in a field position battle hoping to force turnovers and capitalize on good field position against their opponent's elite defense. In an era with very little scoring, teams wouldn't even take the chance of turning the ball over deep in their own zone—they'd just punt it away and play for field position.

The media and fans alike have often overlooked special teams, likely due to lack of data, which leads to an inability to gain an objective basis of understanding the impact of special teams on the game's results. As Aaron Schatz wrote in *Football Outsiders Almanac 2016*, "the most underrated aspect of an NFL team's performance is the field position gained on kicks and punts."[1] Winning field position helps increase your likelihood of scoring and NFL.com's Pat Kirwin found during the 2011 season that teams who scored a special teams touchdown improved their winning percentage to 75%. Add in a great punter and kicker and your special teams can become a weekly advantage helping your offense have a better chance of scoring, while decreasing your opponents. Christopher L. Gasper of *The Boston Globe* pointed out that the elite field goal kickers that Belichick has had have led to them excelling in games decided by three points or less. Since 2001, the Patriots have gone 39-16, a .709 winning percentage, in such games. The next closest are the Colts at .661 with a 41-21 record.[2]

Belichick was a special teams assistant or coordinator for seven of his first eight years in the NFL with the Lions, Broncos, and Giants. That influence likely played a role in his five championship specialists groups—which includes the kicker, punter, and long snapper—averaging 3.73% of the cap versus the other champions averaging 2.14%. While Adam Vinatieri and Stephen Gostowski averaged 2.52% of the cap, other champions have averaged 0.93%. At punter, Belichick's champions have averaged 0.84%, while the group of champions cost 0.87% on average, and that market is one that will be growing in the coming years with the realized importance of field position with punters who are specializing in directional kicks that can confuse returners along with new styles of kicks that pin opponents near their own goal line.

This special teams background paid off on the way to his first Super Bowl as the Patriots' offense scored just three total touchdowns in their three playoff wins. Vinatieri hit six field goals including game tying and winning field goals in the snow against Oakland in the divisional round, plus the historic 48-yarder as time expired against the Rams. In the AFC Championship against the Steelers, Troy Brown started the scoring with a 55-yard punt return for a touchdown in the first quarter and Antwan Harris returned a blocked kick 49-yards for a touchdown to put the Patriots up 21-3 when a made field goal could've made it a 14-6 game. The defense got involved in the scoring with a 47-yard touchdown return by Ty Law to put New England up 7-3 in the second quarter of the Super Bowl. With the Super Bowl win coming with huge contributions from all three phases, this likely confirmed and encouraged his belief in building a roster through depth and balance rather than stars—and it has been reflected in their salary cap spending since that time.

As mentioned in the last chapter, the 2016 Patriots had their money spread in a way that provided them with 25 players making over one percent of the cap with Brady capping the team at 8.87%. That depth over a star system philosophy allows them to afford to spend money on special teams where other teams might not. Teams can have as few as 18 or 19 players making over one percent of the cap, which typically indicates a star system with heavy investments in the top few cap hits that leads to less depth elsewhere. The Seahawks have still been able to compete with just 18 over one percent in 2016 because their biggest investments have paid off as they extended the young core of their 2013 Super Bowl team, players with a high probability of continued success, but those high cap hits have made them heavily reliant on inexpensive rookie contract players. These inexpensive players are vital to any team and few are better than the Seahawks at finding gems, but relying on too many of these players comes with risk across the roster. With Wilson's mobility at quarterback, the Seahawks decided offensive line was a place they'd try to conserve cap space in 2016 with a starting five that cost just 2.54% of the cap and resulted in the worst offensive line ranking in the NFL, according to Pro Football Focus' metrics.[3] That lack of investment was their biggest liability. The lack of investment in any one discipline, whether the offensive line or special teams, can become a liability.

With the way Belichick spreads his money, he was able to afford having his kicker Stephen Gostowski, at 2.64%, his punter, Ryan Allen, at 1.09%, and then three veteran players who only played special teams in Matt Slater at 1.33%, Brandon

Bolden at 0.82%, and Nate Ebner at 0.77%. That totals 6.65% invested in five special teams players with 2.92% of it invested in the three non-kickers. They also traded a 2017 fifth-round pick for the Browns' 6th overall pick in 2013, Barkevius Mingo, who became a huge part of their special teams unit at 0.43% of the cap to bring the total invested in six primarily special teams players to 7.08%. All four of these players were part of the big 4 special teams units, which are kick, kick return, punt and punt return. Ebner had the most snaps of the four, followed by Mingo, Bolden and Slater. At 1.44% of the cap, linebacker Shea McClellin played 48.66% of special teams snaps with a much higher percentage of offensive or defensive snaps than the other four with 36.43%, so he's another investment that was special teams related. Being able to invest that much into special teams becomes an advantage that has led to their being one of the best special teams units in the NFL every year. Rick Gosselin of *The Dallas Morning News* ranked the 2016 Patriots as the sixth best special teams unit in the NFL and PFF named Ebner to their special teams All-Pro punt team noting that he led the NFL with 14 total special teams tackles.[4] This strategy provides the Patriots with three veterans to lead the young players like free safety Brandon King (66.74% of special teams snaps), cornerback Jonathan Jones (68.53%), and defensive end Geneo Grissom (55.80%) who make up the rest of the unit, while establishing and representing the organization's standard for the units.

The 2016 Patriots had seven special teams players who played over 50% of special teams snaps with just 205 total offensive and defensive snaps. McClellin and Patrick Chung, to add to his versatility and value, were both over 40% to add to that group with McClellin's 380 defensive snaps and Chung over 1000 defensive snaps. They had seven roster spots dedicated to non-kicking special teamers, plus McClellin and Chung. That adds up to seven to nine roster spots dedicated to talented players playing special teams almost exclusively.

For young players, particularly late-round picks and undrafted players, special teams are the way onto the field and the path to a bigger role on offense or defense. When a player is on special teams, their offensive or defensive coordinator can rely on that player being dressed every week when they're putting together their game plan. With this, the coach can scheme a way to use the player's strengths at his position, which can grow into a bigger role on that side of the ball. Belichick believes in this approach, so he'll maximize his roster with young, inexpensive special teamers who can potentially grow into larger roles over time. Jonathan Jones is still playing a high percentage of special teams snaps in 2017 , while seeing his role on defense grow. Oftentimes these can become key contributors as back-up running backs, nickel defensive backs, passing down linebackers who can cover running backs, or a second tight end toward the end of his first contract and heading into his second contract. This is another way Belichick, and all NFL coaches in this case, looks to increase roster versatility.

Safety concerns on kickoff are promoting rule changes intended to decrease the number of high impact collisions that occur on the play over the course of the season. A 2011 change moved kicks from the 30 to the 35-yard line, which led to a huge increase in touchbacks from 16.4% in 2010 to 43.5% in 2011 and 55.9% by 2015. The 2016 season was the first with touchbacks coming out to the 25-yard line, rather than the 20, which saw the trend of the touchback rate continuing to increase up near 59%. This saw a decrease in the number of kicks that were fielded in the endzone and returned out and for good reason as the return success rate, a stat that we should use on kicks returned out of the endzone based on if the returner makes it to the touchback line, drastically decreased with the five extra yards of field position needed. This led Jonathan Jones, the writer, not the cornerback, to write a January 2017 article for *Sports Illustrated* titled, "Why NFL playoff teams need to kneel for the touchback whenever possible."

Jones, with a "stat geek college friend" named Kevin Hogan, found a trend toward decreasing returns in touchback opportunities over the last three seasons. In 2014, 808 kicks were brought out of the end zone, which is 38.1% of all kicks that traveled past the goal line. Of those, 464, or 57.4% got to or past the 20-yard line. In 2015, those numbers were 724 and 423 meaning that 32.9% of all kicks that traveled past the goal line were brought out and 58.4% of those made it to the 20 or further.

They found that with the 2016 change, both the number of touchbacks and percentage of kick returns that made it to the touchback line fell drastically. Only 439 kicks, 22.4% of all kicks that traveled past the goal line, were brought out and 127 of those got to or past the new touchback line. This means that 71.1% of returns failed to make it to the 25-yard line. One statistic did increase in 2016, the number of kicks that came up short of the end zone with Jones and Hogan finding, "of all the kickoffs in 2016, 24.4% of them came up short of the goal line compared to just 14.5% in 2015." As Kansas City Chiefs Special Teams Coordinator Dave Toub said at the beginning of the season regarding kickoffs, "no one wants to give up those 25 yards. To me, that's like giving up."[5] Teams are using strategies that used to be more frequently used at the college level where fewer kickers can get the ball into the endzone, so they'll aim a high arching kick toward the pylon to allow their coverage unit to get down there and decrease the return team's ability to set up their blocks.

While it might feel like giving up, Kurt Ballard of the Harvard Sports Analysis Collective did a study of the first two weeks of the 2016 season and isolated all kick returns without a penalty that occurred outside of the last 30 seconds of each quarter. He found that kicks that didn't make it to the end zone saw an average starting field position of 25.5, while kicking it into the end zone resulted in a worse average field position at the 24.5. As Bullard writes, "this is the product of bad decision making; when a kick returner has taken it out of the end zone this year, they've ended up on average at the 22.7 yard line."[6] Over time we will see what the long-term impact of the role and the strategic adjustment that coordinators create dependent on what the data says, but currently it seems that better decision making is needed on kick returns and, in most cases, returners should lean toward kneeling. Belichick has been quoted on the topic saying that the depth of a kick into the end zone is less important than the hang time, "you put a ball nine-yards into the end zone with 3.8 (seconds) of hang time, I don't see any problem bringing that out. You put a ball one-yard deep in the end zone with 4.5 hang time, that's a whole different ball game." The longer the ball is in the air, the closer the cover unit is.

Big kick returns have their obvious impact on the game by either scoring a touchdown to putting the offense closer to one and tipping field position. Kickoffs can have a momentum shifting impact themselves after a touchdown because they can create "runs" by setting the opponent's offense back and increasing your probability of getting good field position yourself. As Belichick has said, runs are created by scoring, covering the next kick well, getting a stop or turnover on defense, then taking advantage of that good field position by scoring again, then another good coverage play on the next kick. This creates the opportunity to score a few times before your opponent has an opportunity to respond.

The increase in touchbacks is decreasing the impact that good kickoff coverage and kick returners can have on the game and, simultaneously, advancements in punting and explosive punt returners are making the punt the more impactful of the two. Dante Hall was one of the most dynamic returners in NFL history for the Chiefs in the early-2000s and he lamented to Robert Klemko in an article titled, "The Unfair Catch: How NFL Return Men Became an Endangered Species," that no way his career would have lasted today as long as it did because he was primarily a returner. During the five years of his prime from 2002 to 2006, Hall averaged 90 special teams touches per season, while the Chiefs new explosive returner Tyreek Hill only had 53 in 2016 because of the changes in the game.[7]

Transitioning toward the punting game, as Pro Football Focus' Gordon McGuinness explains in "The Best Special Teamer in the NFL in 2016," the goal of the punt is to put the opposing offense in the toughest field position possible. The key components are that the snap needs to be clean and the punter needs to get the ball off under the generally accepted operation time for special teams coordinators of 2.10 seconds. The average time in 2016 from long snapper to the punt leaving the punters foot was 1.99 seconds. Traditional stats aren't a true illustration of a punter's performance because it depends where on the field the team is punting from in terms of what the goal is. McGuinness writes, "net yards are frequently touted for punters, but it's important to remember that if a punter is punting from his opponent's side of the field, he's not looking to punt the ball over 50 yards, and instead is looking to hang the ball up and allow his coverage team to make a play to keep the opponent pinned inside their own 10-yard line."[8]

He continues, "from here it's up to the punt coverage team. This is led by the gunners on either edge, who are responsible for keeping initial contain on a return, making tackles, and keeping the ball from bouncing into the end zone. The punt offensive line needs to get enough on any rushers that the punter has the 2.1 seconds needed to get the ball away, and then they too need to hustle downfield, stay in their lanes to prevent big plays, and make tackles or down the ball where necessary."

We take some more Belichickian knowledge from Kirby's *Big Book of Belichick* with his take on the traits that he looks for in gunners and the attributes that teams should look for in their coverage players. On gunners Belichick says he's looking for "some combination of speed, strength and quickness. The more the better of all three; it's a tough position to play. You have to deal with two guys. You have to be strong enough to deal with them or quick enough to deal with them or fast enough to deal with them and then there's all of the techniques of not only dealing with the double teams but also the punts, the returns, the rushes, the wind conditions, knowing where the ball is, trying to defeat two blockers and then locate the ball and the returner and the different returns and so forth. There's a lot of technique and skill that's involved beyond just the physical part of it. I think you need some combination of those three elements to deal with consistent double teams out there."[9]

When asked if the common denominator for special teams players was a mentality that allowed them to excel on the entire unit, kick and punts, Belichick said that there was a mentality of aggressiveness to a degree, an attitude of "trying to make plays as opposed to just trying to stay in your area of responsibility." He goes on, I'd say that just the instinctiveness of being primarily a space player, recognizing how much space there is between you and the runner or how much space you have to defend from the guy you're blocking to where he has to get to the runner, can you get around the guy to the backside to make the play, do you have the front side, or do you have to go through him?" With this, he notes a combination of speed, strength, and explosiveness, which is another way of saying quickness like the gunners. That combination is "so if you have to take people on you can take them on and if you can run around them or avoid them you've got the speed to do it as well. So, it's a combination of space ability, speed, power, explosion, quickness, and judgment in space, which is different than making inline judgments or close quarter type decisions. Those space judgments are your speed, their speed, the angle, what's between you and the guy, whether you're blocking or covering."

Belichick's four big special teams investments of Slater, Bolden, Ebner and Mingo, along with McClellin, Chung, plus rookies Jones and King, made up the Patriots gunners and main special teams tacklers in 2016. Including the kicker or punter on each play, Belichick made conscious investments in almost all of the players on the special teams unit on every play.

A recent major innovation is in the process of revolutionizing the art of punting, which is part of the increasing awareness of a punter's ability to impact a game. Over time, punters have been able to increase their distance and accuracy, but Baltimore's Sam Koch introduced a style of directional punting that is illustrating a new potential for maximizing your team's field position and as a means of maximizing punt coverage by making punts difficult to return. In Week 9 of the 2014 season, Koch was in his ninth NFL season preparing for a match-up with Antonio Brown and the rival Steelers. Kevin Seifert of ESPN wrote in a December 2015 article on Koch's new style of punting. Koch kept thinking "we need something extra" to avoid the explosive returner. Ravens' special teams coordinator Jerry Rosburg was the person who suggested the twist that led to the new style saying, "let's see if we can fool him."[10]

As Seifert writes, this was a huge change, an innovation far outside of anything Koch himself had done before as he "spent the first 8 1/2 years of his career as a right directional punter. On most kicks, he stood offset to the right and attempted to pin the returner on that sideline." Rosburg joined the staff in 2008 and suggested adding a left directional punt, but "there was no real deception involved beyond an offset stance."

With that first punt of Week 9, he angled his body to the right sideline and then torqued his right hip and leg back to the left to send the punt sailing to the left sideline. Brown found himself on the wrong sideline, ran the 50 yards to the other sideline just to watch the ball roll out of bounds at the three-yard line. "You try to get a read off where the punters head is facing. However, when you have a guy who can point his head one way, and punt it the other way, that's a great skill," Brown later said. Koch says that his first eight years in the NFL "were all just trying to get the ball as high as you can, as far as you can, get it to be as pretty as you can, and get it over to the sideline." He points out to Seifert the root question that sparked his innovation, "why would you want to punt it to the returner if you didn't have to?"

Former Chiefs GM John Dorsey is quoted in a 2008 *Wall Street Journal* article by James Wagner titled, "How to Kick Australian" back when he was the Packers director of college scouting saying that while Americans have always looked toward the guy with the strongest leg to punt, Australians have elevated punting "to an art form." One reason for this is that all 18 players on an Australian rules football team have to be able to punt on the run, while only one or two kids per American football team are trained as punters. As Wagner writes, Australian style punters use the drop punt, "which sends the ball spinning end over end instead of in a traditional spiral" and "typically allows punters to pinpoint their kicks to within five yards," while also resulting in fewer off bounces and a lower likelihood of a touchback. He writes that the late 1970s saw foreign-born place-kickers as the norm with their soccer-style technique, which is now the norm in all of football and provides a historical example of how the new innovations of punting will be integrated across the NFL. According to Wagner's article, Darren Bennett introduced this rugby style to the league in the early-2000s; Mike Scifres and Shane Lechler then perfected the art of backward-bouncing punts to get balls to drop down inside the five and stay there. The three of these innovations together will influence the future norm of the game as future punters grow up integrating these styles into their own.[11]

While other punters had brought innovations to the game in the years leading up to Koch's experiment and may have affected his, directional punting was an innovation that came in the same entrepreneurial manner that innovations do in football. As Chris B. Brown wrote in *The Essential Smart Football*, "new ideas in football tend to arise as potential solutions to specific problems," which is what we find in the business world as well: a great company or product solves a problem for their customers.[12] Antonio Brown was the twice a year problem Koch had and now the innovation is making its way around the league due to Koch's great success with it. According to ESPN Stats & Information research, from Koch's rookie year in 2006 through Week 8 of 2014, he averaged 39.03 net yards per punt, which was 28th among qualified punters over that period. Since the change, he has the NFL's top net average at 44.39.

Alok Pattani of ESPN analytics writes about ESPN's "expected points" metric, a formula built on a statistical analysis of 10 years of NFL play-by-play data that "assigns an 'expected points' value to the team with the ball at the start of each play based on the game situation." He writes, "the value it puts out is on a scale from about minus-3 to 7, and it basically represents 'which team is likely to score next, and how many points?' It represents the likely points not just on the current drive but also on the next drive or any subsequent drive until the score changes or the half ends."[13] At the time of Seifert's article, Koch saw his Expected Points Added jump to 0.37 per punt and leading the NFL after changing his punting style after his first 8 1/2 years of his career had him ranked 33rd at 0.03 per punt.

Koch went from punting the same way every time for those first eight seasons to now having a golf bag's worth as Seifert aptly puts it. First are the "more standard 'turnover' kicks, which spiral in the air, and rugby-style punts with backward spin." Next comes the hook and liner punts, both of which use the "torque" technique of angling your head to one side of the field and then kicking it back to the other side. Hook punts are "designed to go 43-47 gross yards and post a hang time between 4.5-4.7 seconds. If the returner does catch up to it, the torque and force of the kick makes it difficult to catch. It will fade back into the field and ultimately drop in the shape of an S." Liner punts "average between 47-50 gross yards with a hang time between 3.6-3.7 seconds" as these have a lower trajectory intended to get the ball on the ground and the coverage there before the returner has a chance to field it.

According to Seifert, many punters have a knuckle punt, but "Koch brings a more severe effect to his in context with the rest of his array." Others will point their knuckles toward the sideline, while Koch punts it toward the middle of the field in an attempt to get a turnover by forcing the returner to catch the ball. The boomerang is his last punt, which Koch says "will look like it's going straight at the returner, but then it'll boomerang and slowly start running away from him." Each week, the Ravens' punt team will meet to game-plan for the next game and they'll decide which type of punt they'll use in each situation dependent on weather, game situation, hash mark positioning, and the week's returner.

Two early adopters mentioned in the Koch article were Denver's Britton Colquitt and Johnny Hekker of the Rams, two players who've since put together an MVP level performance in the Super Bowl and a historic 2016 season respectively. As Chuck Zodda from Inside The Pylon wrote after Super Bowl 50, Colquitt had a serious case that he was the game's MVP with just 509 total yards of offense in the game and the way Colquitt's punts played a big role in their ability to score 24 points with the offense providing just 104 net passing yards and 90 rushing yards.[14] They certainly didn't win because of their offense; the game was won by a defense and special teams unit that kept the field tilted in their favor all game and set up three of their five scores.

Denver had drives of 64 and 54 yards that ended in field goals on their first drive of each half, but their third and fourth longest drives were 36 and 18 yards with both of them ending in turnovers. Their first touchdown was a fumble recovery in the end zone by Malik Jackson off a Von Miller strip-sack to make it 10-0. They had another field goal on a second quarter drive that started on Carolina's 14 yard-line and lost a yard after Jordan Norwood's Super Bowl record 61-yard punt return, then a four-yard touchdown run by C.J. Anderson to make the game 24-10 with 3:08 left that was again set up by a Miller strip sack that was recovered and returned to the four by T.J. Ward. Colquitt lost the MVP vote to a guy whose strip sacks led to the only two Broncos touchdowns of the game, so voters made a good choice. Denver's performance in that Super Bowl game was a perfect example of how an elite pass rush and coverage skills on defense paired with a strong special teams unit can overcome subpar quarterback and offensive play to win a championship if the team hits on their investments or invests well. They even overcame that complete lack of offensive production in the Super Bowl with a top three cap hits of Peyton Manning, Demaryius Thomas, and Ryan Clady on the offensive side of the ball consuming a record 28.82% of the cap because they did such a phenomenal job of finding value on and producing with their defense and special teams.

Colquitt had eight punts for 367 yards, an average of 45.8 per punt. Taking out a 28-yarder that bounced out of bounds with just 54 seconds left intended only to stop Ginn from having a chance to return it, Colquitt average 48.4 per punt, all of which were on open field punts rather than opportunities to pin the opponent deep. Zodda wrote that Colquitt hit 101% of target distance punted (TDP), well above his season's average of 95% in that situation. His hang time was 4.65 per punt compared to 4.38 seconds during the regular season.

According to Zodda, "TDP measures how effectively a punter delivers the distance expected in various field positions—which is not always as far as possible. For open field punts target distance is the league average in open field situations over the course of the time period measured. For pin deep situations, the target distance is the difference between the yard line on which the ball is kicked and the opponent's 10-yard line. Since TDP is designed to calculate only a punter's impact on field position, returns are not included, but touchbacks are counted."

As Zodda goes on, "the real story lies not just in how far Britton Colquitt punted, but in how accurately he punted and how he was able to limit the ability of Ted Ginn, Jr., whose 10.3 yard average was good for fifth in the NFL in 2015. Ginn racked up this yardage despite lacking a return longer than 37 yards this season, while every other returner [in the top 12] had at least one return of 58 yards or greater. More than anything else, this indicates Ginn's consistent ability to produce large chunks of return yards." An indication of Colquitt's impact lies in the fact that "Ginn gained just two yards on the eight punts, and was able to return only three of them at all. To put this in perspective, there were only 11 games all season in which a punt return unit averaged fewer than one-yard per return attempt over three or more returns." That's 11 out of 256 games, putting this performance on the big stage against an elite, consistent returner in the top five percent of all 2015 punt coverage performances.

Colquitt's punts consistently had distance and hang-time that allowed coverage to get down there, while also pinning Ginn toward the sideline on almost every punt. His seventh punt may have been his best and most impactful of the day with 4:51 left on Denver's own 28-yard line needing a great punt to help ensure victory. He boomed a 48-yard punt with 4.82 seconds of hang-time that landed on the right sideline, preventing a Ginn return and starting Carolina out on their own 24-yard line. Three plays later, Miller committed his second strip sack, which led to the Anderson touchdown that effectively ended the game.

Johnny Hekker had a record-setting 2016 season as the second Koch replica and he has quickly become a prototype. An NFL record 51 of his punts landed inside the 20 in 2016, while number two, Dustin Colquitt of the Chiefs, Britton's brother, had just 38. Only one of Hekker's 98 punts on the season crossed the goal line for a touchback. His net average of 46.0 yards was 1.8 yards better than Detroit's Sam Martin and they were the only two with average above 42.7. This number is helped by the opponents gaining an average of just 1.55 yards per return on all of his punts as no other punter held their opponents to a return average of less than 1.82. As former Vikings punter Chris Kluwe told Dom Cosentino of Deadspin, some punters have the ability to punt for distance or the ability to directionally punt, "but it's somewhat rare to see both on a very high level" like we do with Hekker.[15] Pat McAfee of the Colts led the NFL with a gross punt average of 49.3 yards per punt, one and a half yards better than Hekker, and had a good enough season to be named PFF's best punter of 2016, but he tied Dustin Colquitt for the NFL lead with nine touchbacks. This dropped his net average to 42.7.

Hekker has the ability to completely shift field position like he did in Week 4 against the Jets booming a punt to their five-yard line with his heels at the Rams own three and dropping the ball inside the opponent's one. Zodda focuses on "distance control" when evaluating punters and this focuses on how far, how high and how accurately a punter hits the ball in both the open field and pin deep situations. Hekker's year was surely one of the best seasons of distance control in NFL history.

His special teams coordinator over his first five seasons in the NFL with the Rams, Jim Fassel, said that the former high school quarterback and basketball star turned Oregon State and All-Pro punter had steadily progressed from year to year. As Fassel tells it, Hekker would hit a really nice ball on about half of his punts his rookie year, then about 70% the next year, then eight out of every 10 balls were hit well and by 2016 that number got to nine out of 10 punts were "pretty darn good." He says that one of the things that makes Hekker special is "his ability as an athlete to get better faster and to pick up new techniques and implement them into a game. He is as athletic a punter as I've seen—I probably shouldn't say in the history of the NFL—but as far as punters who are athletes, he's in the 99th percentile."[16] Like on the offensive line and across the roster, organizations are trying to find phenomenal athletes who fit the mold for what they need with the base level of skills necessary to succeed at the position and athletic capability to learn and implement the techniques taught by the coaching staff once in the NFL. Coaches want to find players who can carry out their strategy and a team of elite, malleable athletes helps elite coaches execute. Athleticism itself is a form of versatility.

Although Koch sets the Super Bowl record for punters with his 2012 cap hit of 1.83%, the cost of the punter market will be increasing in the near future, likely up to three percent for defensive minded competitors. Just in 2016, three punters were over two percent with Marquette King at 3.25% for the Raiders, Dustin Colquitt at 2.87% for the Chiefs and Koch at two percent. The Raiders and Chiefs both went 12-4, making the playoffs, while the Ravens had a competitive year at 8-8; they lost their first seven games by a total of 40 points, with six of those losses being one score games, before losing the season finale by 17 to the Bengals after being eliminated from playoff contention the week before. I don't think their records are directly correlated to all three having good punters as all three of these teams had a lot of talent and good quarterbacks, but punter can be an inexpensive and impactful investment. Teams should especially invest in a punter when they have a young, inexperienced quarterback or lower tier veteran as a way to increase the team's scoring potential and decrease its opponents through field position.

As *Football Outsiders* writes, "every yard line on the field has a value based on how likely a team is to score from that location on the field as opposed to from a yard further back. The change in value from one yard to the next is the same whether the team has the ball or not. The goal of a defense is not just to prevent scoring, but also to hold the opposition so that the offense can get the ball back with the best possible field position. A bad offense will score as many points as a good offense if it starts each drive five-yards closer to the goal line." And as a corollary to this, "the most underrated aspect of an NFL team's performance is the field position gained on kicks and punts. This is part of why players such as Cordarrelle Patterson and Tyler Lockett can have such an impact on the game, even when they aren't taking a kick or punt all the way back." Nick Saban has an interesting quote in Alex Kirby's *Big Book of Saban*, "I've often said if you accumulate 100 yards of field position, no matter how you get it, usually equates to six points."[17] With the decrease in the impact of kickoff plays, punt and punt return have become the place where this field position battle is fought and won. Saban's quote is also worth considering when thinking about offensive and defensive production. How does this running back that can get us 130 yards per game impact your ability to score and win? How does a defense that holds opponents below 300 yards per game impact your ability to win?

Speaking of this concept of 100 yards of field position usually equating to six points, penalties and the yardage generated by them play a large role in each game. Teams cannot commit a high number of unforced errors in such a competitive league and expect to win championships. The league-wide average per team per season from 1994 through 2016 is 102.5 penalties (6.4 per game) and 847.8

penalty yards (53.0 per game). The Super Bowl champions average is in line with that with 101.4 penalties (6.3 per game) and 864.7 penalty yards (54.0 per game). On the flip side, the average team in the cap era has gained 25.7 first downs per season, which is 1.6 per game, and the Super Bowl champions have gained 27.7 or 1.7 per game.

The 2007 Giants are one of the strangest looking champions on paper with an offense ranked 14th in points scored and 17th in points allowed, especially considering that they beat the previously undefeated Patriots in the Super Bowl, but maybe their being the least penalized team of all champions played a role in that? The Giants had four penalties for 36 yards in that Super Bowl, while the Patriots played an equally smart game with five penalties for 35 yards. The G-Men had just 77 penalties on the season, which is just 4.8 per game, for the second least amount of penalty yards of all champions at 652 (40.8 per game).

The 2012 Ravens, 2013 Seahawks, and 2014 Patriots were the three most penalized champions at 121 (7.6), 128 (8.0), and 120 (7.5), which came to 1127 yards (70.4), 1183 (73.9), and 1080 (67.5). The Seahawks and 2014 Patriots had the two worst differentials between their penalties and penalty yards given up and their opponents. That Seahawks team had 30 more penalties and 304 more penalty yards than their opponents, 1.9 more penalties per game and 19.0 more yards per game. This may be due to their physical style of defense, which has clear advantages, but may also have the disadvantage of slightly more penalties. The 2014 Patriots had 28 more penalties, 1.75 more per game, and 328 more penalty yards, which comes to 20.5 more yards per game. Team penalty stats are compiled in the appendix.

Although the emphasis on field position amplifies the importance of special teams, there is fast becoming less overall chance of impact. In the December 2016 article by *Sports Illustrated's* Robert Klemko mentioned earlier, long-time NFL special teams coordinator Mike Westhoff laments the transformation of how special teams were played during his 12 season tenure with the Jets from 2001 through 2012: "special teams has been put on the back burner, the job that I had for so many years no longer exists anymore." Klemko writes that Westhoff gets yearly calls from General Managers asking him to give up his consultant role with college teams and come back to the NFL as a coordinator, but he doesn't think the job is worth doing any longer, "it used to be that we had 22 actual special teams plays per game, not counting field goals and non-plays. When I was with the Jets, we were a big part of the success. Now we wouldn't be. You want me to coach five or six plays? I don't need it." (Westhoff did return to the New Orleans Saints sideline as their Special Teams Coordinator in the middle of the 2017 season.) This lack of total plays is creating a lack of support in roster decisions for special teams coaches as well. They're told that their best candidate for maybe the gunner job isn't going to make the team because they need the roster spot for someone else. This makes Belichick's emphasis on these primarily special teams playing veterans unique, although it could shift over the next few years if directional punts turn special teams into kicks out of the back of the end zone and punts out of bounds or away from the punt returner, almost exactly where the punter wants it almost every time.

Westhoff is not wrong in his frustration over seeing his craft reduced to an afterthought. Kickoff rules have turned most kickoffs, and therefore kickoff returns as well, into non-plays with half of 2016 NFL teams averaging two kick returns or less per game despite the league maintaining high scoring trends. While new styles of punts have played a part of that reduction of plays, the overall opportunity for special teams impact has been funneled into the punt game. These punting innovations have played a massive role in shifting field position, but the punt return has seemingly become the only opportunity for the explosive, game breaking play that turns a loss into a win or a win into a loss if you're on the wrong end of the play.

Current Dolphins Special Teams Coordinator Darren Rizzi was my head coach my freshman year at Rhode Island, having come from Rutgers where he was Greg Schiano's special teams coach. One of the main messages of strategy and objectives that sticks with me is that he intended for us to win through winning two of three phases of the game with one of those being special teams. If our rebuilding program could do that, then we'd have a chance to compete and win. His confidence in his special team's strategies was for good reason: there were five blocked punts, field goal, or point after attempts that were returned for points in 2016, two were by Miami. After a Week 13 loss to the Ravens set them back to 7-5, a fourth quarter PAT block returned for two points put them up 23-15 with 7:05 left. Arizona tied it at 23 with 3:01 left, but a last second field goal by Andrew Franks gave them the 26-23 win. The next week, up 13-10 against the Jets in the third, a punt blocked and returned for a touchdown by Walt Aikens made it 20-10 and they went on to win 34-13. As a Wild Card team at 10-6, the Dolphins may have lost a game and missed the playoffs to another 9-7 team if they don't make one of those blocks or the other special teams plays the unit made during the season. Three other blocks were returned for points in 2016 and all three earned wins. The Broncos blocked PAT after a Saints touchdown made it 23-23 with 1:22 left to win 25-23. Denver finished 9-7, but this could've been the difference maker to get them in the playoffs the same way Miami's were. The Ravens had two blocks returned for points as well; the first came when they were down 20-0 against Cleveland in Week 2 when a PAT block return made it 20-2 and they later came all the way back to win 25-20. They blocked a punt early in the fourth quarter against the Steelers to make it 21-0, which helped secure the win as their divisional rival scored two touchdowns to make it 21-14 before time expired.

Coordinators like Rizzi and Ravens Head Coach John Harbaugh, a former special teams coordinator himself, create blocks. Can you create a strategy that gets one of your athletes to the block point in less than the time it takes from snap to kick? On a punt that means getting guys there in under two seconds, on field goals that means getting guys to the block point in 1.2 seconds or less or skying high to block it up the middle, and coordinators create strategies to accomplish those objectives. The shift toward 33-yard extra points will likely increase total blocks per year over time due to the lower trajectory of the kick and strategies that attack the middle of the line although the NFL just voted to ban the jump over the interior of the line strategy that has been en vogue the last couple years. Special teams coordinators can have an impact on punt returns as well with the plays they create and having an explosive punt returner is the main place where a special teams unit has a chance to create an explosive play. From 2014 through 2016, the NFL had 36 punt returns for touchdowns versus 20 kick returns. There has been a substantial dip in kick return production during that time with the league averaging 910.1 kick return yards per team in 2014 versus 709.0 in 2016. While just two teams had over 1000 kick return yards in 2016, 15 teams were over that mark in 2014.

Punt returners must have explosive first-step quickness to make defenders miss in space and the acceleration to get moving up field. Athletes who can excel at this tend to have a low-center of gravity that allows them to make defenders miss. Klemko's article on returners highlighted the two Chiefs in the 5'8", 187-pounds Dante Hall and the 5'10", 185 pounds—Tyreek Hill, who are both in the size range of most of the players returning punts today between 5'8" to 6' and 180 to 200 pounds. Darren Sproles has been a long-time great with his 5'6", 180-pound frame helping him move laterally and explode in a way that very few humans can on a field full of monsters who have a higher center of gravity. Why do you think tiny jackrabbits evolved to have such quickness? Well, how could they survive without it?

Belichick has been consistently using slot receivers to return punts as their great hands provide great ball security. Slots, being "possession receivers," tend to have great hands for that reason, but also because, when you're 5'9", you can't afford to drop balls in college training camp like a taller, track speed guy can. Coaches are looking for returners who can produce positive yardage and, speaking in terms of objectives, they're doing the same thing the offense does, trying to produce first down yardage to give the offense one less first down to gain. The occasional touchdown will come, but touchdown production is not the focus; the focus is on finding returners who can consistently produce chunks of yardage. Eight teams averaged 10 or more yards per return in 2016, a full first down closer to the end zone, or another 10 yards of field position, which is one less first down your offense has to earn, even if you don't score. Hill led the NFL averaging 15.2 yards per return, a great way to start a drive. As Gordon McGuinness wrote for PFF, "no one in 2016 was better than Hill with 23 missed tackles and two touchdowns on punt returns alone." That elite quickness in space allowed him to make defenders miss and get downfield.

McGuinness writes that a "punt returner needs good blocking, starts with the vice, often referred to as anti-gunners. They line up opposite the gunners and try to slow their progress downfield. With the importance of this position, teams often line up two vice on either side." He goes on, "the punt defensive line and linebackers are there to rush the punter, and/or slow the release of the punt offensive line, depending on the situation. The blocks are the highlight reel plays, but jamming the left guard of the punt unit can free up a lane for the punt returner that otherwise wouldn't be there." When this unit executes a great scheme from the special teams coordinator to open up a lane, these explosive returners create the big plays.

Lastly are the field goal units and it is of critical importance in close games, which are plentiful as the calendar turns to a new year. As mentioned earlier, Christopher L. Gasper found that the Patriots have a .709 winning percentage in games decided by three or fewer points, the highest win percentage in the NFL for such games. For the last 16 seasons, the Patriots have had Adam Vinatieri hitting 83.6% of his field goals from 2001 through 2005, a rate that would be good for 20th all-time at the end of the 2016 season, then his replacement Stephen Gostowski has hit at a rate of 87.1% from 2005 through 2016, which is fourth all-time. This became a bit of a trend with the Colts and the Broncos being the other two teams with win percentages over 60% at .661 and .610 respectively. The Colts have had two of the best of all-time with Mike Vanderjagt hitting 86.2% of his field goals from 2001 to '05 and Vinatieri at 86.7% from 2006 to 2016, which would both rank fifth of all-time on their own. The Broncos haven't had the same level of play as the other two, but Jason Elam, Matt Prater and Brandon McManus have given them a combined field goal percentage of 83.2% since 2001.

Of the 23 Super Bowl champions of the salary cap era, the Patriots have the four most expensive kickers with Vinatieri at 3.09% in 2003, Gostowski at 2.86% in 2014, then at 2.64% in 2016, and Vinatieri in 2004 at 2.59%. After that is a drop off down to 1.69% with Jeff Reed of the 2008 Steelers and Vinatieri's 2001 cap hit of 1.42% isn't far behind him. The rest of the league seems to be catching on with 11 kickers with cap hits over 2% in 2016 and—I believe, like punter, the top of this market will become three percent for the best three-point shooters in the NFL.

A kicker's field goal percentage can fluctuate from year to year based on the difference between one or two kicks missing rather than making, which can be affected by distance, weather conditions and blocked kicks that could effect accurate data collection. For instance, Robbie Gould's 85.9% field goal percentage during 11 seasons playing home games outside at Soldier Field in Chicago is arguably more impressive than Vanderjagt's career mark of 87.5% because Vanderjagt played in a dome in Indianapolis. New England intends to play their playoff games at home and outside in January, so the high investment in a kicker is a smart investment for Belichick. In 2016, four kickers were over 90% in Justin Tucker at 97.4%, Matt Bryant at 91.9%, Ryan Succop at 91.7%, and Kai Forbath at 100% in seven games going 15 for 15 for Minnesota after Blair Walsh was released after hitting just 12 of his 16 kicks (75.0%) in the first nine games. The top 12 most accurate field goal kickers were over 86%, while the bottom ten were all at 80.0% or less. Chandler Catanzaro hit just 21 of 28 field goals in 2016, only 75.0% for the Cardinals as a part of a special teams unit that Rick Gosselin of *The Dallas Morning News* ranked 31st in the NFL in his annual rankings.

Detroit was the NFC's sixth seed in the playoffs at 9-7 and Arizona went 7-8-1, but without a few special teams mistakes Arizona may have gotten into the playoffs and had a chance to compete for the Super Bowl with an offense that was sixth in points per game at 26.1 and a defense that was second in yards allowed at 305.2 per game. While second in yards allowed, they were 14th in points allowed at 22.6 per game, maybe because of their poor special teams plus an offense that was 26th in the NFL with 28 turnovers. We've already mentioned the 26-23 loss with the punt block touchdown by Miami, but Catanzaro also missed a field goal that game. His tough year started Week 1 with a missed game-winning 47-yard field goal with 41 seconds left on Monday Night Football as the Patriots held on to win 23-21. In Week 7, rather than tie Seattle 6-6, the Cardinals could've won if Catanzaro's 39-yarder in the second quarter wasn't blocked and they definitely would've won if he could've hit the 24-yarder he had with 3:26 left in overtime. If Arizona doesn't make those mistakes on special teams, they might've been 10-6 and not only have made the playoffs, but won the NFC West with the 2-0 record against what would've been a 10-6 Seahawks team. The 2015 NFC runner-up Cardinals would have been in position to make another run.

The 2016 Chargers went 5-11 on Gosselin's 32nd best special teams unit in the NFL. They lost their 11 games by an average of 5.45 points per game as every loss was by 10 points or less with 10 of them being decided by eight points or less. Combine a league leading 35 turnovers on offense with terrible special teams play and you get a team that is 16th in yards allowed, but 29th in points allowed. This combination led to many of those losses.

While the 2016 Patriots made financial investments and kept roster spots open for special teams players, Arizona had just three players playing over 50% of special teams snaps and the Chargers had four. Arizona invested 2.09% in cornerback

Justin Bethel and the Chargers in their last year in San Diego had 1.07% invested in Darrell Stuckey, but they had no other investments in special teamers. It seemed they were content with filling their special teams units with a combination of rookie contract players, many of whom probably played very little special teams in college as the best college players who make it to the NFL might be left off most special teams units to preserve their energy for offense or defense and not deal with the risk of injury on special teams.

Speaking of Cardinals kicker Chandler Catanzaro, his failures in 2016 were hard to foreseeing as he'd hit 57 of 64 field goals his first two seasons, an 89.1% mark, which would've ranked seventh of qualified kickers in 2016. The 25-year old's psyche may have been impacted by the very public miss to start the year, but it may be a great example of the difficulty in projecting year to year performance at one of the most mentally and psychologically challenging positions in sports. You could split the 2016 kickers into three tiers with the top being above 86% and the bottom being below 80% with everyone else in the middle tier, but that wouldn't be accurate due to the small sample size of kicks in a season. Dan Bailey is the second most accurate kicker of all-time at 89.5% behind Tucker's 89.9% rate post-2016, but at 84.4% in 2016 he wouldn't be in the top tier. But if he'd made one more of his 32 kicks, he'd bounce to the top. The goal is to find those kickers who are likely to produce that 86% plus performance over time. Although only six kickers all-time have averaged over 86% for their career, advances in the technical aspects of execution of kicks have increased efficiency at the position. This increase, as well as the 33-yard point after attempts that were introduced in 2015 increase the need for an accurate kicker, will push the market up to three percent and maybe even higher in time. As Tucker illustrates, a 100% three-point shooter if your offense gets to your opponent's 35 or 40-yard line is a deadly weapon and 100% on point after attempts is becoming a luxury with just four perfect kickers, including Tucker, and 11 total with one or less misses. As seen in Super Bowl 51, Gostowski's miss would've cost the Patriots the win if they didn't convert both two-point conversations they had to attempt in their epic comeback, so these longer one-point conversions have already impacted NFL history.

Our last special teams expense is very cheap, but very important—the long snapper. In 2016, the highest cap hit was Miami's John Denney at 0.78%, so if your team had struggles the previous season, it could potentially be worth stealing a good one that hits free agency with a deal near one percent. While they're forgotten until they make a mistake, their accuracy is a vital part of getting punts off in less than two seconds and field goals off in less than 1.2 seconds, the time special teams coordinators shoot for.

We've discussed every offensive and defensive positional market, as well as special teams. These markets and the ranges of spending are important to understand, but a rapidly increasing salary cap over the next few years will open up the opportunity to spending a little bit more on top talent. A disparity is growing between the haves and have nots in the NFL because of the low-rookie wage scale and low veteran minimums due to a salary cap that will be over $200 million very soon. The short careers of certain markets make positions like running back low-cost across time as teams use and discard players after, or shortly after, their rookie deals, while positions like quarterback can have 15 year careers and make 15% of the cap at their peak. Some team or teams will win with record breaking top cap hits over the next few seasons, but this will likely, and hopefully, be adjusted in the next CBA as the players union overcorrected a big problem in the previous CBA, which was the ridiculous contracts that quarterbacks at the top of the first round were receiving toward the end of the agreement. At least now unproven top of first round rookie contract players aren't the ones getting the ridiculous contracts, but the entire rookie pool is getting nowhere near their true value.

Chapter 10: Projecting the Salary Cap, Big Cap Hits and the Need for a Wage Increase in Rookie Contracts Under the Next CBA

During the 2015 offseason, I realized the need for teams to be able to project the future cap to sign players to contracts whose cap hits would fit manageable parameters in future years to help the team compete. On the other hand, I also realized the importance of agents understanding future cap projections and a player's market value because too many contracts were being signed with cap hits much higher in the later years than the player's team would ever pay him with no dead money to dissuade the team from releasing their clients and their overvalued cap hits. Years were just added to make a contract sound bigger than it really was, which would both make the agent look good on ESPN's bottom line ticker to potential clients and help a team seemingly outbid another with a contract they may never pay out.

Dan Snyder has done this continuously with the Redskins and he's done it poorly by creating such bad, overpriced contracts that they would eat up huge chunks of their salary cap in the 2000s with dead money charges. In 2003 the Redskins had $14.5 million in dead money, which was 20.71% of the 2003 cap. In a 2004 Washington Post article, Jason LaCanfora and Nunyo Demasio wrote that the Redskins faced as much as $27 million in dead money in one of Snyder's first years in Washington.[1] All this dead money while he was firing coaches because they couldn't make the playoffs with depleted rosters.

To project future salary caps, I looked at the average annual salary cap increase, which I found to be 7.5% through 2015 and still essentially holds true through 2017 at 7.56%. Then, to check my work, I looked at what the revenue growth rate would have to be to hit Roger Goodell's publicly stated goal of $25 billion in revenues by 2027. Given that league revenues were projected to be $10 billion in 2014, the number I found was that a 7.32% yearly increase would get to that 2027 number. I now assume this could be coincidental, but when these revenue figures were multiplied by 0.47 to represent the player's 47% of revenues, I found the projected salary cap off these numbers was just a few million more than the projected caps using the 7.5% yearly cap increase. The year prior in the 47% of revenues model would have a similar cap figure with the next season's salary cap using the 7.5% yearly cap increase, so I thought they were correlated. I've since adjusted the revenue figures for 2014 through 2016 with 2017's revenue projections included and the projected salary cap is now tens of millions more than the cap with the revenue projections that I did in 2015. I know that the player's 47% is made up by receiving 40% of local revenues (mainly ticket sales); 45% of sponsorship money, revenues from the post-season and NFL Ventures, such as NFL.com and the NFL Network; and 55% of all the revenues from media deals, so maybe something else could cause that gap from revenue to salary cap.

I don't know if any wrongdoing on behalf of the NFL and owners exists, but they did use a loophole to hide $100 million from the player's pool in the early parts of the current CBA, which led to the NFLPA filing a grievance and an independent arbiter forcing the money into the pool to increase the 2016 cap by $1.5 million. That made the year's cap $155.27 million and the 2017 cap $167 million, so my projection was 100% accurate in 2017. This makes me think there could either be more grievances to come or maybe the gap between the salary cap and 47% has to do with the NFL's pension program; maybe the pension program is what makes up the difference. This could be where the Joint Contribution Credit comes in as it is used to fund various programs outside of the game like healthcare for retired players, medical research, and donations to charities of the joint contribution, which is then used as a 47.5% credit toward player costs that decreases the cap slightly. In 2016, the joint contribution credit was $66,852,844, which was then multiplied by 47.5% and subtracted from all other revenues to help create the total player cost. Tens of millions are subtracted from player costs each year because of this joint contribution credit and then that total is divided by the 32 teams to create the salary cap. Multiplying the joint contribution credit by 47.5% should mean only $31,755,101 was subtracted from the player's pool, so I'm unsure why such a gap exists between 47% of revenues and cap costs, which players are only guaranteed 89% of with the 89% Rule.

Here is a table from *Crunching Numbers: An Inside Look at the Salary Cap and Negotiating Player Contracts* by Jason Fitzgerald and Vijay Natarajan that explains what counts as a Salary Cap Charge versus what is a Player Benefit Charge:[2]

Salary Cap Charges	Player Benefit Charges
Paragraph 5 Base Salary	Postseason Salary
Prorated Bonus Money	Preseason Salary
All Offseason Bonuses	Severance Pay
All Tenders	Medical Costs
Earned Incentives	Minimum Salary Benefit
Dead Money	Performance-Based Pay
Termination Pay	Pension Funding
Injury Grievances	Rookie Orientation
Injury Settlements	Meals
Injury Protections (starting in 2016)	Moving Expenses

Travel/Lodging/Expenses for Workout
Program
Insurance
Injury Protections (through 2015)

This is explained in chapter four of *Crunching Numbers*, a great resource for anyone who wants to have a better understanding of the entire Collective Bargaining Agreement (CBA). This chapter is less about the details behind calculating the cap and instead focused on understanding where the salary cap is going.

What follows are the tables that illustrate the NFL salary cap increases and projections that I've just explained.

Historic Salary Cap Increase

Season	Cap	(+/-) Last Cap	% of Last Cap
1994	34,608,000	N/A	N/A
1995	37,100,000	2,492,000	107.20%
1996	40,753,000	3,653,000	109.85%
1997	41,454,000	701,000	101.72%
1998	52,388,000	10,934,000	126.38%
1999	57,288,000	4,900,000	109.35%
2000	62,172,000	4,884,000	108.53%
2001	67,405,000	5,233,000	108.42%
2002	71,101,000	3,696,000	105.48%
2003	75,007,000	3,906,000	105.49%
2004	80,852,000	5,845,000	107.79%
2005	85,500,000	4,648,000	105.75%
2006	102,000,000	16,500,000	119.30%
2007	109,000,000	7,000,000	106.86%
2008	116,000,000	7,000,000	106.42%
2009	123,000,000	7,000,000	106.03%
2010	NO CAP	N/A	N/A
2011	120,000,000	-3,000,000	97.56%
2012	120,600,000	600,000	100.50%
2013	123,000,000	2,400,000	101.99%
2014	133,000,000	10,000,000	108.13%
2015	143,280,000	10,280,000	107.73%
2016	155,270,000	11,990,000	108.37%
2017	167,000,000	11,730,000	107.55%
		1994-2017	107.56%
		2011-2017	104.55%

	2012-2017	105.71%
	1994-2009	108.97%

Projected Revenue Increase to Hit Roger Goodell's Goal of $25 Billion by 2027: Using 107.31% Increase; Projected Salary Cap Equals 47% divided by 32 teams

Year	Projected Revenues	Proj. Player's 47%	Proj. Salary Cap
2014	10,000,000,000	4,700,000,000	146,875,000
2015	10,731,000,000	5,043,570,000	157,611,563
2016	11,515,436,100	5,412,254,967	169,132,968
2017	12,357,214,479	5,807,890,805	181,496,588
2018	13,260,526,857	6,232,447,623	194,763,988
2019	14,229,871,371	6,688,039,544	209,001,236
2020	15,270,074,968	7,176,935,235	224,279,226
2021	16,386,317,448	7,701,569,201	240,674,038
2022	17,584,157,253	8,264,553,909	258,267,310
2023	18,869,559,149	8,868,692,800	277,146,650
2024	20,248,923,922	9,516,994,244	297,406,070
2025	21,729,120,261	10,212,686,523	319,146,454
2026	23,317,518,952	10,959,233,908	342,476,060
2027	25,022,029,588	11,760,353,906	367,511,060

Revised 2014-16 Revenues Still Using 107.31% Increase

Year	Projected Revenues	Proj. Player's 47%	Proj. Salary Cap
2014	12,000,000,000	5,640,000,000	176,250,000
2015	13,000,000,000	6,110,000,000	190,937,500
2016	13,300,000,000	6,251,000,000	195,343,750
2017	14,000,000,000	6,580,000,000	205,625,000
2018	15,023,400,000	7,060,998,000	220,656,188
2019	16,121,610,540	7,577,156,954	236,786,155
2020	17,300,100,270	8,131,047,127	254,095,223
2021	18,564,737,600	8,725,426,672	272,669,584
2022	19,921,819,919	9,363,255,362	292,601,730
2023	21,378,104,955	10,047,709,329	313,990,917
2024	22,940,844,427	10,782,196,881	336,943,653
2025	24,617,820,155	11,570,375,473	361,574,234
2026	26,417,382,808	12,416,169,920	388,005,310
2027	28,348,493,491	13,323,791,941	416,368,498

Using the revised revenues for 2014 through 2016 with average growth rates, we see that revenues should blow past Goodell's $25 billion goal by 2027.
My Original 2015 Cap Projections

Season	(+107.5%) Cap
2015	143,280,000
2016	154,026,000
2017	165,677,950
2018	177,996,296
2019	191,346,018
2020	205,696,970
2021	221,124,243

Rounding To Half Million

Season	(+107.5%) Cap
2015	143,280,000
2016	154,000,000
2017	165,500,000
2018	178,000,000
2019	191,500,000
2020	205,500,000
2021	221,000,000

Even if those salary cap numbers are legitimate, it seems that current NFL players aren't getting a clean 47% of revenues, so the NFLPA should be looking to at least get back to a 50-50 split with owners–the split that was used under the previous CBA. In a July 2013 article in *The Boston Globe* titled, "Now more than ever, we realize NFL owners won," Ben Volin quotes a prominent agent with two decades in the league, who spoke under the condition of anonymity for fear of retribution by the NFLPA and said, "the owners used the bad economy to cry poor, and then they took everything."[3] Volin points this out in the Packers financials as they saw $22.3 million of net income in the two-years prior to the 2011 CBA and $85.5 million in 2011 and 2012. That equates to a 385% increase in net income while the 2011 salary cap saw a contraction of 2.44% as $120 million was just 97.56% of the $123 million cap in 2009. The next year's cap was just 100.5% of the 2011 cap at $120.6 million, still below the 2009 level, so four-years of wage stagnation during a time where the NFL seemed to take over as America's favorite sport. This was after the salary cap increased at an average rate of 108.97% from 1994 to 2009, which leads me to believe the NFLPA should look to, **at minimum**, lock in a 109% yearly cap increase that will restore previous growth rates, while still allowing the NFL to not actually give players even a 47% share of revenue as seen by comparing the table below with the revised chart of Goodell projections. I maintained the 7.5% increase through 2020 with the addition of $1.5 million to each year through 2027 to adjust for the $1.5 million added with the 2016 adjustment as my original projections were correct once accounting for the addition. These are just rough estimates that should be within a couple million at least through 2020. Past 2020 is anyone's guess what happens under a new CBA.

My Cap Projection/Proposal through 2027 Using My 2015 Projections adding $1.5 Million to numbers from 2016 to 2021 and multiplying by 107.5% from 2015-2020 and 109% from 2021-2027
(Full chart with work in Appendix)

Year	2015-2027 Projection
2015	143,280,000
2016	155,270,000
2017	167,000,000
2018	179,500,000
2019	193,000,000
2020	207,000,000
2021	225,500,000
2022	244,500,000
2023	266,500,000
2024	290,500,000
2025	316,500,000
2026	345,000,000
2027	376,000,000

This is just the starting point, though. I don't think the NFLPA should allow negotiations to continue without seeing each team's books to ensure full compensation on a 50-50 split. Factoring in a 109% increase, at minimum considering this would still not represent 47% judging off of Goodell's own projection, we see that the cap could reach $376 million by 2027. This is why 10-12% of the cap for a top quarterback becomes possible in the future; more teams should be able to implement the strategy that Brady and Rodgers are using as some handful of players will likely realize that a $30 million a year average for a decade, along with the continually growing off field business and endorsement opportunities that come from being an elite quarterback, is enough to create and grow generational wealth. Organizations will likely have created a more realistic quarterback market by then and/or an increase in rookie compensation might solve the issue. I'll address, and hopefully provide the solution, or foundation for the solution, of low-rookie contract compensation later in this chapter.

This low, undervalued compensation for a big chunk of NFL rosters has led to the potential for teams to compete for championships with high-cost, first tier players who are paired with rookie contract players. As Jason Fitzgerald wrote in a July 2017 article, "the league is likely on pace to spend about $5 billion in salaries to players this year. About 17% of that total will go to 50 players. 50% of the total will go to just 150 players, about 12% of the entire league population." The 2013 Seahawks and 2015 Broncos had a top of cap construction that was much different than most past champions because of this growing disparity between the haves and the have nots with top 10 cap hits that consumed 61.31% and 62.33% of their caps, which is far above the top three from prior to the 2011 CBA: the 2002 Bucs at 55.97%, the 2006 Colts at 54.07%, and the 1994 49ers at 53.95%. The average top 10 for champions from 1994 to 2009 cost 48.39% of the cap compared to 55.23% since the 2011 CBA.

The Seahawks and Broncos earned championships with a high-cost veterans, low-cost rookies strategy, the 2016 Falcons were up 28-3 in the third quarter against what may have been Bill Belichick's best team to date with Matt Ryan and Julio Jones consuming a cap percentage that was seemingly as insurmountable as the lead the Patriots overcame at 25.54% of the 2016 cap compared to the Super Bowl record of 21.64% by Steve Young and Jerry Rice. The Seahawks and Broncos had acquired much of their rosters through the draft and had them playing on rookie contracts, which allowed them to pair them with multiple first tier veterans. Zach Miller consumed a Super Bowl record 8.94% of the cap for the Seahawks, which was 3.3% higher than the next closest Super Bowl tight end in Aaron Hernandez's accelerated dead money cap hit, and 3.93% higher than Shannon Sharpe's 5.01% for the 1998 Broncos. They also had wide receiver Sidney Rice at 7.89% with him missing most of the season due to injury. Having a starting quarterback at 0.55% of the cap like Russell Wilson was helps allow for this kind of investment. For the Broncos, Peyton Manning and Ryan Clady have the second highest Super Bowl cap hits for their positions, Demaryius Thomas broke Jerry Rice's previous record as a receiver, Von Miller and Demarcus Ware were both over six percent of the cap, but that was paired with valuable rookie contract contributors like Bradley Roby, Malik Jackson, Derek Wolfe, C.J. Anderson, Brandon Marshall, Danny Trevathan, Matt Paradis, Sylvester Williams, and Michael Schofield. The Falcons got their two first-tier, franchise players through the draft who were on the big second contracts their positions require for their level of production and potential, but just didn't have enough to win that final game.

Seattle has since been able to maintain and extend their core with a strategy that has seen them trade out of the first round in four of the last five drafts dating back to 2013. This is almost as a point of necessity considering their now expensive core superstars; they've avoided first round picks and stockpiled second through fourth round picks that can consistently produce starters at less than one percent of the cap for the first four years of their careers. From 2013 through 2017, they had 22 picks in the second through fourth round with 2017 being the best example of this strategy with two second round picks and four third rounders. They've realized this high-probability, low-cost, low-risk strategy, which allows them to then, in a sense, overpay their core due to the increased market costs across positions that are due to the extreme bargains available in the rookie pool.

All three of those organizations had the deep knowledge of what their West Coast offenses and stifling defenses needed to succeed using the same sort of logic described over the last nine chapters. Darrelle Bevell knew Russell Wilson was the perfect fit for their system. Pete Carroll understood what they needed on both sides of the ball and he worked with John Schneider to find the best players they could for it by bringing in hundreds of prospects through the organization during those early years for tryouts; they cycled through players until they found the right players. John Elway managed the end of Peyton Manning's career with the same roster construction strategy the organization used to win two Super Bowls at the end of Elway's career and in the same offensive system under Gary Kubiak. Atlanta found extreme value at running back with Devonta Freeman and Tevin Coleman in Kyle Shanahan's system similar to the way his father did—plus Matt Ryan and Julio Jones leading the passing attack—and Dan Quinn found the prototypes in the draft to fill out the Seahawks—style defense he knows so well.

These three teams have clear alignment between their front office and head coach, which combines a deep knowledge of systems with knowledge of how to make those systems a reality through player acquisition and salary cap decisions. Rookie contracts for second round picks peak near one percent in year four, but drop rapidly to the point where from the third round on, every player costs less than half a percent of the cap. With the advancement of analytics, access to prospect information that teams now have, and knowledge of systems, finding pieces to fill system needs is becoming easier for organizations, which has caused the probability of a team finding a productive player with mid- to late-round picks to increase and it should continue to increase. Being able to find such low-cost production then allows organizations to find ways to cut costs through knowledge of the market value of production specific to their system, which then allows them to spend those cap savings elsewhere.

Like I've already explained, the Patriots know their system can produce rushing and receiving yards for far less money than market costs through knowing how and where to find production for a lower cost. West Coast systems, especially those in the Shanahan tree, look for specific skills at running back that allow for them to find production at the position in a way that has depressed costs at the position for veterans as well. If you want to make tens of millions of dollars as an NFL player, you shouldn't be a running back because unless you're a first round pick, the likelihood of making those millions is low as the position may be the most difficult on the body considering the physics they deal with weekly, which leads to short careers and decreased free agent markets. Mass times acceleration equals force and they deal with some otherworldly math. Yet, a great running back can be one of the most valuable pieces of a Super Bowl run, the pace setter your team relies on, so these low costs aren't equal to the value that great running backs provide.

The supply of running backs that can perform early at that low-cost has destroyed the entire market. Strategies like the Cowboys in recent years with their elite offensive lines can set up a situation where a team can cycle through 1000-yard rushers and ride a player on a rookie deal to the playoffs like they did with Demarco Murray with 392 rushes in the final year of his contract and now Ezekiel Elliott. This is much less expensive than Emmitt Smith's Super Bowl record 9.17% cap hit in 1995 behind his equally stout offensive lines.

Many backs are used up by an organization and never earn a chance at generational wealth. Running back is a position that needs to receive better value in rookie contracts because of the short career length, especially considering that when they do hit the market, it now seems to be capping around five percent of the cap in the case of many high performing backs in recent years.

As discussed in the previous chapters on positional market costs, outside of quarterback, an average veteran starter costs around one and a half to three percent of the cap, so hits on draft picks in the second round or later become huge values—but even first round picks are values. Top picks have a high probability of becoming stars and they should be definite starters, yet Tampa Bay Buccaneers quarterback Jameis Winston is only projected to consume 4.46% of the cap in the fourth year of his contract, far below the market value of a starting quarterback, but also below the value of what a top pick at quarterback should, and is very likely to, provide in year four of his career. If the Eagles didn't release Chase Daniel, his 2017 cap hit on a back-up quarterback contract would have been 4.79%. Teams are getting the #1 pick for back-up, bridge quarterback money, as no team drafts a first round pick at quarterback not expecting him to start by year four. Very few teams plan on not starting that guy in year one, so the three percent they get paid in year one isn't realistic either. This presents a great opportunity for organizations to build up their roster around that quarterback, but such low rookie cap hits are not fair market value. Neither was Sam Bradford's rookie deal that paid him over 10% of the cap with the St. Louis Rams. The happy medium for a first round pick at high-cost positions like cornerback, wide receiver, left tackle and pass rusher in year four would be closer to four to five percent of the cap, much higher than almost all first round picks currently. Rookie quarterback deals should probably hit even higher in year four, at least six percent, while seven to eight percent is even realistic in the current market. Position specific slotted contracts might be said to be too crazy an idea for an industry with 32 franchises worth over $1.5 billion to figure out though.

It gets worse as the first round goes on. Missing on a first round pick has no direct financial risk now; even if the player you drafted with the 20th pick becomes a marginal starter, they're still a strong value. DeVante Parker was the Dolphins 14th pick in 2015 and he'll cost between one and a half and two percent of the cap throughout his rookie contract. While he hasn't broken out yet, 2017 was just his third season and he had to suffer through Jay Cutler and Matt Moore, so we haven't gotten a great look at his full potential. In 2016 he had 56 catches (64.4% catch rate) for 744 yards and four touchdowns, which is the kind of production teams could expect from a player in the bottom of the second tier of the receiver market, just over three percent of the cap. The third tier of the wide receiver market exists between one and a half and three percent to represent an average veteran starter who could be relied on to produce 500 yards. Fourth tier receivers are those under one and a half percent of the cap and these are the kind of guys you'd only rely on for a couple hundred receiving yards, so a 1st round pick at receiver is locked into a production cost far below the probable value of a top 32 draft pick, a player that the NFL admits is a potential top player at his position through his selection in the first round (and fifth-year team options that acknowledge their value as being worth top veteran rates).

With these contracts, teams are able to lock a large percentage, maybe half, of their rosters into contracts far below their value, which then likely leads to overpaying many top veterans. With considerable decreases in rookie contract costs in the entire first round and into the second round, the savings on rookie contracts are being spread to veterans, allowing for the increasing spread between top paid veterans and the average NFL player. Jordy Nelson was the 36th pick in the second round in 2008 and, according to Over The Cap, he had a contract that paid him about 1.5% of the cap in his first two seasons. Today that same pick will not breach one percent until year four. Jake Long was the first round pick in 2008 with a cap hit of 7.8% in year two and over 10% in 2011 and 2012, which is too extreme in the other direction as over 10% of the cap is clearly an overvaluation of rookie contract players, after the uncapped 2010 season. As mentioned earlier, #1 picks don't pass four percent until year four. Players coming out of college are more prepared than they've ever been with many coming in and contributing as starters in year one. The current CBA's rookie contracts are robbing these players of getting fair value in a league where the average career is between three to four years. NFL teams get to own the average player's rights for longer than the average career is. They're dictating labor costs, not the market.

Until the 2021 CBA hopefully solves the issue for these far below market rate contracts, there will be teams competing for Super Bowls like the Seahawks, Broncos, and Falcons teams mentioned, so teams may win in these next few years with cap hit(s) that break Super Bowl records. With low-cost draft picks at key positions, the 2013 Seahawks and 2015 Broncos drafted good rosters and brought in more than one key first tier free agent, which is something that a small number of Super Bowl teams have done, a fact that might have surprised you prior to reading this book considering how much attention goes to the most expensive, splashy free agent signings. Free agent signings do win Super Bowls, but they're the right ones, for the right value, and, especially if they're for first tier players, at the right time.

On 22 Super Bowl champions during salary capped seasons there have been 13 free agent acquisitions with cap hits at or over six percent who were still playing on their initial contracts they signed with the team. Of those 13, three were on Seattle (Zach Miller, 8.94%; Sidney Rice, 7.89%; Chris Clemons, 6.64%;), two on the 2015 Broncos (Peyton Manning, 12.21%; Demarcus Ware, 6.05%), two on the 2002 Buccaneers (Brad Johnson, 9.57%; Simeon Rice, 8.44%), and two on the 1995 Cowboys (Charles Haley, 6.01%; Deion Sanders. 5.98%).

The 2002 Buccaneers' two eight percent plus free agent cap hits of Johnson and Rice make them a good example of a successful free agent strategy. Johnson had second tier costs, but he was accurate and didn't throw interceptions, providing a great example of what a system manager at quarterback with a great defense can accomplish. Worth noting considering one of the main arguments of this book being the different strategies for building a roster other than overpaying a quarterback.

Four of these 22 teams had nine total free agents over 6% of the cap, while the other 18 teams had four such free agents. Two pass rushers were signed as premium free agents with Reggie White consuming 8.90% of the cap for the 1996 Packers and Chris Canty at 6.00% for the 2011 Giants, while Adam Timmerman was the right guard for the 1999 championship Rams after signing that offseason with a cap hit of 6.11% as an elite offensive lineman. Drew Brees had a second tier quarterback cap hit of 8.67% in 2009 as he signed with the team in the 2006 offseason after a shoulder injury that many thought he'd struggle to come back from, so the Chargers decided to move on from him and into the Phillip Rivers era.

While 2010 was an uncapped year (so he doesn't necessarily count towards this group), Charles Woodson was in the middle of a seven year deal that had a potential worth of as much as $52 million according to ESPN's Michael Smith at the time and his cap hit in 2010 would have been seven percent of a $120 million cap. Ryan Pickett signed as a free agent in 2006 and was re-signed to a frontloaded contract that took advantage of this uncapped year with a cap hit of almost $8,437,500, which would have been 7.03% of the next season's $120 million salary cap, so he's not really a first tier free agent in this scenario with it being his second contract with the team. With Rodgers on a contract that would be considered third tier at 5.42% of a $120 million cap, the Packers were able to afford these two, plus three homegrown players in safety Nick Collins at over nine percent of the cap, defensive tackle B.J. Raji, and Chad Clifton over six percent.

Five veterans acquired through trades cost over six percent of the cap for their Super Bowl teams with all five of them playing on contracts they'd signed after being acquired by their teams, which brings the total of players acquired as veterans over six percent of the cap up to 17 on the 22 salary capped teams with 10 of those teams having the 17 players—which does lend support to the idea of the right big acquisition coming at the right time having the right impact. Since each of these players were a part of Super Bowl teams on deals signed after their trades, they're in a bit of a different scenario than most of the players mentioned who were signed as free agents.

In April 1987, seven and a half years before he achieved Super Bowl glory for the 49ers, Steve Young was traded from the Buccaneers to the 49ers for second- and fourth-round choices in the 1987 draft. On February 10th, 1992, the Packers traded a first-round pick in that year's draft to Atlanta for Brett Favre. While these two were over 10% of the cap for their Super Bowl winning teams, they earned these championships after signing new contracts and after spending just two and one year in their previous cities respectively.

Marshawn Lynch came to the Seahawks in 2010 through a trade with the Bills that sent a 2011 fourth-round pick and a conditional pick in 2012 as he re-signed with the team in 2012 to the contract that had him consuming 6.91% of the cap for the 2013 team. Marshall Faulk was traded by the Colts prior to the 1999 season for the Rams' second- and fifth-round picks in the 1999 draft where they drafted Edgerrin James in the first-round. Faulk then held out of training camp for 12 days before signing a seven-year, $45.15 million contract that had him consuming 7.42% of the 1999 cap. Anquan Boldin was traded from the Cardinals with a fifth-round pick in 2010 for the Ravens third- and fourth-round draft picks, then re-signed to a three-year, $25 million extension as he was entering the last year of his contract turning his contract into a four year $28 million deal that he was released from after the 2012 season as he wouldn't take a pay cut. He cost 6.24% of the cap for the 2012 championship team.

The strategy of an expensive top of roster combined with low-cost rookies has become a viable strategy for success in this CBA because the NFLPA was successful in their mission to increase veteran pay, but the bulk of that pay goes to a small group of players in expensive markets like quarterback, wide receiver, cornerback, pass rusher, and offensive linemen. In a way this is because these are positions that have a little more longevity. Positions like running back and inside linebacker, two of the sports most violent, have seen their market value shrink while teams find cheaper, younger, and/or healthier alternatives. This isn't just an issue for those two positions; non-elite veterans can get squeezed out of the league after rookie deals for new prospects without ever making a million in a year. Analytics will help teams continue to cut costs on these fringe and lower tier veterans. Others continue to play, yet never get what would be considered a big pay day in free agency, even though they're a starter, because of these low-market rates.

Jason Fitzgerald wrote a November 2017 article on guaranteed contracts that included an analysis of the top 15 passing yard leaders, top 20 rushing yard leaders, top 30 receiving yard and sack leaders, top 75 tacklers, top 49 in interceptions, and top 87 in passes defended. With most players just getting off their rookie deals around 26 years old, he found that many of the top performers at most everything except pass yards and sacks were right around this threshold. As seen below in rush yards, tackles, interceptions, and passes defended, very few players over 28 years old are performing at this high level, which means that most free agent money is going to players past their primes, while top performing young players on rookie contracts are being underpaid. The market needs to be stabilized for performance.

Position	Pass Yds	Rush Yds	Rec. Yds	Sacks	Tackles	INTs	PDs
Avg. Age	31.7	25.5	26.6	28	26.2	26.9	25.5
28+	80.0%	20.0%	43.3%	66.7%	26.7%	18.4%	20.7%
30+	53.3%	10.0%	10.0%	23.3%	9.1%	36.7%	10.3%

The Raiders became a playoff team in 2016 with a big three that consisted of players on rookie deals at expensive positions in quarterback Derek Carr, wide receiver Amari Cooper, and edge rusher Khalil Mack. As a group these players will likely be overpaid on the back-end, but fair rookie contracts present an opportunity to stabilize spending across a career through creating rookie contracts closer to true value as it decreases the need to take all you can as a veteran because you need to secure as much as you can considering the risks involved. These contracts could lead to reasonable, realistic second contracts, in terms of a player's true financial value as markets would stabilize towards these levels, which could keep a player in a city for the length of his career while streamlining the re-negotiating and extension process through this knowledge of market values.

In an April 2016 article by Jason Fitzgerald for Over The Cap titled "Drafting Decisions and the Salary Cap 2016," he presents a draft valuation chart that uses Pro Football Reference's Approximate Value metric to assign a market price for a player before he steps on the field.[4] This was explained in the discussion of the quarterback position in chapter three and, as explained there, Jared Goff and Carson Wentz will just make the $8.5 million that is Jason's average value for the #1 overall pick's value in that 2016 season—and that average for each draft slot doesn't even come until 2019, year four of their contracts. Even at their peak, after three seasons that would place their costs in the bottom 50% of production regardless of their level of production, the top two picks can only gain half of their total potential value that Jason found to be just under $16 million. Wentz was the Eagles Week 1 starter in 2016 and is a perfect system fit, a potentially more mobile and accurate version of Donovan McNabb, the quarterback who brought them to four straight NFC Championship Games.

The value for a draft pick is the Approximate Value (AV) of past players from years one through four of their career to match rookie contract length. Jason writes,

> "To come up with the average score I looked at every draft from 1994 through 2012 and compiled the combined AV for every draft pick made in that time frame. Each slot was then broken into quartiles to determine performance ranges that we can expect for the players. We set our upper limits using the inter-quartile range (IQR) for each slot (the lower limit in almost all cases was going to be 0). Originally I was going to adjust for outliers, but once I started looking at the data, in many cases, that didn't seem to make sense since there is no logical reason for say a player drafted at 13 to be an outlier for that individual selection, but be fine for pick 14 to 20.
>
> Similarly, I looked at every veteran player that has been in the NFL since 2012 and determined their combined AV for that four year period. Each player's APY was then used as the salary basis for the player. The one limitation of that is that for some players that had multiple contracts over that time period I am using their most current negotiated deal. While that may not be perfect, I think for the sake of these posts it's fair to use."

As Jason explains, "the interquartile range is a descriptive term to show the difference between the upper and lower quartile of data. Normally, when doing statistical process controls you use the IQR to help set normal bounds of operation. Here, Jason used it to set an upper level of performance such that no team should ever expect to get a Tom Brady in the 6th round when making decisions even if it may happen once in 1000 tries."

Jason then used the matrix below to determine the average veteran salary that corresponds to the expected AV range for each draft pick. This matrix represents the value range for the first pick.

Draft Pick AV Range	Average Veteran Salary Per Year
48.0-84	$15,965,567

35.0-48.0	$9,761,615
24.0-35.0	$6,074,002
0-24.0	$2,195,682
AVERAGE	$8,499,217

The corresponding monetary values associated with each Draft Pick's AV Range become the four quartiles of potential value with the dollar figure being their value.

Jason used the matrix to calculate the value that teams can gain by utilizing the draft and, "because every draft pick is slotted, we can get a very accurate estimate of the rookie salary over four years before the draft even occurs. In almost every case the average expectation is going to be below what it would cost to sign a veteran. Those savings, theoretically, can be used to sign more veterans at other positions to best build the team. The following chart will show you the expected contribution in salary versus the actual annual cost of the contract." That expected contribution in salary is an estimation of a player's true economic value.

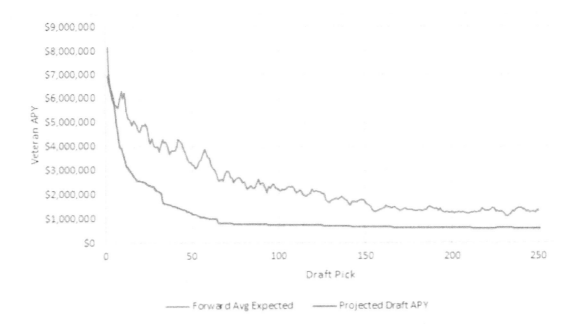

Jason goes on, "the area between the blue and red line is the savings that are realized by drafting players rather than signing them. As you can see the NFL, once we get beyond the first few picks, drastically undervalues the performance of these players. When we visualize this way we should get a better understanding of why teams should look to maximize their number of draft selections. When we sign a player for $15 million, the odds are we will never get more than $15 million in value. There is however downside in those players as you may only get $6 million in value from such a player. It is no upside use of salary." Meanwhile, "the draft gives us limited downside, but significant upside. Here are the projected "profits" and "losses" that a team realizes if their draft picks rank in the upper 25% or in the bottom 25%."

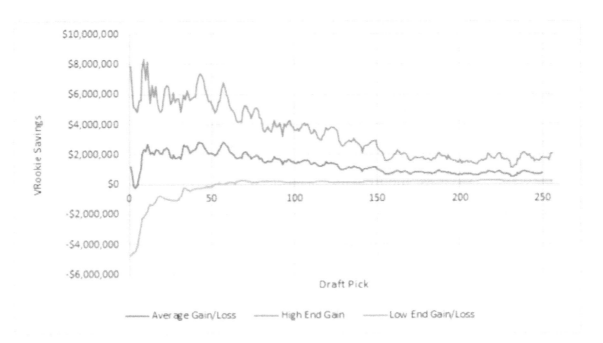

This difference shows that the teams have extreme value potential throughout the draft and the lack of risk that teams have to take on, which isn't new, but has definitely been exacerbated by the 2011 CBA. The previous CBA underpaid these rounds as well, but now we have the math to explain how underpaid they are. Jason wrote that "the only picks that really carry any potential downside are the ones in the first forty or so of the draft. Everywhere else we basically are drawing even with what we would pay a veteran for that performance even in the event the player is a bust. That is why the bust label is somewhat misused. While we expect great things from our draft picks and certain players bust relative to expectations, the team is still, more often than not, driving value from the player. The problem is that too often teams continue to chase the higher upside when it's clear that it does not exist. If those 'busts' are put in the positions they belong, there is still a gain for most teams."

If teams really want to exploit a "moneyball" aspect of building a team, the draft is where to do that. For example, the Titans made a 2016 trade with the Rams that gave the Rams the #1 pick to take Jared Goff along with a fourth and sixth round pick in 2016, while providing the Titans with the Rams #15 pick, two second round picks (2016), a third-round pick (2016), a first-round pick (2017) and another third-round pick (2017). According to Jason, this theoretically gave the

Titans something like $23 million per year in expected value, but at a cost of just $13 million per year. That is $10 million in savings to use on rookies, free agents, and player retention. While a player signed for $10 million still has potential downsides, that savings is essentially the same as being able to sign the same talent level of a number one overall pick and a third rounder. So not only did the Titans add a ton of draft capital, but also the profits gained in the draft should fuel one or two big additions in free agency in 2017. That does not mean the Titans will do that, but in theory, that is the way that teams should be maneuvering to maximize their budgets to get the most value on a team in a given year." In 2017, the Titans signed cornerback Logan Ryan to a deal worth $10 million per year, safety Jonathan Cyprien to a $6.25 million per year deal, and defensive tackle Sylvester Williams to a deal worth $5.5 million per year. Wide receiver Eric Decker signed to a one-year deal worth $4 million. Together those four cost $22 million against the cap with the cap space earned through the trade helping facilitate the spending spree.

This extreme value in the 70 to 90 picks that come after the first round of the draft has made the second through fourth rounds extremely value rich for teams and a huge loss of value for sixty to eighty players per year, and 240 to 320 per four year cycle, who are represented by the NFLPA. These badlands should be their biggest concern in the next CBA. This area of the draft and later is playing a key role in building championship rosters.

As one agent pointed out at the NFLPA's annual agents meeting at the 2017 NFL Combine, agents must be involved in the next negotiation. As one player who is one of his teams' three NFLPA reps told me, "I play football. I don't really understand the CBA." Considering how bad the current CBA is, the NFLPA can't afford to not include agents who are incentivized to understand contracts better than anyone outside the NFL and incentivized to maximize league-wide player earnings considering the large number of players they represent.

Jason's graph showed that the top 40 picks were the only place where teams could actually lose value, but even at the beginning of the second round, year four of contracts are around one percent of the cap, which is an extremely low-cost for a player who should be a high-performing starter for you if your organization knows what it is doing. As explained in the positional chapters, average starters at most positions cost between one and a half and three percent of the cap, but by looking at the slotted costs of the 2015 Draft below, only 24 picks are projected to even earn over one and a half percent in year four of their contract. Year four is when those top 24 picks should be high performing starters and many of them will have become stars.

One.Cool.Customer of SB Nation's BloggingTheBoys.com wrote a March 2016 article that provides an analysis of team-by-team draft success in the first three rounds from 2010 through the 2015 drafts. He agrees that "the first three rounds of the NFL draft are where teams should expect to draft immediate or eventual starters."[5] He writes that the NFL's own site, NFL.com, grades prospective draft picks in five tiers, which acknowledges that a first round pick should be an immediate starter and that players drafted in round two and three should eventually become starters. As he correctly points out, the real actual downside of a missed draft pick, considering that the contract itself has no substantial economic risk, is that getting it right in the earlier rounds is critical "because when teams fail to get starters in the Top 100 picks of a draft, they usually end up having to fill those voids with expensive free agents." As Jason pointed out though, there are very few situations where a pick in the top three rounds can't be used in some way that provides the value of the minimal cap space the players provide. Think about it this way too: if an organization hits on their first round pick with a top ten player at their position, then two quality special teamers or role players with their second and third round picks, they'll still get more or equal production value to the cost. In OCC's article, he judges a successful pick as a player who becomes a "primary starter," which is someone who has started at least eight games in at least one of the last six seasons, which was from 2010 to 2015 at the time of the article. This means that even those drafted in 2014 and 2015 were judged off this, so a percentage of these picks likely became primary starters for the first time during the 2016 or 2017 seasons.

Here's what he found from his analysis:

Primary Starters by Round, 2010-2015 Drafts

	Round 1	Round 2	Round 3	Round 4	Round 5	Round 6	Round 7
# of Players	192	190	206	220	219	231	275
Pr. Starters	159	122	101	66	50	34	29
In %	83%	62%	49%	30%	23%	15%	11%

Assuming that many of those 2014 and 2015 picks have matured into starters, those numbers are likely even higher. The numbers for the later rounds are likely higher too considering the growth that later round players have to undergo to become starters and the timeframe we're looking at. Later round draft picks all the way back to 2013 could have just developed into starters in 2016 like fifth round pick Malik Jackson did for the Broncos in 2015. This data means a huge percentage of players are starting for NFL teams on rookie contracts that drop below half a percent of the cap as every draftee after the first pick in the third round makes less than half a percent of the cap, much less for most.

As explained in previous chapters, the cost of an average to slightly above average veteran starter is between one and a half and three percent of the cap, while first tier players in low-cost markets and second tier players in high-cost markets like wide receiver, edge rusher, and cornerback, but third tier for quarterback, cost between three and six percent of the cap. Yet, using Table A in the appendix, just 24 draft slots even have cap hits over one and a half percent of the cap in their first four years. Of all slotted contracts in the NFL draft, according to Jason's salary cap projections based on 2015's base slotted contracts, just 69 of 1012 contract years, 0.68%, are over one and a half percent of the cap. Only the first 11 draft picks in the draft have four years over one and a half percent and considering how many players in expensive markets go at the top of the draft, many of them are still undervalued as they're getting third tier money, which is average starter money for one of the top 11 prospects coming out of college each year. Are there just 24 of 253 players per draft who become starters during their rookie contracts? Are there just 11 players who can become better than third tier options at one and a half percent in these expensive markets during their rookie seasons? This all essentially means that NFL teams, billion dollar organizations, have to take on almost zero risk of these draftees performing at less than their contract costs, while the players spend a huge chunk of their career at a contract far below their value. This paragraph has some information that the NFLPA can beat over the public's head for the next four years to win the PR battle for the 2021 CBA negotiations.

Three tables for this chapter are in the appendix. Table A is what the standard slotted contracts are projected to look like against the cap. This is a suggested figure and agents can negotiate for more or less for their client within a general range established by the CBA. The first 21 picks in the 2017 draft have fully guaranteed contracts, and most draft picks have cap hits that are made up of signing bonus money and guaranteed money, but that can't make up for deals that are nowhere near true value. As Andrew Brandt points out in a May 2017 article titled, "The Fine Print of Rookie Contracts in the NFL," current rookie contracts are being signed at a record pace with the Panthers having all their picks signed in a week, which is likely due to the fact that no matter what the teams offer players within the range denoted from the CBA, they're underpaying them. Brandt writes, "when I negotiated rookie contracts for the Packers, from 1999 through 2009, I would call agents in May and June and try and do deals, only to hear that they wanted to wait until the market filled in and they would be "safe." Some teams wouldn't even call agents until the week of training camp."[6] By safe Brandt means that agents didn't want to risk players who were drafted after their client receiving more favorable deals.

Slots have a benefit of increasing the speed at which teams and players sign, which is a beneficial concept for both parties as having a player prepared for Week 1 is in the best interest for both sides, but the value needs to be realistic. The team wants to know the player is signed, the player wants to be prepared to play physically and mentally to ensure himself the best opportunity to succeed in the

NFL. Table B is the chart that I created based on the quartiles that Jason presented in the second post of his two-part article titled, "Drafting Decisions and the Salary Cap 2016."[7] I made 2018, year three of the contracts, the Expected Average Per Year that Jason discovered through his research. I then made the 2016 figure 75% of this total, which brings us to figures that are just slightly higher than the 25% to 50% quartile that represents players who performed slightly below the average value per Jason's research. The 2017 figure is 90% of the Expected Value to split the difference between 2016 and 2018. Year four is 135% of this Expected Value, which means it is still a few million less than Jason's top quartile of value for top picks and maintains this split from the top quartile throughout the draft. These decreases in salary from that top quartile is four years after Jason did the calculation, which means that expected value will have, in theory, grown in correlation to a percent of the salary cap as veteran player cap costs will continue to increase. This is all still far below the value for Jason's top quartile of value, so NFL teams will still take on very little risk of underperformance in regard to the player's costs compared to his actual market value. Players will get closer to true value, with some reasonable adjustments throughout the draft.

I maintain a slight downward adjustment over the course of the four years by taking Jason's Expected Value, even though I found the average projected salary and the 2016 percentage of cap figure, and I instead maintained that dollar figure for 2018 rather than the cap percentage. If I were to make the 2018 cap figure, our baseline based off the average Expected Value figure, based on the percentage of cap, it would have increased cap hits by about a half percent yearly in the first round with slighter increases as the draft progressed. I've also made adjustments in the later rounds to acknowledge that, while Jason's chart helps create a point of reference for the potential value of the pick, we should adjust for the potential of that player washing out of the league. A good percentage of later round picks never complete their rookie contracts and even less would with this increase in their cost as an increase in cost will turn a percentage of low-performers into bad values and result in a slight increase in releases. While rookie contract players may provide X in veteran value, that rookie contract value should reflect that these are still unproven commodities, which is why I allowed the downward adjustment in this proposal. Rookies should be paid fair value, but we should also maintain some of the cap space available for proven veterans.

Looking at Table B, we can create a rough spending range for each round and that range is displayed below. As seen from Table B as well, this new proposal gets rid of the fifth-year team option for first-round picks.

Cap Hit Range:

Round	Year 1	Year 4
1st: Top 10	3.0-4.0%	4.0-5.0%

1st: 11-32	2.0-3.0%	2.6-4.0%
2nd: 33-64	1.35-2.0%	2.0-3.0%
3rd: 65-98	1.1-1.35%	1.6-2.0%
4th: 99-139	0.85-1.1%	1.2-1.6%
5th: 140-175	0.70-0.85%	0.95-1.2%
6th: 176-221	0.60-0.70%	0.85-0.95%
7th: 222-256	0.50-0.60%	0.80-0.85%

These values should be slotted with the top of the round getting the top of the range and the bottom, the bottom. Yearly salaries should increase in cost over the years towards reaching its peak in year four. Looking across the rounds, the totals show a correlation with starter data from OCC and a separate, position specific analysis by Western Chief of SB Nation's Arrowhead Pride. The similar cost ranges for the bottom three rounds illustrate the lower percentage of draft picks that produce value with these picks, a huge decrease from the fourth round. Many seventh round picks have higher values in Jason's analysis than sixth rounders because these late picks are a crapshoot; the success of picks here is even more random than at the top.

The big takeaway from this chart is that it supports an increase in the league minimum. The minimum in 2017 is 0.28%, which is pushing the income disparity between rookie contract players, plus players on veteran minimums that max at 0.37%, and expensive veterans. These lower earnings from a percentage of the salary cap standpoint were more reasonable for league minimum players when MVP quarterback Steve Young's 13% of the cap was just $4,525,000. By 2019, the league minimum for first year players will be $495,000 or 0.25% of the projected cap of $193 million. Defensive tackle Ndamukong Suh's contract with the Dolphins is slated to consume $28.1 million of the 2019 cap, which is 14.56% of the cap. This income disparity for rookies with no bargaining power is absurd; rookie contracts are a built in four-year extension of continuing to underpay these players after they weren't paid in college. The disparity is especially absurd considering the value that Jason proves rookies create and the elite value that teams can get hitting on any draft pick that develops into a starter.

The current league minimum percentages will produce absurd disparities when the cap gets up near $350 million in the middle of the next decade when a disparity between 0.25% and 14.56% would mean a league minimum of $875,000 and $50.96 million at 14.56% of the cap. Even ten percent for a quarterback will be worth a cap hit of $35 million. A league minimum of 0.50% would be $1,750,000, a big jump that brings the after tax income close to a million dollars. Anyone who plays a year in the NFL is given real financial security to start and plan their own life even if they only play one season. Three or four years at this league minimum rate would provide a player with the income to chart their own entrepreneurial path to life after football, take care of any future potential medical costs versus the current total over four, which is roughly $2.3 million for the final pick in the draft. Say the new league minimum averages out to $1.5 million over four years in the early 2020s, that means a player who plays that out retires with $6 million, enough to start whatever future they want, a fair reward for reaching the pinnacle of simulated war for mass entertainment that could leave them physically and mentally debilitated. League pension programs are helpful to players once they hit 55-years old, but they're only helpful to players who meet the requirements. Hundreds of former NFL players leave after a year or two without much financially to show for the time they invested in the sport, no pension, and typically sub-par educational experiences in college as football demands most of their time, which results in most players choosing easier majors to ensure they stay eligible with ample time to dedicate to football. A violent sport needs to make as many wealthy players as possible rather than keeping a system that will continue this growing income gap that doesn't even represent the value that both rookie contract and top paid veteran players provide.

Jason's findings confirm that the value that rookies could receive in this system will likely be earned by player performance. Players should also get a raise as a form of some compensation for the free labor in college, a feeder system the NFL doesn't have to pay for. Although a million dollars is a subjective metric of wealth, everyone who makes it to the NFL for a year should at least become a millionaire before taxes, especially considering a November 2017 Business Insider article by Cork Gaines that found the average University of Texas player's fair market value was $666,000, which is even higher than the NFL's current league minimum.[8] In September 2017, according to the Wall Street Journal, the Ohio State, Texas, and Oklahoma football programs have all been valued at over $1 billion. Ohio State was valued at $1.51 billion, which is just $90 million less than the Buffalo Bills at $1.6 billion.[9] Now, this is off the topic of this book, but if Buffalo can afford a salary cap of $167 million, how does Ohio State get away with paying their athletes in the form of scholarships for educations worth about $25,000 per year (when considering in-state tuition, room-and-board, books and supplies, and other expenses) that the players can't even fully realize due to their full-time job playing football?

Increasing minimums are a big improvement, but the high costs of the new rookie contract structure means that less money will be able to go to veterans, so these rookie contracts must have some sort of decreasing mechanism for players who underperform as to allow teams to clear space to allocate that money to more deserving veterans. If you take a team drafting near the middle of each round with a fifth round compensatory selection to give them the league average of eight picks per year, their four year cap costs for 32 players using the new rookie structure would be about 42% of the cap. If a team is drafting at the beginning of the round in the top five picks, this cost would be around 47% over four years. A team drafting at the end of he round would be around 37%. Under the current structure, a team drafting at the top of the first round for four years would have a total four year cost of about 26% of the cap for 32 players, while those drafting in the middle are around 18% and drafting at the bottom of the round for four years would cost 16% for 32 players.

Looking at the new chart's costs, there seems to be a bit of an issue as the new structure could leave as little as 53% of the cap for the theoretically 21 remaining players on the 53-man roster for a team drafting near the top of the first round, which comes to 2.52% of the cap per player, but doesn't account for any of the potential dead money mistakes that teams make each year. It wouldn't allow for top performing veterans to get their true financial value as the high rookie costs would place a ceiling on veteran markets. The league could introduce maximum contracts league wide or position specific max contracts based on percentages of the cap, but I don't think the league is ready for that, nor do I believe an auction is necessary to a solution. Teams drafting in the middle of rounds, setting a sort of league median, would have 58% of the cap for these 21 players and teams at the end of the round would have 63%. None of these teams would have anywhere close to the 72.04% of the cap that the top 21 cap hits for the 23 champions have cost on average. The prior CBA's champions had a lower cost at 70.11%, while the current CBA, with the continued low-costs of the rookie pool, and teams having more success drafting through improving processes over time, has gotten much more expensive at 77.19% going to the top 21 for the six champions since. Most of this increase in cost comes from the top, supporting the idea that the NFL is becoming a haves-and-have nots league with the top tens for Super Bowl champions from 2011 through 2016 averaging 7.34% more of the cap than the champions from 1994 through 2009.

	1994-2009	2011-2016	Difference
Top 1	8.89%	10.41%	1.52%
Top 2	15.44%	17.84%	2.41%
Top 3	21.04%	24.32%	3.28%
Top 5	30.76%	35.55%	4.78%
Top 10	47.89%	55.23%	7.34%
Top 15	59.92%	67.88%	7.96%
Top 20	68.54%	75.95%	7.41%
Top 25	74.88%	81.43%	6.55%
Top 30	79.83%	85.32%	5.49%

This 72% number is driven by the low-rookie costs throughout the salary cap era; not just since 2011, so it still might not be a realistic barometer of value. This is still the reality that the league exists in, so a massive adjustment from what has been done in the past like what the chart proposes is unrealistic for both NFL owners and players. Under the new structure, rookie contract players are getting closer to true value, which is important, but it can't be to the detriment of veteran pay. Using the new structure, some adjustments can be made to clear space for veterans, while still maintaining an overall increase in rookie pay. The easiest and simplest solution to clear space in the first place seems to be to drop all fifth through seventh round picks to the 0.50% minimum as it would still increase their pay significantly from current costs, drop costs to more manageable levels than the original proposal's numbers, and be more realistic about the low probability of high performance out of late-round picks. And, to be fair to the teams in a negotiation of the entire rookie wage scale, if a team finds a productive player in the last three rounds, they deserve to receive some value savings for that find. As a concession for these low costs, players picked after the first four rounds should only have three-year contracts to allow the best among them to have a shot at earning bigger money in free agency earlier. Teams will also still be able to accumulate these late round picks to build up their roster and the most well-managed organizations will still be able to find competitive advantages. Even early round picks still have the potential for value if teams find starters, so the current strategies of building through the draft will still be viable.

With the 0.50% adjustment for the last three rounds, teams drafting at the top of the round over four years would see their four year costs at 42%, mid-round picks would result in 32 player costs of 38%, and end of round picks would cost 33% over four. The 42% at the top of rounds seems high, but teams consistently drafting early because they're not good shouldn't be spending much in free agency as they should instead be focusing on building their roster through the draft. The 0.50% minimum won't have a big impact on the cap with an increase of 0.2% or less over current rookie contract cap hits, but it will have a big impact on the earnings of these individual players. The theoretically nine to 12 players drafted over a three to four season window, depending on if the contracts are three of four years, would have a minimal impact on costs, only adding about 1.35% to 1.6% on cap costs each year.

Draft picks will still be valuable, but since players will be making closer to their true value, and with higher risks associated with their higher contracts, there will likely be a decrease in trading of draft picks. Although, most of these trades for draft picks seem to deal with picks after the third round, so many trades would likely still occur as there is the potential for value. Picking the right player in the draft will always have the potential for value. Maybe the same amount of draft day trades would happen for picks in the top rounds as teams would still make plays for prospects they love if they're available. The increased contracts for rookies may also inspire teams to trade more based on a player being perceived to be worth less than his cap costs in their city, while another team may see him as a potential value for how they intend to use him as they had him graded as a great pick for them in the draft process.

Using 38% as a barometer for where teams would end up with their four-year costs if they were to keep all 32 players drafted under contract, which is very unlikely, teams have 62% of the cap to spend on those 21 players, 2.95% of the cap per player. Teams drafting at the top of the first round for four straight years will only have 57% of the cap for their 21 non-drafted players, which isn't a lot, but they should be in rebuilding mode anyway then and keeping top of cap costs low. (There could be a slight downward adjustment to cap costs in the second through fourth rounds as well if the NFL or NFLPA wanted to increase money available for veterans, but the NFLPA should aim to keep these costs close to potential veteran starter costs.)

Considering that teams should be abiding by more reasonable veteran contracts in the next CBA, closer to true production value, especially due to this proposed increase in rookie spending, this adjustment toward 0.50% seems more realistic than the original proposal as it will leave cap space, but not the same level that currently exists to promote an average of over 77% of the cap going to just 21 players on these last five champs. The 2013 Seahawks had 86.30% of the cap going to their top 21 cap hits, while the many rookie contract stars that made up their core made less than one percent of the cap for the first four years of their careers. Meanwhile, Zach Miller and Sidney Rice combined to make 16.83% of the cap because of this broken system. In many cases, the rookies can be undervalued, while veterans can be overvalued, which just leads to money being invested in the wrong players.

This rookie contract structure with the 0.50% adjustment will decrease the top end of player contracts; it could potential end the insanity of 17 quarterbacks making over 10% of the cap like in 2016; it'll stop teams from investing double digits in positions that can't provide nearly that value; and it will raise pay across the league. Prior to the 2011 CBA, the average top cap hit for a champion was 8.95%, while it has jumped to 10.41% since. Increasing pay across the league is the point of a union, to represent all of their members and increase pay across the board. This would do that and it would incentivize more realistic positional markets that are closer to true production value.

The 2001 Patriots provide an example of this cap structure being possible with 63.90% of the cap going to 21 players. They still had quarterback Drew Bledsoe at 10.29%, cornerback Ty Law at 7.47%, defensive end/outside linebacker Willie McGinest at 6.47%, and inside linebacker Ted Johnson at 5.90% with 24 players over one percent of the cap.

That 62% number, or 58% or 67% at either end of the round, isn't the end of adjustments either. That can be expanded towards 70% with a realistic assessment of how many of those, potentially, 32 drafted players per year will be on the roster each year. Teams will let go of unproductive rookies. Current first round costs are so low that the Patriots released 2014 first-round pick Dominique Easley before 2016 with a 1.87% dead money charge. Taking that into account regarding late rounders, and all picks really in this proposal, teams can still stockpile draft picks to create value if they do a good job scouting, especially considering how often late round picks are dealt. The consequence of higher rookie costs will incentivize NFL franchises to allocate more resources to scouting too, something they don't currently have to do as discussed in chapter three, which might be a sign of the lack of direct financial consequence for a bad draft pick. Teams may have to spend more on a veteran if they miss on a draft pick, but being wrong on the actual player has little consequence, just replacement costs.

With the 32 picks from the example, all of the players in the first four rounds, 16 picks in this case, are over one percent of the cap. Averaging out Super Bowl cap hits, 27 cap hits average 0.97% or higher, so in theory teams would have about 11 more spots for veterans to make over one percent of the cap, although there will be more with teams releasing underperformers. More than half of the 16 draft contract cap hits reside in the one to two percent of the cap range, depending on where the team is drafting it can be anywhere from eight to 13 of these cap hits in this range. This means that most of them will be in the range between a team's 15th to 25th highest cap hits, meaning teams will still have the cap space to sign plenty of high level veteran starters, the top earning players will still be veterans. At least top five picks won't have the potential to make over 10% of the cap on their first contract under this CBA compared to the one prior to 2011.

Looking at the Super Bowl champions, the average for players over 1% of the cap is 26.2 for the whole group. Looking at the data set prior to the 2011 CBA, the average was 27.0 with the 1998 Broncos with 31, the 2003 and 2004 Patriots with 30 and 29, the 2005 Steelers with 30, and the 2009 Saints with 32 due to them utilizing cap rollover to increase their cap space that year. The six champions since have averaged just 24.2 players over 1% of the cap as league spending has morphed into the haves-and-have nots income disparity mentioned. Teams are more than capable of adjusting their spending to accommodate this suggested rookie spending increase.

Undrafted free agents can't be forgotten about. Before the start of the 2016 season, more undrafted free agents made up NFL rosters than first and second round picks combined by a margin of 481 to 480. Each year, each team finds a couple of these players who make the team and eventually become contributors.

In a September 2017 article, Robert Klemko of *Sports Illustrated* explained how the last CBA is contributing to a decrease in the level of play in the first two weeks of NFL games due to less practice time, but also a higher emphasis on these undrafted free agents and rookie contract players, rather than veterans due to the economics created by this CBA. Kevin Clark at The Ringer wrote in 2016 "executives and coaches agreed that players were more inexperienced than ever." Klemko writes, "in 2012, before the realities of the new bargaining agreement dawned on roster builders, there were 412 undrafted free agents on opening-day rosters. The difference of more than two players per team comes at the expense of veterans who might have previously enjoyed modest second contracts in exchange for competent, effective performance. More cynically, that 481 number is evidence of a new class of players who might owe their roster spots more to the warped economics of the 2011 CBA than to their own merit."[10] A decline in level of play that might be due to the inexperience of lesser talents making rosters because of economics is an issue that both the NFL and NFLPA should be concerned with.

Fair value for rookies has to come from somewhere, so overall veteran pay will decrease, but for good reason and for one that will increase player income and maximize player earnings in their short window of maximum earning potential. Again, the rapidly increasing cap means everyone could be getting rich, so more reasonable positional markets will still maintain high wages for those outlier, elite players. Even with the veteran minimum salary benefit from the 2011 CBA that intended to make veterans with at least four credited seasons more affordable by making players on one-year minimum salaries more affordable to teams by making their cap hits less than their salaries, veterans are still getting priced out of the league. Maybe an increase in rookie minimum pay could help keep a few more around; there could even still be a veteran minimum salary benefit.

Before the 2011 CBA more rookies were in the top 21 cap hits for their teams, but not to the level this proposal has with many rookie contract players over one percent of the cap. This means that many of those will be in the top 21 of their team's cap charges. Teams acknowledge that they understand the potential value of first round picks in their fifth-year if they develop with fifth-year player options that pay top picked players pretty fair market rates. NFL teams know these picks have more value than the current structure; they don't just only think first round picks are suddenly worth 6.81% of the cap like Von Miller in 2015 or 4.99% for Dont'a Hightower in 2016 in their fifth years. Hightower's cap hit jumped from 1.72% in 2015 to 4.99% as these later first round rates are really undervalued. They know that the first pick in the second round isn't worth less than one percent of the cap, but they were dealing with an NFLPA that likely didn't have the data to articulate and support a stance for increasing rookie pay. They were also dealing with representatives who saw how much top picks at quarterback were getting paid and were clamoring for more pay to be allocated for veterans. This likely made figuring out fair rookie pay more of an afterthought to what seemed to be more pressing matters, but it has created problems for the players they represent now, which is why entry level pay is the most pressing issue of the next CBA.

The new rates that we propose for rookie contracts have to have some built in mechanisms through the first four rounds to decrease pay if players underperform like, barring injury, not being a starter or not performing at an established and predetermined production level built into the contract. Rookies need to be paid, but not so much so that it can go to players who aren't performing or haven't earned it in the same way a veteran who is plugging away in year seven does. This proposal of decreasing pay for underperforming rookies is the right position for the NFLPA to take not because it would appease NFL teams, but because it would allocate that money to more deserving veterans, while still retaining the value that players should receive for being top draft picks. If a team flops so completely on a second round pick that earns over one and a half percent of the cap over his first two years, that mistake should cost the billion-dollar organization. The productive second round pick shouldn't pay an economic consequence because billion dollar organizations want to pay them 0.50% of the cap in year one to a probable starter with the reasoning being that the billion dollar organization might make a bad hiring decision, so they don't want to take on the appropriate market costs and risks associated with it, nor do they care to actually spend the averages other industries spend on the scouting and talent acquisition process.

To decrease these cap costs in later years for underperformers, one proposal could be decreasing mechanisms in each round where players see their year three and/or year four pay decrease depending on certain metrics or percentage of snap count percentages, barring injury. These contracts, or a portion of them, could be guaranteed for injury to protect players. Even if it saw first round picks decrease to one and a half percent of the cap in those years and every pick after that shrunk to 0.50%, there would still be a sizeable pay increase for every player over the course of the contract. Teams would still get fair value and that money can be used elsewhere. Another aspect of the proposal could be no guaranteed money in years three and four of any rookie contract to allow teams to rid themselves of underperforming players, while players who are released then have the opportunity to sign a deal where the league minimum is 0.50% after earning much more in their first two seasons than under the 2011 CBA.

Another mechanism could be signing bonuses prorated over two or three years, which would make players who aren't worth their year four costs expendable and the team gets to release him or work out a restructure. This would increase the cap hits for earlier years, but this is an option both sides could entertain or they could pass a rule that just doesn't count prorated signing bonuses in year four as dead money against the cap if the team releases the player. It would increase player's earnings, so they would benefit, while also providing the organization the benefit of not counting the dead money against their cap. That player and agent can then decide to enter free agency a year early if he doesn't want a restructure or, even if outright released, he can sign to a league minimum of 0.50% if he is worth re-signing.

Conversely, players should once again be able to sign extensions after year two, so that the agents of players who have already proven themselves on the field as top talents can negotiate an extension that pays them near their true market value earlier rather than waiting until after year four. The last CBA saw Rob Gronkowski and Antonio Brown sign extensions after their second seasons, which still allowed the teams to pay them less than the value they ended up providing the teams over the years of the contracts, while also paying the players closer to their true worth earlier rather than the second and sixth round rookie contracts they signed. This helps player pay and extensions help keep player costs slightly lower for teams in future years by extending them and increasing their costs earlier. Locking high-performing players into at least three years of below market costs under this CBA, without allowing extensions until after year three, isn't reasonable when we know that outliers can outperform their value. Along with decreasing costs or no consequence releases for underperforming players with no potential dead money after year two, this will help further allocate value to the proper players in this new system.

Position specific adjustments would be a good addition to the negotiating process and could be incorporated into the next CBA as built in position market specific costs in correlation with the market cost and even the likelihood of the player becoming a contributor at his position. Western Chief from Arrowhead Pride wrote an article in February 2015 that created a simple criteria for determining if a draft pick was successful: "how many players were drafted by position and round over the last decade and how many went on to become a starter." As he writes, he "did not distinguish superstars from regular starters. The determination of a starter comes from whether the player started at least half of his career. Obviously, this will range from below average to high performing starters. The reality is that if you can start in this league for at least half of your playing career, you are better than most."[11] This process isn't perfect, but it provides a foundation for thinking about a position specific adjustment to draft slots and gives us a definition of a successful draft pick, while still maintaining the slots as they provide a basis to start negotiations at. Again, whatever the proposal ends up being for the next CBA, any slotted contracts should be much more flexible than they are today. There should be a suggested value for each slot, but agents should be able to make value and market based arguments to increase a player's worth.

In the Appendix, Table C displays the percentage of players at each position drafted between 2005 and 2014 that developed into starters. These picks are judged by a slightly different criteria than what OCC used, which is why these two charts have a difference in percentage of picks that are deemed a "success." While OCC's research found that 49% of third round picks were a primary starter for at least one year, Western Chief's research found that offensive line was the most successful third round pick with 40% of those picks turning into players who starter for over half of their career.

Using this with positional markets that will increase costs for some positions and decrease them for others; we can also use the probability of that position becoming a contributor to adjust numbers further. For example, 83% of offensive linemen drafted in the first round are starters for at least half of their career. That positional market wouldn't call for much of an increase over the average, but this gives agents a strong argument for increasing the amount of guaranteed money their client receives as a first round pick in this system. Looking at the second round, 70% of offensive linemen there develop into starters, so there being a high probability of them being a starter for your organization might be a reason to increase pay.

In the fourth round, 37% of defensive linemen become starters, which actually outpaces their success in the second (26%) and third round (27%). Interestingly, they are tied for last with wide receiver and running back with just a 58% success rate in the first round. It doesn't make sense that fourth round defensive linemen would be more successful, but the economic value could be accounted for with a position specific draft structure based off of what has already been proposed that creates position specific drafting tables based off of mathematical formulas that combined Table B, positional market costs, and probability of players at that position developing into a starter or some other agreed upon metric for success.

The goal with this is to eventually move towards an auction draft in the next CBA. Prior to the 2016 season, I wrote an article for Over The Cap exploring the possibility of an auction draft, but that concept is far too radical a proposal considering current rookie contracts and positional market costs. After another decade long CBA with slotted contracts, plus advancements in data collection that that will increase draft success and properly estimate the true value that all players provide, an auction draft should be a viable option. Jason and I both believe that an auction would increase pay for players that would have been drafted in the fifth round or later under the 2011 CBA since teams would be bidding over players with current costs far below their true value, which is mentioned in Jason's "Drafting Decisions" article mentioned earlier.

For example, the Steelers know what they're doing when it comes to drafting receivers with Antonio Brown and Martavis Bryant being two recent examples. They didn't know they would become elite players, but knowing their offensive system, they likely knew that both players would have a high probability of success. Under the old structure they were simply paid near minimum contracts. Under my proposal Brown would've made 0.50% and Bryant would've been on a fourth round deal that capped around one and a half percent in year four. If the league had an auction draft format, the Steelers in this case would likely be willing to increase what they were willing to pay these players.

Each player is a case-by-case basis in terms of his potential costs. I'm unsure what would happen on a macro-economic level to salaries at the top of the draft, but for a player like Carson Wentz with the Eagles, I see plenty that makes me think he'd make much more money under this system. Doug Peterson runs the same system Andy Reid ran in Philadelphia with Donovan McNabb. Peterson looks at Wentz's skillset, compares it to what McNabb accomplished with the Eagles and his 59.0% completion percentage in Philadelphia, plus mobility, and realizes that he could build a similar system around Wentz. While every player comes into the league with risk, Wentz was a great fit for the Eagles offensive system, so he'd likely earn a contract even higher than what the new rookie contract structure I propose would pay. Every year players would benefit from being ideal system fits with increased rookie contracts through an auction format.

NFL teams have years to prepare their draft classes; they have over four months to analyze the entire process; they can figure out how to bid over their labor like other industries have to. Again, this is why they need to increase their expenses invested in the scouting process. This proposal and the various potential adjustments, or proposals similar to it, could lay the foundation for real change in the next CBA. It will be up to the NFLPA to make the case.

Acknowledgements

Thank you to the coaches I played for growing up who fostered my love of sports along with my parents and cousins. A few deserve special mention. Coach John Sandberg and Coach Brian Remo who added fuel to the fire I already came to them with. Coach Jeff Brown always encouraged me to be myself. And Ramapo High School head coach Drew Gibbs built a football program that motivated me to be the best football player and athlete I could be. He has helped place countless players in college football programs, myself included. Thank you too, to all of my teachers along the way as well from elementary school up through graduate school. You, along with my parents, helped instill a passion for learning in me that continue to inspire me.

Thank you to the coaches at the University of Rhode Island who gave me a chance to continue my career and experiences that put me on the path I'm on today. Specifically, thank you to Darren Rizzi, Chris Pincince, and Mark Fabish for recruiting me as well as Ari Confesor for giving me the opportunity to compete. Thank you to Dr. Kevin Elko for teaching me about "process" and Joe DeFranco for the years of training at his gym during my college career. You both played a big part in inspiring me to write about football.

Thank you to Jason Fitzgerald at Over The Cap for creating the best NFL salary cap resource available to fans and for having the confidence in me to allow me to write for him. A huge thank you also goes out to him for providing me with the salary cap information to write this. Thank you to Vijay Natarajan, Jason's co-author on *Crunching Numbers: An Inside Look at the Salary Cap and Negotiating Player Contracts*, who helped me understand the publishing process. Thank you to Drew Vigen for being so kind as to prepare this book for publishing. Thank you to Adam Doyle for his artwork, which is displayed on the front of this book.

Thank you to the many writers who provided so much of the education that made this book possible. Thank you to the podcasters who've provided me with countless hours of a free education that have helped give me the ability to articulate the information this book. Thank you to Hardik Sanghavi and Troy Chapman for their feedback on this book. Thank you to Andy Benoit for his help as well. Thank you to Hardik and Austin Zak for helping me compile Excel sheets when I needed the help. Thank you to my sister, Mackenzie Moore, for doing a class project for statistics on quarterback costs that ended up having a place in this book.

Thank you to my family, my friends, and my girlfriend who kept me grounded and supported me during this entire process. Thank you to my jiujitsu teams at Silver Fox Brazilian JiuJitsu in Saddle Brook, New Jersey and 10th Planet Jiujitsu at the Onnit Academy in Austin, Texas for keeping me motivated and focused on my goals, while providing me with a community of people that continue to keep me accountable to those goals.

Most of all, thank you to my parents for supporting this project of mine as I wouldn't have been able to do this without either of you. Thank you to my father for helping edit this book and for teaching me how to do it for myself as well. Thank you to my mother for always encouraging me to chase my dreams and goals. As stated in the dedication, thank you to my four grandparents for creating lives that were far bigger than what they were given, which instilled in me the ability to dream bigger, while providing for me a life that has given me the opportunity to accomplish those dreams.

Appendix

CHAPTER 3 DATA

Draft Picks from 1994-2015; Ranked by Avg Number of Picks				
Rank	Team	# of Picks	Avg # of Picks	Winning %
1	Patriots	201	8.74	0.685
2	Packers	197	8.57	0.643
3	Titans	194	8.43	0.483
4	Rams	193	8.39	0.415
5	Eagles	192	8.35	0.551
6	Steelers	188	8.17	0.629
7	Bills	185	8.04	0.452
8	Bengals	184	8.00	0.446
9	49ers	183	7.96	0.536
10	Dolphins	180	7.83	0.500
11	Texans (15)	117	7.80	0.433
12	Seahawks	179	7.78	0.534
13	Ravens (21)	162	7.71	0.542
14	Vikings	177	7.70	0.531
15	Cowboys	177	7.70	0.528
16	Bears	176	7.65	0.477
17	Jaguars	176	7.65	0.452
18	Cardinals	176	7.65	0.432
19	Browns (20)	153	7.65	0.339
20	Broncos	173	7.52	0.611
21	Chiefs	173	7.52	0.511
22	Buccaneers	173	7.52	0.455
23	Raiders	170	7.39	0.398
24	Colts	169	7.35	0.605
25	Falcons	169	7.35	0.496
26	Panthers (22)	161	7.32	0.472
27	Chargers	165	7.17	0.497
28	Lions	163	7.09	0.378
29	Jets	162	7.04	0.472
30	Giants	162	7.04	0.513
31	Redskins	157	6.83	0.425
32	Saints	148	6.43	0.486

The top 10 teams had a combined winning percentage of .534. The middle 12 had a winning percentage of .487. The bottom 10 had a winning percentage of .474. The top half had a winning percentage of .520, while the bottom half had a winning percentage of .470.

Draft Picks from 1994-2016; Ranked by Avg Number of Picks				
Rank	Team	# of Picks	Avg # of Picks	Winning %
1	Patriots	210	9.13	0.693
2	Packers	204	8.87	0.641
3	Titans	204	8.87	0.486
4	Eagles	200	8.70	0.543
5	Rams	200	8.70	0.407
6	Steelers	195	8.48	0.630
7	49ers	194	8.43	0.516
8	Bills	192	8.35	0.451
9	Browns (20)	167	8.35	0.325
10	Bengals	191	8.30	0.440
11	Ravens (21)	173	8.24	0.539
12	Seahawks	189	8.22	0.538
13	Texans (15)	123	8.20	0.442
14	Dolphins	188	8.17	0.505
15	Cowboys	186	8.09	0.540
16	Bears	185	8.04	0.465
17	Vikings	185	8.04	0.528
18	Jaguars	183	7.96	0.440
19	Chiefs	182	7.91	0.522
20	Cardinals	182	7.91	0.432
21	Broncos	181	7.87	0.609
22	Buccaneers	180	7.83	0.459
23	Colts	177	7.70	0.603
24	Raiders	177	7.70	0.413
25	Falcons	175	7.61	0.502
26	Panthers (22)	166	7.55	0.466
27	Lions	173	7.52	0.386
28	Chargers	173	7.52	0.489
29	Jets	169	7.35	0.464
30	Giants	168	7.30	0.519
31	Redskins	164	7.13	0.424
32	Saints	153	6.65	0.484

The top 10 teams had a combined winning percentage of .513, while the bottom 10 had a winning percentage of .475. The top half of teams had a .510 winning percentage, while the bottom half had a .480 winning percentage.

Draft Picks from 1994 through 2016

1994-2016		Total				Average		
AFC East	# of Draft Picks	W	L	T	W %	W	L	T
Bills	192	159	193	0	0.452	7.2	8.8	0.0
Dolphins	188	176	176	0	0.500	8.0	8.0	0.0
Jets	169	166	186	0	0.472	7.5	8.5	0.0
Patriots	210	241	111	0	0.685	11.0	5.0	0.0
AFC North								
Bengals	191	156	194	2	0.446	7.1	8.8	0.1
Browns (20 drafts)	167	103	201	0	0.339	5.4	10.6	0.0
Ravens (21)	173	173	146	1	0.542	8.7	7.3	0.1
Steelers	195	221	130	1	0.629	10.0	5.9	0.0
AFC South								
Colts	177	213	139	0	0.605	9.7	6.3	0.0
Jaguars (22)	183	152	184	0	0.452	7.2	8.8	0.0
Texans (15)	123	97	127	0	0.433	6.9	9.1	0.0
Titans	177	170	182	0	0.483	7.7	8.3	0.0
AFC West								
Broncos	181	215	137	0	0.611	9.8	6.2	0.0
Chargers	173	175	177	0	0.497	8.0	8.0	0.0
Chiefs	182	180	172	0	0.511	8.2	7.8	0.0
Raiders	177	140	212	0	0.398	6.4	9.6	0.0
NFC East								
Cowboys	186	186	166	0	0.528	8.5	7.5	0.0
Eagles	200	193	157	2	0.551	8.8	7.1	0.1
Giants	168	180	171	1	0.513	8.2	7.8	0.0
Redskins	164	149	202	1	0.425	6.8	9.2	0.0
NFC North								
Bears	185	168	184	0	0.477	7.6	8.4	0.0
Lions	173	133	219	0	0.378	6.0	10.0	0.0
Packers	204	226	125	1	0.643	10.3	5.7	0.0
Vikings	185	187	165	1	0.531	8.5	7.5	0.0
NFC South								
Buccaneers	180	160	192	0	0.455	7.3	8.7	0.0
Falcons	175	174	177	1	0.496	7.9	8.0	0.0
Panthers (22)	166	158	177	1	0.472	7.5	8.4	0.0
Saints	153	171	181	0	0.486	7.8	8.2	0.0
NFC West								
49ers	194	188	163	1	0.536	8.5	7.4	0.0
Cardinals	182	152	200	1	0.432	6.9	9.1	0.0
Rams	200	146	206	1	0.415	6.6	9.4	0.0
Seahawks	189	188	164	0	0.534	8.5	7.5	0.0

CHAPTER 5 DATA

Peyton Manning Cap Hits

Year	Salary Cap	Age	Salary	% of Cap	Season		Playoffs		Round Eliminated
					W	L	W	L	
1998	52,388,000	22	2,077,333	3.97	3	13			
1999	57,288,000	23	3,363,333	5.87	13	3	0	1	Divisional
2000	62,172,000	24	6,699,333	10.78	10	6	0	1	Wild Card
2001	67,405,000	25	8,485,333	12.59	6	10			
2002	71,101,000	26	10,331,333	14.53	10	6	0	1	Wild Card
2003	75,007,000	27	15,375,333	20.50	12	4	2	1	Championship
2004	80,852,000	28	8,301,666	10.27	12	4	1	1	Championship
2005	85,500,000	29	8,431,666	9.86	14	2	0	1	Divisional
2006	102,000,000	30	10,566,668	10.36	12	4	4	0	CHAMPIONS
2007	109,000,000	31	8,200,000	7.52	13	3	0	1	Divisional
2008	116,000,000	32	18,700,000	16.12	12	4	0	1	Wild Card
2009	123,000,000	33	21,200,000	17.24	14	2	2	1	Super Bowl
2010	NO CAP	34	19,266,666		10	6	0	1	Wild Card
2011	120,000,000	35	16,000,000	13.33	0	0			
2012	120,600,000	36	18,000,000	14.93	13	3	0	1	Divisional
2013	123,000,000	37	17,500,000	14.23	13	3	2	1	Super Bowl
2014	133,000,000	38	17,500,000	13.16	12	4	0	1	Divisional
2015	143,280,000	39	17,500,000	12.21	12	4	3	0	CHAMPIONS
	(1998-2015)			12.20	191	81	14	13	0.702 / 0.519
	(2001-2015)			13.35	165	59	14	11	0.737 / 0.560
	Super Bowl Avg			11.29					
	2009-2015			14.18					
	2005-2015			12.90					
	98-11			11.76					
	2000-09			13.30					

Tom Brady Cap Hits

					Season		Playoffs		
Year	Salary Cap	Age	Salary	% of Cap	W	L	W	L	Round Eliminated
1998	52,388,000								
1999	57,288,000								
2000	62,172,000	23	205,833	0.33	0	0			
2001	67,405,000	24	314,933	0.47	11	3	3	0	CHAMPIONS
2002	71,101,000	25	1,087,833	1.53	9	7			
2003	75,007,000	26	3,318,750	4.42	14	2	3	0	CHAMPIONS
2004	80,852,000	27	5,058,750	6.26	14	2	3	0	CHAMPIONS
2005	85,500,000	28	8,423,750	9.85	10	6	1	1	Divisional
2006	102,000,000	29	13,823,750	13.55	12	4	2	1	Championship
2007	109,000,000	30	7,340,000	6.73	16	0	2	1	Super Bowl
2008	116,000,000	31	14,620,000	12.60	1	0			
2009	123,000,000	32	14,620,000	11.89	10	6	0	1	Wild Card
2010	NO CAP	33	17,420,000		14	2	0	1	Divisional
2011	120,000,000	34	13,200,000	11.00	13	3	2	1	Super Bowl
2012	120,600,000	35	8,000,000	6.63	12	4	1	1	Championship
2013	123,000,000	36	13,800,000	11.22	12	4	1	1	Championship
2014	133,000,000	37	14,800,000	11.13	12	4	3	0	CHAMPIONS
2015	143,280,000	38	14,000,000	9.77	12	4	1	1	Championship
2016	155,270,000	39	13,764,706	8.87	14	2	3	0	CHAMPIONS
2017	167,000,000	40	14,000,000	8.38					

Label	% of Cap	Season W	Season L	Win%	Playoff W	Playoff L	Win%
(2001-2015)	8.36	172	51	0.771	22	9	0.710
Career	7.92	186	53	0.778	25	9	0.735
Super Bowl Avg	6.85						
Excluding 2001	8.63						
Using Bledsoe	9.04						
Post-Gis 2009-2015	9.77						
2005-2015	10.34						
2005-2016	10.16						
2002-09	9.33						

Super Bowl Top QB Cap Hit				
Year	Year's Salary Cap	Player	Salary	% of Cap
1994	34,608,000	Steve Young	4,525,000	13.08
1995	37,100,000	Troy Aikman	2,493,500	6.72
1996	40,753,000	Brett Favre	4,175,720	10.25
1997	41,454,000	John Elway	2,141,475	5.17
1998	52,388,000	John Elway	2,624,315	5.01
1999	57,288,000	Trent Green	3,128,290	5.46
2000	62,172,000	Tony Banks	2,263,140	3.64
2001	67,405,000	Drew Bledsoe	6,936,391	10.29
2002	71,101,000	Brad Johnson	6,981,530	9.82
2003	75,007,000	Tom Brady	3,323,450	4.43
2004	80,852,000	Tom Brady	5,062,950	6.26
2005	85,500,000	Ben Roethlisberger	4,225,090	4.94
2006	102,000,000	Peyton Manning	10,566,668	10.36
2007	109,000,000	Eli Manning	10,046,666	9.22
2008	116,000,000	Ben Roethlisberger	7,971,920	6.87
2009	123,000,000	Drew Brees	10,660,400	8.67
2010	NO CAP	Aaron Rodgers	6,500,000	
2011	120,000,000	Eli Manning	14,100,000	11.75
2012	120,600,000	Joe Flacco	8,000,000	6.63
2013	123,000,000	Russell Wilson	681,085	0.55
2014	133,000,000	Tom Brady	14,800,000	11.13
				7.51

Super Bowl Starting Quarterbacks				
Year	Year's Salary Cap	Player	Salary	% of Cap
1994	34,608,000	Steve Young	4,525,000	13.08
1995	37,100,000	Troy Aikman	2,493,500	6.72
1996	40,753,000	Brett Favre	4,175,720	10.25
1997	41,454,000	John Elway	2,141,475	5.17
1998	52,388,000	John Elway	2,624,315	5.01
1999	57,288,000	Kurt Warner	753,920	1.32
2000	62,172,000	Trent Dilfer	1,000,320	1.61
2001	67,405,000	Tom Brady	314,933	0.47
2002	71,101,000	Brad Johnson	6,981,530	9.82
2003	75,007,000	Tom Brady	3,323,450	4.43
2004	80,852,000	Tom Brady	5,062,950	6.26
2005	85,500,000	Ben Roethlisberger	4,225,090	4.94
2006	102,000,000	Peyton Manning	10,566,668	10.36
2007	109,000,000	Eli Manning	10,046,666	9.22
2008	116,000,000	Ben Roethlisberger	7,971,920	6.87
2009	123,000,000	Drew Brees	10,660,400	8.67
2010	NO CAP	Aaron Rodgers	6,500,000	
2011	120,000,000	Eli Manning	14,100,000	11.75
2012	120,600,000	Joe Flacco	8,000,000	6.63
2013	123,000,000	Russell Wilson	681,085	0.55
2014	133,000,000	Tom Brady	14,800,000	11.13
				6.71

Peyton Manning Earnings Per Spotrac			
Year	Salary Cap	Age	Total Cash
1998	52,388,000	22	12,744,000
1999	57,288,000	23	1,430,000
2000	62,172,000	24	11,066,000
2001	67,405,000	25	4,452,000
2002	71,101,000	26	6,298,000
2003	75,007,000	27	11,342,000
2004	80,852,000	28	35,035,000
2005	85,500,000	29	665,000
2006	102,000,000	30	10,000,000
2007	109,000,000	31	11,000,000
2008	116,000,000	32	11,500,000
2009	123,000,000	33	14,000,000
2010	NO CAP	34	15,800,000
2011	120,000,000	35	26,400,000
2012	120,600,000	36	18,000,000
2013	123,000,000	37	25,000,000
2014	133,000,000	38	15,000,000
2015	143,280,000	39	19,000,000
2016	155,270,000	40	
2017	165,500,000	41	
	1998-2015		248,732,000
	2004-15		201,400,000
	1998-2003		47,332,000
	2010-15 AVG		19,866,667

Tom Brady Career Earnings per Spotrac				
Year	Salary Cap	Age	Total Cash	Signing Bonus?
1998	52,388,000			
1999	57,288,000			
2000	62,172,000	23	231,500	YES
2001	67,405,000	24	372,160	
2002	71,101,000	25	3,878,780	YES
2003	75,007,000	26	9,129,700	
2004	80,852,000	27	6,004,200	
2005	85,500,000	28	12,004,180	YES
2006	102,000,000	29	14,004,840	YES
2007	109,000,000	30	12,505,160	
2008	116,000,000	31	8,001,320	
2009	123,000,000	32	8,000,000	
2010	NO CAP	33	16,500,000	YES
2011	120,000,000	34	19,750,000	YES
2012	120,600,000	35	12,000,000	NO - ROSTER+RESTRUCTURE B
2013	123,000,000	36	13,000,000	YES
2014	133,000,000	37	19,000,000	YES
2015	143,280,000	38	12,010,663	YES
2016	155,270,000	39	28,774,301	YES
2017	167,000,000	40	1,000,000	
2018	179,500,000	41	*15,000,000*	
2019	193,000,000	42	*15,000,000*	
	2000-19		226,166,804	
	2000-17		196,166,804	
	2005-2017		176,550,464	
	2000-04		19,616,340	
	2010-16 AVG		17,290,709	

Manning's Defense Points Allowed						
Year	Team	Pts Allowed	Pts/Game	Ranking	NFL Teams	Coach
1998	Colts	444	27.8	29	30	Jim Mora
1999	Colts	333	20.8	17	31	Jim Mora
2000	Colts	326	20.4	15	31	Jim Mora
2001	Colts	486	30.4	31	31	Jim Mora
2002	Colts	313	19.6	7	32	Tony Dungy
2003	Colts	336	21.0	20	32	Tony Dungy
2004	Colts	351	21.9	19	32	Tony Dungy
2005	Colts	247	15.4	2	32	Tony Dungy
2006	Colts	360	22.5	23	32	Tony Dungy
2007	Colts	262	16.4	1	32	Tony Dungy
2008	Colts	298	18.6	7	32	Tony Dungy
2009	Colts	307	19.2	8	32	Jim Caldwell
2010	Colts	388	24.3	23	32	Jim Caldwell
2011	Colts	430	26.9	28	32	Jim Caldwell
2012	Broncos	289	18.1	4	32	John Fox
2013	Broncos	399	24.9	22	32	John Fox
2014	Broncos	354	22.1	16	32	John Fox
2015	Broncos	296	18.5	4	32	Gary Kubiak
		345.5	21.6	15.3		
	IND	348.6	21.8	16.4		
	DEN	334.5	20.9	11.5		

Brady's Defense Points Allowed						
Year	Team	Pts Allowed	Pts/Game	Ranking	NFL Teams	Coach
2001	Patriots	272	17.0	6	31	Bill Belichick
2002	Patriots	346	21.6	17	32	Bill Belichick
2003	Patriots	238	14.9	1	32	Bill Belichick
2004	Patriots	260	16.3	2	32	Bill Belichick
2005	Patriots	338	21.1	17	32	Bill Belichick
2006	Patriots	237	14.8	2	32	Bill Belichick
2007	Patriots	274	17.1	4	32	Bill Belichick
2008	Patriots	309	19.3	8	32	Bill Belichick
2009	Patriots	285	17.8	5	32	Bill Belichick
2010	Patriots	313	19.6	8	32	Bill Belichick
2011	Patriots	342	21.4	15	32	Bill Belichick
2012	Patriots	331	20.7	9	32	Bill Belichick
2013	Patriots	338	21.1	10	32	Bill Belichick
2014	Patriots	313	19.6	8	32	Bill Belichick
2015	Patriots	315	19.7	10	32	Bill Belichick
2016	Patriots	250	15.6	1	32	Bill Belichick
		297.6	18.6	7.7		

CHAPTER 6 DATA

Patriots Two Running Back Roles
Patriots Lead Rusher Role

Player	Height	Inches	Weight
Antowain Smith	6' 2"	74	232
Corey Dillon	6' 1"	73	225
Laurence Maroney	5' 11"	71	210
BenJarvus Green-Ellis	5' 11"	71	215
Stevan Ridley	5' 11"	71	230
LeGarrette Blount	6' 1"	73	245
		72.2	226.2

Patriots Pass Catcher Role

Player	Height	Inches	Weight
Kevin Faulk	5' 8"	68	202
Danny Woodhead	5' 9"	69	200
Shane Vereen	5' 10"	70	200
Dion Lewis	5' 8"	68	195
James White	5' 10"	70	205
		69	200.4

Patriots Leading Rusher Role - Rushing Stats

Year	Player	Age	G	Rush Att	Rush Yds	Yds/Att	Yds/Gm	Att/Gm	TDs
2001	Antowain Smith	29	16	287	1157	4.0	72.3	17.9	12
2002	Antowain Smith	30	16	252	982	3.9	61.4	15.8	6
2003	Antowain Smith	31	13	182	642	3.5	49.4	11.4	3
2004	Corey Dillon	30	15	345	1635	4.7	109.0	21.6	12
2005	Corey Dillon	31	12	209	733	3.5	61.1	13.1	12
2006	Corey Dillon	32	16	199	812	4.1	50.8	12.4	13
	Laurence Maroney	21	14	175	745	4.3	53.2	10.9	6
			30	374	1557	4.2	51.9	23.4	19
2007	Laurence Maroney	22	13	185	835	4.5	64.2	11.6	6
	Sammy Morris	30	6	85	384	4.5	64.0	5.3	3
			19	270	1219	4.5	64.2	16.9	9
2008	Sammy Morris	31	13	156	727	4.7	55.9	9.8	7
	LaMont Jordan	30	8	80	363	4.5	45.4	5.0	4
	BenJarvus Green-Ellis	23	9	74	275	3.7	30.6	4.6	5
			30	310	1365	4.4	45.5	19.4	16
2009	Laurence Maroney	24	15	194	757	3.9	50.5	12.1	9
	Sammy Morris	32	12	73	319	4.4	26.6	4.6	2
	Fred Taylor	33	6	63	269	4.3	44.8	3.9	4
	BenJarvus Green-Ellis	24	12	26	114	4.4	9.5	1.6	0
			45	356	1459	4.1	32.4	22.3	15
2010	BenJarvus Green-Ellis	25	16	229	1008	4.4	63.0	14.3	13
	Fred Taylor	34	7	43	155	3.6	22.1	2.7	0
			23	272	1163	4.3	50.6	17.0	13
2011	BenJarvus Green-Ellis	26	16	181	667	3.7	41.7	11.3	11
	Stevan Ridley	22	16	87	441	5.1	27.6	5.4	1
			32	268	1108	4.1	34.6	16.8	12
2012	Stevan Ridley	23	16	290	1263	4.4	78.9	18.1	12
	Brandon Bolden	22	10	56	274	4.9	27.4	3.5	2
			26	346	1537	4.4	59.1	21.6	14
2013	Stevan Ridley	24	14	178	773	4.3	55.2	11.1	7
	LeGarrette Blount	27	16	153	772	5.0	48.3	9.6	7
	Brandon Bolden	23	12	55	271	4.9	22.6	3.4	3
			42	386	1816	4.7	43.2	24.1	17
2014	Stevan Ridley	25	6	94	340	3.6	56.7	5.9	2
	Jonas Gray	24	8	89	412	4.6	51.5	5.6	5
	LeGarrette Blount	28	5	60	281	4.7	56.2	3.8	3
			19	243	1033	4.3	54.4	15.2	10
2015	LeGarrette Blount	29	12	165	703	4.3	58.6	10.3	6
	Brandon Bolden	25	15	63	207	3.3	13.8	3.9	0
			27	228	910	4.0	33.7	14.3	6
2016	LeGarrette Blount	30	16	299	1161	3.9	72.6	18.7	18
	AVERAGE		16	289.2	1217.3	4.2	76.1	18.1	12.1

240

Patriots Leading Rusher Role - Receiving Stats							Catch		
Year	Player	G	Rec	Tgts	Rec Yds	Yds/Rec	Yds/T	Rate	Yds/G	TDs
2001	Antowain Smith	16	19	28	192	10.1	6.9	67.9%	12.0	1
2002	Antowain Smith	16	31	42	243	7.8	5.8	73.8%	15.2	2
2003	Antowain Smith	13	14	16	92	6.6	5.8	87.5%	7.1	0
2004	Corey Dillon	15	15	21	103	6.9	4.9	71.4%	6.9	1
2005	Corey Dillon	12	22	26	181	8.2	7.0	84.6%	15.1	1
2006	Corey Dillon	16	15	16	147	9.8	9.2	93.8%	9.2	0
	Laurence Maroney	14	22	30	194	8.8	6.5	73.3%	13.9	1
		30	37	46	341	9.2	7.4	80.4%	11.4	1
2007	Laurence Maroney	13	4	8	116	29.0	14.5	50.0%	8.9	0
	Sammy Morris	6	6	8	35	5.8	4.4	75.0%	5.8	0
		19	10	16	151	15.1	9.4	62.5%	7.9	0
2008	Sammy Morris	13	17	24	161	9.5	6.7	70.8%	12.4	0
	LaMont Jordan	8	0	0	0	0.0	0.0	0.0%	0.0	0
	BenJarvus Green-Ellis	9	3	6	37	12.3	6.2	50.0%	4.1	0
		30	20	30	198	9.9	6.6	66.7%	6.6	0
2009	Laurence Maroney	15	14	18	99	7.1	5.5	77.8%	6.6	0
	Sammy Morris	12	19	27	180	9.5	6.7	70.4%	15.0	0
	Fred Taylor	6	2	3	17	8.5	5.7	66.7%	2.8	0
	BenJarvus Green-Ellis	12	2	5	11	5.5	2.2	40.0%	0.9	0
		45	37	53	307	8.3	5.8	69.8%	6.8	0
2010	BenJarvus Green-Ellis	16	12	16	85	7.1	5.3	75.0%	5.3	0
	Fred Taylor	7	2	3	6	3.0	2.0	66.7%	0.9	0
		23	14	19	91	6.5	4.8	73.7%	4.0	0
2011	BenJarvus Green-Ellis	16	9	13	159	17.7	12.2	69.2%	9.9	0
	Stevan Ridley	16	3	5	13	4.3	2.6	60.0%	0.8	0
		32	12	18	172	14.3	9.6	66.7%	5.4	0
2012	Stevan Ridley	16	6	14	51	8.5	3.6	42.9%	3.2	0
	Brandon Bolden	10	2	2	11	5.5	5.5	100.0%	1.1	0
		26	8	16	62	7.8	3.9	50.0%	2.4	0
2013	Stevan Ridley	14	10	12	62	6.2	5.2	83.3%	4.4	0
	LeGarrette Blount	16	2	5	38	19.0	7.6	40.0%	2.4	0
	Brandon Bolden	12	21	29	152	7.2	5.2	72.4%	12.7	0
		42	33	46	252	7.6	5.5	71.7%	6.0	0
2014	Stevan Ridley	6	4	5	20	5.0	4.0	80.0%	3.3	0
	Jonas Gray	8	1	3	7	7.0	2.3	33.3%	0.9	0
	LeGarrette Blount	5	4	4	18	4.5	4.5	100.0%	3.6	0
		19	9	12	45	5.0	3.8	75.0%	2.4	0
2015	LeGarrette Blount	12	6	7	43	7.2	6.1	85.7%	3.6	1
	Brandon Bolden	15	19	30	180	9.5	6.0	63.3%	12.0	2
		27	25	37	223	8.9	6.0	67.6%	8.3	3
2016	LeGarrette Blount	16	7	8	38	5.4	4.8	87.5%	2.4	0
	AVERAGE	16	##	27.1	168.2	8.6	6.2	72.1%	10.5	0.6

Patriots Pass Catcher Role - Rushing Stats									
Year	Player	Age	Games	Rush Att	Rush Yds	Yds/Att	Yds/Gm	Att/Gm	TDs
2001	Kevin Faulk	25	15	41	169	4.1	11.3	2.6	1
2002	Kevin Faulk	26	15	52	271	5.2	18.1	3.3	2
2003	Kevin Faulk	27	15	178	638	3.6	42.5	11.1	0
2004	Kevin Faulk	28	11	54	255	4.7	23.2	3.4	2
2005	Kevin Faulk	29	8	51	145	2.8	18.1	3.2	0
2006	Kevin Faulk	30	15	25	123	4.9	8.2	1.6	1
2007	Kevin Faulk	31	16	62	265	4.3	16.6	3.9	0
2008	Kevin Faulk	32	15	83	507	6.1	33.8	5.2	3
2009	Kevin Faulk	33	15	62	335	5.4	22.3	3.9	2
2010	Danny Woodhead	25	14	97	547	5.6	39.1	6.1	5
2011	Danny Woodhead	26	15	77	351	4.6	23.4	4.8	1
2012	Danny Woodhead	27	16	76	301	4.0	18.8	4.8	4
	Shane Vereen	23	13	62	251	4.0	19.3	3.9	3
			29	138	552	4.0	19.0	8.6	7
2013	Shane Vereen	24	8	44	208	4.7	26.0	2.8	1
2014	Shane Vereen	25	16	96	391	4.1	24.4	6.0	2
2015	Dion Lewis	25	7	49	234	4.8	33.4	3.1	2
	James White	23	14	22	56	2.5	4.0	1.4	2
			21	71	290	4.1	13.8	4.4	4
2016	Dion Lewis	26	7	64	283	4.4	40.4	4.0	0
	James White	24	16	39	166	4.3	10.4	2.4	0
			23	103	449	4.4	19.5	6.4	0
	AVERAGE		16	77.1	343.5	4.5	21.5	4.8	1.9

Patriots Pass Catcher Role - Receiving Stats								Catch		
Year	Player	G	Rec	Tgts	Rec Yds	Yds/Rec	Yds/T	Rate	Yds/G	TDs
2001	Kevin Faulk	15	30	36	189	6.3	5.3	83.3%	12.6	2
2002	Kevin Faulk	15	37	53	379	10.2	7.2	69.8%	25.3	3
2003	Kevin Faulk	15	48	67	440	9.2	6.6	71.6%	29.3	0
2004	Kevin Faulk	11	26	30	248	9.5	8.3	86.7%	22.5	1
2005	Kevin Faulk	8	29	37	260	0.0	0.0	0.0%	32.5	0
2006	Kevin Faulk	15	43	56	356	8.3	6.4	76.8%	23.7	2
2007	Kevin Faulk	16	47	61	383	8.1	6.3	77.0%	23.9	1
2008	Kevin Faulk	15	58	74	486	8.4	6.6	78.4%	32.4	3
2009	Kevin Faulk	15	37	53	301	8.1	5.7	69.8%	20.1	1
2010	Danny Woodhead	14	34	44	379	11.1	8.6	77.3%	27.1	1
2011	Danny Woodhead	15	18	31	157	8.7	5.1	58.1%	10.5	0
2012	Danny Woodhead	16	40	55	446	11.2	8.1	72.7%	27.9	3
	Shane Vereen	13	8	13	149	18.6	11.5	61.5%	11.5	1
		29	48	68	595	12.4	8.8	70.6%	20.5	4
2013	Shane Vereen	8	47	69	427	9.1	6.2	68.1%	53.4	3
2014	Shane Vereen	16	52	77	447	8.6	5.8	67.5%	27.9	3
2015	Dion Lewis	7	36	50	388	10.8	7.8	72.0%	55.4	2
	James White	14	40	54	410	10.3	7.6	74.1%	29.3	4
		21	76	104	798	10.5	7.7	73.1%	38.0	6
2016	Dion Lewis	7	17	24	94	5.5	3.9	70.8%	13.4	0
	James White	16	60	86	551	9.2	6.4	69.8%	34.4	5
		23	77	110	645	8.4	5.9	70.0%	28.0	5
	AVERAGE	16	44.2	60.6	405.6	9.2	6.7	72.9%	25.4	2.2

CHAPTER 10 DATA

Cap Projection/Proposal through 2027 Using My 2015 Projections

Uses a 107.5% increase from 2015 through 2020, then a 109% increase from 2021 through 2027.

Year	(*107.5%)	Nearest 1/2 M	Plus $1.5 M (2016)	Using *107.5% & 109%	Nearest 1/2 M	Plus $1.5 M to '21
2015	143,280,000	143,280,000	143,280,000	143,280,000	143,280,000	143,280,000
2016	154,026,000	154,000,000	155,270,000	154,026,000	154,000,000	155,270,000
2017	165,577,950	165,500,000	167,000,000	165,577,950	165,500,000	167,000,000
2018	177,996,296	178,000,000	179,500,000	177,996,296	178,000,000	179,500,000
2019	191,346,018	191,500,000	193,000,000	191,346,018	191,500,000	193,000,000
2020	205,696,970	205,500,000	207,000,000	205,696,970	205,500,000	207,000,000
2021	221,124,243	221,000,000	222,500,000	224,209,697	224,000,000	225,500,000
2022	237,708,561	237,500,000	239,000,000	244,388,570	244,500,000	244,500,000
2023	255,536,703	255,500,000	257,000,000	266,383,541	266,500,000	266,500,000
2024	274,701,956	274,500,000	276,000,000	290,358,060	290,500,000	290,500,000
2025	295,304,602	295,500,000	297,000,000	316,490,285	316,500,000	316,500,000
2026	317,452,447	317,500,000	319,000,000	344,974,411	345,000,000	345,000,000
2027	341,261,381	341,500,000	343,000,000	376,022,108	376,000,000	376,000,000

Table A

Round	Pick	Overall	Signing Bonus	2015 Cap	% of Cap	2016 Cap	% of Cap	2017 Cap		2018 Cap		Total
1	1	1	$15,547,712	$4,321,928	3.02%	$5,402,410	3.48%	$6,482,892	3.88%	$7,563,374	4.21%	$23,770,604
1	2	2	$14,777,528	$4,129,382	2.88%	$5,161,728	3.32%	$6,194,074	3.71%	$7,226,420	4.03%	$22,711,604
1	3	3	$14,287,416	$4,006,854	2.80%	$5,008,568	3.23%	$6,010,282	3.60%	$7,011,996	3.91%	$22,037,700
1	4	4	$13,727,284	$3,866,821	2.70%	$4,833,526	3.11%	$5,800,231	3.47%	$6,766,936	3.77%	$21,267,514
1	5	5	$12,747,052	$3,621,763	2.53%	$4,527,204	2.92%	$5,432,645	3.25%	$6,338,086	3.53%	$19,919,698
1	6	6	$10,996,640	$3,184,160	2.22%	$3,980,200	2.56%	$4,776,240	2.86%	$5,572,280	3.10%	$17,512,880
1	7	7	$9,596,312	$2,834,078	1.98%	$3,542,598	2.28%	$4,251,118	2.55%	$4,959,638	2.76%	$15,587,432
1	8	8	$8,195,980	$2,483,995	1.73%	$3,104,994	2.00%	$3,725,993	2.23%	$4,346,992	2.42%	$13,661,974
1	9	9	$8,125,964	$2,466,491	1.72%	$3,083,114	1.99%	$3,699,737	2.22%	$4,316,360	2.40%	$13,565,702
1	10	10	$7,740,872	$2,370,218	1.65%	$2,962,773	1.91%	$3,555,328	2.13%	$4,147,883	2.31%	$13,036,202
1	11	11	$7,145,732	$2,221,433	1.55%	$2,776,791	1.79%	$3,332,149	2.00%	$3,887,507	2.17%	$12,217,880
1	12	12	$6,305,532	$2,011,383	1.40%	$2,514,229	1.62%	$3,017,075	1.81%	$3,519,921	1.96%	$11,062,608
1	13	13	$6,095,484	$1,958,871	1.37%	$2,448,589	1.58%	$2,938,307	1.76%	$3,428,025	1.91%	$10,773,792
1	14	14	$5,745,404	$1,871,351	1.31%	$2,339,189	1.51%	$2,807,027	1.68%	$3,274,865	1.82%	$10,292,432
1	15	15	$5,605,372	$1,836,343	1.28%	$2,295,429	1.48%	$2,754,515	1.65%	$3,213,601	1.79%	$10,099,888
1	16	16	$5,185,272	$1,731,318	1.21%	$2,164,148	1.39%	$2,596,978	1.56%	$3,029,808	1.69%	$9,522,252
1	17	17	$5,045,236	$1,696,309	1.18%	$2,120,386	1.37%	$2,544,463	1.52%	$2,968,540	1.65%	$9,329,698
1	18	18	$4,870,200	$1,652,550	1.15%	$2,065,688	1.33%	$2,478,826	1.48%	$2,891,964	1.61%	$9,089,028
1	19	19	$4,765,168	$1,626,292	1.14%	$2,032,865	1.31%	$2,439,438	1.46%	$2,846,011	1.59%	$8,944,606
1	20	20	$4,730,164	$1,617,541	1.13%	$2,021,926	1.30%	$2,426,311	1.45%	$2,830,696	1.58%	$8,896,474
1	21	21	$4,695,156	$1,608,789	1.12%	$2,010,986	1.30%	$2,413,183	1.45%	$2,815,380	1.57%	$8,848,338
1	22	22	$4,625,136	$1,591,284	1.11%	$1,989,105	1.28%	$2,386,926	1.43%	$2,784,747	1.55%	$8,752,062
1	23	23	$4,555,124	$1,573,781	1.10%	$1,967,226	1.27%	$2,360,671	1.41%	$2,754,116	1.53%	$8,655,794
1	24	24	$4,415,088	$1,538,772	1.07%	$1,923,465	1.24%	$2,308,158	1.38%	$2,692,851	1.50%	$8,463,246
1	25	25	$4,345,076	$1,521,269	1.06%	$1,901,586	1.22%	$2,281,903	1.37%	$2,662,220	1.48%	$8,366,978
1	26	26	$4,275,056	$1,503,764	1.05%	$1,879,705	1.21%	$2,255,646	1.35%	$2,631,587	1.47%	$8,270,702
1	27	27	$4,205,040	$1,486,260	1.04%	$1,857,825	1.20%	$2,229,390	1.33%	$2,600,955	1.45%	$8,174,430
1	28	28	$4,170,032	$1,477,508	1.03%	$1,846,885	1.19%	$2,216,262	1.33%	$2,585,639	1.44%	$8,126,294
1	29	29	$3,889,108	$1,407,277	0.98%	$1,759,096	1.13%	$2,110,915	1.26%	$2,462,734	1.37%	$7,740,022
1	30	30	$3,740,336	$1,370,084	0.96%	$1,712,605	1.10%	$2,055,126	1.23%	$2,397,647	1.34%	$7,535,462
1	31	31	$3,615,724	$1,338,931	0.93%	$1,673,664	1.08%	$2,008,397	1.20%	$2,343,130	1.31%	$7,364,122
1	32	32	$3,535,484	$1,318,871	0.92%	$1,648,589	1.06%	$1,978,307	1.18%	$2,308,025	1.29%	$7,253,792
2	1	33	$2,524,644	$1,066,161	0.74%	$1,332,701	0.86%	$1,599,241	0.96%	$1,865,781	1.04%	$5,863,884

246

Table A

Round	Pick	Overall	Signing Bonus	2015 Cap	% of Cap	2016 Cap	% of Cap	2017 Cap		2018 Cap		Total
1	1	1	$15,547,712	$4,321,928	3.02%	$5,402,410	3.48%	$6,482,892	3.88%	$7,563,374	4.21%	$23,770,604
1	2	2	$14,777,528	$4,129,382	2.88%	$5,161,728	3.32%	$6,194,074	3.71%	$7,226,420	4.03%	$22,711,604
1	3	3	$14,287,416	$4,006,854	2.80%	$5,008,568	3.23%	$6,010,282	3.60%	$7,011,996	3.91%	$22,037,700
1	4	4	$13,727,284	$3,866,821	2.70%	$4,833,526	3.11%	$5,800,231	3.47%	$6,766,936	3.77%	$21,267,514
1	5	5	$12,747,052	$3,621,763	2.53%	$4,527,204	2.92%	$5,432,645	3.25%	$6,338,086	3.53%	$19,919,698
1	6	6	$10,996,640	$3,184,160	2.22%	$3,980,200	2.56%	$4,776,240	2.86%	$5,572,280	3.10%	$17,512,880
1	7	7	$9,596,312	$2,834,078	1.98%	$3,542,598	2.28%	$4,251,118	2.55%	$4,959,638	2.76%	$15,587,432
1	8	8	$8,195,980	$2,483,995	1.73%	$3,104,994	2.00%	$3,725,993	2.23%	$4,346,992	2.42%	$13,661,974
1	9	9	$8,125,964	$2,466,491	1.72%	$3,083,114	1.99%	$3,699,737	2.22%	$4,316,360	2.40%	$13,565,702
1	10	10	$7,740,872	$2,370,218	1.65%	$2,962,773	1.91%	$3,555,328	2.13%	$4,147,883	2.31%	$13,036,202
1	11	11	$7,145,732	$2,221,433	1.55%	$2,776,791	1.79%	$3,332,149	2.00%	$3,887,507	2.17%	$12,217,880
1	12	12	$6,305,532	$2,011,383	1.40%	$2,514,229	1.62%	$3,017,075	1.81%	$3,519,921	1.96%	$11,062,608
1	13	13	$6,095,484	$1,958,871	1.37%	$2,448,589	1.58%	$2,938,307	1.76%	$3,428,025	1.91%	$10,773,792
1	14	14	$5,745,404	$1,871,351	1.31%	$2,339,189	1.51%	$2,807,027	1.68%	$3,274,865	1.82%	$10,292,432
1	15	15	$5,605,372	$1,836,343	1.28%	$2,295,429	1.48%	$2,754,515	1.65%	$3,213,601	1.79%	$10,099,888
1	16	16	$5,185,272	$1,731,318	1.21%	$2,164,148	1.39%	$2,596,978	1.56%	$3,029,808	1.69%	$9,522,252
1	17	17	$5,045,236	$1,696,309	1.18%	$2,120,386	1.37%	$2,544,463	1.52%	$2,968,540	1.65%	$9,329,698
1	18	18	$4,870,200	$1,652,550	1.15%	$2,065,688	1.33%	$2,478,826	1.48%	$2,891,964	1.61%	$9,089,028
1	19	19	$4,765,168	$1,626,292	1.14%	$2,032,865	1.31%	$2,439,438	1.46%	$2,846,011	1.59%	$8,944,606
1	20	20	$4,730,164	$1,617,541	1.13%	$2,021,926	1.30%	$2,426,311	1.45%	$2,830,696	1.58%	$8,896,474
1	21	21	$4,695,156	$1,608,789	1.12%	$2,010,986	1.30%	$2,413,183	1.45%	$2,815,380	1.57%	$8,848,338
1	22	22	$4,625,136	$1,591,284	1.11%	$1,989,105	1.28%	$2,386,926	1.43%	$2,784,747	1.55%	$8,752,062
1	23	23	$4,555,124	$1,573,781	1.10%	$1,967,226	1.27%	$2,360,671	1.41%	$2,754,116	1.53%	$8,655,794
1	24	24	$4,415,088	$1,538,772	1.07%	$1,923,465	1.24%	$2,308,158	1.38%	$2,692,851	1.50%	$8,463,246
1	25	25	$4,345,076	$1,521,269	1.06%	$1,901,586	1.22%	$2,281,903	1.37%	$2,662,220	1.48%	$8,366,978
1	26	26	$4,275,056	$1,503,764	1.05%	$1,879,705	1.21%	$2,255,646	1.35%	$2,631,587	1.47%	$8,270,702
1	27	27	$4,205,040	$1,486,260	1.04%	$1,857,825	1.20%	$2,229,390	1.33%	$2,600,955	1.45%	$8,174,430
1	28	28	$4,170,032	$1,477,508	1.03%	$1,846,885	1.19%	$2,216,262	1.33%	$2,585,639	1.44%	$8,126,294
1	29	29	$3,889,108	$1,407,277	0.98%	$1,759,096	1.13%	$2,110,915	1.26%	$2,462,734	1.37%	$7,740,022
1	30	30	$3,740,336	$1,370,084	0.96%	$1,712,605	1.10%	$2,055,126	1.23%	$2,397,647	1.34%	$7,535,462
1	31	31	$3,615,724	$1,338,931	0.93%	$1,673,664	1.08%	$2,008,397	1.20%	$2,343,130	1.31%	$7,364,122
1	32	32	$3,535,484	$1,318,871	0.92%	$1,648,589	1.06%	$1,978,307	1.18%	$2,308,025	1.29%	$7,253,792
2	1	33	$2,524,644	$1,066,161	0.74%	$1,332,701	0.86%	$1,599,241	0.96%	$1,865,781	1.04%	$5,863,884

3	5	69	$732,584	$618,146	0.43%	$708,146	0.46%	$798,146	0.48%	$888,146	0.49%	$3,012,584
3	6	70	$718,836	$614,709	0.43%	$704,709	0.45%	$794,709	0.48%	$884,709	0.49%	$2,998,836
3	7	71	$709,464	$612,366	0.43%	$702,366	0.45%	$792,366	0.47%	$882,366	0.49%	$2,989,464
3	8	72	$702,848	$610,712	0.43%	$700,712	0.45%	$790,712	0.47%	$880,712	0.49%	$2,982,848
3	9	73	$693,936	$608,484	0.42%	$698,484	0.45%	$788,484	0.47%	$878,484	0.49%	$2,973,936
3	10	74	$689,520	$607,380	0.42%	$697,380	0.45%	$787,380	0.47%	$877,380	0.49%	$2,969,520
3	11	75	$682,692	$605,673	0.42%	$695,673	0.45%	$785,673	0.47%	$875,673	0.49%	$2,962,692
3	12	76	$663,384	$600,846	0.42%	$690,846	0.44%	$780,846	0.47%	$870,846	0.49%	$2,943,384
3	13	77	$661,204	$600,301	0.42%	$690,301	0.44%	$780,301	0.47%	$870,301	0.48%	$2,941,204
3	14	78	$657,312	$599,328	0.42%	$689,328	0.44%	$779,328	0.47%	$869,328	0.48%	$2,937,312
3	15	79	$649,360	$597,340	0.42%	$687,340	0.44%	$777,340	0.47%	$867,340	0.48%	$2,929,360
3	16	80	$641,328	$595,332	0.42%	$685,332	0.44%	$775,332	0.46%	$865,332	0.48%	$2,921,328
3	17	81	$633,296	$593,324	0.41%	$683,324	0.44%	$773,324	0.46%	$863,324	0.48%	$2,913,296
3	18	82	$627,612	$591,903	0.41%	$681,903	0.44%	$771,903	0.46%	$861,903	0.48%	$2,907,612
3	19	83	$616,028	$589,007	0.41%	$679,007	0.44%	$769,007	0.46%	$859,007	0.48%	$2,896,028
3	20	84	$607,792	$586,948	0.41%	$676,948	0.44%	$766,948	0.46%	$856,948	0.48%	$2,887,792
3	21	85	$603,180	$585,795	0.41%	$675,795	0.44%	$765,795	0.46%	$855,795	0.48%	$2,883,180
3	22	86	$595,352	$583,838	0.41%	$673,838	0.43%	$763,838	0.46%	$853,838	0.48%	$2,875,352
3	23	87	$588,036	$582,009	0.41%	$672,009	0.43%	$762,009	0.46%	$852,009	0.47%	$2,868,036
3	24	88	$584,040	$581,010	0.41%	$671,010	0.43%	$761,010	0.46%	$851,010	0.47%	$2,864,040
3	25	89	$582,712	$580,678	0.41%	$670,678	0.43%	$760,678	0.46%	$850,678	0.47%	$2,862,712
3	26	90	$582,048	$580,512	0.41%	$670,512	0.43%	$760,512	0.46%	$850,512	0.47%	$2,862,048
3	27	91	$581,384	$580,346	0.41%	$670,346	0.43%	$760,346	0.46%	$850,346	0.47%	$2,861,384
3	28	92	$578,064	$579,516	0.40%	$669,516	0.43%	$759,516	0.45%	$849,516	0.47%	$2,858,064
3	29	93	$571,424	$577,856	0.40%	$667,856	0.43%	$757,856	0.45%	$847,856	0.47%	$2,851,424
3	30	94	$564,784	$576,196	0.40%	$666,196	0.43%	$756,196	0.45%	$846,196	0.47%	$2,844,784
3	31	95	$558,144	$574,536	0.40%	$664,536	0.43%	$754,536	0.45%	$844,536	0.47%	$2,838,144
3	32	96	$551,508	$572,877	0.40%	$662,877	0.43%	$752,877	0.45%	$842,877	0.47%	$2,831,508
4	1	97	$532,260	$568,065	0.40%	$658,065	0.42%	$748,065	0.45%	$838,065	0.47%	$2,812,260
4	2	98	$520,452	$565,113	0.39%	$655,113	0.42%	$745,113	0.45%	$835,113	0.47%	$2,800,452
4	3	99	$518,764	$564,691	0.39%	$654,691	0.42%	$744,691	0.45%	$834,691	0.47%	$2,798,764
4	4	100	$515,576	$563,894	0.39%	$653,894	0.42%	$743,894	0.45%	$833,894	0.46%	$2,795,576
4	5	101	$510,812	$562,703	0.39%	$652,703	0.42%	$742,703	0.44%	$832,703	0.46%	$2,790,812
4	6	102	$508,060	$562,015	0.39%	$652,015	0.42%	$742,015	0.44%	$832,015	0.46%	$2,788,060
4	7	103	$506,196	$561,549	0.39%	$651,549	0.42%	$741,549	0.44%	$831,549	0.46%	$2,786,196

4	104	$503,588	0.39%	$560,897	0.42%	$650,897	0.44%	$740,897	0.46%	$2,783,588
4	105	$500,696	0.39%	$560,174	0.42%	$650,174	0.44%	$740,174	0.46%	$2,780,696
4	106	$497,168	0.39%	$559,292	0.42%	$649,292	0.44%	$739,292	0.46%	$2,777,168
4	107	$488,812	0.39%	$557,203	0.42%	$647,203	0.44%	$737,203	0.46%	$2,768,812
4	108	$487,680	0.39%	$556,920	0.42%	$646,920	0.44%	$736,920	0.46%	$2,767,680
4	109	$485,756	0.39%	$556,439	0.42%	$646,439	0.44%	$736,439	0.46%	$2,765,756
4	110	$485,276	0.39%	$556,319	0.42%	$646,319	0.44%	$736,319	0.46%	$2,765,276
4	111	$482,864	0.39%	$555,716	0.42%	$645,716	0.44%	$735,716	0.46%	$2,762,864
4	112	$476,760	0.39%	$554,190	0.41%	$644,190	0.44%	$734,190	0.46%	$2,756,760
4	113	$474,808	0.39%	$553,702	0.41%	$643,702	0.44%	$733,702	0.46%	$2,754,808
4	114	$470,356	0.39%	$552,589	0.41%	$642,589	0.44%	$732,589	0.46%	$2,750,356
4	115	$465,688	0.38%	$551,422	0.41%	$641,422	0.44%	$731,422	0.46%	$2,745,688
4	116	$462,720	0.38%	$550,680	0.41%	$640,680	0.44%	$730,680	0.46%	$2,742,720
4	117	$459,732	0.38%	$549,933	0.41%	$639,933	0.44%	$729,933	0.46%	$2,739,732
4	118	$455,344	0.38%	$548,836	0.41%	$638,836	0.44%	$728,836	0.46%	$2,735,344
4	119	$449,888	0.38%	$547,472	0.41%	$637,472	0.44%	$727,472	0.46%	$2,729,888
4	120	$449,888	0.38%	$547,472	0.41%	$637,472	0.44%	$727,472	0.46%	$2,729,888
4	121	$445,392	0.38%	$546,348	0.41%	$636,348	0.43%	$726,348	0.45%	$2,725,392
4	122	$441,804	0.38%	$545,451	0.41%	$635,451	0.43%	$725,451	0.45%	$2,721,804
4	123	$436,508	0.38%	$544,127	0.41%	$634,127	0.43%	$724,127	0.45%	$2,716,508
4	124	$434,212	0.38%	$543,553	0.41%	$633,553	0.43%	$723,553	0.45%	$2,714,212
4	125	$428,932	0.38%	$542,233	0.41%	$632,233	0.43%	$722,233	0.45%	$2,708,932
4	126	$425,236	0.38%	$541,309	0.41%	$631,309	0.43%	$721,309	0.45%	$2,705,236
4	127	$419,252	0.38%	$539,813	0.41%	$629,813	0.43%	$719,813	0.45%	$2,699,252
4	128	$412,988	0.38%	$538,247	0.40%	$628,247	0.43%	$718,247	0.45%	$2,692,988
5	1	$230,788	0.34%	$492,697	0.38%	$582,697	0.40%	$672,697	0.42%	$2,510,788
5	2	$228,756	0.34%	$492,189	0.37%	$582,189	0.40%	$672,189	0.42%	$2,508,756
5	3	$227,028	0.34%	$491,757	0.37%	$581,757	0.40%	$671,757	0.42%	$2,507,028
5	4	$226,012	0.34%	$491,503	0.37%	$581,503	0.40%	$671,503	0.42%	$2,506,012
5	5	$221,568	0.34%	$490,392	0.37%	$580,392	0.40%	$670,392	0.42%	$2,501,568
5	6	$216,288	0.34%	$489,072	0.37%	$579,072	0.40%	$669,072	0.42%	$2,496,288
5	7	$214,712	0.34%	$488,678	0.37%	$578,678	0.40%	$668,678	0.42%	$2,494,712
5	8	$213,108	0.34%	$488,277	0.37%	$578,277	0.40%	$668,277	0.42%	$2,493,108
5	9	$212,572	0.34%	$488,143	0.37%	$578,143	0.40%	$668,143	0.42%	$2,492,572
5	10	$212,036	0.34%	$488,009	0.37%	$578,009	0.40%	$668,009	0.42%	$2,492,036

5	11	139	$208,236	$487,059	0.34%	$577,059	0.37%	$667,059	0.40%	$757,059	0.42%	$2,488,236
5	12	140	$206,468	$486,617	0.34%	$576,617	0.37%	$666,617	0.40%	$756,617	0.42%	$2,486,468
5	13	141	$205,612	$486,403	0.34%	$576,403	0.37%	$666,403	0.40%	$756,403	0.42%	$2,485,612
5	14	142	$205,344	$486,336	0.34%	$576,336	0.37%	$666,336	0.40%	$756,336	0.42%	$2,485,344
5	15	143	$204,860	$486,215	0.34%	$576,215	0.37%	$666,215	0.40%	$756,215	0.42%	$2,484,860
5	16	144	$204,712	$486,178	0.34%	$576,178	0.37%	$666,178	0.40%	$756,178	0.42%	$2,484,712
5	17	145	$203,524	$485,881	0.34%	$575,881	0.37%	$665,881	0.40%	$755,881	0.42%	$2,483,524
5	18	146	$202,268	$485,567	0.34%	$575,567	0.37%	$665,567	0.40%	$755,567	0.42%	$2,482,268
5	19	147	$200,524	$485,131	0.34%	$575,131	0.37%	$665,131	0.40%	$755,131	0.42%	$2,480,524
5	20	148	$199,976	$484,994	0.34%	$574,994	0.37%	$664,994	0.40%	$754,994	0.42%	$2,479,976
5	21	149	$198,112	$484,528	0.34%	$574,528	0.37%	$664,528	0.40%	$754,528	0.42%	$2,478,112
5	22	150	$197,248	$484,312	0.34%	$574,312	0.37%	$664,312	0.40%	$754,312	0.42%	$2,477,248
5	23	151	$195,356	$483,839	0.34%	$573,839	0.37%	$663,839	0.40%	$753,839	0.42%	$2,475,356
5	24	152	$194,528	$483,632	0.34%	$573,632	0.37%	$663,632	0.40%	$753,632	0.42%	$2,474,528
5	25	153	$191,188	$482,797	0.34%	$572,797	0.37%	$662,797	0.40%	$752,797	0.42%	$2,471,188
5	26	154	$190,732	$482,683	0.34%	$572,683	0.37%	$662,683	0.40%	$752,683	0.42%	$2,470,732
5	27	155	$189,012	$482,253	0.34%	$572,253	0.37%	$662,253	0.40%	$752,253	0.42%	$2,469,012
5	28	156	$183,636	$480,909	0.34%	$570,909	0.37%	$660,909	0.40%	$750,909	0.42%	$2,463,636
5	29	157	$180,828	$480,207	0.34%	$570,207	0.37%	$660,207	0.40%	$750,207	0.42%	$2,460,828
5	30	158	$176,484	$479,121	0.33%	$569,121	0.37%	$659,121	0.39%	$749,121	0.42%	$2,456,484
5	31	159	$174,340	$478,585	0.33%	$568,585	0.37%	$658,585	0.39%	$748,585	0.42%	$2,454,340
5	32	160	$171,664	$477,916	0.33%	$567,916	0.37%	$657,916	0.39%	$747,916	0.42%	$2,451,664
6	1	161	$137,952	$469,488	0.33%	$559,488	0.36%	$649,488	0.39%	$739,488	0.41%	$2,417,952
6	2	162	$133,984	$468,496	0.33%	$558,496	0.36%	$648,496	0.39%	$738,496	0.41%	$2,413,984
6	3	163	$131,828	$467,957	0.33%	$557,957	0.36%	$647,957	0.39%	$737,957	0.41%	$2,411,828
6	4	164	$129,148	$467,287	0.33%	$557,287	0.36%	$647,287	0.39%	$737,287	0.41%	$2,409,148
6	5	165	$126,292	$466,573	0.33%	$556,573	0.36%	$646,573	0.39%	$736,573	0.41%	$2,406,292
6	6	166	$123,996	$465,999	0.33%	$555,999	0.36%	$645,999	0.39%	$735,999	0.41%	$2,403,996
6	7	167	$122,320	$465,580	0.32%	$555,580	0.36%	$645,580	0.39%	$735,580	0.41%	$2,402,320
6	8	168	$121,496	$465,374	0.32%	$555,374	0.36%	$645,374	0.39%	$735,374	0.41%	$2,401,496
6	9	169	$119,940	$464,985	0.32%	$554,985	0.36%	$644,985	0.39%	$734,985	0.41%	$2,399,940
6	10	170	$118,332	$464,583	0.32%	$554,583	0.36%	$644,583	0.39%	$734,583	0.41%	$2,398,332
6	11	171	$117,860	$464,465	0.32%	$554,465	0.36%	$644,465	0.39%	$734,465	0.41%	$2,397,860
6	12	172	$115,304	$463,826	0.32%	$553,826	0.36%	$643,826	0.39%	$733,826	0.41%	$2,395,304
6	13	173	$113,728	$463,432	0.32%	$553,432	0.36%	$643,432	0.39%	$733,432	0.41%	$2,393,728

6	14	174	$113,300	$463,325	0.32%	$553,325	0.36%	$643,325	0.39%	$733,325	0.41%	$2,393,300
6	15	175	$112,772	$463,193	0.32%	$553,193	0.36%	$643,193	0.39%	$733,193	0.41%	$2,392,772
6	16	176	$112,284	$463,071	0.32%	$553,071	0.36%	$643,071	0.39%	$733,071	0.41%	$2,392,284
6	17	177	$111,608	$462,902	0.32%	$552,902	0.36%	$642,902	0.38%	$732,902	0.41%	$2,391,608
6	18	178	$111,448	$462,862	0.32%	$552,862	0.36%	$642,862	0.38%	$732,862	0.41%	$2,391,448
6	19	179	$111,228	$462,807	0.32%	$552,807	0.36%	$642,807	0.38%	$732,807	0.41%	$2,391,228
6	20	180	$111,144	$462,786	0.32%	$552,786	0.36%	$642,786	0.38%	$732,786	0.41%	$2,391,144
6	21	181	$110,464	$462,616	0.32%	$552,616	0.36%	$642,616	0.38%	$732,616	0.41%	$2,390,464
6	22	182	$109,444	$462,361	0.32%	$552,361	0.36%	$642,361	0.38%	$732,361	0.41%	$2,389,444
6	23	183	$108,880	$462,220	0.32%	$552,220	0.36%	$642,220	0.38%	$732,220	0.41%	$2,388,880
6	24	184	$107,408	$461,852	0.32%	$551,852	0.36%	$641,852	0.38%	$731,852	0.41%	$2,387,408
6	25	185	$105,908	$461,477	0.32%	$551,477	0.36%	$641,477	0.38%	$731,477	0.41%	$2,385,908
6	26	186	$104,340	$461,085	0.32%	$551,085	0.35%	$641,085	0.38%	$731,085	0.41%	$2,384,340
6	27	187	$103,876	$460,969	0.32%	$550,969	0.35%	$640,969	0.38%	$730,969	0.41%	$2,383,876
6	28	188	$103,448	$460,862	0.32%	$550,862	0.35%	$640,862	0.38%	$730,862	0.41%	$2,383,448
6	29	189	$100,720	$460,180	0.32%	$550,180	0.35%	$640,180	0.38%	$730,180	0.41%	$2,380,720
6	30	190	$99,068	$459,767	0.32%	$549,767	0.35%	$639,767	0.38%	$729,767	0.41%	$2,379,068
6	31	191	$97,452	$459,363	0.32%	$549,363	0.35%	$639,363	0.38%	$729,363	0.41%	$2,377,452
6	32	192	$94,488	$458,622	0.32%	$548,622	0.35%	$638,622	0.38%	$728,622	0.41%	$2,374,488
7	1	193	$74,024	$453,506	0.32%	$543,506	0.35%	$633,506	0.38%	$723,506	0.40%	$2,354,024
7	2	194	$73,784	$453,446	0.32%	$543,446	0.35%	$633,446	0.38%	$723,446	0.40%	$2,353,784
7	3	195	$72,284	$453,071	0.32%	$543,071	0.35%	$633,071	0.38%	$723,071	0.40%	$2,352,284
7	4	196	$71,712	$452,928	0.32%	$542,928	0.35%	$632,928	0.38%	$722,928	0.40%	$2,351,712
7	5	197	$69,768	$452,442	0.32%	$542,442	0.35%	$632,442	0.38%	$722,442	0.40%	$2,349,768
7	6	198	$68,248	$452,062	0.32%	$542,062	0.35%	$632,062	0.38%	$722,062	0.40%	$2,348,248
7	7	199	$67,176	$451,794	0.31%	$541,794	0.35%	$631,794	0.38%	$721,794	0.40%	$2,347,176
7	8	200	$66,876	$451,719	0.31%	$541,719	0.35%	$631,719	0.38%	$721,719	0.40%	$2,346,876
7	9	201	$66,660	$451,665	0.31%	$541,665	0.35%	$631,665	0.38%	$721,665	0.40%	$2,346,660
7	10	202	$66,204	$451,551	0.31%	$541,551	0.35%	$631,551	0.38%	$721,551	0.40%	$2,346,204
7	11	203	$64,896	$451,224	0.31%	$541,224	0.35%	$631,224	0.38%	$721,224	0.40%	$2,344,896
7	12	204	$64,528	$451,132	0.31%	$541,132	0.35%	$631,132	0.38%	$721,132	0.40%	$2,344,528
7	13	205	$64,520	$451,130	0.31%	$541,130	0.35%	$631,130	0.38%	$721,130	0.40%	$2,344,520
7	14	206	$63,636	$450,909	0.31%	$540,909	0.35%	$630,909	0.38%	$720,909	0.40%	$2,343,636
7	15	207	$63,612	$450,903	0.31%	$540,903	0.35%	$630,903	0.38%	$720,903	0.40%	$2,343,612
7	16	208	$63,368	$450,842	0.31%	$540,842	0.35%	$630,842	0.38%	$720,842	0.40%	$2,343,368

7	17	209	$61,948	$450,487	0.31%	$540,487	0.35%	$630,487	0.38%	$720,487	0.40%	$2,341,948
7	18	210	$60,876	$450,219	0.31%	$540,219	0.35%	$630,219	0.38%	$720,219	0.40%	$2,340,876
7	19	211	$59,920	$449,980	0.31%	$539,980	0.35%	$629,980	0.38%	$719,980	0.40%	$2,339,920
7	20	212	$57,412	$449,353	0.31%	$539,353	0.35%	$629,353	0.38%	$719,353	0.40%	$2,337,412
7	21	213	$55,036	$448,759	0.31%	$538,759	0.35%	$628,759	0.38%	$718,759	0.40%	$2,335,036
7	22	214	$54,488	$448,622	0.31%	$538,622	0.35%	$628,622	0.38%	$718,622	0.40%	$2,334,488
7	23	215	$53,920	$448,480	0.31%	$538,480	0.35%	$628,480	0.38%	$718,480	0.40%	$2,333,920
7	24	216	$53,356	$448,339	0.31%	$538,339	0.35%	$628,339	0.38%	$718,339	0.40%	$2,333,356
7	25	217	$52,936	$448,234	0.31%	$538,234	0.35%	$628,234	0.38%	$718,234	0.40%	$2,332,936
7	26	218	$52,472	$448,118	0.31%	$538,118	0.35%	$628,118	0.38%	$718,118	0.40%	$2,332,472
7	27	219	$52,044	$448,011	0.31%	$538,011	0.35%	$628,011	0.38%	$718,011	0.40%	$2,332,044
7	28	220	$51,616	$447,904	0.31%	$537,904	0.35%	$627,904	0.38%	$717,904	0.40%	$2,331,616
7	29	221	$50,964	$447,741	0.31%	$537,741	0.35%	$627,741	0.38%	$717,741	0.40%	$2,330,964
7	30	222	$50,492	$447,623	0.31%	$537,623	0.35%	$627,623	0.38%	$717,623	0.40%	$2,330,492
7	31	223	$49,808	$447,452	0.31%	$537,452	0.35%	$627,452	0.38%	$717,452	0.40%	$2,329,808
7	32	224	$49,148	$447,287	0.31%	$537,287	0.35%	$627,287	0.38%	$717,287	0.40%	$2,329,148

Table B – Table does not include signing bonuses, but each year's figure in this chart is a cap hit that would include signing bonus

Pick	Expected APY	2016	%	2017	%	2018	%	2019	%	Average	Total
1	$8,168,242	$6,126,182	3.95%	$7,351,418	4.40%	$8,168,242	4.55%	$11,027,127	5.71%	8,168,242	$32,672,968
2	$7,097,059	$5,322,794	3.43%	$6,387,353	3.82%	$7,097,059	3.95%	$9,581,030	4.96%	7,097,059	$28,388,236
3	$6,315,369	$4,736,527	3.05%	$5,683,832	3.40%	$6,315,369	3.52%	$8,525,748	4.42%	6,315,369	$25,261,476
4	$5,980,861	$4,485,646	2.89%	$5,382,775	3.22%	$5,980,861	3.33%	$8,074,162	4.18%	5,980,861	$23,923,444
5	$5,745,837	$4,309,378	2.78%	$5,171,253	3.10%	$5,745,837	3.20%	$7,756,880	4.02%	5,745,837	$22,983,348
6	$5,715,291	$4,286,468	2.76%	$5,143,762	3.08%	$5,715,291	3.18%	$7,715,643	4.00%	5,715,291	$22,861,164
7	$5,616,433	$4,212,325	2.71%	$5,054,790	3.03%	$5,616,433	3.13%	$7,582,185	3.93%	5,616,433	$22,465,732
8	$6,005,441	$4,504,081	2.90%	$5,404,897	3.24%	$6,005,441	3.35%	$8,107,345	4.20%	6,005,441	$24,021,764
9	$6,293,448	$4,720,086	3.04%	$5,664,103	3.39%	$6,293,448	3.51%	$8,496,155	4.40%	6,293,448	$25,173,792
10	$6,022,544	$4,516,908	2.91%	$5,420,290	3.25%	$6,022,544	3.36%	$8,130,434	4.21%	6,022,544	$24,090,176
11	$6,238,351	$4,678,763	3.01%	$5,614,516	3.36%	$6,238,351	3.48%	$8,421,774	4.36%	6,238,351	$24,953,404
12	$5,499,746	$4,124,810	2.66%	$4,949,771	2.96%	$5,499,746	3.06%	$7,424,657	3.85%	5,499,746	$21,998,984
13	$5,166,515	$3,874,886	2.50%	$4,649,864	2.78%	$5,166,515	2.88%	$6,974,795	3.61%	5,166,515	$20,666,060
14	$5,121,208	$3,840,906	2.47%	$4,609,087	2.76%	$5,121,208	2.85%	$6,913,631	3.58%	5,121,208	$20,484,832
15	$4,877,696	$3,658,272	2.36%	$4,389,926	2.63%	$4,877,696	2.72%	$6,584,890	3.41%	4,877,696	$19,510,784
16	$5,099,060	$3,824,295	2.46%	$4,589,154	2.75%	$5,099,060	2.84%	$6,883,731	3.57%	5,099,060	$20,396,240
17	$4,949,195	$3,711,896	2.39%	$4,454,276	2.67%	$4,949,195	2.76%	$6,681,413	3.46%	4,949,195	$19,796,780
18	$4,889,231	$3,666,923	2.36%	$4,400,308	2.63%	$4,889,231	2.72%	$6,600,462	3.42%	4,889,231	$19,556,924
19	$4,633,993	$3,475,495	2.24%	$4,170,594	2.50%	$4,633,993	2.58%	$6,255,891	3.24%	4,633,993	$18,535,972
20	$4,586,957	$3,440,218	2.22%	$4,128,261	2.47%	$4,586,957	2.56%	$6,192,392	3.21%	4,586,957	$18,347,828
21	$4,899,025	$3,674,269	2.37%	$4,409,123	2.64%	$4,899,025	2.73%	$6,613,684	3.43%	4,899,025	$19,596,100
22	$4,850,312	$3,637,734	2.34%	$4,365,281	2.61%	$4,850,312	2.70%	$6,547,921	3.39%	4,850,312	$19,401,248
23	$4,920,602	$3,690,452	2.38%	$4,428,542	2.65%	$4,920,602	2.74%	$6,642,813	3.44%	4,920,602	$19,682,408
24	$4,695,365	$3,521,524	2.27%	$4,225,829	2.53%	$4,695,365	2.62%	$6,338,743	3.28%	4,695,365	$18,781,460
25	$4,214,545	$3,160,909	2.04%	$3,793,091	2.27%	$4,214,545	2.35%	$5,689,636	2.95%	4,214,545	$16,858,180
26	$4,127,889	$3,095,917	1.99%	$3,715,100	2.22%	$4,127,889	2.30%	$5,572,650	2.89%	4,127,889	$16,511,556
27	$4,342,177	$3,256,633	2.10%	$3,907,959	2.34%	$4,342,177	2.42%	$5,861,939	3.04%	4,342,177	$17,368,708
28	$4,049,240	$3,036,930	1.96%	$3,644,316	2.18%	$4,049,240	2.26%	$5,466,474	2.83%	4,049,240	$16,196,960
29	$3,968,565	$2,976,424	1.92%	$3,571,709	2.14%	$3,968,565	2.21%	$5,357,563	2.78%	3,968,565	$15,874,260
30	$4,020,285	$3,015,214	1.94%	$3,618,257	2.17%	$4,020,285	2.24%	$5,427,385	2.81%	4,020,285	$16,081,140
31	$3,798,392	$2,848,794	1.83%	$3,418,553	2.05%	$3,798,392	2.12%	$5,127,829	2.66%	3,798,392	$15,193,568
32	$4,067,762	$3,050,822	1.96%	$3,660,986	2.19%	$4,067,762	2.27%	$5,491,479	2.85%	4,067,762	$16,271,048
33	$4,295,423	$3,221,567	2.07%	$3,865,881	2.31%	$4,295,423	2.39%	$5,798,821	3.00%	4,295,423	$17,181,692

34	$4,142,409	$3,106,807	2.00%	$3,728,168	2.23%	$4,142,409	2.31%	$5,592,252	2.90%	4,142,409	$16,569,636
35	$4,204,768	$3,153,576	2.03%	$3,784,291	2.27%	$4,204,768	2.34%	$5,676,437	2.94%	4,204,768	$16,819,072
36	$4,010,896	$3,008,172	1.94%	$3,609,806	2.16%	$4,010,896	2.23%	$5,414,710	2.81%	4,010,896	$16,043,584
37	$3,669,666	$2,752,250	1.77%	$3,302,699	1.98%	$3,669,666	2.04%	$4,954,049	2.57%	3,669,666	$14,678,664
38	$3,812,558	$2,859,419	1.84%	$3,431,302	2.05%	$3,812,558	2.12%	$5,146,953	2.67%	3,812,558	$15,250,232
39	$3,808,240	$2,856,180	1.84%	$3,427,416	2.05%	$3,808,240	2.12%	$5,141,124	2.66%	3,808,240	$15,232,960
40	$3,830,630	$2,872,973	1.85%	$3,447,567	2.06%	$3,830,630	2.13%	$5,171,351	2.68%	3,830,630	$15,322,520
41	$4,022,420	$3,016,815	1.94%	$3,620,178	2.17%	$4,022,420	2.24%	$5,430,267	2.81%	4,022,420	$16,089,680
42	$4,291,729	$3,218,797	2.07%	$3,862,556	2.31%	$4,291,729	2.39%	$5,793,834	3.00%	4,291,729	$17,166,916
43	$4,233,623	$3,175,217	2.04%	$3,810,261	2.28%	$4,233,623	2.36%	$5,715,391	2.96%	4,233,623	$16,934,492
44	$4,163,582	$3,122,687	2.01%	$3,747,224	2.24%	$4,163,582	2.32%	$5,620,836	2.91%	4,163,582	$16,654,328
45	$3,899,507	$2,924,630	1.88%	$3,509,556	2.10%	$3,899,507	2.17%	$5,264,334	2.73%	3,899,507	$15,598,028
46	$3,741,420	$2,806,065	1.81%	$3,367,278	2.02%	$3,741,420	2.08%	$5,050,917	2.62%	3,741,420	$14,965,680
47	$3,513,831	$2,635,373	1.70%	$3,162,448	1.89%	$3,513,831	1.96%	$4,743,672	2.46%	3,513,831	$14,055,324
48	$3,330,347	$2,497,760	1.61%	$2,997,312	1.79%	$3,330,347	1.86%	$4,495,968	2.33%	3,330,347	$13,321,388
49	$3,344,804	$2,508,603	1.62%	$3,010,324	1.80%	$3,344,804	1.86%	$4,515,485	2.34%	3,344,804	$13,379,216
50	$3,257,694	$2,443,271	1.57%	$2,931,925	1.76%	$3,257,694	1.81%	$4,397,887	2.28%	3,257,694	$13,030,776
51	$3,221,451	$2,416,088	1.56%	$2,899,306	1.74%	$3,221,451	1.79%	$4,348,959	2.25%	3,221,451	$12,885,804
52	$3,091,248	$2,318,436	1.49%	$2,782,123	1.67%	$3,091,248	1.72%	$4,173,185	2.16%	3,091,248	$12,364,992
53	$3,161,756	$2,371,317	1.53%	$2,845,580	1.70%	$3,161,756	1.76%	$4,268,371	2.21%	3,161,756	$12,647,024
54	$3,385,023	$2,538,767	1.64%	$3,046,521	1.82%	$3,385,023	1.89%	$4,569,781	2.37%	3,385,023	$13,540,092
55	$3,456,609	$2,592,457	1.67%	$3,110,948	1.86%	$3,456,609	1.93%	$4,666,422	2.42%	3,456,609	$13,826,436
56	$3,723,184	$2,792,388	1.80%	$3,350,866	2.01%	$3,723,184	2.07%	$5,026,298	2.60%	3,723,184	$14,892,736
57	$3,900,967	$2,925,725	1.88%	$3,510,870	2.10%	$3,900,967	2.17%	$5,266,305	2.73%	3,900,967	$15,603,868
58	$3,772,099	$2,829,074	1.82%	$3,394,889	2.03%	$3,772,099	2.10%	$5,092,334	2.64%	3,772,099	$15,088,396
59	$3,547,140	$2,660,355	1.71%	$3,192,426	1.91%	$3,547,140	1.98%	$4,788,639	2.48%	3,547,140	$14,188,560
60	$3,537,739	$2,653,304	1.71%	$3,183,965	1.91%	$3,537,739	1.97%	$4,775,948	2.47%	3,537,739	$14,150,956
61	$3,180,786	$2,385,590	1.54%	$2,862,707	1.71%	$3,180,786	1.77%	$4,294,061	2.22%	3,180,786	$12,723,144
62	$3,092,733	$2,319,550	1.49%	$2,783,460	1.67%	$3,092,733	1.72%	$4,175,190	2.16%	3,092,733	$12,370,932
63	$2,991,339	$2,243,504	1.44%	$2,692,205	1.61%	$2,991,339	1.67%	$4,038,308	2.09%	2,991,339	$11,965,356
64	$2,812,419	$2,109,314	1.36%	$2,531,177	1.52%	$2,812,419	1.57%	$3,796,766	1.97%	2,812,419	$11,249,676
65	$2,568,772	$1,926,579	1.24%	$2,311,895	1.38%	$2,568,772	1.43%	$3,467,842	1.80%	2,568,772	$10,275,088
66	$2,547,477	$1,910,608	1.23%	$2,292,729	1.37%	$2,547,477	1.42%	$3,439,094	1.78%	2,547,477	$10,189,908
67	$2,623,783	$1,967,837	1.27%	$2,361,405	1.41%	$2,623,783	1.46%	$3,542,107	1.84%	2,623,783	$10,495,132
68	$2,573,085	$1,929,814	1.24%	$2,315,777	1.39%	$2,573,085	1.43%	$3,473,665	1.80%	2,573,085	$10,292,340

69	$2,870,710	$2,153,033	1.39%	$2,583,639	1.55%	$2,870,710	1.60%	$3,875,459	2.01%	2,870,710	$11,482,840
70	$2,959,442	$2,219,582	1.43%	$2,663,498	1.59%	$2,959,442	1.65%	$3,995,247	2.07%	2,959,442	$11,837,768
71	$2,940,988	$2,205,741	1.42%	$2,646,889	1.58%	$2,940,988	1.64%	$3,970,334	2.06%	2,940,988	$11,763,952
72	$2,697,276	$2,022,957	1.30%	$2,427,548	1.45%	$2,697,276	1.50%	$3,641,323	1.89%	2,697,276	$10,789,104
73	$2,653,182	$1,989,887	1.28%	$2,387,864	1.43%	$2,653,182	1.48%	$3,581,796	1.86%	2,653,182	$10,612,728
74	$2,492,072	$1,869,054	1.20%	$2,242,865	1.34%	$2,492,072	1.39%	$3,364,297	1.74%	2,492,072	$9,968,288
75	$2,585,852	$1,939,389	1.25%	$2,327,267	1.39%	$2,585,852	1.44%	$3,490,900	1.81%	2,585,852	$10,343,408
76	$2,675,902	$2,006,927	1.29%	$2,408,312	1.44%	$2,675,902	1.49%	$3,612,468	1.87%	2,675,902	$10,703,608
77	$2,717,678	$2,038,259	1.31%	$2,445,910	1.46%	$2,717,678	1.51%	$3,668,865	1.90%	2,717,678	$10,870,712
78	$2,629,826	$1,972,370	1.27%	$2,366,843	1.42%	$2,629,826	1.47%	$3,550,265	1.84%	2,629,826	$10,519,304
79	$2,480,339	$1,860,254	1.20%	$2,232,305	1.34%	$2,480,339	1.38%	$3,348,458	1.73%	2,480,339	$9,921,356
80	$2,514,174	$1,885,631	1.21%	$2,262,757	1.35%	$2,514,174	1.40%	$3,394,135	1.76%	2,514,174	$10,056,696
81	$2,273,315	$1,704,986	1.10%	$2,045,984	1.23%	$2,273,315	1.27%	$3,068,975	1.59%	2,273,315	$9,093,260
82	$2,224,912	$1,668,684	1.07%	$2,002,421	1.20%	$2,224,912	1.24%	$3,003,631	1.56%	2,224,912	$8,899,648
83	$2,302,388	$1,726,791	1.11%	$2,072,149	1.24%	$2,302,388	1.28%	$3,108,224	1.61%	2,302,388	$9,209,552
84	$2,359,799	$1,769,849	1.14%	$2,123,819	1.27%	$2,359,799	1.31%	$3,185,729	1.65%	2,359,799	$9,439,196
85	$2,266,664	$1,699,998	1.09%	$2,039,998	1.22%	$2,266,664	1.26%	$3,059,996	1.59%	2,266,664	$9,066,656
86	$2,249,207	$1,686,905	1.09%	$2,024,286	1.21%	$2,249,207	1.25%	$3,036,429	1.57%	2,249,207	$8,996,828
87	$2,429,686	$1,822,265	1.17%	$2,186,717	1.31%	$2,429,686	1.35%	$3,280,076	1.70%	2,429,686	$9,718,744
88	$2,640,236	$1,980,177	1.28%	$2,376,212	1.42%	$2,640,236	1.47%	$3,564,319	1.85%	2,640,236	$10,560,944
89	$2,423,295	$1,817,471	1.17%	$2,180,966	1.31%	$2,423,295	1.35%	$3,271,448	1.70%	2,423,295	$9,693,180
90	$2,428,621	$1,821,466	1.17%	$2,185,759	1.31%	$2,428,621	1.35%	$3,278,638	1.70%	2,428,621	$9,714,484
91	$2,476,083	$1,857,062	1.20%	$2,228,475	1.33%	$2,476,083	1.38%	$3,342,712	1.73%	2,476,083	$9,904,332
92	$2,288,445	$1,716,334	1.11%	$2,059,601	1.23%	$2,288,445	1.27%	$3,089,401	1.60%	2,288,445	$9,153,780
93	$2,079,546	$1,559,660	1.00%	$1,871,591	1.12%	$2,079,546	1.16%	$2,807,387	1.45%	2,079,546	$8,318,184
94	$2,325,320	$1,743,990	1.12%	$2,092,788	1.25%	$2,325,320	1.30%	$3,139,182	1.63%	2,325,320	$9,301,280
95	$2,262,690	$1,697,018	1.09%	$2,036,421	1.22%	$2,262,690	1.26%	$3,054,632	1.58%	2,262,690	$9,050,760
96	$2,411,350	$1,808,513	1.16%	$2,170,215	1.30%	$2,411,350	1.34%	$3,255,323	1.69%	2,411,350	$9,645,400
97	$2,397,865	$1,798,399	1.16%	$2,158,079	1.29%	$2,397,865	1.34%	$3,237,118	1.68%	2,397,865	$9,591,460
98	$2,270,812	$1,703,109	1.10%	$2,043,731	1.22%	$2,270,812	1.27%	$3,065,596	1.59%	2,270,812	$9,083,248
99	$2,261,366	$1,696,025	1.09%	$2,035,229	1.22%	$2,261,366	1.26%	$3,052,844	1.58%	2,261,366	$9,045,464
100	$2,168,813	$1,626,610	1.05%	$1,951,932	1.17%	$2,168,813	1.21%	$2,927,898	1.52%	2,168,813	$8,675,252
101	$2,136,077	$1,602,058	1.03%	$1,922,469	1.15%	$2,136,077	1.19%	$2,883,704	1.49%	2,136,077	$8,544,308
102	$2,228,271	$1,671,203	1.08%	$2,005,444	1.20%	$2,228,271	1.24%	$3,008,166	1.56%	2,228,271	$8,913,084
103	$2,169,078	$1,626,809	1.05%	$1,952,170	1.17%	$2,169,078	1.21%	$2,928,255	1.52%	2,169,078	$8,676,312

104	$2,225,104	1.07%	$1,668,828	$2,225,104	1.20%	$2,002,594	1.24%	$3,003,890	1.56%	2,225,104	$8,900,416
105	$2,294,253	1.11%	$1,720,690	$2,294,253	1.24%	$2,064,828	1.28%	$3,097,242	1.60%	2,294,253	$9,177,012
106	$2,338,650	1.13%	$1,753,988	$2,338,650	1.26%	$2,104,785	1.30%	$3,157,178	1.64%	2,338,650	$9,354,600
107	$2,278,910	1.10%	$1,709,183	$2,278,910	1.23%	$2,051,019	1.27%	$3,076,529	1.59%	2,278,910	$9,115,640
108	$2,343,527	1.13%	$1,757,645	$2,343,527	1.26%	$2,109,174	1.31%	$3,163,761	1.64%	2,343,527	$9,374,108
109	$2,224,926	1.07%	$1,668,695	$2,224,926	1.20%	$2,002,433	1.24%	$3,003,650	1.56%	2,224,926	$8,899,704
110	$2,091,563	1.01%	$1,568,672	$2,091,563	1.13%	$1,882,407	1.17%	$2,823,610	1.46%	2,091,563	$8,366,252
111	$2,094,223	1.01%	$1,570,667	$2,094,223	1.13%	$1,884,801	1.17%	$2,827,201	1.46%	2,094,223	$8,376,892
112	$2,186,464	1.06%	$1,639,848	$2,186,464	1.18%	$1,967,818	1.22%	$2,951,726	1.53%	2,186,464	$8,745,856
113	$2,127,729	1.03%	$1,595,797	$2,127,729	1.15%	$1,914,956	1.19%	$2,872,434	1.49%	2,127,729	$8,510,916
114	$2,004,697	0.97%	$1,503,523	$2,004,697	1.08%	$1,804,227	1.12%	$2,706,341	1.40%	2,004,697	$8,018,788
115	$1,966,068	0.95%	$1,474,551	$1,966,068	1.06%	$1,769,461	1.10%	$2,654,192	1.38%	1,966,068	$7,864,272
116	$1,929,823	0.93%	$1,447,367	$1,929,823	1.04%	$1,736,841	1.08%	$2,605,261	1.35%	1,929,823	$7,719,292
117	$2,015,364	0.97%	$1,511,523	$2,015,364	1.09%	$1,813,828	1.12%	$2,720,741	1.41%	2,015,364	$8,061,456
118	$2,019,087	0.98%	$1,514,315	$2,019,087	1.09%	$1,817,178	1.12%	$2,725,767	1.41%	2,019,087	$8,076,348
119	$2,212,266	1.07%	$1,659,200	$2,212,266	1.19%	$1,991,039	1.23%	$2,986,559	1.55%	2,212,266	$8,849,064
120	$2,122,455	1.03%	$1,591,841	$2,122,455	1.14%	$1,910,210	1.18%	$2,865,314	1.48%	2,122,455	$8,489,820
121	$2,137,342	1.03%	$1,603,007	$2,137,342	1.15%	$1,923,608	1.19%	$2,885,412	1.50%	2,137,342	$8,549,368
122	$2,147,884	1.04%	$1,610,913	$2,147,884	1.16%	$1,933,096	1.20%	$2,899,643	1.50%	2,147,884	$8,591,536
123	$2,114,037	1.02%	$1,585,528	$2,114,037	1.14%	$1,902,633	1.18%	$2,853,950	1.48%	2,114,037	$8,456,148
124	$2,103,351	1.02%	$1,577,513	$2,103,351	1.13%	$1,893,016	1.17%	$2,839,524	1.47%	2,103,351	$8,413,404
125	$2,053,508	0.99%	$1,540,131	$2,053,508	1.11%	$1,848,157	1.14%	$2,772,236	1.44%	2,053,508	$8,214,032
126	$2,051,574	0.99%	$1,538,681	$2,051,574	1.11%	$1,846,417	1.14%	$2,769,625	1.44%	2,051,574	$8,206,296
127	$1,788,061	0.86%	$1,341,046	$1,788,061	0.96%	$1,609,255	1.00%	$2,413,882	1.25%	1,788,061	$7,152,244
128	$1,698,447	0.82%	$1,273,835	$1,698,447	0.92%	$1,528,602	0.95%	$2,292,903	1.19%	1,698,447	$6,793,788
129	$1,663,364	0.80%	$1,247,523	$1,663,364	0.90%	$1,497,028	0.93%	$2,245,541	1.16%	1,663,364	$6,653,456
130	$1,719,872	0.83%	$1,289,904	$1,719,872	0.93%	$1,547,885	0.96%	$2,321,827	1.20%	1,719,872	$6,879,488
131	$1,764,622	0.85%	$1,323,467	$1,764,622	0.95%	$1,588,160	0.98%	$2,382,240	1.23%	1,764,622	$7,058,488
132	$1,821,641	0.88%	$1,366,231	$1,821,641	0.98%	$1,639,477	1.01%	$2,459,215	1.27%	1,821,641	$7,286,564
133	$1,867,061	0.90%	$1,400,296	$1,867,061	1.01%	$1,680,355	1.04%	$2,520,532	1.31%	1,867,061	$7,468,244
134	$1,823,654	0.88%	$1,367,741	$1,823,654	0.98%	$1,641,289	1.02%	$2,461,933	1.28%	1,823,654	$7,294,616
135	$1,866,084	0.90%	$1,399,563	$1,866,084	1.01%	$1,679,476	1.04%	$2,519,213	1.31%	1,866,084	$7,464,336
136	$1,923,230	0.93%	$1,442,423	$1,923,230	1.04%	$1,730,907	1.07%	$2,596,361	1.35%	1,923,230	$7,692,920
137	$1,849,959	0.89%	$1,387,469	$1,849,959	1.00%	$1,664,963	1.03%	$2,497,445	1.29%	1,849,959	$7,399,836
138	$1,821,452	0.88%	$1,366,089	$1,821,452	0.98%	$1,639,307	1.01%	$2,458,960	1.27%	1,821,452	$7,285,808

139	$1,334,410	0.86%	$1,601,292	0.96%	$1,779,213	0.99%	$2,401,938	1.24%	1,779,213	$7,116,852
140	$1,260,992	0.81%	$1,513,191	0.91%	$1,681,323	0.94%	$2,269,786	1.18%	1,681,323	$6,725,292
141	$1,175,561	0.76%	$1,410,673	0.84%	$1,567,414	0.87%	$2,116,009	1.10%	1,567,414	$6,269,656
142	$1,264,236	0.81%	$1,517,083	0.91%	$1,685,648	0.94%	$2,275,625	1.18%	1,685,648	$6,742,592
143	$1,266,814	0.82%	$1,520,177	0.91%	$1,689,085	0.94%	$2,280,265	1.18%	1,689,085	$6,756,340
144	$1,262,842	0.81%	$1,515,410	0.91%	$1,683,789	0.94%	$2,273,115	1.18%	1,683,789	$6,735,156
145	$1,284,611	0.83%	$1,541,534	0.92%	$1,712,815	0.95%	$2,312,300	1.20%	1,712,815	$6,851,260
146	$1,307,213	0.84%	$1,568,655	0.94%	$1,742,950	0.97%	$2,352,983	1.22%	1,742,950	$6,971,800
147	$1,332,182	0.86%	$1,598,618	0.96%	$1,776,242	0.99%	$2,397,927	1.24%	1,776,242	$7,104,968
148	$1,334,380	0.86%	$1,601,256	0.96%	$1,779,173	0.99%	$2,401,884	1.24%	1,779,173	$7,116,692
149	$1,339,488	0.86%	$1,607,386	0.96%	$1,785,984	0.99%	$2,411,078	1.25%	1,785,984	$7,143,936
150	$1,238,247	0.80%	$1,485,896	0.89%	$1,650,996	0.92%	$2,228,845	1.15%	1,650,996	$6,603,984
151	$1,198,835	0.77%	$1,438,602	0.86%	$1,598,447	0.89%	$2,157,903	1.12%	1,598,447	$6,393,788
152	$1,165,226	0.75%	$1,398,271	0.84%	$1,553,634	0.87%	$2,097,406	1.09%	1,553,634	$6,214,536
153	$1,120,349	0.72%	$1,344,419	0.81%	$1,493,799	0.83%	$2,016,629	1.04%	1,493,799	$5,975,196
154	$1,033,247	0.67%	$1,239,896	0.74%	$1,377,662	0.77%	$1,859,844	0.96%	1,377,662	$5,510,648
155	$976,618	0.63%	$1,171,941	0.70%	$1,302,157	0.73%	$1,757,912	0.91%	1,302,157	$5,208,628
156	$979,431	0.63%	$1,175,317	0.70%	$1,305,908	0.73%	$1,762,976	0.91%	1,305,908	$5,223,632
157	$989,514	0.64%	$1,187,417	0.71%	$1,319,352	0.74%	$1,781,125	0.92%	1,319,352	$5,277,408
158	$1,013,366	0.65%	$1,216,039	0.73%	$1,351,154	0.75%	$1,824,058	0.95%	1,351,154	$5,404,616
159	$1,044,019	0.67%	$1,252,823	0.75%	$1,392,025	0.78%	$1,879,234	0.97%	1,392,025	$5,568,100
160	$1,072,054	0.69%	$1,286,465	0.77%	$1,429,405	0.80%	$1,929,697	1.00%	1,429,405	$5,717,620
161	$1,102,289	0.71%	$1,322,747	0.79%	$1,469,719	0.82%	$1,984,121	1.03%	1,469,719	$5,878,876
162	$1,154,259	0.74%	$1,385,111	0.83%	$1,539,012	0.86%	$2,077,666	1.08%	1,539,012	$6,156,048
163	$1,121,254	0.72%	$1,345,505	0.81%	$1,495,005	0.83%	$2,018,257	1.05%	1,495,005	$5,980,020
164	$1,096,712	0.71%	$1,316,054	0.79%	$1,462,282	0.81%	$1,974,081	1.02%	1,462,282	$5,849,128
165	$1,079,322	0.70%	$1,295,186	0.78%	$1,439,096	0.80%	$1,942,780	1.01%	1,439,096	$5,756,384
166	$1,111,694	0.72%	$1,334,032	0.80%	$1,482,258	0.83%	$2,001,048	1.04%	1,482,258	$5,929,032
167	$1,096,106	0.71%	$1,315,327	0.79%	$1,461,474	0.81%	$1,972,990	1.02%	1,461,474	$5,845,896
168	$1,059,781	0.68%	$1,271,737	0.76%	$1,413,041	0.79%	$1,907,605	0.99%	1,413,041	$5,652,164
169	$1,030,797	0.66%	$1,236,956	0.74%	$1,374,396	0.77%	$1,855,435	0.96%	1,374,396	$5,497,584
170	$999,428	0.64%	$1,199,313	0.72%	$1,332,570	0.74%	$1,798,970	0.93%	1,332,570	$5,330,280
171	$1,019,633	0.66%	$1,223,559	0.73%	$1,359,510	0.76%	$1,835,339	0.95%	1,359,510	$5,438,040
172	$1,048,577	0.68%	$1,258,293	0.75%	$1,398,103	0.78%	$1,887,439	0.98%	1,398,103	$5,592,412
173	$1,073,379	0.69%	$1,288,055	0.77%	$1,431,172	0.80%	$1,932,082	1.00%	1,431,172	$5,724,688

174	$1,384,241	$1,038,181	0.67%	$1,245,817	0.75%	$1,384,241	0.77%	$1,868,725	0.97%	1,384,241	$5,536,964
175	$1,376,707	$1,032,530	0.66%	$1,239,036	0.74%	$1,376,707	0.77%	$1,858,554	0.96%	1,376,707	$5,506,828
176	$1,380,723	$1,035,542	0.67%	$1,242,651	0.74%	$1,380,723	0.77%	$1,863,976	0.97%	1,380,723	$5,522,892
177	$1,381,101	$1,035,826	0.67%	$1,242,991	0.74%	$1,381,101	0.77%	$1,864,486	0.97%	1,381,101	$5,524,404
178	$1,342,912	$1,007,184	0.65%	$1,208,621	0.72%	$1,342,912	0.75%	$1,812,931	0.94%	1,342,912	$5,371,648
179	$1,315,972	$986,979	0.64%	$1,184,375	0.71%	$1,315,972	0.73%	$1,776,562	0.92%	1,315,972	$5,263,888
180	$1,336,489	$1,002,367	0.65%	$1,202,840	0.72%	$1,336,489	0.74%	$1,804,260	0.93%	1,336,489	$5,345,956
181	$1,351,787	$1,013,840	0.65%	$1,216,608	0.73%	$1,351,787	0.75%	$1,824,912	0.95%	1,351,787	$5,407,148
182	$1,327,925	$995,944	0.64%	$1,195,133	0.72%	$1,327,925	0.74%	$1,792,699	0.93%	1,327,925	$5,311,700
183	$1,315,373	$986,530	0.64%	$1,183,836	0.71%	$1,315,373	0.73%	$1,775,754	0.92%	1,315,373	$5,261,492
184	$1,378,630	$1,033,973	0.67%	$1,240,767	0.74%	$1,378,630	0.77%	$1,861,151	0.96%	1,378,630	$5,514,520
185	$1,361,265	$1,020,949	0.66%	$1,225,139	0.73%	$1,361,265	0.76%	$1,837,708	0.95%	1,361,265	$5,445,060
186	$1,457,990	$1,093,493	0.70%	$1,312,191	0.79%	$1,457,990	0.81%	$1,968,287	1.02%	1,457,990	$5,831,960
187	$1,526,715	$1,145,036	0.74%	$1,374,044	0.82%	$1,526,715	0.85%	$2,061,065	1.07%	1,526,715	$6,106,860
188	$1,485,311	$1,113,983	0.72%	$1,336,780	0.80%	$1,485,311	0.83%	$2,005,170	1.04%	1,485,311	$5,941,244
189	$1,426,221	$1,069,666	0.69%	$1,283,599	0.77%	$1,426,221	0.79%	$1,925,398	1.00%	1,426,221	$5,704,884
190	$1,415,894	$1,061,921	0.68%	$1,274,305	0.76%	$1,415,894	0.79%	$1,911,457	0.99%	1,415,894	$5,663,576
191	$1,422,576	$1,066,932	0.69%	$1,280,318	0.77%	$1,422,576	0.79%	$1,920,478	1.00%	1,422,576	$5,690,304
192	$1,338,854	$1,004,141	0.65%	$1,204,969	0.72%	$1,338,854	0.75%	$1,807,453	0.94%	1,338,854	$5,355,416
193	$1,425,400	$1,069,050	0.69%	$1,282,860	0.77%	$1,425,400	0.79%	$1,924,290	1.00%	1,425,400	$5,701,600
194	$1,328,675	$996,506	0.64%	$1,195,808	0.72%	$1,328,675	0.74%	$1,793,711	0.93%	1,328,675	$5,314,700
195	$1,291,144	$968,358	0.62%	$1,162,030	0.70%	$1,291,144	0.72%	$1,743,044	0.90%	1,291,144	$5,164,576
196	$1,266,759	$950,069	0.61%	$1,140,083	0.68%	$1,266,759	0.71%	$1,710,125	0.89%	1,266,759	$5,067,036
197	$1,287,222	$965,417	0.62%	$1,158,500	0.69%	$1,287,222	0.72%	$1,737,750	0.90%	1,287,222	$5,148,888
198	$1,254,500	$940,875	0.61%	$1,129,050	0.68%	$1,254,500	0.70%	$1,693,575	0.88%	1,254,500	$5,018,000
199	$1,250,749	$938,062	0.60%	$1,125,674	0.67%	$1,250,749	0.70%	$1,688,511	0.87%	1,250,749	$5,002,996
200	$1,294,540	$970,905	0.63%	$1,165,086	0.70%	$1,294,540	0.72%	$1,747,629	0.91%	1,294,540	$5,178,160
201	$1,223,313	$917,485	0.59%	$1,100,982	0.66%	$1,223,313	0.68%	$1,651,473	0.86%	1,223,313	$4,893,252
202	$1,259,258	$944,444	0.61%	$1,133,332	0.68%	$1,259,258	0.70%	$1,699,998	0.88%	1,259,258	$5,037,032
203	$1,259,489	$944,617	0.61%	$1,133,540	0.68%	$1,259,489	0.70%	$1,700,310	0.88%	1,259,489	$5,037,956
204	$1,295,139	$971,354	0.63%	$1,165,625	0.70%	$1,295,139	0.72%	$1,748,438	0.91%	1,295,139	$5,180,556
205	$1,259,356	$944,517	0.61%	$1,133,420	0.68%	$1,259,356	0.70%	$1,700,131	0.88%	1,259,356	$5,037,424
206	$1,274,675	$956,006	0.62%	$1,147,208	0.69%	$1,274,675	0.71%	$1,720,811	0.89%	1,274,675	$5,098,700
207	$1,267,645	$950,734	0.61%	$1,140,881	0.68%	$1,267,645	0.71%	$1,711,321	0.89%	1,267,645	$5,070,580
208	$1,223,853	$917,890	0.59%	$1,101,468	0.66%	$1,223,853	0.68%	$1,652,202	0.86%	1,223,853	$4,895,412

209	$1,223,853	$917,890	0.59%	$1,101,468	0.66%	$1,223,853	0.68%	$1,652,202	0.86%	1,223,853	$4,895,412
210	$1,201,220	$900,915	0.58%	$1,081,098	0.65%	$1,201,220	0.67%	$1,621,647	0.84%	1,201,220	$4,804,880
211	$1,249,530	$937,148	0.60%	$1,124,577	0.67%	$1,249,530	0.70%	$1,686,866	0.87%	1,249,530	$4,998,120
212	$1,246,599	$934,949	0.60%	$1,121,939	0.67%	$1,246,599	0.69%	$1,682,909	0.87%	1,246,599	$4,986,396
213	$1,278,365	$958,774	0.62%	$1,150,529	0.69%	$1,278,365	0.71%	$1,725,793	0.89%	1,278,365	$5,113,460
214	$1,267,289	$950,467	0.61%	$1,140,560	0.68%	$1,267,289	0.71%	$1,710,840	0.89%	1,267,289	$5,069,156
215	$1,300,981	$975,736	0.63%	$1,170,883	0.70%	$1,300,981	0.72%	$1,756,324	0.91%	1,300,981	$5,203,924
216	$1,288,053	$966,040	0.62%	$1,159,248	0.69%	$1,288,053	0.72%	$1,738,872	0.90%	1,288,053	$5,152,212
217	$1,432,530	$1,074,398	0.69%	$1,289,277	0.77%	$1,432,530	0.80%	$1,933,916	1.00%	1,432,530	$5,730,120
218	$1,397,221	$1,047,916	0.67%	$1,257,499	0.75%	$1,397,221	0.78%	$1,886,248	0.98%	1,397,221	$5,588,884
219	$1,338,585	$1,003,939	0.65%	$1,204,727	0.72%	$1,338,585	0.75%	$1,807,090	0.94%	1,338,585	$5,354,340
220	$1,334,485	$1,000,864	0.64%	$1,201,037	0.72%	$1,334,485	0.74%	$1,801,555	0.93%	1,334,485	$5,337,940
221	$1,318,037	$988,528	0.64%	$1,186,233	0.71%	$1,318,037	0.73%	$1,779,350	0.92%	1,318,037	$5,272,148
222	$1,369,428	$1,027,071	0.66%	$1,232,485	0.74%	$1,369,428	0.76%	$1,848,728	0.96%	1,369,428	$5,477,712
223	$1,428,941	$1,071,706	0.69%	$1,286,047	0.77%	$1,428,941	0.80%	$1,929,070	1.00%	1,428,941	$5,715,764
224	$1,438,176	$1,078,632	0.69%	$1,294,358	0.78%	$1,438,176	0.80%	$1,941,538	1.01%	1,438,176	$5,752,704
225	$1,300,321	$975,241	0.63%	$1,170,289	0.70%	$1,300,321	0.72%	$1,755,433	0.91%	1,300,321	$5,201,284
226	$1,324,365	$993,274	0.64%	$1,191,929	0.71%	$1,324,365	0.74%	$1,787,893	0.93%	1,324,365	$5,297,460
227	$1,294,033	$970,525	0.63%	$1,164,630	0.70%	$1,294,033	0.72%	$1,746,945	0.91%	1,294,033	$5,176,132
228	$1,303,819	$977,864	0.63%	$1,173,437	0.70%	$1,303,819	0.73%	$1,760,156	0.91%	1,303,819	$5,215,276
229	$1,290,891	$968,168	0.62%	$1,161,802	0.70%	$1,290,891	0.72%	$1,742,703	0.90%	1,290,891	$5,163,564
230	$1,223,393	$917,545	0.59%	$1,101,054	0.66%	$1,223,393	0.68%	$1,651,581	0.86%	1,223,393	$4,893,572
231	$1,101,568	$826,176	0.53%	$991,411	0.59%	$1,101,568	0.61%	$1,487,117	0.77%	1,101,568	$4,406,272
232	$1,117,927	$838,445	0.54%	$1,006,134	0.60%	$1,117,927	0.62%	$1,509,201	0.78%	1,117,927	$4,471,708
233	$1,176,185	$882,139	0.57%	$1,058,567	0.63%	$1,176,185	0.66%	$1,587,850	0.82%	1,176,185	$4,704,740
234	$1,183,874	$887,906	0.57%	$1,065,487	0.64%	$1,183,874	0.66%	$1,598,230	0.83%	1,183,874	$4,735,496
235	$1,315,861	$986,896	0.64%	$1,184,275	0.71%	$1,315,861	0.73%	$1,776,412	0.92%	1,315,861	$5,263,444
236	$1,298,147	$973,610	0.63%	$1,168,332	0.70%	$1,298,147	0.72%	$1,752,498	0.91%	1,298,147	$5,192,588
237	$1,412,065	$1,059,049	0.68%	$1,270,859	0.76%	$1,412,065	0.79%	$1,906,288	0.99%	1,412,065	$5,648,260
238	$1,451,403	$1,088,552	0.70%	$1,306,263	0.78%	$1,451,403	0.81%	$1,959,394	1.02%	1,451,403	$5,805,612
239	$1,458,082	$1,093,562	0.70%	$1,312,274	0.79%	$1,458,082	0.81%	$1,968,411	1.02%	1,458,082	$5,832,328
240	$1,430,097	$1,072,573	0.69%	$1,287,087	0.77%	$1,430,097	0.80%	$1,930,631	1.00%	1,430,097	$5,720,388
241	$1,365,217	$1,023,913	0.66%	$1,228,695	0.74%	$1,365,217	0.76%	$1,843,043	0.95%	1,365,217	$5,460,868
242	$1,403,146	$1,052,360	0.68%	$1,262,831	0.76%	$1,403,146	0.78%	$1,894,247	0.98%	1,403,146	$5,612,584
243	$1,307,333	$980,500	0.63%	$1,176,600	0.70%	$1,307,333	0.73%	$1,764,900	0.91%	1,307,333	$5,229,332

244	$1,329,103	$996,827	0.64%	$1,196,193	0.72%	$1,329,103	0.74%	$1,794,289	0.93%	1,329,103	$5,316,412
245	$1,260,926	$945,695	0.61%	$1,134,833	0.68%	$1,260,926	0.70%	$1,702,250	0.88%	1,260,926	$5,043,704
246	$1,289,086	$966,815	0.62%	$1,160,177	0.69%	$1,289,086	0.72%	$1,740,266	0.90%	1,289,086	$5,156,344
247	$1,282,407	$961,805	0.62%	$1,154,166	0.69%	$1,282,407	0.71%	$1,731,249	0.90%	1,282,407	$5,129,628
248	$1,269,973	$952,480	0.61%	$1,142,976	0.68%	$1,269,973	0.71%	$1,714,464	0.89%	1,269,973	$5,079,892
249	$1,356,522	$1,017,392	0.66%	$1,220,870	0.73%	$1,356,522	0.76%	$1,831,305	0.95%	1,356,522	$5,426,088
250	$1,330,806	$998,105	0.64%	$1,197,725	0.72%	$1,330,806	0.74%	$1,796,588	0.93%	1,330,806	$5,323,224
251	$1,329,074	$996,806	0.64%	$1,196,167	0.72%	$1,329,074	0.74%	$1,794,250	0.93%	1,329,074	$5,316,296
252	$1,331,102	$998,327	0.64%	$1,197,992	0.72%	$1,331,102	0.74%	$1,796,988	0.93%	1,331,102	$5,324,408
253	$1,309,448	$982,086	0.63%	$1,178,503	0.71%	$1,309,448	0.73%	$1,767,755	0.92%	1,309,448	$5,237,792
254	$1,253,351	$940,013	0.61%	$1,128,016	0.68%	$1,253,351	0.70%	$1,692,024	0.88%	1,253,351	$5,013,404
255	$1,390,407	$1,042,805	0.67%	$1,251,366	0.75%	$1,390,407	0.77%	$1,877,049	0.97%	1,390,407	$5,561,628
256	$1,390,407	$1,042,805	0.67%	$1,251,366	0.75%	$1,390,407	0.77%	$1,877,049	0.97%	1,390,407	$5,561,628

Table C

Draft Success by Position; Success equals that a player became or has become a starter for over half of his playing career.

Source: Western Chief from Arrowhead Pride

Round	QB	RB	WR	TE	OL	DL	LB	DB
1st Round	63%	58%	58%	67%	83%	58%	70%	64%
2nd Round	27%	25%	49%	50%	70%	26%	55%	46%
3rd Round	17%	16%	25%	39%	40%	27%	34%	24%
4th Round	8%	11%	12%	33%	29%	37%	16%	11%
5th Round	0%	9%	16%	32%	16%	13%	4%	17%
6th Round	0%	6%	9%	26%	16%	13%	5%	8%
7th Round	6%	0%	5%	0%	9%	3%	2%	11%

Players over 1% on Super Bowl Champions		
Year	Team	#
1994	49ers	25
1995	Cowboys	28
1996	Packers	22
1997	Broncos	28
1998	Broncos	31
1999	Rams	27
2000	Ravens	24
2001	Patriots	24
2002	Bucs	26
2003	Patriots	30
2004	Patriots	29
2005	Steelers	30
2006	Colts	24
2007	Giants	26
2008	Steelers	26
2009	Saints	32
2010	Packers	
2011	Giants	25
2012	Ravens	26
2013	Seahawks	20
2014	Patriots	24
2015	Broncos	24
2016	Patriots	26
	AVG	26.2
	1994-2009	27
	2011-16	24.2

Super Bowl Top 30 Cap Hits

*The data in this section was compiled by Jason Fitzgerald of Over The Cap. The data from 1994 through 2009 was sourced from USA Today as they used to cover all NFL salary cap data online, while the data since has been put together by Jason through the years from information compiled from agents, team representatives, and other sources as a part of what he does for Over The Cap

#	1994 49ers	Position	Cap Hit	% of Cap	S.B. AVG.	Difference
1	Steve Young	QB	$4,525,000	13.08%	9.35%	3.73%
2	Jerry Rice	WR	$2,963,333	8.56%	6.93%	1.64%
3	Steve Wallace	OL	$1,987,256	5.74%	5.97%	-0.23%
4	Harris Barton	OL	$1,959,510	5.66%	5.33%	0.33%
5	Tim McDonald	S	$1,551,000	4.48%	4.84%	-0.36%
6	John Taylor	WR	$1,451,257	4.19%	4.34%	-0.14%
7	Deion Sanders	CB	$1,134,000	3.28%	3.78%	-0.50%
8	Richard Dent	DE	$1,050,000	3.03%	3.54%	-0.51%
9	Brent Jones	TE	$1,030,400	2.98%	3.23%	-0.26%
10	Bryant Young	DE	$1,018,333	2.94%	2.95%	-0.01%
11	Jesse Sapolu	OL	$930,608	2.69%	2.78%	-0.09%
12	Ricky Watters	RB	$866,000	2.50%	2.59%	-0.09%
13	Ken Norton	LB	$788,733	2.28%	2.39%	-0.11%
14	Dana Hall	S	$750,000	2.17%	2.21%	-0.04%
15	Ralph Tamm	OL	$700,200	2.02%	2.07%	-0.04%
16	Eric Davis	CB	$700,000	2.02%	1.94%	0.09%
17	Dana Stubblefield	DT	$627,400	1.81%	1.79%	0.03%
18	Merton Hanks	S	$606,700	1.75%	1.65%	0.10%
19	William Floyd	FB	$560,000	1.62%	1.54%	0.08%
20	Todd Kelly	DE	$556,375	1.61%	1.46%	0.15%
21	Gary Plummer	LB	$515,400	1.49%	1.36%	0.13%
22	Harry Boatswain	OL	$510,400	1.47%	1.28%	0.20%
23	Dennis Brown	DE	$400,400	1.16%	1.20%	-0.04%
24	Bart Oates	OL	$395,000	1.14%	1.14%	0.00%
25	Dexter Carter	RB	$350,200	1.01%	1.08%	-0.07%
26	Bill Romanowski	LB	$333,333	0.96%	1.03%	-0.07%
27	Kevin Mitchell	LB	$324,000	0.94%	0.99%	-0.05%
28	Tyronne Drakeford	CB	$313,000	0.90%	0.93%	-0.02%
29	Marc Logan	RB	$300,400	0.87%	0.88%	-0.01%
30	Mark Thomas	DE	$267,066	0.77%	0.84%	-0.06%

	SF	S.B. AVG.	SF +/-
Top 1	13.08%	9.37%	3.70%
Top 2	21.64%	16.31%	5.33%
Top 3	27.38%	22.32%	5.05%
Top 5	37.52%	32.57%	4.95%
Top 10	53.95%	50.43%	3.52%
Top 15	65.61%	62.36%	3.25%
Top 20	74.42%	70.66%	3.77%
Top 25	80.70%	76.72%	3.98%
Top 30	85.14%	81.36%	3.78%
Team	98.12%	100.45%	-2.33%

*Note: Top 30s include dead money cap hits for players who have been released.

#	1995 Cowboys	Position	Cap Hit	% of Cap	S.B. AVG.	Difference
1	Emmitt Smith	RB	$3,400,000	9.17%	9.35%	-0.18%
2	Troy Aikman	QB	$2,493,500	6.72%	6.93%	-0.20%
3	Charles Haley	DE	$2,230,950	6.01%	5.97%	0.04%
4	Deion Sanders	CB	$2,217,442	5.98%	5.33%	0.65%
5	Michael Irvin	WR	$1,972,440	5.32%	4.84%	0.47%
6	Russell Maryland	DT	$1,820,800	4.91%	4.34%	0.57%
7	Daryl Johnston	FB	$1,402,900	3.78%	3.78%	0.00%
8	Jay Novacek	TE	$1,400,000	3.77%	3.54%	0.23%
9	Erik Williams	OL	$1,374,329	3.70%	3.23%	0.47%
10	Kevin Smith	CB	$1,365,050	3.68%	2.95%	0.73%
11	Tony Tolbert	DE	$1,343,300	3.62%	2.78%	0.84%
12	Leon Lett	DT	$1,173,800	3.16%	2.59%	0.57%
13	Robert Jones	LB	$875,200	2.36%	2.39%	-0.03%
14	Ray Donaldson	OL	$818,750	2.21%	2.21%	0.00%
15	Nathaniel Newton	OL	$809,933	2.18%	2.07%	0.12%
16	Mark Tuinei	OL	$728,100	1.96%	1.94%	0.03%
17	Shante Carver	DE	$726,200	1.96%	1.79%	0.17%
18	Darren Woodson	S	$670,900	1.81%	1.65%	0.15%
19	Chad Hennings	DT	$646,300	1.74%	1.54%	0.20%
20	Dixon Edwards	LB	$526,600	1.42%	1.46%	-0.04%
21	Kevin Williams	WR	$515,550	1.39%	1.36%	0.03%
22	Larry Brown	CB	$500,200	1.35%	1.28%	0.07%
23	Godfrey Myles	LB	$452,550	1.22%	1.20%	0.02%
24	Charles Wilson	QB	$450,550	1.21%	1.14%	0.07%
25	Darrin Smith	LB	$426,400	1.15%	1.08%	0.07%
26	Larry Allen	OL	$416,600	1.12%	1.03%	0.09%
27	Sherman Williams	RB	$405,000	1.09%	0.99%	0.11%
28	Clayton Holmes	CB	$402,400	1.08%	0.93%	0.16%
29	Kendell Watkins	TE	$332,333	0.90%	0.88%	0.02%
30	Shane Hannah	OL	$325,000	0.88%	0.84%	0.04%

	DAL	S.B. AVG.	DAL +/-
Top 1	9.17%	9.37%	-0.21%
Top 2	15.89%	16.31%	-0.42%
Top 3	21.90%	22.32%	-0.42%
Top 5	33.19%	32.57%	0.62%
Top 10	53.04%	50.43%	2.61%
Top 15	66.57%	62.36%	4.22%
Top 20	75.46%	70.66%	4.81%
Top 25	81.78%	76.72%	5.07%
Top 30	86.86%	81.36%	5.49%
Team	100.14%	100.45%	-0.31%

#	1996 Packers	Position	CAP HIT	% of Cap	S.B. AVG.	Difference		GB	S.B. AVG.	GB +/-
1	Brett Favre	QB	$4,175,720	10.25%	9.35%	0.90%	Top 1	10.25%	9.37%	0.88%
2	Reggie White	DE	$3,625,000	8.90%	6.93%	1.97%	Top 2	19.14%	16.31%	2.83%
3	Sean Jones	DE	$1,750,000	4.29%	5.97%	-1.67%	Top 3	23.44%	22.32%	1.11%
4	Robert Brooks	WR	$1,700,900	4.17%	5.33%	-1.15%	Top 5	31.78%	32.57%	-0.79%
5	Leroy Butler	S	$1,700,480	4.17%	4.84%	-0.67%	Top 10	48.49%	50.43%	-1.94%
6	Santana Dotson	DT	$1,567,326	3.85%	4.34%	-0.49%	Top 15	60.37%	62.36%	-1.99%
7	Mark Chmura	TE	$1,503,300	3.69%	3.78%	-0.09%	Top 20	69.33%	70.66%	-1.33%
8	Edgar Bennett	RB	$1,300,480	3.19%	3.54%	-0.35%	Top 25	74.70%	76.72%	-2.02%
9	George Koonce	LB	$1,287,740	3.16%	3.23%	-0.07%	Top 30	78.47%	81.36%	-2.89%
10	Ron Cox	LB	$1,150,420	2.82%	2.95%	-0.13%				
11	Keith Jackson	TE	$1,050,000	2.58%	2.78%	-0.20%	Team	95.99%	100.45%	-4.46%
12	Andre Rison	WR	$1,000,000	2.45%	2.59%	-0.14%				
13	Aaron Taylor	OL	$966,280	2.37%	2.39%	-0.02%				
14	Frank Winters	OL	$917,147	2.25%	2.21%	0.04%				
15	Earl Dotson	OL	$907,390	2.23%	2.07%	0.16%				
16	Wayne Simmons	LB	$881,660	2.16%	1.94%	0.23%				
17	John Michels	OL	$751,250	1.84%	1.79%	0.06%				
18	Eugene Robinson	S	$700,000	1.72%	1.65%	0.06%				
19	Craig Newsome	CB	$667,520	1.64%	1.54%	0.10%				
20	Doug Evans	CB	$650,660	1.60%	1.46%	0.14%				
21	Chris Jacke	K	$628,780	1.54%	1.36%	0.18%				
22	Bruce Wilkerson	OL	$450,420	1.11%	1.28%	-0.17%				
23	Jim McMahon	QB	$400,000	0.98%	1.20%	-0.22%				
24	Derrick Mayes	WR	$385,000	0.94%	1.14%	-0.20%				
25	Don Beebe	WR	$325,660	0.80%	1.08%	-0.28%				
26	Lindsay Knapp	OL	$315,800	0.77%	1.03%	-0.26%				
27	Darius Holland	DT	$313,403	0.77%	0.99%	-0.22%				
28	William Henderson	FB	$308,346	0.76%	0.93%	-0.17%				
29	Desmond Howard	WR	$300,000	0.74%	0.88%	-0.14%				
30	Brian Williams	LB	$299,553	0.74%	0.84%	-0.10%				

#	1997 Broncos	Position	CAP HIT	% of Cap	S.B. AVG.	Difference
1	Ray Crockett	CB	$2,281,814	5.50%	9.35%	-3.84%
2	Steve Atwater	S	$2,261,080	5.45%	6.93%	-1.47%
3	John Elway	QB	$2,141,475	5.17%	5.97%	-0.80%
4	Shannon Sharpe	TE	$1,750,240	4.22%	5.33%	-1.11%
5	Bill Romanowski	LB	$1,600,240	3.86%	4.84%	-0.98%
6	Alfred Williams	DE	$1,600,240	3.86%	4.34%	-0.48%
7	Neil Smith	DE	$1,515,420	3.66%	3.78%	-0.12%
8	Anthony Miller	WR	$1,325,000	3.20%	3.54%	-0.35%
9	John Mobley	LB	$1,099,480	2.65%	3.23%	-0.58%
10	Tom Nalen	OL	$1,000,480	2.41%	2.95%	-0.54%
11	Michael Perry	DT	$1,000,000	2.41%	2.78%	-0.36%
12	Tony Jones	OL	$951,080	2.29%	2.59%	-0.30%
13	Brian Habib	OL	$950,240	2.29%	2.39%	-0.10%
14	Gary Zimmerman	OL	$926,667	2.24%	2.21%	0.02%
15	James Geathers	DT	$901,380	2.17%	2.07%	0.11%
16	Terrell Davis	RB	$815,246	1.97%	1.94%	0.03%
17	Trevor Pryce	DE	$721,500	1.74%	1.79%	-0.05%
18	Ed McCaffrey	WR	$675,740	1.63%	1.65%	-0.02%
19	Tyrone Braxton	S	$601,320	1.45%	1.54%	-0.09%
20	Howard Griffith	FB	$600,420	1.45%	1.46%	-0.01%
21	Jason Elam	K	$597,520	1.44%	1.36%	0.08%
22	Tory James	CB	$534,130	1.29%	1.28%	0.01%
23	Willie Green	WR	$500,780	1.21%	1.20%	0.01%
24	Harley Hager	LB	$500,000	1.21%	1.14%	0.06%
25	Michael Pritchard	WR	$500,000	1.21%	1.08%	0.12%
26	Harry Swayne	OL	$450,780	1.09%	1.03%	0.05%
27	Darrien Gordon	CB	$433,993	1.05%	0.99%	0.06%
28	James Jones	DT	$416,666	1.01%	0.93%	0.08%
29	Rod Smith	WR	$403,060	0.97%	0.88%	0.09%
30	Mark Schlereth	OL	$401,200	0.97%	0.84%	0.13%

	DEN	S.B. AVG.	DEN +/-
Top 1	5.50%	9.37%	-3.87%
Top 2	10.96%	16.31%	-5.35%
Top 3	16.12%	22.32%	-6.20%
Top 5	24.21%	32.57%	-8.36%
Top 10	39.99%	50.43%	-10.44%
Top 15	51.39%	62.36%	-10.96%
Top 20	59.63%	70.66%	-11.03%
Top 25	65.98%	76.72%	-10.74%
Top 30	71.06%	81.36%	-10.30%
Team	94.45%	100.45%	-6.00%

#	1998 Broncos	Position	CAP HIT	% of Cap	S.B. AVG.	Difference
1	Steve Atwater	S	$2,702,590	5.16%	9.35%	-4.19%
2	Shannon Sharpe	TE	$2,625,350	5.01%	6.93%	-1.91%
3	John Elway	QB	$2,624,315	5.01%	5.97%	-0.96%
4	Tony Jones	OL	$2,576,990	4.92%	5.33%	0.41%
5	Terrell Davis	RB	$2,393,036	4.57%	4.84%	-0.28%
6	Bill Romanowski	LB	$2,260,000	4.31%	4.34%	-0.02%
7	Alfred Williams	DE	$2,242,890	4.28%	3.78%	0.50%
8	Darrien Gordon	CB	$2,217,646	4.23%	3.54%	0.69%
9	Anthony Miller	WR	$1,450,000	2.77%	3.23%	-0.47%
10	Mark Schlereth	OL	$1,404,095	2.68%	2.95%	-0.27%
11	Rod Smith	WR	$1,404,095	2.68%	2.78%	-0.10%
12	Tom Nalen	OL	$1,400,910	2.67%	2.59%	0.08%
13	Ray Crockett	CB	$1,360,490	2.60%	2.39%	0.20%
14	Neil Smith	DE	$1,302,240	2.49%	2.21%	0.27%
15	John Mobley	LB	$1,206,190	2.30%	2.07%	0.24%
16	Harry Swayne	OL	$1,001,330	1.91%	1.94%	-0.03%
17	Maa Tanuvasa	DE	$981,212	1.87%	1.79%	0.09%
18	Keith Traylor	DT	$967,786	1.85%	1.65%	0.19%
19	Ed McCaffrey	WR	$901,680	1.72%	1.54%	0.18%
20	Willie Green	WR	$875,280	1.67%	1.46%	0.21%
21	Trevor Pryce	DE	$860,260	1.64%	1.36%	0.28%
22	Howard Griffith	FB	$800,280	1.53%	1.28%	0.25%
23	Marcus Nash	WR	$789,000	1.51%	1.20%	0.31%
24	Seth Joyner	LB	$750,000	1.43%	1.14%	0.29%
25	Tyrone Braxton	S	$703,605	1.34%	1.08%	0.26%
26	Gary Zimmerman	OL	$700,000	1.34%	1.03%	0.30%
27	Jason Elam	K	$695,280	1.33%	0.99%	0.34%
28	Tory James	CB	$606,735	1.16%	0.93%	0.23%
29	Glenn Cadrez	LB	$594,180	1.13%	0.88%	0.25%
30	Harald Hasselbach	DE	$587,078	1.12%	0.84%	0.29%

	DEN	S.B. AVG.	DEN +/-
Top 1	5.16%	9.37%	-4.21%
Top 2	10.17%	16.31%	-6.14%
Top 3	15.18%	22.32%	-7.15%
Top 5	24.67%	32.57%	-7.90%
Top 10	42.94%	50.43%	-7.48%
Top 15	55.68%	62.36%	-6.68%
Top 20	64.71%	70.66%	-5.95%
Top 25	72.16%	76.72%	-4.56%
Top 30	78.23%	81.36%	-3.13%
Team	96.37%	100.45%	-4.08%

#	1999 Rams	Position	CAP HIT	% of Cap	S.B. AVG.	Difference		STL	S.B. AVG.	STL +/-
1	Marshall Faulk	RB	$4,309,370	7.52%	9.35%	-1.83%	Top 1	7.52%	9.37%	-1.85%
2	Adam Timmerman	OL	$3,502,450	6.11%	6.93%	-0.81%	Top 2	13.64%	16.31%	-2.67%
3	Todd Lyght	CB	$3,377,500	5.90%	5.97%	-0.07%	Top 3	19.53%	22.32%	-2.79%
4	Orlando Pace	OL	$3,313,666	5.78%	5.33%	0.46%	Top 5	30.78%	32.57%	-1.79%
5	Trent Green	QB	$3,128,290	5.46%	4.84%	0.62%	Top 10	48.58%	50.43%	-1.84%
6	Isaac Bruce	WR	$2,925,000	5.11%	4.34%	0.77%	Top 15	60.98%	62.36%	-1.38%
7	Grant Winstrom	DE	$1,868,000	3.26%	3.78%	-0.52%	Top 20	68.81%	70.66%	-1.85%
8	Kevin Carter	DE	$1,862,483	3.25%	3.54%	-0.29%	Top 25	74.69%	76.72%	-2.03%
9	Mike Jones	LB	$1,850,000	3.23%	3.23%	0.00%	Top 30	79.57%	81.36%	-1.80%
10	Torry Holt	WR	$1,696,000	2.96%	2.95%	0.01%				
11	Keith Lyle	S	$1,575,000	2.75%	2.78%	-0.03%	Team	100.54%	100.45%	0.09%
12	Ricky Proehl	WR	$1,500,000	2.62%	2.59%	0.02%				
13	D'Marco Farr	DT	$1,410,502	2.46%	2.39%	0.07%				
14	Ray Agnew	DT	$1,366,666	2.39%	2.21%	0.17%				
15	Amp Lee	RB	$1,250,000	2.18%	2.07%	0.12%				
16	Robert Jones	LB	$1,130,000	1.97%	1.94%	0.04%				
17	Todd Collins	LB	$950,000	1.66%	1.79%	-0.13%				
18	Eddie Kennison	WR	$850,000	1.48%	1.65%	-0.17%				
19	Devin Bush	S	$800,000	1.40%	1.54%	-0.14%				
20	Kurt Warner	QB	$800,000	1.32%	1.46%	-0.14%				
21	John Flannery	OL	$753,920	1.29%	1.36%	-0.08%				
22	Lorenzo Styles	LB	$737,500	1.28%	1.28%	0.00%				
23	Rick Tuten	P	$731,250	1.14%	1.20%	-0.07%				
24	Craig Heyward	RB	$650,350	1.13%	1.14%	-0.01%				
25	Jeff Wilkins	K	$650,000	1.05%	1.08%	-0.03%				
26	Robert Holcombe	RB	$600,350	1.05%	1.03%	0.01%				
27	Dexter McCleon	CB	$593,000	1.04%	0.99%	0.05%				
28	Andy McCollum	OL	$552,520	0.96%	0.93%	0.04%				
29	Eric Hill	LB	$525,000	0.92%	0.88%	0.04%				
30	Ernie Conwell	TE	$523,750	0.91%	0.84%	0.08%				

#	2000 Ravens	Position	CAP HIT	% of Cap	S.B. AVG.	Difference
1	Jonathan Ogden	OL	$4,021,605	6.47%	9.35%	-2.88%
2	Ray Lewis	LB	$3,311,920	5.33%	6.93%	-1.60%
3	Michael McCrary	DE	$3,196,473	5.14%	5.97%	-0.83%
4	Rod Woodson	S	$2,966,986	4.77%	5.33%	-0.56%
5	Peter Boulware	LB	$2,801,600	4.51%	4.84%	-0.34%
6	Harry Swayne	OL	$2,500,320	4.02%	4.34%	-0.32%
7	Tony Banks	QB	$2,263,140	3.64%	3.78%	-0.14%
8	Jeff Blackshear	OL	$2,183,333	3.51%	3.54%	-0.03%
9	Jamal Lewis	RB	$1,878,000	3.02%	3.23%	-0.21%
10	Duane Starks	CB	$1,698,780	2.73%	2.95%	-0.22%
11	Jermaine Lewis	WR	$1,668,453	2.68%	2.78%	-0.09%
12	Rob Burnett	DE	$1,625,320	2.61%	2.59%	0.02%
13	Shannon Sharpe	TE	$1,625,320	2.61%	2.39%	0.22%
14	Chris McAlister	CB	$1,520,655	2.45%	2.21%	0.23%
15	Travis Taylor	WR	$1,453,000	2.34%	2.07%	0.27%
16	Tony Siragusa	DT	$1,325,000	2.13%	1.94%	0.19%
17	Sam Adams	DT	$1,125,640	1.81%	1.79%	0.02%
18	Jamie Sharper	LB	$1,029,560	1.66%	1.65%	0.00%
19	Jeff Mitchell	OL	$1,027,640	1.65%	1.54%	0.11%
20	Trent Dilfer	QB	$1,000,320	1.61%	1.46%	0.15%
21	Qadry Ismail	WR	$825,320	1.33%	1.36%	-0.04%
22	Ben Coates	TE	$750,000	1.21%	1.28%	-0.07%
23	Larry Webster	DT	$711,296	1.14%	1.20%	-0.06%
24	Matt Stover	K	$690,320	1.11%	1.14%	-0.03%
25	Patrick Johnson	WR	$616,600	0.99%	1.08%	-0.09%
26	Spencer Folau	OL	$604,160	0.97%	1.03%	-0.06%
27	Frank Wainright	TE	$603,520	0.97%	0.99%	-0.01%
28	Sam Gash	FB	$600,000	0.97%	0.93%	0.04%
29	James Trapp	CB	$526,280	0.85%	0.88%	-0.03%
30	Bill Davis	WR	$525,640	0.85%	0.84%	0.01%

	BAL	S.B. AVG.	BAL +/-
Top 1	6.47%	9.37%	-2.90%
Top 2	11.80%	16.31%	-4.51%
Top 3	16.94%	22.32%	-5.39%
Top 5	26.22%	32.57%	-6.35%
Top 10	43.14%	50.43%	-7.28%
Top 15	55.84%	62.36%	-6.52%
Top 20	64.70%	70.66%	-5.96%
Top 25	70.48%	76.72%	-6.24%
Top 30	75.08%	81.36%	-6.29%
Team	95.12%	100.45%	-5.32%

#	2001 Patriots	Position	CAP HIT	% of Cap	S.B. AVG.	Difference		NE	S.B. AVG.	NE +/-
1	Drew Bledsoe	QB	$6,936,391	10.29%	9.35%	0.94%	Top 1	10.29%	9.37%	0.92%
2	Ty Law	CB	$5,033,771	7.47%	6.93%	0.54%	Top 2	17.76%	16.31%	1.45$
3	Willie McGinest	LB	$4,364,366	6.47%	5.97%	0.51%	Top 3	24.23%	22.32%	1.91%
4	Ted Johnson	LB	$3,976,450	5.90%	5.33%	0.57%	Top 5	34.03%	32.57%	1.47%
5	Terry Glenn	WR	$2,630,179	3.90%	4.84%	-0.94%	Top 10	47.13%	50.43%	-3.30%
6	Richard Seymour	DE	$2,000,000	2.97%	4.34%	-1.37%	Top 15	55.73%	62.36%	-6.62%
7	Chris Slade	LB	$1,980,000	2.94%	3.78%	-0.84%	Top 20	62.82%	70.66%	-7.83%
8	Max Lane	OL	$1,848,267	2.74%	3.54%	-0.80%	Top 25	67.97%	76.72%	-8.75%
9	Lawyer Milloy	S	$1,765,017	2.62%	3.23%	-0.62%	Top 30	72.60%	81.36%	-8.77%
10	Tedy Bruschi	LB	$1,230,200	1.83%	2.95%	-1.12%				
11	Troy Brown	WR	$1,215,200	1.80%	2.78%	-0.97%	Team	97.79%	100.45%	-2.66%
12	Damien Woody	OL	$1,183,160	1.76%	2.59%	-0.84%				
13	Tebucky Jones	S	$1,167,150	1.73%	2.39%	-0.66%				
14	Todd Rucci	OL	$1,120,000	1.66%	2.21%	-0.55%				
15	Andy Katzenmoyer	LB	$1,117,415	1.66%	2.07%	-0.41%				
16	Henry Thomas	DT	$1,100,000	1.63%	1.94%	-0.30%				
17	Grant Williams	OL	$1,092,200	1.62%	1.79%	-0.17%				
18	Adam Vinatieri	K	$955,200	1.42%	1.65%	-0.24%				
19	David Patten	WR	$829,000	1.23%	1.54%	-0.31%				
20	Bryan Cox	LB	$800,000	1.19%	1.46%	-0.27%				
21	Robert Edwards	RB	$724,800	1.08%	1.36%	-0.29%				
22	Bobby Hamilton	DE	$705,200	1.05%	1.28%	-0.23%				
23	Mike Compton	OL	$689,866	1.02%	1.20%	-0.18%				
24	Kevin Faulk	RB	$687,200	1.02%	1.14%	-0.12%				
25	Otis Smith	CB	$662,700	0.98%	1.08%	-0.10%				
26	Damon Huard	QB	$655,200	0.97%	1.03%	-0.06%				
27	Marc Edwards	FB	$630,200	0.93%	0.99%	-0.05%				
28	Adrian Klemm	OL	$624,160	0.93%	0.93%	0.00%				
29	Joe Andruzzi	OL	$605,700	0.90%	0.88%	0.02%				
30	Rod Rutledge	TE	$604,200	0.90%	0.84%	0.06%				

#	2002 Buccaneers	Position	CAP HIT	% of Cap	S.B. AVG.	Difference		TB	S.B. AVG.	TB +/-
1	Warren Sapp	DT	$6,981,530	9.82%	9.35%	0.47%	Top 1	9.82%	9.37%	0.45%
2	Brad Johnson	QB	$6,803,150	9.57%	6.93%	2.64%	Top 2	19.39%	16.31%	3.08%
3	Simeon Rice	DE	$6,000,000	8.44%	5.97%	2.47%	Top 3	27.83%	22.32%	5.50%
4	Derrick Brooks	LB	$3,935,493	5.54%	5.33%	0.21%	Top 5	38.36%	32.57%	5.79%
5	Jeff Christy	OL	$3,551,890	5.00%	4.84%	0.15%	Top 10	55.97%	50.43%	5.54%
6	Keyshawn Johnson	WR	$3,357,592	4.72%	4.34%	0.38%	Top 15	64.51%	62.36%	2.16%
7	Marcus Jones	DE	$2,692,436	3.79%	3.78%	0.01%	Top 20	71.10%	70.66%	0.45%
8	John Lynch	S	$2,684,863	3.78%	3.54%	0.23%	Top 25	76.49%	76.72%	-0.23%
9	Mike Alstott	FB	$1,895,176	2.67%	3.23%	-0.57%	Top 30	81.08%	81.36%	-0.29%
10	Ronde Barber	CB	$1,891,430	2.66%	2.95%	-0.29%				
11	Kenyatta Walker	OL	$1,336,123	1.88%	2.78%	-0.90%	Team	100.00%	100.45%	-0.45%
12	Anthony McFarland	DT	$1,275,870	1.79%	2.59%	-0.80%				
13	Keenan McCardell	WR	$1,250,000	1.76%	2.39%	-0.63%				
14	Kerry Jenkins	OL	$1,123,240	1.58%	2.21%	-0.63%				
15	Shelton Quarles	LB	$1,091,370	1.53%	2.07%	-0.53%				
16	Martin Gramatica	K	$1,027,435	1.45%	1.94%	-0.49%				
17	Donnie Abraham	CB	$1,000,000	1.41%	1.79%	-0.38%				
18	Brian Kelly	CB	$910,043	1.28%	1.65%	-0.37%				
19	Michael Pittman	RB	$876,260	1.23%	1.54%	-0.31%				
20	Alshermond Singleton	LB	$870,536	1.22%	1.46%	-0.24%				
21	Ken Dilger	TE	$852,250	1.20%	1.36%	-0.17%				
22	Joe Jurevicius	WR	$777,160	1.09%	1.28%	-0.19%				
23	Jerry Wunsch	OL	$743,600	1.05%	1.20%	-0.16%				
24	Todd Washington	OL	$728,960	1.03%	1.14%	-0.12%				
25	Shaun King	QB	$728,150	1.02%	1.08%	-0.26%				
26	Charles Lee	WR	$721,765	1.02%	1.03%	-0.02%				
27	Cosey Coleman	OL	$666,700	0.94%	0.99%	-0.05%				
28	Randall McDaniel	OL	$666,666	0.94%	0.93%	0.01%				
29	Gregory Spires	DE	$628,870	0.88%	0.88%	0.00%				
30	Karl Williams	WR	$578,150	0.81%	0.84%	-0.02%				

#	2003 Patriots	Position	CAP HIT	% of Cap	S.B. AVG.	Difference
1	Ty Law	CB	$8,806,965	11.74%	9.35%	2.39%
2	Ted Johnson	LB	$3,642,416	4.86%	6.93%	-2.07%
3	Brandon Gorin	OL	$3,380,950	4.51%	5.97%	-1.46%
4	Tom Brady	QB	$3,323,450	4.43%	5.33%	-0.90%
5	Damien Woody	OL	$2,790,600	3.72%	4.84%	-1.12%
6	Richard Seymour	DT	$2,528,200	3.37%	4.34%	-0.97%
7	Troy Brown	WR	$2,451,433	3.27%	3.78%	-0.51%
8	Adam Vinatieri	K	$2,320,676	3.09%	3.54%	-0.45%
9	Antowain Smith	RB	$2,305,600	3.07%	3.23%	-0.16%
10	Mike Vrabel	LB	$2,053,800	2.74%	2.95%	-0.21%
11	Willie McGinest	LB	$1,979,400	2.64%	2.78%	-0.14%
12	Roman Phifer	LB	$1,750,100	2.33%	2.59%	-0.26%
13	Ted Washington	DT	$1,650,000	2.20%	2.39%	-0.19%
14	Mike Compton	OL	$1,588,266	2.12%	2.21%	-0.09%
15	Rosevelt Colvin	LB	$1,554,700	2.07%	2.07%	0.01%
16	Tedy Bruschi	LB	$1,520,966	2.03%	1.94%	0.09%
17	Lawyer Milloy	S	$1,456,806	1.94%	1.79%	0.16%
18	David Patten	WR	$1,354,300	1.81%	1.65%	0.15%
19	Daniel Graham	TE	$1,283,350	1.71%	1.54%	0.17%
20	Ty Warren	DE	$1,265,000	1.69%	1.46%	0.23%
21	Rodney Harrison	S	$1,155,799	1.54%	1.36%	0.18%
22	Tyrone Poole	CB	$1,105,100	1.47%	1.28%	0.19%
23	Anthony Pleasant	DE	$1,079,932	1.44%	1.20%	0.24%
24	Christian Fauria	TE	$970,966	1.29%	1.14%	0.15%
25	Kevin Faulk	RB	$914,700	1.22%	1.08%	0.14%
26	Bobby Hamilton	DE	$860,600	1.15%	1.03%	0.11%
27	Joe Andruzzi	OL	$857,200	1.14%	0.99%	0.16%
28	Damon Huard	QB	$829,700	1.11%	0.93%	0.18%
29	Ken Walter	P	$819,350	1.09%	0.88%	0.21%
30	Adrian Klemm	OL	$775,600	1.03%	0.84%	0.20%

	NE	S.B. AVG.	NE +/-
Top 1	11.74%	9.37%	2.37%
Top 2	16.60%	16.31%	0.29%
Top 3	21.11%	22.32%	-1.22%
Top 5	29.26%	32.57%	-3.31%
Top 10	44.80%	50.43%	-5.63%
Top 15	56.16%	62.36%	-6.19%
Top 20	65.34%	70.66%	-5.32%
Top 25	72.30%	76.72%	-4.41%
Top 30	77.83%	81.36%	-3.54%
Team	99.60%	100.45%	-0.85%

#	2004 Patriots	Position	CAP HIT	% of Cap	S.B. AVG.	Difference		NE	S.B. AVG.	NE +/-
1	Ty Law	CB	$10,206,965	12.67%	9.35%	3.32%	Top 1	12.67%	9.37%	3.30%
2	Tom Brady	QB	$5,062,950	6.28%	6.93%	-0.64%	Top 2	18.95%	16.31%	2.64%
3	Lawyer Milloy	S	$4,053,623	5.03%	5.97%	-0.94%	Top 3	23.98%	22.32%	1.65%
4	Willie McGinest	LB	$3,667,300	4.55%	5.33%	-0.78%	Top 5	32.50%	32.57%	-0.07%
5	Troy Brown	WR	$3,201,434	3.97%	4.84%	-0.87%	Top 10	46.41%	50.43%	-4.01%
6	Richard Seymour	DE	$2,507,800	3.11%	4.34%	-1.23%	Top 15	58.14%	62.36%	-4.22%
7	Tedy Bruschi	LB	$2,246,268	2.79%	3.78%	-0.99%	Top 20	66.54%	70.66%	-4.11%
8	Rodney Harrison	S	$2,200,199	2.73%	3.54%	-0.81%	Top 25	73.56%	76.72%	-3.15%
9	Mike Vrabel	LB	$2,158,100	2.68%	3.23%	-0.56%	Top 30	79.00%	81.36%	-2.37%
10	Adam Vinatieri	K	$2,095,777	2.60%	2.95%	-0.35%				
11	Antowain Smith	RB	$2,025,000	2.51%	2.78%	-0.26%	Team	98.25%	100.45%	-2.20%
12	Tyrone Poole	CB	$1,955,816	2.43%	2.59%	-0.17%				
13	Rosevelt Colvin	LB	$1,853,000	2.30%	2.39%	-0.09%				
14	Ty Warren	DE	$1,843,333	2.29%	2.21%	0.08%				
15	Ted Johnson	LB	$1,771,266	2.20%	2.07%	0.13%				
16	David Patten	WR	$1,504,600	1.87%	1.94%	-0.07%				
17	Daniel Graham	TE	$1,432,550	1.78%	1.79%	-0.01%				
18	Joe Andruzzi	OL	$1,343,100	1.67%	1.65%	0.01%				
19	Roman Phifer	LB	$1,255,600	1.56%	1.54%	0.02%				
20	Rodney Bailey	DE	$1,238,134	1.54%	1.46%	0.08%				
21	Corey Dillon	RB	$1,206,400	1.50%	1.36%	0.13%				
22	Matt Light	OL	$1,198,366	1.49%	1.28%	0.21%				
23	Vince Wilfork	DT	$1,150,000	1.43%	1.20%	0.23%				
24	Christian Fauria	TE	$1,101,268	1.37%	1.14%	0.22%				
25	Keith Traylor	DT	$1,000,400	1.24%	1.08%	0.16%				
26	Benjamin Watson	TE	$950,000	1.18%	1.03%	0.14%				
27	Kevin Faulk	RB	$930,600	1.15%	0.99%	0.17%				
28	Josh Miller	P	$863,000	1.07%	0.93%	0.15%				
29	Adrian Klemm	OL	$850,600	1.06%	0.88%	0.18%				
30	Larry Izzo	LB	$783,350	0.97%	0.84%	0.14%				

#	2005 Steelers	Position	CAP HIT	% of Cap	S.B. AVG.	Difference
1	Alan Faneca	OL	$5,497,750	6.43%	9.35%	-2.92%
2	Aaron Smith	DE	$5,115,066	5.98%	6.93%	-0.94%
3	Joey Porter	LB	$4,888,403	5.72%	5.97%	-0.25%
4	Ben Roethlisberger	QB	$4,225,090	4.94%	5.33%	-0.39%
5	Jeff Hartings	OL	$4,094,166	4.79%	4.84%	-0.06%
6	Kimo Von Oelhoffen	DE	$3,245,880	3.80%	4.34%	-0.54%
7	Marvel Smith	OL	$2,738,580	3.20%	3.78%	-0.58%
8	Jason Gildon	DE	$2,597,864	3.04%	3.54%	-0.51%
9	Jerome Bettis	RB	$2,400,000	2.81%	3.23%	-0.43%
10	Hines Ward	WR	$2,168,960	2.54%	2.95%	-0.41%
11	Jerame Tuman	TE	$2,146,900	2.51%	2.78%	-0.27%
12	Casey Hampton	DT	$2,035,790	2.38%	2.59%	-0.21%
13	Troy Polamalu	S	$1,988,700	2.33%	2.39%	-0.07%
14	James Farrior	LB	$1,926,830	2.25%	2.21%	0.04%
15	Duce Staley	RB	$1,837,130	2.15%	2.07%	0.08%
16	Chad Scott	CB	$1,800,000	2.11%	1.94%	0.17%
17	Clark Haggans	LB	$1,779,306	2.08%	1.79%	0.29%
18	DeShea Townsend	CB	$1,467,710	1.72%	1.65%	0.06%
19	Tommy Maddox	QB	$1,351,760	1.58%	1.54%	0.04%
20	Kendall Simmons	OL	$1,239,624	1.45%	1.46%	-0.01%
21	Travis Kirschke	DE	$1,221,413	1.43%	1.36%	0.06%
22	Chris Gardocki	P	$1,214,700	1.42%	1.28%	0.14%
23	Larry Foote	LB	$1,108,960	1.30%	1.20%	0.10%
24	Heath Miller	TE	$1,092,000	1.28%	1.14%	0.13%
25	Cedrick Wilson	WR	$1,043,520	1.22%	1.08%	0.14%
26	Mike Logan	S	$1,000,973	1.17%	1.03%	0.14%
27	Dan Kreider	FB	$987,640	1.16%	0.99%	0.17%
28	Clint Kriewaldt	LB	$943,960	1.10%	0.93%	0.18%
29	Ricardo Colclough	CB	$903,343	1.06%	0.88%	0.18%
30	Jeff Reed	K	$853,080	1.00%	0.84%	0.16%

	PIT	S.B. AVG.	PIT +/-
Top 1	6.43%	9.37%	-2.94%
Top 2	12.41%	16.31%	-3.90%
Top 3	18.13%	22.32%	-4.19%
Top 5	27.86%	32.57%	-4.71%
Top 10	43.24%	50.43%	-7.18%
Top 15	54.86%	62.36%	-7.50%
Top 20	63.80%	70.66%	-6.86%
Top 25	70.44%	76.72%	-6.28%
Top 30	75.92%	81.36%	-5.44%
Team	92.90%	100.45%	-7.55%

#	2006 Colts	Position	CAP HIT	% of Cap	S.B. AVG.	Difference
1	Peyton Manning	QB	$10,571,068	10.36%	9.35%	1.02%
2	Tarik Glenn	OL	$6,900,666	6.77%	6.93%	-0.16%
3	Dwight Freeney	DE	$6,733,708	6.60%	5.97%	0.63%
4	Marvin Harrison	WR	$6,400,000	6.27%	5.33%	0.95%
5	Reggie Wayne	WR	$5,100,440	5.00%	4.84%	0.16%
6	Ryan Diem	OL	$4,805,720	4.71%	4.34%	0.37%
7	Jeff Saturday	OL	$3,939,506	3.86%	3.78%	0.08%
8	Corey Simon	DT	$3,692,195	3.62%	3.54%	0.08%
9	Raheem Brock	DE	$3,554,840	3.49%	3.23%	0.25%
10	Brandon Stokley	WR	$3,465,613	3.39%	2.95%	0.44%
11	Dominic Rhodes	RB	$3,038,960	2.98%	2.78%	0.20%
12	Montae Reagor	DT	$2,933,784	2.88%	2.59%	0.28%
13	Anthony McFarland	DT	$2,911,765	2.85%	2.39%	0.46%
14	Josh Williams	DT	$2,400,000	2.35%	2.21%	0.14%
15	Robert Mathis	DE	$2,124,840	2.08%	2.07%	0.02%
16	Gary Brackett	LB	$1,998,590	1.96%	1.94%	0.02%
17	Ricky Proehl	WR	$1,852,941	1.82%	1.79%	0.03%
18	Adam Vinatieri	K	$1,682,200	1.65%	1.65%	0.00%
19	Cato June	LB	$1,578,280	1.55%	1.54%	0.01%
20	Nicholas Harper	CB	$1,403,960	1.38%	1.46%	-0.08%
21	Marlin Jackson	CB	$1,245,720	1.22%	1.36%	-0.14%
22	Dallas Clark	TE	$1,195,697	1.17%	1.28%	-0.11%
23	Joseph Addai	RB	$1,075,000	1.05%	1.20%	-0.15%
24	Matt Ulrich	OL	$1,020,588	1.00%	1.14%	-0.14%
25	Justin Snow	LB	$939,395	0.92%	1.08%	-0.16%
26	Hunter Smith	P	$884,508	0.87%	1.03%	-0.17%
27	Aaron Moorehead	WR	$726,000	0.71%	0.99%	-0.27%
28	Mike Doss	S	$724,840	0.71%	0.93%	-0.21%
29	Bob Sanders	S	$700,186	0.69%	0.88%	-0.19%
30	Kelvin Hayden	CB	$636,970	0.62%	0.84%	-0.21%

	IND	S.B. AVG.	IND +/-
Top 1	10.36%	9.37%	0.99%
Top 2	17.13%	16.31%	0.82%
Top 3	23.73%	22.32%	1.41%
Top 5	35.01%	32.57%	2.44%
Top 10	54.07%	50.43%	3.65%
Top 15	67.22%	62.36%	4.86%
Top 20	75.57%	70.66%	4.91%
Top 25	80.94%	76.72%	4.22%
Top 30	84.54%	81.36%	3.17%
Team	99.58%	100.45%	-0.87%

#	2007 Giants	Position	CAP HIT	% of Cap	S.B. AVG.	Difference		NYG	S.B. AVG.	NYG +/-
1	Eli Manning	QB	$10,046,666	9.22%	9.35%	-0.13%	Top 1	9.22%	9.37%	-0.15%
2	Michael Strahan	DE	$6,730,445	6.17%	6.93%	-0.75%	Top 2	15.39%	16.31%	-0.91%
3	Kareem McKenzie	OL	$5,350,000	4.91%	5.97%	-1.06%	Top 3	20.30%	22.32%	-2.02%
4	Amani Toomer	WR	$4,953,960	4.54%	5.33%	-0.78%	Top 5	29.36%	32.57%	-3.21%
5	Plaxico Burress	WR	$4,925,000	4.52%	4.84%	-0.33%	Top 10	49.23%	50.43%	-1.19%
6	Antonio Pierce	LB	$4,550,000	4.17%	4.34%	-0.16%	Top 15	61.91%	62.36%	-0.45%
7	Jeremy Shockey	TE	$4,371,667	4.01%	3.78%	0.23%	Top 20	70.13%	70.66%	-0.53%
8	William James	CB	$4,304,852	3.95%	3.54%	0.41%	Top 25	75.94%	76.72%	-0.78%
9	Osi Umenyiora	DE	$4,232,500	3.88%	3.23%	0.65%	Top 30	80.48%	81.36%	-0.89%
10	LaVar Arrington	LB	$4,200,000	3.85%	2.95%	0.90%				
11	Fred Robbins	DT	$4,126,666	3.79%	2.78%	1.01%	Team	100.33%	100.45%	-0.12%
12	Luke Petitgout	OL	$3,580,000	3.28%	2.59%	0.69%				
13	R.W. McQuarters	CB	$2,100,000	1.93%	2.39%	-0.47%				
14	David Diehl	OL	$2,010,000	1.84%	2.21%	-0.37%				
15	Tiki Barber	RB	$2,000,000	1.83%	2.07%	-0.23%				
16	Shaun O'Hara	OL	$2,000,000	1.83%	1.94%	0.10%				
17	Carlos Emmons	LB	$1,993,750	1.83%	1.79%	0.04%				
18	Rich Seubert	OL	$1,858,750	1.71%	1.65%	0.05%				
19	Sam Madison	CB	$1,600,000	1.47%	1.54%	-0.07%				
20	Reuben Droughns	RB	$1,503,840	1.38%	1.46%	-0.08%				
21	Mathias Kiwanuka	DE	$1,348,790	1.24%	1.36%	-0.13%				
22	William Joseph	DT	$1,328,774	1.22%	1.28%	-0.06%				
23	Gibril Wilson	S	$1,303,480	1.20%	1.20%	-0.01%				
24	David Tyree	WR	$1,180,000	1.08%	1.14%	-0.06%				
25	Aaron Ross	CB	$1,175,000	1.08%	1.08%	0.00%				
26	Jeff Feagles	P	$1,103,840	1.01%	1.03%	-0.02%				
27	Anthony Wright	QB	$1,036,875	0.95%	0.99%	-0.03%				
28	Kawika Mitchell	LB	$1,000,000	0.92%	0.93%	-0.01%				
29	Chriss Snee	OL	$949,166	0.87%	0.88%	-0.01%				
30	Derrick Ward	RB	$855,280	0.78%	0.84%	-0.05%				

#	2008 Steelers	Position	CAP HIT	% of Cap	S.B. AVG.	Difference
1	Ben Roethlisberger	QB	$7,971,920	6.87%	9.35%	-2.48%
2	Max Starks	OL	$6,899,800	5.95%	6.93%	-0.98%
3	Troy Polamalu	S	$6,820,000	5.88%	5.97%	-0.09%
4	Hines Ward	WR	$6,703,840	5.78%	5.33%	0.45%
5	Marvel Smith	OL	$6,646,940	5.73%	4.84%	0.89%
6	Casey Hampton	DT	$5,378,043	4.64%	4.34%	0.30%
7	Kendall Simmons	OL	$4,971,920	4.29%	3.78%	0.51%
8	Aaron Smith	DE	$4,755,760	4.10%	3.54%	0.56%
9	Willie Parker	RB	$4,091,340	3.53%	3.23%	0.29%
10	James Farrior	LB	$4,061,150	3.50%	2.95%	0.55%
11	Ike Taylor	CB	$3,743,360	3.23%	2.78%	0.45%
12	Larry Foote	LB	$3,390,380	2.92%	2.59%	0.33%
13	Brett Keisel	DE	$3,151,340	2.72%	2.39%	0.32%
14	Ryan Clark	S	$2,217,780	1.91%	2.21%	-0.30%
15	DeShea Townsend	CB	$1,976,820	1.70%	2.07%	-0.36%
16	Jeff Reed	K	$1,963,613	1.69%	1.94%	-0.24%
17	Lawrence Timmons	LB	$1,754,510	1.51%	1.79%	-0.27%
18	Santonio Holmes	WR	$1,741,920	1.50%	1.65%	-0.15%
19	Heath Miller	TE	$1,725,760	1.49%	1.54%	-0.05%
20	Charlie Batch	QB	$1,628,388	1.40%	1.46%	-0.06%
21	James Harrison	LB	$1,550,470	1.34%	1.36%	-0.03%
22	Justin Hartwig	OL	$1,493,260	1.29%	1.28%	0.01%
23	Chris Hoke	DT	$1,481,240	1.28%	1.20%	0.08%
24	Chris Kemoeatu	OL	$1,423,240	1.23%	1.14%	0.08%
25	Nate Washington	WR	$1,419,880	1.22%	1.08%	0.14%
26	Rashard Mendenhall	RB	$1,190,000	1.03%	1.03%	-0.01%
27	Mewelde Moore	RB	$1,105,760	0.95%	0.99%	-0.03%
28	Travis Kirschke	DE	$983,360	0.85%	0.93%	-0.08%
29	Trai Essex	OL	$932,280	0.80%	0.88%	-0.08%
30	Tyrone Carter	S	$845,253	0.73%	0.84%	-0.11%

	PIT	S.B. AVG.	PIT +/-
Top 1	6.87%	9.37%	-2.50%
Top 2	12.82%	16.31%	-3.49%
Top 3	18.70%	22.32%	-3.63%
Top 5	30.21%	32.57%	-2.36%
Top 10	50.26%	50.43%	-0.17%
Top 15	62.74%	62.36%	0.38%
Top 20	70.34%	70.66%	-0.31%
Top 25	76.69%	76.72%	-0.03%
Top 30	81.05%	81.36%	-0.31%
Team	97.44%	100.45%	-3.01%

#	2009 Saints	Position	CAP HIT	% of Cap	S.B. AVG.	Difference
1	Drew Brees	QB	$10,660,400	8.67%	9.35%	-0.68%
2	Reggie Bush	RB	$10,589,940	8.61%	6.93%	1.68%
3	Will Smith	DE	$9,421,666	7.66%	5.97%	1.69%
4	Jammal Brown	OL	$6,273,330	5.10%	5.33%	-0.23%
5	Jabari Greer	CB	$5,950,000	4.84%	4.84%	-0.01%
6	Charles Grant	DE	$5,313,333	4.32%	4.34%	-0.02%
7	Sedrick Ellis	DT	$4,866,000	3.96%	3.78%	0.18%
8	Jon Vilma	LB	$4,500,000	3.66%	3.54%	0.11%
9	Scott Fujita	LB	$4,005,070	3.26%	3.23%	0.02%
10	Marques Colston	WR	$3,681,250	2.99%	2.95%	0.04%
11	Jeremy Shockey	TE	$3,226,820	2.62%	2.78%	-0.15%
12	Scott Shanle	LB	$3,200,000	2.60%	2.59%	0.01%
13	Jonathan Goodwin	OL	$3,183,333	2.59%	2.39%	0.20%
14	Bobby McCray	DE	$2,900,000	2.36%	2.21%	0.15%
15	Duece McAllister	RB	$2,836,665	2.31%	2.07%	0.24%
16	Jahri Evans	OL	$2,795,510	2.27%	1.94%	0.34%
17	Randall Gay	CB	$2,762,500	2.25%	1.79%	0.46%
18	Jamar Nesbit	OL	$2,697,388	2.19%	1.65%	0.54%
19	Brian Young	DT	$2,668,617	2.17%	1.54%	0.63%
20	Jon Stinchcomb	OL	$2,500,000	2.03%	1.46%	0.57%
21	Devery Henderson	WR	$2,375,000	1.93%	1.36%	0.57%
22	Mark Simoneau	LB	$2,253,334	1.83%	1.28%	0.55%
23	Kendrick Clancy	DT	$2,033,334	1.65%	1.20%	0.45%
24	Hollis Thomas	DT	$1,910,000	1.55%	1.14%	0.41%
25	Robert Meachem	WR	$1,866,000	1.52%	1.08%	0.44%
26	Mark Brunell	QB	$1,805,000	1.47%	1.03%	0.43%
27	Darren Sharper	S	$1,704,550	1.39%	0.99%	0.40%
28	Kevin Kaesviharn	S	$1,600,000	1.30%	0.93%	0.38%
29	Malcolm Jenkins	S	$1,570,000	1.28%	0.88%	0.40%
30	Lance Moore	WR	$1,549,680	1.26%	0.84%	0.42%

	NO	S.B. AVG.	NO +/-
Top 1	8.67%	9.37%	-0.70%
Top 2	17.28%	16.31%	0.97%
Top 3	24.94%	22.32%	2.61%
Top 5	34.87%	32.57%	2.30%
Top 10	53.06%	50.43%	2.63%
Top 15	65.53%	62.36%	3.18%
Top 20	76.45%	70.66%	5.79%
Top 25	84.93%	76.72%	8.22%
Top 30	91.62%	81.36%	10.26%
Team	114.24%	100.45%	13.79%

#	2010 Packers	Position	CAP HIT	% of Cap S.B. AVG.	Difference	S.B. AVG.
1	Nick Collins	S	$10,950,000	9.35%	Top 1	9.37%
2	Ryan Pickett	DT	$8,437,500	6.93%	Top 2	16.31%
3	Charles Woodson	CB	$8,400,000	5.97%	Top 3	22.32%
4	B.J. Raji	DT	$7,890,000	5.33%	Top 5	32.57%
5	Chad Clifton	OL	$7,500,000	4.84%	Top 10	50.43%
6	A.J. Hawk	LB	$6,995,000	4.34%	Top 15	62.36%
7	Aaron Rodgers	QB	$6,500,000	3.78%	Top 20	70.66%
8	Donald Driver	WR	$5,959,375	3.54%	Top 25	76.72%
9	Ryan Grant	RB	$5,765,625	3.23%	Top 30	81.36%
10	Greg Jennings	WR	$5,537,500	2.95%		
11	Nick Barnett	LB	$5,100,000	2.78%	Team	100.45%
12	Tramon Williams	CB	$5,043,000	2.59%		
13	Cullen Jenkins	DE	$4,570,000	2.39%		
14	Brandon Chillar	LB	$4,150,000	2.21%		
15	Desmond Bishop	LB	$3,667,550	2.07%		
16	Mark Tauscher	OL	$3,525,000	1.94%		
17	Clay Matthews	LB	$3,100,000	1.79%		
18	Scott Wells	OL	$2,700,000	1.65%		
19	Donald Lee	TE	$2,275,000	1.54%		
20	Brady Poppinga	LB	$2,212,500	1.46%		
21	Justin Harrell	DT	$2,150,875	1.36%		
22	Jason Spitz	OL	$1,760,000	1.28%		
23	Daryn Colledge	OL	$1,759,500	1.20%		
24	Atari Bigby	S	$1,699,500	1.14%		
25	Al Harris	CB	$1,523,529	1.08%		
26	Jarrett Bush	CB	$1,433,333	1.03%		
27	Bryan Bulaga	OL	$1,290,000	0.99%		
28	James Jones	WR	$1,286,564	0.93%		
29	John Kuhn	RB	$1,176,000	0.88%		
30	Mason Crosby	K	$1,124,489	0.84%		

	2011 Giants	Position	CAP HIT	% of Cap	S.B. AVG.	Difference
1	Eli Manning	QB	$14,100,000	11.75%	9.35%	2.40%
2	Corey Webster	CB	$7,845,000	6.54%	6.93%	-0.39%
3	Chris Canty	DT	$7,200,000	6.00%	5.97%	0.03%
4	Kareem McKenzie	OL	$5,300,000	4.42%	5.33%	-0.91%
5	Michael Boley	LB	$5,150,000	4.29%	4.84%	-0.55%
6	Justin Tuck	DE	$5,100,000	4.25%	4.34%	-0.09%
7	Brandon Jacobs	RB	$5,000,000	4.17%	3.78%	0.39%
8	David Diehl	OL	$4,787,500	3.99%	3.54%	0.45%
9	Jason Pierre-Paul	DE	$4,698,000	3.92%	3.23%	0.68%
10	Chris Snee	OL	$3,750,000	3.13%	2.95%	0.18%
11	Osi Umenyiora	DE	$3,625,000	3.02%	2.78%	0.24%
12	Antrel Rolle	S	$3,600,000	3.00%	2.59%	0.41%
13	Mathias Kiwanuka	DE	$3,050,000	2.54%	2.39%	0.15%
14	Sage Rosenfels	QB	$3,000,000	2.50%	2.21%	0.29%
15	Ahmad Bradshaw	RB	$2,750,000	2.29%	2.07%	0.22%
16	David Bass	OL	$2,700,000	2.25%	1.94%	0.31%
17	Aaron Ross	CB	$2,322,000	1.94%	1.79%	0.15%
18	Hakeem Nicks	WR	$1,605,000	1.34%	1.65%	-0.32%
19	Kenny Phillips	S	$1,603,750	1.34%	1.54%	-0.20%
20	Mario Manningham	WR	$1,554,250	1.30%	1.46%	-0.17%
21	Kevin Boothe	OL	$1,500,000	1.25%	1.36%	-0.11%
22	Lawrence Tynes	K	$1,500,000	1.25%	1.28%	-0.03%
23	Prince Amukamara	CB	$1,487,436	1.24%	1.20%	0.04%
24	Rocky Bernard	DT	$1,300,000	1.08%	1.14%	-0.06%
25	Shaun O'Hara	OL	$1,250,000	1.04%	1.08%	-0.04%
26	Deon Grant	S	$1,160,000	0.97%	1.03%	-0.07%
27	Adam Koets	OL	$950,000	0.79%	0.99%	-0.19%
28	Clint Sintim	LB	$927,000	0.77%	0.93%	-0.15%
29	Zak DeOssie	LS	$916,666	0.76%	0.88%	-0.12%
30	Danny Ware	RB	$910,000	0.76%	0.84%	-0.08%

	NYG	S.B. AVG.	NYG +/-
Top 1	11.75%	9.37%	2.38%
Top 2	18.29%	16.31%	1.98%
Top 3	24.29%	22.32%	1.96%
Top 5	33.00%	32.57%	0.43%
Top 10	52.44%	50.43%	2.02%
Top 15	65.80%	62.36%	3.44%
Top 20	73.95%	70.66%	3.30%
Top 25	79.81%	76.72%	3.10%
Top 30	83.87%	81.36%	2.50%
Team	113.13%	100.45%	12.68%

	2012 Ravens	Position	CAP HIT	% of Cap	S.B. AVG.	Difference
1	Terrell Suggs	OLB	$11,520,000	9.55%	9.35%	0.20%
2	Haloti Ngata	DT	$10,400,000	8.62%	6.93%	1.70%
3	Ed Reed	S	$8,500,000	7.05%	5.97%	1.08%
4	Joe Flacco	QB	$8,000,000	6.63%	5.33%	1.31%
5	Anquan Boldin	WR	$7,531,250	6.24%	4.84%	1.40%
6	Ray Lewis	ILB	$6,850,000	5.68%	4.34%	1.34%
7	Ray Rice	RB	$5,000,000	4.15%	3.78%	0.37%
8	Vonta Leach	FB	$4,334,418	3.59%	3.54%	0.05%
9	Willis McGahee	RB	$3,750,000	3.11%	3.23%	-0.12%
10	Marshal Yanda	OL	$3,650,930	3.03%	2.95%	0.08%
11	Bryant McKinnie	OL	$3,202,325	2.66%	2.78%	-0.12%
12	Domonique Foxworth	CB	$3,000,000	2.49%	2.59%	-0.11%
13	Chris Carr	CB	$2,850,000	2.36%	2.39%	-0.03%
14	Lardarius Webb	CB	$2,619,185	2.17%	2.21%	-0.04%
15	Sam Koch	P	$2,204,960	1.83%	2.07%	-0.24%
16	Michael Oher	OL	$2,039,650	1.69%	1.94%	-0.25%
17	Bernard Pollard	S	$1,950,000	1.62%	1.79%	-0.17%
18	Dannell Ellerbe	ILB	$1,931,650	1.60%	1.65%	-0.05%
19	Cary Williams	CB	$1,929,945	1.60%	1.54%	0.06%
20	Jameel McClain	LB	$1,902,790	1.58%	1.46%	0.12%
21	Jimmy Smith	CB	$1,700,026	1.41%	1.36%	0.05%
22	Matt Birk	OL	$1,625,930	1.35%	1.28%	0.07%
23	Jacoby Jones	WR	$1,602,480	1.33%	1.20%	0.13%
24	Bobbie Williams	OL	$1,325,000	1.10%	1.14%	-0.05%
25	Corey Graham	CB	$1,304,340	1.08%	1.08%	0.00%
26	Lee Evans	WR	$1,232,500	1.02%	1.03%	-0.01%
27	Brendon Ayanbadejo	LB	$1,059,573	0.88%	0.99%	-0.11%
28	Ryan McBean	DE	$1,003,100	0.83%	0.93%	-0.09%
29	Courtney Upshaw	OLB	$963,036	0.80%	0.88%	-0.08%
30	Paul Kruger	DE	$867,790	0.72%	0.84%	-0.12%

	BAL	S.B. AVG.	BAL +/-
Top 1	9.55%	9.37%	0.18%
Top 2	18.18%	16.31%	1.87%
Top 3	25.22%	22.32%	2.90%
Top 5	38.10%	32.57%	5.53%
Top 10	57.66%	50.43%	7.23%
Top 15	69.17%	62.36%	6.81%
Top 20	77.25%	70.66%	6.60%
Top 25	83.52%	76.72%	6.80%
Top 30	87.77%	81.36%	6.41%
Team	105.63%	100.45%	5.18%

#	2013 Seahawks	Position	CAP HIT	% of Cap	S.B. AVG.	Difference
1	Zach Miller	TE	$11,000,000	8.94%	9.35%	-0.41%
2	Sidney Rice	WR	$9,700,000	7.89%	6.93%	0.96%
3	Russell Okung	LT	$9,540,000	7.76%	5.97%	1.79%
4	Marshawn Lynch	RB	$8,500,000	6.91%	5.33%	1.58%
5	Chris Clemons	43DE	$8,166,666	6.64%	4.84%	1.79%
6	Red Bryant	43DE	$7,600,000	6.18%	4.34%	1.84%
7	Max Unger	C	$6,000,000	4.88%	3.78%	1.10%
8	Brandon Mebane	43DT	$5,200,000	4.23%	3.54%	0.68%
9	Percy Harvin	WR	$4,900,000	3.98%	3.23%	0.75%
10	Michael Bennett	43DE	$4,800,000	3.90%	2.95%	0.95%
11	Breno Giacomini	RT	$4,750,000	3.86%	2.78%	1.09%
12	Matt Flynn	QB	$4,000,000	3.25%	2.59%	0.66%
13	Kam Chancellor	S	$3,878,404	3.15%	2.39%	0.76%
14	Cliff Avril	43DE	$3,750,000	3.05%	2.21%	0.84%
15	Paul McQuistan	LG	$3,375,000	2.74%	2.07%	0.68%
16	Earl Thomas	S	$2,898,215	2.36%	1.94%	0.42%
17	James Carpenter	LG	$2,084,046	1.69%	1.79%	-0.09%
18	Bruce Irvin	OLB	$1,931,546	1.57%	1.65%	-0.08%
19	Heath Farwell	ILB	$1,666,666	1.36%	1.54%	-0.18%
20	Jon Ryan	P	$1,405,000	1.14%	1.46%	-0.32%
21	Antoine Winfield	CB	$1,000,000	0.81%	1.36%	-0.55%
22	Bobby Wagner	ILB	$979,045	0.80%	1.28%	-0.48%
23	Chris Garagos	S	$955,000	0.78%	1.20%	-0.42%
24	O'Brien Schofield	34OLB	$900,000	0.73%	1.14%	-0.41%
25	Golden Tate	WR	$880,000	0.72%	1.08%	-0.37%
26	Tarvaris Jackson	QB	$840,000	0.68%	1.03%	-0.35%
27	Brandon Browner	CB	$773,756	0.63%	0.99%	-0.36%
28	Clint Gresham	LS	$767,500	0.62%	0.93%	-0.30%
29	Leon Washington	RB	$750,000	0.61%	0.88%	-0.27%
30	Russell Wilson	QB	$681,085	0.55%	0.84%	-0.28%

	SEA	S.B. AVG.	SEA +/-
Top 1	8.94%	9.37%	-0.43%
Top 2	16.83%	16.31%	0.52%
Top 3	24.59%	22.32%	2.26%
Top 5	38.14%	32.57%	5.57%
Top 10	61.31%	50.43%	10.88%
Top 15	77.37%	62.36%	15.01%
Top 20	85.48%	70.66%	14.83%
Top 25	89.32%	76.72%	12.60%
Top 30	92.42%	81.36%	11.05%
Team	108.29%	100.45%	7.84%

#	2014 Patriots	Position	CAP HIT	% of Cap	S.B. AVG.	Difference
1	Tom Brady	QB	$14,800,000	11.13%	9.35%	1.78%
2	Vince Wilfork	DT	$7,588,333	5.71%	6.93%	-1.22%
3	Aaron Hernandez	TE	$7,500,000	5.64%	5.97%	-0.33%
4	Jerod Mayo	ILB	$7,287,500	5.48%	5.33%	0.15%
5	Darrelle Revis	CB	$7,000,000	5.26%	4.84%	0.42%
6	Rob Gronkowski	TE	$5,400,000	4.06%	4.34%	-0.28%
7	Devin McCourty	S	$5,115,000	3.85%	3.78%	0.07%
8	Danny Amendola	WR	$4,700,000	3.53%	3.54%	-0.01%
9	Logan Mankins	OG	$4,250,000	3.20%	3.23%	-0.04%
10	Dan Connolly	LG	$4,083,334	3.07%	2.95%	0.12%
11	Sebastian Vollmer	RT	$4,083,333	3.07%	2.78%	0.29%
12	Stephen Gostowski	K	$3,800,000	2.86%	2.59%	0.26%
13	Kyle Arrington	CB	$3,625,000	2.73%	2.39%	0.33%
14	Matt Slater	WR/ST	$2,933,334	2.21%	2.21%	-0.01%
15	Rob Ninkovich	43DE	$2,850,000	2.14%	2.07%	0.08%
16	Julian Edelman	WR	$2,750,000	2.07%	1.94%	0.13%
17	Nate Solder	LT	$2,717,429	2.04%	1.79%	0.26%
18	Brandon Browner	CB	$2,715,706	2.04%	1.65%	0.39%
19	Chandler Jones	43DE	$2,229,136	1.68%	1.54%	0.14%
20	Dont'a Hightower	ILB	$2,106,546	1.58%	1.46%	0.12%
21	Brandon Lafell	WR	$2,000,000	1.50%	1.36%	0.14%
22	Ryan Wendell	C	$1,625,000	1.22%	1.28%	-0.06%
23	Michael Hoomanawanui	TE	$1,407,500	1.06%	1.20%	-0.14%
24	Dominique Easley	DT	$1,327,918	1.00%	1.14%	-0.15%
25	Tavon Wilson	S	$1,150,335	0.86%	1.08%	-0.22%
26	Shane Vereen	RB	$1,101,275	0.83%	1.03%	-0.21%
27	Patrick Chung	S	$1,070,000	0.80%	0.99%	-0.18%
28	Isaac Sopoaga	DT	$1,000,000	0.75%	0.93%	-0.17%
29	Steven Ridley	RB	$939,750	0.71%	0.88%	-0.17%
30	Jamie Collins	43OLB	$854,773	0.64%	0.84%	-0.19%

	NE	S.B. AVG.	NE +/-
Top 1	11.13%	9.37%	1.76%
Top 2	16.83%	16.31%	0.52%
Top 3	22.47%	22.32%	0.15%
Top 5	33.21%	32.57%	0.65%
Top 10	50.92%	50.43%	0.49%
Top 15	63.92%	62.36%	1.56%
Top 20	73.33%	70.66%	2.68%
Top 25	78.98%	76.72%	2.26%
Top 30	82.72%	81.36%	1.35%
Team	99.82%	100.45%	-0.63%

	2015 Broncos	Position	CAP HIT	% of Cap	S.B. AVG.	Difference
1	Peyton Manning	QB	$17,500,000	12.21%	9.35%	2.87%
2	Demaryius Thomas	WR	$13,200,000	9.21%	6.93%	2.29%
3	Ryan Clady	LT	$10,600,000	7.40%	5.97%	1.43%
4	Von Miller	34OLB	$9,754,000	6.81%	5.33%	1.48%
5	DeMarcus Ware	34OLB	$8,666,666	6.05%	4.84%	1.20%
6	T.J. Ward	S	$7,514,706	5.24%	4.34%	0.91%
7	Aqib Talib	CB	$6,968,750	4.86%	3.78%	1.09%
8	Louis Vasquez	RG	$6,250,000	4.36%	3.54%	0.82%
9	Emmanuel Sanders	WR	$5,850,000	4.08%	3.23%	0.85%
10	Chris Harris, Jr.	CB	$3,000,000	2.09%	2.95%	-0.86%
11	Evan Mathis	LG	$2,921,875	2.04%	2.78%	-0.74%
12	Owen Daniels	TE	$2,750,000	1.92%	2.59%	-0.67%
13	Britton Colquitt	P	$2,350,000	1.64%	2.39%	-0.75%
14	Virgil Green	TE	$2,200,000	1.54%	2.21%	-0.68%
15	Sylvester Williams	34DT	$2,067,750	1.44%	2.07%	-0.62%
16	Antonio Smith	34DE	$2,000,000	1.40%	1.94%	-0.54%
17	Vance Walker	34DE	$1,750,000	1.22%	1.79%	-0.57%
18	Darian Stewart	S	$1,750,000	1.22%	1.65%	-0.43%
19	Shane Ray	34OLB	$1,657,981	1.16%	1.54%	-0.38%
20	David Bruton	S	$1,650,000	1.15%	1.46%	-0.31%
21	Malik Jackson	34DE	$1,595,403	1.11%	1.36%	-0.25%
22	Bradley Roby	CB	$1,580,120	1.10%	1.28%	-0.18%
23	Danny Trevathan	ILB	$1,568,018	1.09%	1.20%	-0.11%
24	Andre Caldwell	WR	$1,550,000	1.08%	1.14%	-0.06%
25	Shelley Smith	LG	$1,421,875	0.99%	1.08%	-0.09%
26	Ryan Harris	LT	$1,420,000	0.99%	1.03%	-0.04%
27	Derek Wolfe	34DE	$1,397,881	0.98%	0.99%	-0.01%
28	Brock Osweiler	QB	$1,118,943	0.78%	0.93%	-0.14%
29	Ronnie Hillman	RB	$942,708	0.66%	0.88%	-0.22%
30	Aaron Brewer	LS	$845,000	0.59%	0.84%	-0.25%

	DEN	S.B. AVG.	DEN +/-
Top 1	12.21%	9.37%	2.84%
Top 2	21.43%	16.31%	5.12%
Top 3	28.82%	22.32%	6.50%
Top 5	41.68%	32.57%	9.11%
Top 10	62.33%	50.43%	11.90%
Top 15	70.91%	62.36%	8.55%
Top 20	77.05%	70.66%	6.40%
Top 25	82.44%	76.72%	5.72%
Top 30	86.43%	81.36%	5.07%
Team	101.62%	100.45%	1.18%

#	2016 Patriots	Position	CAP HIT	% of Cap	S.B. AVG.	Difference			NE	S.B. AVG.	NE +/-
1	Tom Brady	QB	$13,764,705	8.87%	9.35%	-0.48%	Top 1		8.87%	9.37%	-0.48%
2	Nate Solder	OT	$10,322,666	6.65%	6.93%	-0.28%	Top 2		15.51%	16.31%	-0.76%
3	Dont'a Hightower	ILB	$7,751,000	4.99%	5.97%	-0.98%	Top 3		20.51%	22.32%	-1.74%
4	Jabaal Sheard	43DE	$6,812,500	4.39%	5.33%	-0.94%	Top 5		29.16%	32.57%	-3.26%
5	Rob Gronkowski	TE	$6,618,750	4.26%	4.84%	-0.58%	Top 10		46.70%	50.43%	-3.56%
6	Marcus Cannon	RT	$6,154,168	3.96%	4.34%	-0.37%	Top 15		60.13%	62.36%	-2.16%
7	Chris Hogan	WR	$5,500,000	3.54%	3.78%	-0.24%	Top 20		68.62%	70.66%	-2.05%
8	Sebastian Vollmer	OT	$5,208,334	3.35%	3.54%	-0.19%	Top 25		74.51%	76.72%	-2.23%
9	Devin McCourty	S	$5,195,000	3.35%	3.23%	0.11%	Top 30		78.73%	81.36%	-2.67%
10	Martellus Bennett	TE	$5,185,000	3.34%	2.95%	0.39%					
11	Rob Ninkovich	DE/OLB	$4,750,000	3.06%	2.78%	0.28%	Team		92.70%	100.45%	-7.75%
12	Julian Edelman	WR	$4,421,875	2.85%	2.59%	0.25%					
13	Jerod Mayo	ILB	$4,400,000	2.83%	2.39%	0.44%					
14	Stephen Gostowski	K	$4,100,00	2.64%	2.21%	0.43%					
15	Patrick Chung	S	$3,187,500	2.05%	2.07%	-0.01%					
16	Danny Amendola	WR	$2,916,666	1.88%	1.94%	-0.06%					
17	Dominique Easley	43DT	$2,899,795	1.87%	1.79%	0.08%					
18	Alan Branch	43DT	$2,750,000	1.77%	1.65%	0.12%					
19	Chris Long	43DE	$2,375,000	1.53%	1.54%	-0.01%					
20	Shea McClellin	43OLB	$2,233,333	1.44%	1.46%	-0.02%					
21	Matt Slater	WR/ST	$2,066,668	1.33%	1.36%	-0.03%					
22	Logan Ryan	CB	$1,811,813	1.17%	1.28%	-0.11%					
23	Duron Harmon	S	$1,804,400	1.16%	1.20%	-0.04%					
24	Jonathan Freeny	43OLB	$1,737,500	1.12%	1.14%	-0.02%					
25	Malcom Brown	43DT	$1,730,280	1.11%	1.08%	0.03%					
26	Ryan Allen	P	$1,700,000	1.09%	1.03%	0.06%					
27	Michael Floyd	WR	$1,291,765	0.83%	0.99%	-0.15%					
28	Brandon Bolden	RB	$1,272,500	0.82%	0.93%	-0.11%					
29	Nate Ebner	S/ST	$1,200,000	0.77%	0.88%	-0.11%					
30	Dion Lewis	RB	$1,087,500	0.70%	0.84%	-0.14%					

Positional Spending - Offense

Year	Team	Offense	%	QB	%	RB	%	WR	%	TE	%	OL	%
1994	49ers	20,590,636	59.50%	4,828,400	13.95%	4,748,790	13.72%	4,748,790	13.72%	1,255,950	3.63%	7,243,080	20.93%
1995	Cowboys	19,237,090	51.85%	3,124,850	8.42%	5,553,700	14.97%	3,050,890	8.22%	1,979,493	5.34%	5,528,157	14.90%
1996	Packers	20,899,615	51.28%	4,878,940	11.97%	2,634,506	6.46%	4,782,998	11.74%	2,837,560	6.96%	5,755,611	14.12%
1997	Broncos	17,306,790	41.75%	2,679,611	6.46%	2,573,706	6.21%	3,890,246	9.38%	1,948,700	4.70%	6,214,527	14.99%
1998	Broncos	26,220,251	50.05%	3,742,131	7.14%	4,899,041	9.35%	5,699,150	10.88%	2,937,708	5.61%	8,942,221	17.07%
1999	Rams	31,391,298	54.80%	4,514,210	7.88%	7,160,870	12.50%	7,858,199	13.72%	1,265,033	2.21%	10,592,986	18.49%
2000	Ravens	30,428,102	48.94%	3,611,460	5.81%	4,442,675	7.15%	6,059,173	9.75%	3,677,056	5.91%	12,637,738	20.33%
2001	Patriots	29,149,731	43.25%	8,106,584	12.03%	3,408,860	5.06%	6,859,113	10.18%	1,275,761	1.89%	9,499,413	14.09%
2002	Bucs	33,799,575	47.54%	8,409,270	11.83%	3,967,311	5.58%	7,816,127	10.99%	3,090,649	4.35%	10,516,218	14.79%
2003	Patriots	31,408,963	41.87%	4,686,183	6.25%	5,475,006	7.30%	6,011,757	8.01%	2,734,016	3.65%	12,502,001	16.67%
2004	Patriots	28,663,219	35.45%	5,980,450	7.40%	5,205,129	6.44%	6,796,881	8.41%	4,204,406	5.20%	6,476,353	8.01%
2005	Steelers	37,310,735	43.64%	6,005,085	7.02%	6,192,170	7.24%	5,213,712	6.10%	3,673,102	4.30%	16,226,665	18.98%
2006	Colts	55,426,361	54.34%	11,021,748	10.81%	4,858,360	4.76%	17,963,194	17.61%	2,552,223	2.50%	19,040,835	18.67%
2007	Giants	54,799,833	50.28%	11,667,034	10.70%	7,145,206	6.56%	13,061,354	11.98%	4,895,167	4.49%	18,031,072	16.54%
2008	Steelers	58,631,894	50.54%	10,423,641	8.99%	7,467,591	6.44%	11,397,409	9.83%	3,256,303	2.81%	26,086,950	22.49%
2009	Saints	66,999,234	54.47%	12,465,400	10.13%	16,440,646	13.37%	11,662,972	9.48%	5,622,220	4.57%	20,807,996	16.92%
2010	Packers	56,157,923		6,986,043		9,674,264		14,280,339		3,815,032		21,402,244	
2011	Giants	66,737,235	55.61%	18,050,000	15.04%	10,661,988	8.88%	8,917,518	7.43%	2,891,250	2.41%	26,216,479	21.85%
2012	Ravens	43,042,489	35.69%	8,491,327	7.04%	12,358,075	10.25%	10,800,136	8.96%	9,137,866	7.58%	9,137,866	7.58%
2013	Seahawks	75,563,517	61.43%	5,521,085	4.49%	11,549,653	9.39%	17,478,142	14.21%	12,778,788	10.39%	28,235,849	22.96%
2014	Patriots	69,726,686	52.43%	15,613,305	11.74%	4,620,691	3.47%	14,398,193	10.83%	15,248,859	11.47%	19,845,638	14.92%
2015	Broncos	76,431,159	53.34%	19,067,139	13.31%	2,155,242	1.50%	23,083,075	16.11%	5,970,401	4.17%	26,155,302	18.25%
2016	Patriots	80,302,503	51.72%	15,259,304	9.83%	5,075,025	3.27%	19,814,674	12.76%	13,945,867	8.98%	26,207,633	16.88%
	Average		49.54%		9.47%		7.72%		10.92%		5.14%		16.84%

Positional Spending - Defense

Year	Team	Defense	%	DT	%	DE	%	LB	%	S	%	CB	%
1994	49ers	10,554,040	30.50%	1,008,150	2.91%	3,763,724	10.88%	2,712,466	7.84%	3,069,700	8.87%	2,436,200	7.04%
1995	Cowboys	17,518,208	47.22%	3,826,400	10.31%	4,579,750	12.34%	2,712,200	7.31%	1,386,100	3.74%	5,013,758	13.51%
1996	Packers	17,292,819	42.43%	2,326,255	5.71%	5,968,866	14.65%	4,197,193	10.30%	2,826,960	6.94%	1,973,545	4.84%
1997	Broncos	20,466,192	49.37%	3,547,425	8.56%	4,855,850	11.71%	4,394,200	10.60%	3,284,793	7.92%	4,383,924	10.58%
1998	Broncos	22,367,610	42.70%	1,318,556	2.52%	6,489,203	12.39%	5,466,795	10.44%	3,986,817	7.61%	5,106,239	9.75%
1999	Rams	23,326,165	40.72%	3,914,668	6.83%	4,606,953	8.04%	6,150,260	10.74%	3,819,074	6.67%	4,835,210	8.44%
2000	Ravens	24,502,526	39.41%	4,235,392	6.81%	5,323,393	8.56%	5,676,560	9.13%	4,721,346	7.59%	4,545,835	7.31%
2001	Patriots	33,794,935	50.14%	2,132,733	3.16%	3,590,011	5.33%	15,891,303	23.58%	5,181,061	7.69%	6,999,827	10.38%
2002	Bucs	34,449,174	48.45%	9,219,928	12.97%	9,518,865	13.39%	7,036,161	9.90%	4,337,036	6.10%	4,337,183	6.10%
2003	Patriots	38,516,661	51.35%	4,962,900	6.62%	3,591,898	4.79%	14,298,190	19.06%	4,924,283	6.57%	10,739,390	14.32%
2004	Patriots	45,256,049	56.16%	3,158,047	3.92%	6,555,535	8.14%	14,468,986	17.96%	7,897,723	9.80%	13,175,757	16.35%
2005	Steelers	38,528,153	45.06%	2,772,736	3.24%	12,841,503	15.02%	11,718,735	13.71%	4,461,542	5.22%	6,733,637	7.88%
2006	Colts	41,852,032	41.03%	12,954,110	12.70%	13,674,710	13.41%	8,287,706	8.13%	2,416,706	2.37%	4,518,801	4.43%
2007	Giants	50,311,683	46.16%	7,924,376	7.27%	13,594,486	12.47%	13,865,867	12.72%	3,411,683	3.13%	11,119,645	10.20%
2008	Steelers	46,255,167	39.88%	7,059,283	6.09%	10,239,218	8.83%	10,893,407	9.39%	10,505,707	9.06%	7,557,551	6.52%
2009	Saints	70,440,490	57.27%	12,309,089	10.01%	18,929,019	15.39%	16,824,545	13.68%	7,431,939	6.04%	14,944,899	12.15%
2010	Packers	74,351,002		19,458,963		6,144,953		25,865,103		4,824,033		18,057,950	
2011	Giants	65,279,077	54.40%	12,153,550	10.13%	18,579,159	15.48%	9,045,605	7.54%	8,990,411	7.49%	15,593,686	12.99%
2012	Ravens	51,900,000	43.03%	13,356,519	11.08%	1,850,668	1.53%	19,766,666	16.39%	11,183,333	9.27%	5,742,814	4.76%
2013	Seahawks	53,698,962	43.66%	7,121,284	5.79%	27,538,319	22.39%	5,549,313	4.51%	8,936,207	7.27%	4,553,839	3.70%
2014	Patriots	58,011,790	43.62%	12,206,615	9.18%	6,222,932	4.68%	13,369,809	10.05%	11,017,180	8.28%	15,195,254	11.43%
2015	Broncos	59,206,275	41.32%	3,129,839	2.18%	6,743,284	4.71%	24,762,516	17.28%	10,914,706	7.62%	13,655,930	9.53%
2016	Patriots	58,538,466	37.70%	8,019,030	5.16%	15,065,176	9.70%	17,924,710	11.54%	12,755,434	8.22%	4,774,116	3.07%
	Average		45.07%		6.96%		10.63%		11.90%		6.98%		8.88%
	4-3 D		45.07%		7.45%		11.51%		11.00%		6.62%		8.84%
	3-4 D		45.09%		5.30%		7.64%		14.95%		8.19%		9.01%

Super Bowl Top Positional Cap Hits

Quarterback

Year	Cap Hit	Player	Age	Cap Hit	% of Cap
1994	1	Steve Young	33	$4,525,000	13.08%
1995	2	Troy Aikman	29	$2,493,500	6.72%
1996	1	Brett Favre	27	$4,175,720	10.25%
1997	3	John Elway	37	$2,141,475	5.17%
1998	3	John Elway	38	$2,624,315	5.01%
1999	5	Trent Green	29	$3,128,290	5.46%
2000	7	Tony Banks	27	$2,263,140	3.64%
2001	1	Drew Bledsoe	29	$6,936,391	10.29%
2002	2	Brad Johnson	34	$6,803,150	9.57%
2003	4	Tom Brady	26	$3,323,450	4.43%
2004	2	Tom Brady	27	$5,062,950	6.26%
2005	4	Ben Roethlisberger	23	$4,225,090	4.94%
2006	1	Peyton Manning	30	$10,571,068	10.36%
2007	1	Eli Manning	26	$10,046,666	9.22%
2008	1	Ben Roethlisberger	26	$7,971,920	6.87%
2009	1	Drew Brees	30	$10,660,400	8.67%
2010	7	Aaron Rodgers	27	$6,500,000	N/A
2011	1	Eli Manning	30	$14,100,000	11.75%
2012	4	Joe Flacco	27	$8,000,000	6.63%
2013	12	Matt Flynn	28	$4,000,000	3.25%
2014	1	Tom Brady	37	$14,800,000	11.13%
2015	1	Peyton Manning	39	$17,500,000	12.21%
2016	1	Tom Brady	39	$13,764,705	8.87%
	2.9		30.3	$7,200,749	7.90%

Running Back

Year	Cap Hit	Player	Age	Cap Hit	% of Cap
1994	12	Ricky Watters	25	$866,000	2.50%
1995	1	Emmitt Smith	26	$3,400,600	9.17%
1996	8	Edgar Bennett	27	$1,300,480	3.19%
1997	16	Terrell Davis	25	$815,246	1.97%
1998	5	Terrell Davis	26	$2,393,036	4.57%
1999	1	Marshall Faulk	26	$4,309,370	7.52%
2000	9	Jamal Lewis	21	$1,878,000	3.02%
2001	21	Robert Edwards	27	$724,800	1.08%
2002	9	Mike Alstott	29	$1,895,176	2.67%
2003	9	Antowain Smith	31	$2,305,600	3.07%
2004	11	Antowain Smith	32	$2,025,000	2.50%
2005	9	Jerome Bettis	33	$2,400,000	2.81%
2006	11	Dominic Rhodes	27	$3,038,960	2.98%
2007	15	Tiki Barber	32	$2,000,000	1.83%
2008	9	Willie Parker	28	$4,091,340	3.53%
2009	2	Reggie Bush	24	$10,589,940	8.61%
2010	9	Ryan Grant	28	$5,765,625	
2011	7	Brandon Jacobs	29	$5,000,000	4.17%
2012	7	Ray Rice	25	$5,000,000	4.15%
2013	4	Marshawn Lynch	27	$8,500,000	6.91%
2014	26	Shane Vereen	25	$1,101,275	0.83%
2015	29	Ronnie Hillman	24	$942,708	0.66%
2016	29	Brandon Bolden	26	$1,272,500	0.82%
	11.3		27.1	$3,113,724	3.57%

Wide Receiver

Year	Cap Hit	Player	Age	Cap Hit	% of Cap
1994	2	Jerry Rice	32	$2,963,333	8.56%
1995	5	Michael Irvin	29	$1,972,440	5.32%
1996	4	Robert Brooks	26	$1,700,900	4.17%
1997	8	Anthony Miller	32	$1,325,000	3.20%
1998	9	Anthony Miller	33	$1,450,000	2.77%
1999	6	Isaac Bruce	27	$2,925,000	5.11%
2000	11	Jermaine Lewis	26	$1,668,453	2.68%
2001	5	Terry Glenn	27	$2,630,179	3.90%
2002	6	Keyshawn Johnson	30	$3,356,592	4.72%
2003	7	Troy Brown	32	$2,451,433	3.27%
2004	5	Troy Brown	33	$3,201,434	3.96%
2005	10	Hines Ward	29	$2,168,960	2.54%
2006	4	Marvin Harrison	34	$6,400,000	6.27%
2007	4	Amani Toomer	33	$4,953,960	4.54%
2008	4	Hines Ward	32	$6,703,840	5.78%
2009	10	Marques Colston	26	$3,681,250	2.99%
2010	8	Donald Driver	35	$5,959,375	
2011	18	Hakeem Nicks	23	$1,605,000	1.34%
2012	5	Anquan Boldin	32	$7,532,250	6.24%
2013	2	Sidney Rice	27	$9,700,000	7.89%
2014	8	Danny Amendola	29	$4,700,000	3.53%
2015	2	Demaryius Thomas	28	$13,200,000	9.21%
2016	7	Chris Hogan	28	$5,500,000	3.54%
	6.5		29.7	$4,249,974	4.62%

Tight End					
Year	Cap Hit	Player	Age	Cap Hit	% of Cap
1994	9	Brent Jones	31	$1,030,400	2.98%
1995	8	Jay Novacek	33	$1,400,000	3.77%
1996	7	Mark Chmura	27	$1,503,300	3.69%
1997	4	Shannon Sharpe	29	$1,750,240	4.22%
1998	2	Shannon Sharpe	30	$2,625,350	5.01%
1999	30	Ernie Conwell	27	$523,750	0.91%
2000	13	Shannon Sharpe	32	$1,625,320	2.61%
2001	30	Rod Rutledge	26	$604,200	0.90%
2002	21	Ken Dilger	31	$852,250	1.20%
2003	19	Daniel Graham	25	$1,283,250	1.71%
2004	17	Daniel Graham	26	$1,432,550	1.77%
2005	11	Jerame Tuman	29	$2,146,900	2.51%
2006	22	Dallas Clark	27	$1,195,697	1.17%
2007	7	Jeremy Shockey	27	$4,371,667	4.01%
2008	19	Heath Miller	26	$1,725,760	1.49%
2009	11	Jeremy Shockey	29	$3,226,820	2.62%
2010	19	Donald Lee	30	$2,275,000	
2011	40	Travis Beckum	24	$678,250	0.57%
2012	30	Ed Dickson	25	$765,174	0.63%
2013	1	Zach Miller	28	$11,000,000	8.94%
2014	3	Aaron Hernandez	25	$7,500,000	5.64%
2015	12	Owen Daniels	33	$2,750,000	1.92%
2016	5	Rob Gronkowski	27	$6,618,750	4.26%
	14.8		28.1	$2,560,206	2.84%

Offensive Line

Year	Cap Hit	Player	Age	Cap Hit	% of Cap
1994	3	Steve Wallace – LT	30	$1,987,256	5.74%
1995	9	Erik Williams – RT	27	$1,374,329	3.70%
1996	13	Aaron Taylor – LG	24	$966,280	2.37%
1997	10	Tom Nalen – C	26	$1,000,480	2.41%
1998	4	Tony Jones – LT	32	$2,576,990	4.92%
1999	2	Adam Timmerman – RG	28	$3,502,450	6.11%
2000	1	Jonathan Ogden – LT	26	$4,021,605	6.47%
2001	8	Max Lane – G/T	30	$1,848,267	2.74%
2002	5	Jeff Christy – C	33	$3,551,890	5.00%
2003	3	Brandin Gorin – OT	25	$3,380,950	4.51%
2004	18	Joe Andruzzi – LG	29	$1,343,100	1.66%
2005	1	Alan Faneca – LG	29	$5,497,750	6.43%
2006	2	Tarik Glenn – LT	30	$6,900,666	6.77%
2007	3	Kareem McKenzie – RT	28	$5,350,000	4.91%
2008	2	Max Starks – LT	26	$6,899,800	5.95%
2009	4	Jammal Brown – OT	28	$6,273,330	5.10%
2010	5	Chad Clifton – LT	34	$7,500,000	
2011	4	Kareem McKenzie – RT	32	$5,300,000	4.42%
2012	9	Marshal Yanda – RG	28	$3,650,930	3.03%
2013	2	Russell Okung – LT	26	$9,540,000	7.76%
2014	9	Logan Mankins – LG	32	$4,250,000	3.20%
2015	3	Ryan Clady – LT	29	$10,600,000	7.40%
2016	2	Nate Solder – LT	28	$10,322,666	6.65%
	5.3		28.7	$4,679,945	4.87%

Wide Receiver 2

Year	Cap Hit	Player	Age	Cap Hit	% of Cap
1994	6	John Taylor	32	$1,451,257	4.19%
1995	21	Kevin Williams	24	$515,550	1.39%
1996	12	Andre Rison	29	$1,000,000	2.45%
1997	18	Ed McCaffrey	29	$675,740	1.63%
1998	11	Rod Smith	28	$1,404,095	2.68%
1999	10	Torry Holt	23	$1,696,000	2.96%
2000	15	Travis Taylor	21	$1,453,000	2.34%
2001	11	Troy Brown	30	$1,215,200	1.80%
2002	13	Keenan McCardell	32	$1,250,000	1.76%
2003	18	David Patten	29	$1,354,300	1.81%
2004	16	David Patten	30	$1,504,600	1.86%
2005	25	Cedrick Wilson	27	$1,043,520	1.22%
2006	5	Reggie Wayne	28	$5,100,440	5.00%
2007	5	Plaxico Burress	30	$4,925,000	4.52%
2008	18	Santonio Holmes	24	$1,741,920	1.50%
2009	21	Devery Henderson	27	$2,375,000	1.93%
2010	10	Greg Jennings	27	$5,537,500	
2011	20	Mario Manningham	25	$1,554,250	1.30%
2012	23	Jacoby Jones	28	$1,602,480	1.33%
2013	9	Percy Harvin	25	$4,900,000	3.98%
2014	16	Julian Edelman	28	$2,750,000	2.07%
2015	9	Emmanuel Sanders	28	$5,850,000	4.08%
2016	12	Julian Edelman	30	$4,421,875	2.85%
	26.4		27.6	$1,208,571	1.33%

Wide Receiver 3

Year	Cap Hit	Player	Age	Cap Hit	% of Cap
1994	34	Nate Singleton	26	$172,200	0.50%
1995	46	Cory Fleming	24	$168,400	0.45%
1996	24	Derrick Mayes	22	$385,000	0.94%
1997	23	Willie Green	31	$500,780	1.21%
1998	19	Ed McCaffrey	30	$901,680	1.72%
1999	12	Ricky Proehl	31	$1,500,000	2.62%
2000	21	Qadray Ismail	30	$825,320	1.33%
2001	19	David Patten	27	$829,000	1.23%
2002	22	Joe Jerevicius	28	$777,160	1.09%
2003	33	Bethel Johnson	24	$624,000	0.83%
2004	32	Bethel Johnson	25	$696,800	0.86%
2005	34	Antwaan Randle El	26	$691,830	0.81%
2006	10	Brandon Stokley	30	$3,456,613	3.39%
2007	24	David Tyree	27	$1,180,000	1.08%
2008	25	Nate Washington	25	$1,419,880	1.22%
2009	25	Robert Meachem	25	$1,866,000	1.52%
2010	28	James Jones	26	$1,286,564	
2011	31	Dominik Hixon	27	$850,000	0.71%
2012	26	Lee Evans	31	$1,232,500	1.02%
2013	23	Golden Tate	25	$880,000	0.72%
2014	21	Brandon Lafell	28	$2,000,000	1.50%
2015	24	Andre Caldwell	20	$1,550,000	1.08%
2016	16	Danny Amendola	31	$2,916,666	1.88%
	24.9		26.9	$1,208,571	1.33%

Defensive End

Year	Cap Hit	Player	Age	Cap Hit	% of Cap
1994	8	Richard Dent	34	$1,050,000	3.03%
1995	3	Charles Haley	31	$2,230,950	6.01%
1996	2	Reggie White	35	$3,625,000	8.90%
1997	6	Alfred Williams	29	$1,600,240	3.86%
1998	7	Alfred Williams	30	$2,242,890	4.28%
1999	7	Grant Winstrom	23	$1,868,000	3.26%
2000	3	Michael McCrary	30	$3,196,473	5.14%
2001	6	Richard Seymour	22	$2,000,000	2.97%
2002	3	Simeon Rice	28	$6,000,000	8.44%
2003	20	Ty Warren	22	$1,265,000	1.69%
2004	6	Richard Seymour	25	$2,507,800	3.10%
2005	2	Aaron Smith	29	$5,115,066	5.98%
2006	3	Dwight Freeney	26	$6,733,708	6.60%
2007	2	Michael Strahan	36	$6,730,445	6.17%
2008	8	Aaron Smith	32	$4,755,760	4.10%
2009	3	Will Smith	28	$9,421,666	7.66%
2010	2	Ryan Pickett	31	$8,437,500	
2011	9	Jason Pierre-Paul	22	$4,698,000	3.92%
2012	24	Ryan McBean	28	$1,003,100	0.83%
2013	5	Chris Clemons	32	$8,166,666	6.64%
2014	15	Rob Ninkovich	30	$2,850,000	2.14%
2015	16	Antonio Smith	34	$2,000,000	1.40%
2016	4	Jabaal Sheard	27	$6,812,500	4.39%
	7.1		28.9	$4,100,468	4.57%

Defensive Tackle

Year	Cap Hit	Player	Age	Cap Hit	% of Cap
1994	17	Dana Stubblefield	24	$627,400	1.81%
1995	6	Russell Maryland	26	$1,820,800	4.91%
1996	6	Santana Dotson	27	$1,567,326	3.85%
1997	11	Michael Perry	32	$1,000,000	2.41%
1998	18	Keith Traylor	29	$967,786	1.85%
1999	13	D'Marco Farr	28	$1,410,502	2.46%
2000	16	Tony Siragusa	33	$1,325,000	2.13%
2001	16	Henry Thomas	36	$1,100,000	1.63%
2002	1	Warren Sapp	30	$6,981,530	9.82%
2003	6	Richard Seymour	24	$2,528,200	3.37%
2004	23	Vince Wilfork	23	$1,150,000	1.42%
2005	12	Casey Hampton	28	$2,035,790	2.38%
2006	12	Montae Reagor	29	$2,933,784	2.88%
2007	11	Fred Robbins	30	$4,126,666	3.79%
2008	6	Casey Hampton	31	$5,378,043	4.64%
2009	7	Sedrick Ellis	24	$4,866,000	3.96%
2010	4	B.J. Raji	24	$7,890,000	
2011	3	Chris Canty	29	$7,200,000	6.00%
2012	2	Haloti Ngata	28	$10,400,000	8.62%
2013	8	Brandon Mebane	28	$5,200,000	4.23%
2014	2	Vince Wilfork	33	$7,588,333	5.71%
2015	15	Sylvester Williams	27	$2,067,750	1.44%
2016	17	Dominique Easley	24	$2,89,795	1.87%
	10.1		28.1	$3,611,509	3.69%

Linebacker

Year	Cap Hit	Player	Age	Cap Hit	% of Cap
1994	13	Ken Norton	28	$788,733	2.28%
1995	13	Robert Jones	26	$875,200	2.36%
1996	9	George Koonce	28	$1,287,740	3.16%
1997	5	Bill Romanowski	31	$1,600,240	3.86%
1998	6	Bill Romanowski	32	$2,260,000	4.31%
1999	9	Mike Jones	30	$1,850,000	3.23%
2000	2	Ray Lewis	25	$3,311,920	5.33%
2001	3	Willie McGinest	30	$4,364,366	6.47%
2002	4	Derrick Brooks	29	$3,935,493	5.54%
2003	2	Ted Johnson	31	$3,642,416	4.86%
2004	4	Willie McGinest	33	$3,667,300	4.54%
2005	3	Joey Porter	28	$4,888,403	5.72%
2006	16	Gary Brackett	26	$1,998,590	1.96%
2007	6	Antonio Pierce	29	$4,550,000	4.17%
2008	10	James Farrior	33	$4,061,150	3.50%
2009	8	Jon Vilma	27	$4,500,000	3.66%
2010	6	A.J. Hawk	26	$6,995,000	
2011	5	Michael Boley	29	$5,150,000	4.29%
2012	1	Terrell Suggs	30	$11,520,000	9.55%
2013	18	Bruce Irvin	26	$1,931,546	1.57%
2014	4	Jerod Mayo	28	$7,287,500	5.48%
2015	4	Von Miller	26	$9,754,000	6.81%
2016	3	Dont'a Hightower	26	$7,751,000	4.99%
	6.7		28.6	$4,259,591	4.44%

Cornerback

Year	Cap Hit	Player	Age	Cap Hit	% of Cap
1994	7	Deion Sanders	27	$1,134,000	3.28%
1995	4	Deion Sanders	28	$2,217,442	5.98%
1996	19	Craig Newsome	25	$667,520	1.64%
1997	1	Ray Crockett	30	$2,281,814	5.50%
1998	8	Darrien Gordon	28	$2,217,646	4.23%
1999	3	Todd Lyght	30	$3,377,500	5.90%
2000	10	Duane Starks	26	$1,698,780	2.73%
2001	2	Ty Law	27	$5,033,771	7.47%
2002	10	Ronde Barber	27	$1,891,430	2.66%
2003	1	Ty Law	29	$8,806.97	11.74%
2004	1	Ty Law	30	$10,206,965	12.62%
2005	16	Chad Scott	31	$1,800,000	2.11%
2006	20	Nicholas Harper	32	$1,403,960	1.38%
2007	8	William James	28	$4,304,852	3.95%
2008	11	Ike Taylor	28	$3,743,360	3.23%
2009	5	Jabari Greer	27	$5,950,000	4.84%
2010	3	Charles Woodson	34	$8,400,000	
2011	2	Corey Webster	29	$7,845,000	6.54%
2012	12	Domonique Foxworth	29	$3,000,000	2.49%
2013	21	Antoine Winfield	36	$1,000,000	0.81%
2014	5	Darrelle Revis	29	$7,000,000	5.26%
2015	7	Aqib Talib	29	$6,968,750	4.86%
2016	20	Logan Ryan	25	$1,811,813	1.17%
	8.5		28.9	$4,033,112	4.56%

Safety

Year	Cap Hit	Player	Age	Cap Hit	% of Cap
1994	5	Tim McDonald	29	$1,551,000	4.48%
1995	18	Darren Woodson	26	$670,900	1.81%
1996	5	Leroy Butler	28	$1,700,480	4.17%
1997	2	Steve Atwater	31	$2,261,080	5.45%
1998	1	Steve Atwater	32	$2,702,590	5.16%
1999	11	Keith Lyle	27	$1,575,000	2.75%
2000	4	Rod Woodson	35	$2,966,986	4.77%
2001	9	Lawyer Milloy	28	$1,765,017	2.62%
2002	8	John Lynch	31	$2,684,863	3.78%
2003	17	Lawyer Milloy	30	$1,456,806	1.94%
2004	3	Lawyer Milloy	31	$4,053,623	5.01%
2005	13	Troy Polamalu	24	$1,988,700	2.33%
2006	28	Mike Doss	25	$724,840	0.71%
2007	23	Gibril Wilson	26	$1,303,840	1.20%
2008	3	Troy Polamalu	27	$6,820,000	5.88%
2009	27	Darren Sharper	34	$1,704,550	1.39%
2010	1	Nick Collins	27	$10,950,000	
2011	12	Antrel Rolle	29	$3,600,000	3.00%
2012	3	Ed Reed	34	$8,500,000	7.05%
2013	13	Kam Chancellor	25	$3,878,404	3.15%
2014	7	Devin McCourty	27	$5,115,000	3.85%
2015	6	T.J. Ward	29	$7,514,706	5.24%
2016	9	Devin McCourty	29	$5,195,000	3.35%
	9.9		28.9	$3,507,973	3.59%

Kicker

Year	Cap Hit	Player	Age	Cap Hit	% of Cap
1994	35	Doug Brien	24	$170,000	0.49%
1995	49	Chris Boniol	24	$151,359	0.41%
1996	21	Chris Jacke	30	$628,780	1.54%
1997	21	Jason Elam	27	$597,520	1.44%
1998	27	Jason Elam	28	$695,280	1.33%
1999	25	Jeff Wilkins	27	$600,350	1.05%
2000	24	Matt Stover	32	$690,320	1.11%
2001	18	Adam Vinatieri	29	$955,200	1.42%
2002	16	Martin Gramatica	27	$1,027,435	1.45%
2003	8	Adam Vinatieri	31	$2,320,676	3.09%
2004	10	Adam Vinatieri	32	$2,095,777	2.59%
2005	30	Jeff Reed	26	$835,080	1.00%
2006	18	Adam Vinatieri	34	$1,682,200	1.65%
2007	36	Lawrence Tynes	29	$650,840	0.60%
2008	16	Jeff Reed	29	$1,963,613	1.69%
2009	58	John Carney	45	$455,882	0.37%
2010	30	Mason Crosby	26	$1,124,489	
2011	22	Lawrence Tynes	33	$1,500,000	1.25%
2012	39	Bill Cundiff	32	$604,340	0.50%
2013	34	Steven Hauschka	28	$620,000	0.50%
2014	12	Stephen Gostowski	30	$3,800,000	2.86%
2015	44	Brandon McManus	24	$510,000	0.36%
2016	14	Stephen Gostowski	32	$4,100,000	2.64%
	26.4		29.5	$1,208,571	1.33%

Non-Patriots Kickers: 0.93%
Patriots Kickers: 2.52%

Punter					
Year	Cap Hit	Player	Age	Cap Hit	% of Cap
1994	38	Klaus Wilmsmeyer	27	$162,200	0.47%
1995	41	John Jett	27	$180,550	0.49%
1996	43	Craig Hentrich	25	$219,773	0.54%
1997	36	Tom Rouen	29	$359,018	0.87%
1998	32	Tom Rouen	30	$460,333	0.88%
1999	23	Rick Tuten	23	$650,350	1.14%
2000	43	Kyle Richardson	27	$388,520	0.62%
2001	46	Lee Johnson	40	$392,734	0.58%
2002	36	Tom Tupa	36	$476,260	0.67%
2003	29	Ken Walter	31	$819,350	1.09%
2004	28	Josh Miller	34	$863,000	1.07%
2005	22	Chris Gardocki	35	$1,214,700	1.42%
2006	26	Hunter Smith	29	$884,508	0.87%
2007	26	Jeff Feagles	41	$1,103,840	1.01%
2008	42	Daniel Sepulveda	24	$490,760	0.42%
2009	63	Thomas Morstead	23	$351,250	0.29%
2010	58	Tim Masthay	23	$320,000	
2011	32	Steve Weatherford	29	$850,000	0.71%
2012	15	Sam Koch	30	$2,204,960	1.83%
2013	20	Jon Ryan	32	$1,405,000	1.14%
2014	50	Ryan Allen	24	$495,500	0.37%
2015	13	Britton Colquitt	30	$2,350,000	1.64%
2016	27	Ryan Allen	26	$1,700,000	1.09%
	34.3		29.3	$797,505	0.87%

Super Bowl Average for Top Cap Hits with 2017 Cap		
Position	Cap Hit	Cap Hit w/$167 M Cap
QB	7.85%	$13,109,500
RB	3.70%	$6,179,000
WR	4.67%	$7,798,900
TE	2.78%	$4,642,600
OL	4.79%	$7,999,300
	23.79%	$39,729,300
DE	4.58%	$7,648,600
DT	3.78%	$6,312,600
LB	4.41%	$7,364,700
CB	4.72%	$7,882,400
S	3.61%	$6,028,700
	21.10%	$35,237,000
K	1.27%	$2,120,900
P	0.86%	$1,436,200

Offensive Line Costs

1994 49ers Offense	West Coast		34,608,000		
LT	Steve Wallace	30	$1,987,256	5.74%	
LG	Jesse Sapolu	33	$930,608	2.69%	
C	Bart Oates	36	$395,000	1.14%	
RG	Derrick Deese	24	$209,300	0.60%	
RT	Harris Barton	30	$1,959,510	5.66%	15.84%
1995 Cowboys Offense	Air Coryell		37,100,000		
LT	Mark Tuinei	35	$728,100	1.96%	
LG	Nate Newton	34	$809,933	2.18%	
C	Ray Donaldson	37	$818,750	2.21%	
RG	Larry Allen	24	$416,600	1.12%	
RT	Erik Williams	27	$1,374,329	3.70%	11.18%
1996 Packers Offense	West Coast		40,753,000		
LT	John Michels	23	$751,250	1.84%	
LG	Aaron Taylor	24	$966,280	2.37%	
C	Frank Winters	32	$917,147	2.25%	
RG	Adam Timmerman	25	$175,666	0.43%	
RT	Earl Dotson	26	$907,390	2.23%	9.12%
1997 Broncos Offense	West Coast		41,454,000		
LT	Gary Zimmerman	36	$926,667	2.24%	
LG	Mark Schlereth	31	$401,200	0.97%	
C	Tom Nalen	26	$1,000,480	2.41%	
RG	Brian Habib	33	$950,240	2.29%	
RT	Tony Jones	31	$951,080	2.29%	10.20%
1998 Broncos Offense	West Coast		52,388,000		
LT	Tony Jones	32	$2,576,990	4.92%	
LG	Mark Schlereth	32	$1,404,095	2.68%	
C	Tom Nalen	27	$1,400,910	2.67%	
RG	Dan Neil	25	$341,270	0.65%	
RT	Harry Swayne	33	$1,001,330	1.91%	12.84%
1999 Rams	Air Coryell		57,288,000		

Offense					
LT	Orlando Pace	24	$3,313,666	5.78%	
LG	Tom Nutten	28	$335,000	0.58%	
C	Mike Gruttadauria	27	$432,430	0.75%	
RG	Adam Timmerman	28	$3,502,450	6.11%	
RT	Fred Miller	26	$432,150	0.75%	13.99%
2000 Ravens	West Coast		62,172,000		
Offense					
LT	Jonathan Ogden	26	$4,021,605	6.47%	
LG	Edwin Mulitalo	26	$284,160	0.46%	
C	Jeff Mitchell	26	$1,027,640	1.65%	
RG	Mike Flynn	26	$385,960	0.62%	
RT	Harry Swayne	35	$2,500,320	4.02%	13.22%
2001 Patriots	Erhardt-Perkins		67,405,000		
Offense					
LT	Matt Light	23	$587,500	0.87%	
LG	Mike Compton	31	$689,866	1.02%	
C	Damien Woody	24	$1,183,160	1.76%	
RG	Joe Andruzzi	26	$605,700	0.90%	
RT	Greg Randall	23	$364,950	0.54%	5.09%
2002 Bucs	West Coast		71,101,000		
Offense					
LT	Roman Oben	30	$476,980	0.67%	
LG	Kerry Jenkins	29	$1,123,240	1.58%	
C	Jeff Christy	33	$3,551,890	5.00%	
RG	Cosey Coleman	24	$666,700	0.94%	
RT	Kenyatta Walker	23	$1,336,123	1.88%	10.06%
2003 Patriots	Erhardt-Perkins		75,007,000		
Offense					
LT	Matt Light	25	$721,600	0.96%	
LG	Damien Woody	26	$2,790,600	3.72%	
C	Dan Koppen	24	$254,000	0.34%	
RG	Joe Andruzzi	28	$857,200	1.14%	
RT	Tom Ashworth	26	$304,700	0.41%	6.57%
2004 Patriots	Erhardt-Perkins		80,852,000		
Offense					
LT	Matt Light	26	$1,198,366	1.48%	
LG	Joe Andruzzi	29	$1,343,100	1.66%	

C	Dan Koppen	25	$369,000	0.46%	
RG	Steve Neal	28	$460,000	0.57%	
RT	Brandon Gorin	26	$386,250	0.48%	4.65%
2005 Steelers Offense	Erhardt-Perkins		85,500,000		
LT	Marvel Smith	27	$2,738,580	3.20%	
LG	Alan Faneca	29	$5,497,750	6.43%	
C	Jeff Hartings	33	$4,094,166	4.79%	
RG	Kendall Simmons	26	$1,239,624	1.45%	
RT	Max Starks	23	$486,506	0.57%	16.44%
2006 Colts Offense	Air Coryell		102,000,000		
LT	Tarik Glenn	30	$6,900,666	6.77%	
LG	Dylan Gandy	24	$454,033	0.45%	
C	Jeff Saturday	31	$3,939,506	3.86%	
RG	Jake Scott	25	$472,138	0.46%	
RT	Ryan Diem	27	$4,805,720	4.71%	16.25%
2007 Giants Offense	Erhardt-Perkins		109,000,000		
LT	David Diehl	27	$2,010,000	1.84%	
LG	Rich Seubert	28	$1,858,750	1.71%	
C	Shaun O'Hara	30	$2,000,000	1.83%	
RG	Chris Snee	25	$949,166	0.87%	
RT	Kareem McKenzie	28	$5,350,000	4.91%	11.16%
2008 Steelers Offense	Air Coryell		116,000,000		
LT	Max Starks	26	$6,899,800	5.95%	
LG	Chris Kemoeatu	25	$1,423,240	1.23%	
C	Justin Hartwig	30	$1,493,260	1.29%	
RG	Darnell Stapleton	23	$378,906	0.33%	
RT	Willie Colon	25	$546,220	0.47%	9.26%
2009 Saints Offense	Air Coryell		123,000,000		
LT	Jermon Bushrod	25	$569,340	0.46%	
LG	Carl Nicks	24	$429,060	0.35%	
C	Jonathan Goodwin	31	$3,183,333	2.59%	
RG	Jahri Evans	26	$2,795,510	2.27%	
RT	Jon Stinchcomb	30	$2,500,000	2.03%	7.71%
2010 Packers Offense	West Coast		NO CAP		
LT	Chad Clifton	34	$7,500,000		

2011 Giants Offense	Erhardt-Perkins		120,000,000		
LT	Will Beatty	26	$755,000	0.63%	
LG	David Diehl	31	$4,787,500	3.99%	
C	David Baas	30	$2,700,000	2.25%	
RG	Chris Snee	29	$3,750,000	3.13%	
RT	Kareem McKenzie	32	$5,300,000	4.42%	14.41%
2012 Ravens Offense	Air Coryell		120,600,000		
LT	Michael Oher	26	$2,035,000	1.69%	
LG	Jah Reid	24	$605,810	0.50%	
C	Matt Birk	36	$1,625,930	1.35%	
RG	Marshal Yanda	28	$3,650,000	3.03%	
RT	Kelechi Osemele	23	$608.340	0.50%	7.07%
2013 Seahawks Offense	West Coast		123,000,000		
LT	Russell Okung	26	9,540,000	7.76%	
LG	James Carpenter	24	2,084,046	1.69%	
C	Max Unger	27	6,000,000	4.88%	
RG	J.R. Sweezy	24	494,212	0.40%	
RT	Breno Giacomini	28	4,750,000	3.86%	18.59%
2014 Patriots Offense	Erhardt-Perkins		133,000,000		
LT	Nate Solder	26	2,717,429	2.04%	
LG	Dan Connolly	32	4,083,334	3.07%	
C	Bryan Stork	24	539,250	0.41%	
RG	Ryan Wendell	28	1,625,000	1.22%	
RT	Sebastian Vollmer	30	4,083,333	3.07%	9.81%
2015 Broncos Offense	West Coast		143,280,000		
LT	Ryan Harris	30	1,420,000	0.99%	
LG	Evan Mathis	34	2,921,875	2.04%	
C	Matt Paradis	26	435,000	0.30%	
RG	Louis Vasquez	28	6,250,000	4.36%	
RT	Michael Scofield	25	652,300	0.46%	8.15%
2016 Patriots Offense	Erhardt-Perkins		155,270,000		
LT	Nate Solder	28	10,322,666	6.65%	
LG	Joe Thuney	24	643,357	0.41%	
C	David Andrews	24	440,000	0.28%	
RG	Shaq Mason	23	545,881	0.35%	

RT	Marcus Cannon	28	4,754,168	3.06%	10.76%

OL Averages					
Averages					
LT		27.9	$2,744,354	3.22%	
LG		28.5	$1,681,022	1.90%	
C		29.3	$1,820,948	2.02%	
RG		26.2	$1,397,347	1.51%	
RT		27.2	$1,904,116	2.36%	11.03%

Pats Average					
LT		25	$1,306,224	2.40%	
LG		29.5	$2,226,725	1.98%	
C		24.3	$586,353	0.65%	
RG		27.5	$886,975	0.84%	
RT		26.3	$1,284,808	1.51%	7.38%

West Coast Avg			Excluding 2010		
LT		29.7	$3,244,528	3.83%	
LG		29.1	$1,319,389	1.81%	
C		29.1	$1,936,452	2.54%	
RG		25.9	$1,115,483	1.29%	
RT		28	$1,705,339	2.79%	12.25%

Air Coryell Avg					
LT		27.7	$3,407,762	3.77%	
LG		26.5	$676,179	0.88%	
C		32	$1,915,535	2.01%	
RG		25.7	$1,869,267	2.22%	
RT		26.3	$1,711,127	2.03%	10.91%

Erhardt-Perkins Avg					
LT		25.7	$1,532,639	2.21%	
LG		29.4	$3,007,271	2.75%	
C		27.1	$1,591,368	1.51%	
RG		27.1	$1,355,241	1.20%	
RT		26.9	$2,325,106	2.18%	9.86%

Super Bowl Passing Game and Offensive Skil Spending

Year	Team	WR1	WR2	WR3	Total	TE	Total	QB	Total	RB	Total
1994	49ers	8.56%	4.19%	0.50%	13.25%	2.98%	16.23%	13.08%	29.31%	2.50%	31.81%
1995	Cowboys	5.32%	1.39%	0.45%	7.16%	3.77%	10.93%	6.72%	17.65%	9.17%	26.82%
1996	Packers	4.17%	2.45%	0.94%	7.56%	3.69%	11.25%	10.25%	21.50%	3.19%	24.69%
1997	Broncos	3.20%	1.63%	1.21%	6.04%	4.22%	10.26%	5.17%	15.43%	1.97%	17.40%
1998	Broncos	2.77%	2.68%	1.72%	7.17%	5.01%	12.18%	5.01%	17.19%	4.57%	21.76%
1999	Rams	5.11%	2.96%	2.62%	10.69%	0.91%	11.60%	5.46%	17.06%	7.52%	24.58%
2000	Ravens	2.68%	2.34%	1.33%	6.35%	2.61%	8.96%	3.64%	12.60%	3.02%	15.62%
2001	Patriots	3.90%	1.80%	1.23%	6.93%	0.90%	7.83%	10.29%	18.12%	1.08%	19.20%
2002	Bucs	4.72%	1.76%	1.09%	7.57%	1.20%	8.77%	9.57%	18.34%	2.67%	21.01%
2003	Patriots	3.27%	1.81%	0.83%	5.91%	1.71%	7.62%	4.43%	12.05%	3.07%	15.12%
2004	Patriots	3.96%	1.86%	0.86%	6.68%	1.77%	8.45%	6.26%	14.71%	2.50%	17.21%
2005	Steelers	2.54%	1.22%	0.81%	4.57%	2.51%	7.08%	4.94%	12.02%	2.81%	14.83%
2006	Colts	6.27%	5.00%	3.39%	14.66%	1.17%	15.83%	10.36%	26.19%	2.98%	29.17%
2007	Giants	4.54%	4.52%	1.08%	10.14%	4.01%	14.15%	9.22%	23.37%	1.83%	25.20%
2008	Steelers	5.78%	1.50%	1.22%	8.50%	1.49%	9.99%	6.87%	16.86%	3.53%	20.39%
2009	Saints	2.99%	1.93%	1.52%	6.44%	2.62%	9.06%	8.67%	17.73%	8.61%	26.34%
2010	Packers										
2011	Giants	1.34%	1.30%	0.71%	3.35%	0.57%	3.92%	11.75%	15.67%	4.17%	19.84%
2012	Ravens	6.24%	1.33%	1.02%	8.59%	0.63%	9.22%	6.63%	15.85%	4.15%	20.00%
2013	Seahawks	7.89%	3.98%	0.72%	12.59%	8.94%	21.53%	3.25%	24.78%	6.91%	31.69%
2014	Patriots	3.53%	2.07%	1.50%	7.10%	5.64%	12.74%	11.13%	23.87%	0.83%	24.70%
2015	Broncos	9.21%	4.08%	1.08%	14.37%	1.92%	16.29%	12.21%	28.50%	0.66%	29.16%
	Averages	4.67%	2.47%	1.23%	8.36%	2.77%	11.14%	7.85%	18.99%	3.70%	22.69%

Statistics for Super Bowl Winners

*All data from Pro Football Reference unless otherwise noted

Offensive Yards Per Attempt

Year	Team	Points	Pts/Gm	Rank	Total Yds	Yds/Gm	Rank	Plays	P/Gm	Yds/P	Rank
1994	49ers	505	31.6	1	6060	378.8	2	1037	64.8	5.8	1
1995	Cowboys	435	27.2	3	5824	364	5	1007	62.9	5.8	2
1996	Packers	456	28.5	1	5535	345.9	5	1053	65.8	5.3	4
1997	Broncos	472	29.5	1	5872	367	1	1068	66.8	5.5	3
1998	Broncos	501	31.3	2	6092	380.8	3	1041	65.1	5.9	3
1999	Rams	526	32.9	1	6412	400.8	1	994	62.1	6.5	1
2000	Ravens	333	20.8	14	5014	313.4	16	1058	66.1	4.7	20
2001	Patriots	371	23.2	6	4882	305.1	19	1001	62.6	4.9	20
2002	Buccaneers	346	21.6	18	5002	312.6	24	1022	63.9	4.9	23
2003	Patriots	348	21.8	12	5039	314.9	17	1042	65.1	4.8	12
2004	Patriots	437	27.3	4	5722	357.6	7	1035	64.7	5.5	9
2005	Steelers	389	24.3	9	5149	321.8	15	960	60	5.4	9
2006	Colts	427	26.7	2	6070	379.4	3	1011	63.2	6	2
2007	Giants	373	23.3	14	5302	331.4	16	1041	65.1	5.1	19
2008	Steelers	347	21.7	20	4991	311.9	22	1015	63.4	4.9	25
2009	Saints	510	31.9	1	6461	403.8	1	1032	64.5	6.3	1
2010	Packers	388	24.3	10	5730	358.1	9	1000	62.5	5.7	6
2011	Giants	394	24.6	9	6161	385.1	8	1028	64.3	6	8
2012	Ravens	398	24.9	10	5640	352.5	16	1042	65.1	5.4	16
2013	Seahawks	417	26.1	8	5424	339	17	973	60.8	5.6	9
2014	Patriots	468	29.3	4	5848	365.5	11	1073	67.1	5.5	12
2015	Broncos	355	22.2	19	5688	355.5	16	1056	66	5.4	18
2016	Patriots	441	27.6	3	6180	386.3	4	1056	66	5.9	5
Average		419	26.2	7.5	5656.4	353.5	10.3	1028	64.3	5.5	9.9

Offensive Passing Yards Per Attempt (QB Passing Yds; does not account for sack loss)

Year	Team	QB P Yds	P Yds/Gm	Comp	Pass Att	Att/Game	Comp %	P Yds/Att	Rank
1994	49ers	4362	272.6	359	511	31.9	70.30%	8.5	1
1995	Cowboys	3741	233.8	322	494	30.9	65.20%	7.6	3
1996	Packers	3938	246.1	328	548	34.3	59.90%	7.2	7
1997	Broncos	3704	231.5	287	513	32.1	55.90%	7.2	6
1998	Broncos	3808	238	290	491	30.7	59.10%	7.8	5
1999	Rams	4580	286.3	343	530	33.1	64.70%	8.6	1
2000	Ravens	3102	193.9	287	504	31.5	56.90%	6.2	21
2001	Patriots	3326	207.9	306	482	30.1	63.50%	6.9	14
2002	Bucs	3665	229.1	348	567	35.4	61.40%	6.5	19
2003	Patriots	3651	228.2	320	537	33.6	59.60%	6.8	13
2004	Patriots	3750	234.4	293	485	30.3	60.40%	7.7	9
2005	Steelers	3104	194	228	379	23.7	60.20%	8.2	1
2006	Colts	4397	274.8	362	557	34.8	65.00%	7.9	3
2007	Giants	3376	211	302	544	34	55.50%	6.2	28
2008	Steelers	3607	225.4	303	506	31.6	59.90%	7.1	14
2009	Saints	4490	280.6	378	544	34	69.50%	8.3	3
2010	Packers	4355	272.2	352	541	33.8	65.10%	8	3
2011	Giants	4933	308.3	359	589	36.8	61.00%	8.4	3
2012	Ravens	3996	249.8	334	560	35	59.60%	7.1	14
2013	Seahawks	3508	219.3	267	420	26.3	63.60%	8.4	2
2014	Patriots	4291	268.2	392	609	38.1	64.40%	7	20
2015	Broncos	4216	263.5	368	606	37.9	60.70%	7	22
2016	Patriots	4456	278.5	368	550	34.4	66.90%	8.1	3
Average		3928.5	245.5	325.9	524.7	32.8	62.10%	7.5	9.3
1994-2008		3740.7	233.8	311.9	509.9	31.9	61.20%	7.4	9.7
2009-16		4280.6	267.5	352.3	552.4	34.5	63.80%	7.8	8.8

Offensive Pass Yds Per Attempt (Team Pass Yards = QB Pass Yds - Sack Yard Loss)

Year	Team	Sack Loss	Sacks	Team P Yds	T P Yds/Gm	Rank	Net Y/PA	Rank
1994	49ers	199	35	4163	260.2	4	7.6	1
1995	Cowboys	118	18	3623	226.4	13	7.1	1
1996	Packers	241	40	3697	231.1	5	6.3	6
1997	Broncos	210	35	3494	218.4	9	6.4	4
1998	Broncos	184	25	3624	226.5	7	7	3
1999	Rams	227	33	4353	272.1	1	7.7	1
2000	Ravens	287	43	2815	175.9	22	5.1	24
2001	Patriots	237	46	3089	193.1	22	5.9	15
2002	Bucs	220	41	3445	215.3	15	5.7	21
2003	Patriots	219	32	3432	214.5	9	6	13
2004	Patriots	162	26	3588	224.3	11	7	7
2005	Steelers	178	32	2926	182.9	24	7.1	2
2006	Colts	89	15	4308	269.3	2	7.5	1
2007	Giants	222	28	3154	197.1	21	5.5	22
2008	Steelers	306	49	3301	206.3	17	5.9	20
2009	Saints	135	20	4355	272.2	4	7.7	2
2010	Packers	231	38	4124	257.8	5	7.1	3
2011	Giants	199	28	4734	295.9	5	7.7	4
2012	Ravens	257	38	3739	233.7	15	6.3	15
2013	Seahawks	272	44	3236	202.3	26	7	6
2014	Patriots	170	26	4121	257.6	9	6.5	17
2015	Broncos	246	39	3970	248.1	14	6.2	21
2016	Patriots	148	24	4308	269.3	4	7.5	3
Average		206.8	32.8	3721.7	232.6	11.5	6.7	9.2
1994-2008		206.6	33.2	3534.1	220.9	12.1	6.5	9.4
2009-16		207.3	32.1	4073.4	254.6	10.3	7	8.9

Rushing Yards Per Attempt

Year	Team	Rush Yds	R Yds/Gm	Rank	Att	Att/Gm	R Yd/Att	Rank
1994	49ers	1897	118.6	6	491	30.7	3.9	7
1995	Cowboys	2201	137.6	2	495	30.9	4.4	4
1996	Packers	1838	114.9	11	465	29.1	4	12
1997	Broncos	2378	148.6	4	520	32.5	4.6	2
1998	Broncos	2468	154.3	2	525	32.8	4.7	2
1999	Rams	2059	128.7	5	431	26.9	4.8	2
2000	Ravens	2199	137.4	5	511	31.9	4.3	8
2001	Patriots	1793	112.1	13	473	29.6	3.8	24
2002	Buccaneers	1557	97.3	27	414	25.9	3.8	28
2003	Patriots	1607	100.4	27	473	29.6	3.4	30
2004	Patriots	2134	133.4	7	524	32.8	4.1	18
2005	Steelers	2223	138.9	5	549	34.3	4	12
2006	Colts	1762	110.1	18	439	27.4	4	16
2007	Giants	2148	134.3	4	469	29.3	4.6	4
2008	Steelers	1690	105.6	23	460	28.8	3.7	29
2009	Saints	2106	131.6	6	468	29.3	4.5	7
2010	Packers	1606	100.4	24	421	26.3	3.8	25
2011	Giants	1427	89.2	32	411	25.7	3.5	32
2012	Ravens	1901	118.8	11	444	27.8	4.3	12
2013	Seahawks	2188	136.8	4	509	31.8	4.3	12
2014	Patriots	1727	107.9	18	438	27.4	3.9	22
2015	Broncos	1718	107.4	17	411	25.7	4.2	13
2016	Patriots	1872	117	7	482	30.1	3.9	24
	Average	1934.7	120.9	12.1	470.6	29.4	4.1	15
	1994-2008	1996.9	124.8	10.6	482.6	30.2	4.1	13.2
	2009-16	1818.1	113.6	14.9	448	28	4	18.4

Offensive Touchdowns and Turnovers

Year	Team	Pass TDs	Rank	INTs	Rank	Rush TDs	Rank	Total TDs
1994	49ers	37	1	11	3	23	2	60
1995	Cowboys	18	22	10	1	29	1	47
1996	Packers	39	1	13	5	9	19	48
1997	Broncos	27	4	11	6	18	5	45
1998	Broncos	32	4	14	8	26	1	58
1999	Rams	42	1	15	7	13	10	55
2000	Ravens	20	15	19	20	9	24	29
2001	Patriots	21	11	15	11	15	7	36
2002	Buccaneers	23	14	10	2	6	31	29
2003	Patriots	23	11	13	6	9	24	32
2004	Patriots	29	5	14	11	15	8	44
2005	Steelers	21	12	14	9	21	5	42
2006	Colts	31	1	9	2	17	6	48
2007	Giants	23	14	20	23	15	7	38
2008	Steelers	19	18	15	16	16	11	35
2009	Saints	34	1	12	6	21	3	55
2010	Packers	31	4	13	9	11	18	42
2011	Giants	29	6	16	19	17	6	46
2012	Ravens	22	18	11	6	17	6	39
2013	Seahawks	27	10	9	3	14	13	41
2014	Patriots	34	5	9	4	13	12	47
2015	Broncos	19	28	23	32	13	12	32
2016	Patriots	32	6	2	1	19	5	51
	Average	27.5	9.2	13	9.1	15.9	10.3	43.4

316

Defensive Yards Per Attempt

Year	Team	Pts	Pts/Gm	Rank	Total Yds	Yds/Gm	Rank	Plays	P/Gm	Yds/Play	Rank
1994	49ers	296	18.5	6	4839	302.4	8	996	62.3	4.9	12
1995	Cowboys	291	18.2	3	5044	315.3	9	1001	62.6	5	13
1996	Packers	210	13.1	1	4156	259.8	1	981	61.3	4.2	1
1997	Broncos	287	17.9	6	4671	291.9	5	951	59.4	4.9	15
1998	Broncos	309	19.3	8	4935	308.4	11	999	62.4	4.9	11
1999	Rams	242	15.1	4	4698	293.6	6	991	61.9	4.7	7
2000	Ravens	165	10.3	1	3967	247.9	2	924	57.8	4.3	2
2001	Patriots	272	17	6	5352	334.5	24	1016	63.5	5.3	24
2002	Buccaneers	196	12.3	1	4044	252.8	1	963	60.2	4.2	1
2003	Patriots	238	14.9	1	4666	291.6	7	1060	66.3	4.4	4
2004	Patriots	260	16.3	2	4972	310.8	9	988	61.8	5	11
2005	Steelers	258	16.1	3	4544	284	4	998	62.4	4.6	4
2006	Colts	360	22.5	23	5316	332.3	21	959	59.9	5.5	28
2007	Giants	351	21.9	17	4880	305	7	984	61.5	5	9
2008	Steelers	223	13.9	1	3795	237.2	1	974	60.9	3.9	1
2009	Saints	341	21.3	20	5724	357.8	25	1044	65.3	5.5	21
2010	Packers	240	15	2	4945	309.1	5	969	60.6	5.1	12
2011	Giants	400	25	25	6022	376.4	27	1072	67	5.6	22
2012	Ravens	344	21.5	12	5615	350.9	17	1086	67.9	5.2	12
2013	Seahawks	231	14.4	1	4378	273.6	1	990	61.9	4.4	1
2014	Patriots	313	19.6	8	5506	344.1	13	1033	64.6	5.3	12
2015	Broncos	296	18.5	4	4530	283.1	1	1033	64.6	4.4	1
2016	Patriots	240	15	1	5223	326.4	8	998	62.4	5.2	10
	Average	276.7	17.3	6.8	4861.8	303.9	9.3	1000.4	62.5	4.9	10.2

Defensive Passing Yards (QB Passing Yards; does not include sack loss)

Year	Team	Pass Yds	P Yds/Gm	Comp	Att	Att/Game	Comp %	P Yds/Att	Rank
1994	49ers	3756	234.8	329	583	36.4	56.40%	6.4	6
1995	Cowboys	3491	218.2	293	523	32.7	56.00%	6.7	16
1996	Packers	2942	183.9	283	544	34	52.00%	5.4	1
1997	Broncos	3166	197.9	290	526	32.9	55.10%	6	4
1998	Broncos	3983	248.9	345	596	37.3	57.90%	6.7	11
1999	Rams	3867	241.7	319	596	37.3	53.50%	6.5	7
2000	Ravens	3175	198.4	295	528	33	55.90%	6	4
2001	Patriots	3731	233.2	299	546	34.1	54.80%	6.8	17
2002	Bucs	2785	174.1	259	510	31.9	50.80%	5.5	1
2003	Patriots	3485	217.8	328	618	38.6	53.10%	5.6	1
2004	Patriots	3711	231.9	315	538	33.6	58.60%	6.9	15
2005	Steelers	3480	217.5	315	549	34.3	57.40%	6.3	5
2006	Colts	2705	169.1	266	415	25.9	64.10%	6.5	8
2007	Giants	3666	229.1	306	523	32.7	58.50%	7	11
2008	Steelers	2861	178.8	301	533	33.3	56.50%	5.4	1
2009	Saints	3961	247.6	330	574	35.9	57.50%	6.9	15
2010	Packers	3440	215	296	527	32.9	56.20%	6.5	7
2011	Giants	4417	276.1	361	589	36.8	61.30%	7.5	20
2012	Ravens	3900	243.8	335	557	34.8	60.10%	7	17
2013	Seahawks	3050	190.6	309	524	32.8	59.00%	5.8	1
2014	Patriots	4119	257.4	342	574	35.9	59.60%	7.2	15
2015	Broncos	3544	221.5	344	573	35.8	60.00%	6.2	2
2016	Patriots	4033	252.1	368	596	37.3	61.70%	6.8	8
	Average	3533.4	220.8	314.3	549.7	34.4	57.20%	6.4	8.4

318

Defensive Passing Yards Per Attempt (Team Pass Yards = QB Passing Yards - Sack Yard Loss)

Year	Team	Sack Loss	Sacks	Team P Yds	Yd/Gm	Rank	Net Y/PA	Rank
1994	49ers	255	38	3501	218.8	17	5.6	6
1995	Cowboys	219	36	3272	204.5	8	5.9	13
1996	Packers	202	37	2740	171.3	1	4.7	1
1997	Broncos	298	44	2868	179.3	5	5	5
1998	Broncos	335	47	3648	228	26	5.7	12
1999	Rams	358	57	3509	219.3	20	5.4	6
2000	Ravens	178	35	2997	187.3	8	5.3	7
2001	Patriots	234	41	3497	218.6	24	6	19
2002	Bucs	295	43	2490	155.6	1	4.5	1
2003	Patriots	253	41	3232	202	15	4.9	2
2004	Patriots	311	45	3400	212.5	17	5.8	10
2005	Steelers	312	47	3168	198	16	5.3	3
2006	Colts	157	25	2548	159.3	2	5.8	13
2007	Giants	349	53	3317	207.3	11	5.8	10
2008	Steelers	350	51	2511	156.9	1	4.3	1
2009	Saints	192	35	3769	235.6	26	6.2	20
2010	Packers	333	47	3107	194.2	5	5.4	3
2011	Giants	335	48	4082	255.1	29	6.4	20
2012	Ravens	250	37	3650	228.1	17	6.1	16
2013	Seahawks	298	44	2752	172	1	4.8	1
2014	Patriots	282	40	3837	239.8	17	6.2	16
2015	Broncos	351	52	3193	199.6	1	5.1	1
2016	Patriots	227	34	3806	237.9	12	6	6
Average		277.1	42.5	3256.3	203.5	12.2	5.5	8.3

Defensive Rushing Yards

Year	Team	Rush Yds	R Yds/Gm	Rank	Att	Att/Game	R Yd/Att	Rank
1994	49ers	1338	83.6	2	375	23.4	3.6	8
1995	Cowboys	1772	110.8	16	442	27.6	4	18
1996	Packers	1416	88.5	4	400	25	3.5	5
1997	Broncos	1803	112.7	16	381	23.8	4.7	30
1998	Broncos	1287	80.4	3	356	22.3	3.6	7
1999	Rams	1189	74.3	1	338	21.1	3.5	6
2000	Ravens	970	60.6	1	361	22.6	2.7	1
2001	Patriots	1855	115.9	19	429	26.8	4.3	21
2002	Bucs	1554	97.1	5	410	25.6	3.8	5
2003	Patriots	1434	89.6	4	401	25.1	3.6	6
2004	Patriots	1572	98.3	6	405	25.3	3.9	11
2005	Steelers	1376	86	3	402	25.1	3.4	1
2006	Colts	2768	173	32	519	32.4	5.3	32
2007	Giants	1563	97.7	8	408	25.5	3.8	9
2008	Steelers	1284	80.3	2	390	24.4	3.3	1
2009	Saints	1955	122.2	21	435	27.2	4.5	26
2010	Packers	1838	114.9	18	395	24.7	4.7	28
2011	Giants	1940	121.3	19	435	27.2	4.5	23
2012	Ravens	1965	122.8	20	492	30.8	4	8
2013	Seahawks	1626	101.6	7	422	26.4	3.9	7
2014	Patriots	1669	104.3	9	419	26.2	4	9
2015	Broncos	1337	83.6	3	408	25.5	3.3	1
2016	Patriots	1417	88.6	3	368	23	3.9	25
	Average	1605.6	100.3	9.7	408.3	25.5	3.9	12.5

Defensive Passing Touchdowns-to-Interceptions, plus Rushing Touchdowns

Year	Team	Pass TDs	Rank	INT	Rank	Rush TDs	Rank	Total TDs
1994	49ers	15	2	23	1	16	23	31
1995	Cowboys	17	7	19	8	13	16	30
1996	Packers	12	3	26	2	7	5	19
1997	Broncos	20	11	18	8	10	6	30
1998	Broncos	28	28	19	10	8	4	36
1999	Rams	19	7	29	2	4	1	23
2000	Ravens	11	2	23	5	5	1	16
2001	Patriots	15	6	22	6	7	4	22
2002	Bucs	10	1	31	1	8	3	18
2003	Patriots	11	1	29	1	10	6	21
2004	Patriots	18	7	20	7	9	8	27
2005	Steelers	15	2	15	19	10	7	25
2006	Colts	16	5	15	20	20	30	36
2007	Giants	24	20	15	20	12	17	36
2008	Steelers	12	2	20	6	7	2	19
2009	Saints	15	5	26	3	19	28	34
2010	Packers	16	4	24	2	6	3	22
2011	Giants	28	25	20	6	15	23	43
2012	Ravens	15	2	13	19	15	23	30
2013	Seahawks	16	2	28	1	4	1	20
2014	Patriots	24	12	16	12	6	2	30
2015	Broncos	19	3	14	13	10	10	29
2016	Patriots	21	15	13	15	6	1	27
	Average	17.3	7.5	20.8	8.1	9.9	9.7	27.1

321

Turnover Ratios

Year	Team	Giveaways	Rank	Takeaways	Rank	Ratio	Rank
1994	49ers	24	5	35	5	11	3
1995	Cowboys	23	5	25	24	2	11
1996	Packers	24	2	39	3	15	2
1997	Broncos	21	6	31	9	10	4
1998	Broncos	20	3	30	13	10	5
1999	Rams	31	13	36	6	5	9
2000	Ravens	26	9	49	1	23	1
2001	Patriots	28	13	35	8	7	9
2002	Bucs	21	6	38	3	17	1
2003	Patriots	24	7	41	2	17	2
2004	Patriots	27	14	36	3	9	8
2005	Steelers	23	6	30	11	7	9
2006	Colts	19	4	26	21	7	6
2007	Giants	34	23	25	22	-9	26
2008	Steelers	25	15	29	9	4	11
2009	Saints	28	16	39	2	11	3
2010	Packers	22	10	32	6	10	4
2011	Giants	24	16	31	5	7	7
2012	Ravens	16	2	25	14	9	8
2013	Seahawks	19	4	39	1	20	1
2014	Patriots	13	1	25	14	12	2
2015	Broncos	31	29	27	8	-4	19
2016	Patriots	11	1	23	14	12	3
	Average	23.2	9.1	32.4	8.9	9.2	6.7

First Downs Per Game

Year	Team	O 1st Downs	Per Game	Rank	D 1st Downs	Per Game	Rank
1994	49ers	362	22.6	1	285	17.8	10
1995	Cowboys	364	22.8	1	303	18.9	11
1996	Packers	338	21.1	2	248	15.5	1
1997	Broncos	340	21.3	1	258	16.1	2
1998	Broncos	347	21.7	2	283	17.7	12
1999	Rams	335	20.9	2	263	16.4	7
2000	Ravens	288	18	18	216	13.5	2
2001	Patriots	292	18.3	13	303	18.9	25
2002	Bucs	287	17.9	23	236	14.8	1
2003	Patriots	294	18.4	16	293	18.3	17
2004	Patriots	344	21.5	6	290	18.1	10
2005	Steelers	297	18.6	17	275	17.2	9
2006	Colts	376	23.5	1	325	20.3	28
2007	Giants	321	20.1	7	288	18	10
2008	Steelers	290	18.1	20	240	15	2
2009	Saints	348	21.8	2	310	19.4	22
2010	Packers	312	19.5	13	270	16.9	4
2011	Giants	331	20.7	10	338	21.1	26
2012	Ravens	314	19.6	15	326	20.4	21
2013	Seahawks	307	19.2	20	282	17.6	3
2014	Patriots	361	22.6	4	329	20.6	22
2015	Broncos	314	19.6	19	289	18.1	5
2016	Patriots	351	21.9	5	294	18.4	3
	Average	326.7	20.4	9.5	284.5	17.8	11

323

Offensive Third Down Converstion Rate (Source: NFL.com)

Year	Team	O Made	O Att	3rd D %	Rank
1994	49ers	102	200	51.00%	1
1995	Cowboys	83	186	44.60%	6
1996	Packers	97	219	44.30%	2
1997	Broncos	92	217	42.40%	3
1998	Broncos	90	207	43.50%	5
1999	Rams	91	194	46.90%	1
2000	Ravens	95	236	40.30%	11
2001	Patriots	91	221	41.20%	8
2002	Bucs	79	222	35.60%	26
2003	Patriots	84	227	37.00%	15
2004	Patriots	93	206	45.10%	5
2005	Steelers	68	192	35.40%	23
2006	Colts	105	187	56.10%	1
2007	Giants	91	219	41.60%	12
2008	Steelers	92	224	41.10%	14
2009	Saints	88	197	44.70%	6
2010	Packers	85	205	41.50%	8
2011	Giants	77	206	37.40%	14
2012	Ravens	80	217	36.90%	20
2013	Seahawks	76	204	37.30%	17
2014	Patriots	98	221	44.30%	6
2015	Broncos	79	224	35.30%	25
2016	Patriots	104	227	45.80%	4
	Average	88.7	211.2	42.10%	10.1

Defensive Third Down Conversion Rate (Source: NFL.com)

Year	Team	O Made	O Att	3rd D %	Rank
1994	49ers	87	221	39.40%	13
1995	Cowboys	97	216	44.90%	26
1996	Packers	74	226	32.70%	2
1997	Broncos	65	207	31.40%	1
1998	Broncos	88	225	39.10%	21
1999	Rams	77	228	33.80%	10
2000	Ravens	72	211	34.10%	5
2001	Patriots	80	215	37.20%	15
2002	Bucs	75	223	33.60%	3
2003	Patriots	81	235	34.50%	7
2004	Patriots	81	209	38.80%	21
2005	Steelers	92	232	39.70%	20
2006	Colts	90	191	47.10%	32
2007	Giants	73	211	34.60%	5
2008	Steelers	71	226	31.40%	1
2009	Saints	82	216	38.00%	14
2010	Packers	77	213	36.20%	9
2011	Giants	84	220	38.20%	17
2012	Ravens	83	232	35.80%	7
2013	Seahawks	76	216	35.20%	10
2014	Patriots	84	209	40.20%	16
2015	Broncos	80	227	35.20%	7
2016	Patriots	76	206	36.90%	37
Average		80.2	218	36.90%	13

Offensive Fourth Down Conversion Rate (Source: NFL.com)

Year	Team	O Made	O Att	4th D %	Rank
1994	49ers	11	18	61.10%	4
1995	Cowboys	8	13	61.50%	7
1996	Packers	5	11	45.50%	14
1997	Broncos	7	16	43.80%	20
1998	Broncos	4	10	40.00%	18
1999	Rams	5	8	62.00%	5
2000	Ravens	1	6	16.70%	31
2001	Patriots	7	17	41.20%	20
2002	Bucs	6	9	66.70%	6
2003	Patriots	6	14	42.90%	21
2004	Patriots	4	10	40.00%	24
2005	Steelers	5	12	41.70%	20
2006	Colts	0	4	0.00%	32
2007	Giants	6	17	35.30%	27
2008	Steelers	3	12	25.00%	32
2009	Saints	6	15	40.00%	25
2010	Packers	5	13	38.50%	25
2011	Giants	4	13	30.80%	26
2012	Ravens	6	14	42.90%	22
2013	Seahawks	6	11	54.50%	13
2014	Patriots	7	13	53.80%	8
2015	Broncos	7	14	50.00%	15
2016	Patriots	8	12	66.70%	7
	Average	5.5	12.3	43.50%	18.3

Defensive Fourth Down Conversion Rate (Source: NFL.com)

Year	Team	O Made	O Att	4th D %	Rank
1994	49ers	11	19	57.90%	24
1995	Cowboys	8	19	42.10%	6
1996	Packers	14	22	63.60%	27
1997	Broncos	8	19	42.10%	9
1998	Broncos	10	19	52.60%	22
1999	Rams	12	25	48.00%	20
2000	Ravens	4	19	21.10%	4
2001	Patriots	5	15	33.30%	8
2002	Bucs	8	13	61.50%	26
2003	Patriots	6	16	37.50%	7
2004	Patriots	13	30	43.30%	14
2005	Steelers	6	17	35.30%	8
2006	Colts	11	14	78.60%	30
2007	Giants	10	16	62.50%	29
2008	Steelers	10	21	47.60%	13
2009	Saints	11	24	45.80%	9
2010	Packers	6	20	30.00%	4
2011	Giants	10	18	55.60%	26
2012	Ravens	6	12	50.00%	17
2013	Seahawks	4	11	36.40%	8
2014	Patriots	8	23	34.80%	6
2015	Broncos	5	14	35.70%	8
2016	Patriots	7	18	38.90%	10
	Average	8.4	18.4	45.80%	14.6

Offensive Red Zone Percentage - Score meands TD, FGs do not count toward RZ % (only has data to 1999)

Year	Team	RZ Score	RZ Att	RZ %	Rank
1999	Rams	37	56	66.07%	2
2000	Ravens	20	50	40.00%	26
2001	Patriots	25	52	48.08%	16
2002	Buccaneers	23	51	45.10%	28
2003	Patriots	22	50	44.00%	27
2004	Patriots	37	63	58.73%	7
2005	Steelers	34	56	60.71%	5
2006	Colts	41	62	66.13%	2
2007	Giants	30	55	54.55%	12
2008	Steelers	27	49	55.10%	15
2009	Saints	41	71	57.75%	6
2010	Packers	32	53	60.38%	6
2011	Giants	32	56	57.14%	8
2012	Ravens	28	49	57.14%	11
2013	Seahawks	32	57	56.14%	12
2014	Patriots	39	67	58.21%	9
2015	Broncos	21	44	47.73%	28
2016	Patriots	38	60	63.33%	8
	Average	31.1	55.6	55.30%	12.7

Defensive Red Zone Percentage - Score meands TD, FGs do not count toward RZ % (only has data to 1999)

Year	Team	RZ Score	RZ Att	RZ %	Rank
1999	Rams	19	36	52.78%	23
2000	Ravens	8	27	29.63%	2
2001	Patriots	19	49	38.78%	3
2002	Buccaneers	12	35	34.29%	1
2003	Patriots	18	46	39.13%	4
2004	Patriots	20	49	40.82%	3
2005	Steelers	23	48	47.92%	10
2006	Colts	30	51	58.82%	31
2007	Giants	25	42	59.52%	28
2008	Steelers	14	42	33.33%	1
2009	Saints	22	56	39.29%	2
2010	Packers	15	31	48.39%	12
2011	Giants	34	61	55.74%	21
2012	Ravens	23	53	43.40%	2
2013	Seahawks	13	36	36.11%	1
2014	Patriots	22	46	47.83%	6
2015	Broncos	22	37	59.46%	20
2016	Patriots	23	44	52.27%	8
	Average	20.1	43.8	45.40%	9.9

Team Sacks

Year	Team	O Sacks	Per Game	Yards	D Sacks	Per Game	Yards
1994	49ers	35	2.2	199	38	2.4	255
1995	Cowboys	18	1.1	118	36	2.3	219
1996	Packers	40	2.5	241	37	2.3	202
1997	Broncos	35	2.2	210	44	2.8	298
1998	Broncos	25	1.6	184	47	2.9	335
1999	Rams	33	2.1	227	57	3.6	358
2000	Ravens	43	2.7	287	35	2.2	178
2001	Patriots	46	2.9	237	41	2.6	234
2002	Bucs	41	2.6	220	43	2.7	295
2003	Patriots	32	2	219	41	2.6	253
2004	Patriots	26	1.6	162	45	2.8	311
2005	Steelers	32	2	178	47	2.9	312
2006	Colts	15	0.9	89	25	1.6	157
2007	Giants	28	1.8	222	53	3.3	349
2008	Steelers	49	3.1	306	51	3.2	350
2009	Saints	20	1.3	135	35	2.2	192
2010	Packers	38	2.4	231	47	2.9	333
2011	Giants	28	1.8	199	48	3	335
2012	Ravens	38	2.4	257	37	2.3	250
2013	Seahawks	44	2.8	272	44	2.8	298
2014	Patriots	26	1.6	170	40	2.5	282
2015	Broncos	39	2.4	246	52	3.3	351
2016	Patriots	24	1.5	148	34	2.1	227
Average		32.8	2.1	206.8	42.5	2.7	277.1

Big Plays of 20+ Yards (Source: NFL.com)

Year	Team	O Passing	Rank	O Rushing	Rank	Total	Per Game	D Passing	Rank	D Rushing	Rank	Total	Per Game
1994	49ers	53	4	11	4	64	4	36	7	3	1	39	2.4
1995	Cowboys	44	14	13	3	57	3.6	43	12	8	12	51	3.2
1996	Packers	50	3	4	27	54	3.4	32	3	7	11	39	2.4
1997	Broncos	53	5	8	17	61	3.8	35	4	17	31	52	3.3
1998	Broncos	48	7	17	2	65	4.1	49	21	13	22	62	3.9
1999	Rams	62	3	14	4	76	4.8	48	19	5	3	53	3.3
2000	Ravens	37	21	11	11	48	3	33	4	3	2	36	2.3
2001	Patriots	38	24	10	17	48	3	50	25	8	6	58	3.6
2002	Bucs	37	23	9	19	46	2.9	40	10	4	1	44	2.8
2003	Patriots	44	14	5	28	49	3.1	37	8	2	1	39	2.4
2004	Patriots	53	11	9	15	62	3.9	44	14	4	3	48	3
2005	Steelers	44	10	11	9	55	3.4	38	12	7	7	45	2.8
2006	Colts	53	6	3	30	56	3.5	27	1	18	32	45	2.8
2007	Giants	36	25	11	11	47	2.9	47	21	9	13	56	3.5
2008	Steelers	39	20	8	26	47	2.9	23	1	4	1	27	1.7
2009	Saints	58	8	14	8	72	4.5	48	19	11	18	59	3.7
2010	Packers	57	6	3	31	60	3.8	44	10	10	10	54	3.4
2011	Giants	67	5	4	32	71	4.4	60	29	11	16	71	4.4
2012	Ravens	62	5	10	18	72	4.5	49	17	8	7	57	3.6
2013	Seahawks	52	13	11	10	63	3.9	30	1	6	4	36	2.3
2014	Patriots	46	22	7	20	53	3.3	62	28	2	1	64	4
2015	Broncos	41	29	11	13	52	3.3	41	2	5	3	46	2.9
2016	Patriots	56	8	8	17	64	4	53	20	3	1	56	3.5
Average		49.1	12.4	9.2	16.2	58.3	3.6	42.1	12.5	7.3	9	49.4	3.1

Kicking Percentage

Year	Team	FGA	FGM	FG %	XPA	XPM	XP%
1994	49ers	15	20	75.00%	60	62	96.80%
1995	Cowboys	27	28	96.40%	46	48	95.80%
1996	Packers	21	27	77.80%	51	53	96.20%
1997	Broncos	28	39	71.80%	50	50	100.00%
1998	Broncos	23	27	85.20%	58	59	98.30%
1999	Rams	20	28	71.40%	64	64	100.00%
2000	Ravens	35	39	89.70%	30	30	100.00%
2001	Patriots	24	30	80.00%	41	42	97.60%
2002	Bucs	32	39	82.10%	32	32	100.00%
2003	Patriots	25	34	73.50%	37	38	97.40%
2004	Patriots	31	33	93.90%	48	48	100.00%
2005	Steelers	24	29	82.80%	45	45	100.00%
2006	Colts	26	29	89.70%	47	48	97.90%
2007	Giants	23	27	85.20%	40	42	95.20%
2008	Steelers	27	31	87.10%	36	37	97.30%
2009	Saints	22	28	78.60%	60	63	95.20%
2010	Packers	22	28	78.60%	46	46	100.00%
2011	Giants	19	24	79.20%	43	43	100.00%
2012	Ravens	30	33	90.90%	42	42	100.00%
2013	Seahawks	33	35	94.30%	44	44	100.00%
2014	Patriots	35	37	94.60%	51	51	100.00%
2015	Broncos	30	35	85.70%	35	36	97.20%
2016	Patriots	27	32	84.40%	46	49	93.90%
	Average	26	31	83.80%	45.7	46.6	98.20%

Punting Stats

Year	Team	Punts	Per Game	Yards	Per Game	Block	Yds/Punt
1994	49ers	54	3.4	2235	139.7	0	41.4
1995	Cowboys	55	3.4	2243	140.2	0	40.8
1996	Packers	68	4.3	2886	180.4	0	42.4
1997	Broncos	60	3.8	2598	162.4	0	43.3
1998	Broncos	66	4.1	3097	193.6	1	46.9
1999	Rams	60	3.8	2464	154	0	41.1
2000	Ravens	86	5.4	3457	216.1	0	40.2
2001	Patriots	74	4.6	3042	190.1	0	41.1
2002	Bucs	91	5.7	3879	242.4	0	42.6
2003	Patriots	87	5.4	3266	204.1	1	37.5
2004	Patriots	56	3.5	2350	146.9	0	42
2005	Steelers	69	4.3	2875	179.7	0	41.7
2006	Colts	47	2.9	2085	130.3	1	44.4
2007	Giants	71	4.4	2865	179.1	1	40.4
2008	Steelers	78	4.9	3107	194.2	0	39.8
2009	Saints	58	3.6	2528	158	0	43.6
2010	Packers	71	4.4	3114	194.6	0	43.9
2011	Giants	82	5.1	3745	234.1	0	45.7
2012	Ravens	83	5.2	3911	244.4	0	47.1
2013	Seahawks	74	4.6	3159	197.4	2	42.7
2014	Patriots	66	4.1	3060	191.3	1	46.4
2015	Broncos	85	5.3	3704	231.5	0	43.6
2016	Patriots	72	4.5	3217	201.1	0	44.7
Average		70.1	4.4	2995.1	187.2	0.3	42.7

Punt Return Stats

Year	Team	PR #	Yds	TD	Lng	Yds/PR
1994	49ers	40	334	0	26	8.4
1995	Cowboys	23	255	0	43	11.1
1996	Packers	58	875	3	92	15.1
1997	Broncos	41	555	3	94	13.6
1998	Broncos	38	399	0	44	10.5
1999	Rams	52	498	1	84	9.6
2000	Ravens	45	713	2	89	15.8
2001	Patriots	33	440	2	85	13.3
2002	Bucs	44	430	1	56	9.8
2003	Patriots	50	462	0	23	9.2
2004	Patriots	40	230	0	23	5.8
2005	Steelers	46	470	2	81	10.2
2006	Colts	23	207	1	82	9
2007	Giants	43	319	0	27	7.4
2008	Steelers	41	247	0	35	6
2009	Saints	33	152	0	23	4.6
2010	Packers	41	325	0	52	7.9
2011	Giants	28	171	0	18	6.1
2012	Ravens	43	404	1	63	9.4
2013	Seahawks	52	579	0	71	11.1
2014	Patriots	41	431	1	84	10.5
2015	Broncos	29	283	1	83	9.8
2016	Patriots	45	309	0	30	6.9
Average		40.4	395.1	0.8	56.9	9.6

Opponent's Punt Returns

Year	Team	PR #	Yds	TD	Yds/PR
1994	49ers	28	242	0	8.6
1995	Cowboys	22	216	0	9.8
1996	Packers	29	237	0	8.2
1997	Broncos	26	235	1	9
1998	Broncos	43	381	0	8.9
1999	Rams	21	134	0	6.4
2000	Ravens	40	373	0	9.3
2001	Patriots	26	124	0	4.8
2002	Bucs	42	433	0	10.3
2003	Patriots	38	240	1	6.3
2004	Patriots	31	365	1	11.8
2005	Steelers	37	336	0	9.1
2006	Colts	25	327	1	13.1
2007	Giants	28	173	0	6.2
2008	Steelers	40	247	0	6.2
2009	Saints	25	358	1	14.3
2010	Packers	31	341	1	11
2011	Giants	41	407	0	9.9
2012	Ravens	49	383	0	7.8
2013	Seahawks	21	82	0	3.9
2014	Patriots	29	267	0	9.2
2015	Broncos	36	247	0	6.9
2016	Patriots	27	134	0	5
Average		32	273.1	0.3	8.5

Kick Return Stats

Year	Team	KR #	Yds	TD	Long	Yd/KR
1994	49ers	58	1244	1	96	21.4
1995	Cowboys	58	1276	0	46	22
1996	Packers	47	1038	1	90	22.1
1997	Broncos	54	1203	0	61	22.3
1998	Broncos	58	1402	1	95	24.2
1999	Rams	54	1354	2	101	25.1
2000	Ravens	45	1005	0	41	22.3
2001	Patriots	59	1184	0	42	20.1
2002	Bucs	45	1085	0	67	24.1
2003	Patriots	60	1428	1	92	23.8
2004	Patriots	56	1302	1	93	23.3
2005	Steelers	56	1208	0	74	21.6
2006	Colts	58	1368	0	70	23.6
2007	Giants	66	1579	1	74	23.9
2008	Steelers	50	1013	0	43	20.3
2009	Saints	57	1393	1	97	24.4
2010	Packers	62	1249	0	51	20.1
2011	Giants	52	1209	0	40	23.3
2012	Ravens	60	1636	2	108	27.3
2013	Seahawks	33	698	0	58	21.2
2014	Patriots	31	693	0	81	22.4
2015	Broncos	27	588	0	41	21.8
2016	Patriots	29	542	0	73	18.7
Average		51.1	1160.7	0.5	71	22.6

Opponent Kick Return Stats

Year	Team	KR #	Yds	TD	Yd/KR
1994	49ers	89	1912	0	21.5
1995	Cowboys	85	1661	0	19.5
1996	Packers	76	1649	0	21.7
1997	Broncos	89	1827	0	20.5
1998	Broncos	89	2006	0	22.5
1999	Rams	85	2115	0	24.9
2000	Ravens	73	1558	0	21.3
2001	Patriots	75	1658	0	22.1
2002	Bucs	72	1567	0	21.8
2003	Patriots	77	1623	0	21.1
2004	Patriots	86	2003	1	23.3
2005	Steelers	77	1685	0	21.9
2006	Colts	78	2029	2	26
2007	Giants	69	1596	1	23.1
2008	Steelers	71	1357	0	19.1
2009	Saints	74	1813	0	24.5
2010	Packers	76	1658	0	21.8
2011	Giants	46	1053	0	22.9
2012	Ravens	37	859	0	23.2
2013	Seahawks	44	1056	0	24
2014	Patriots	45	955	0	21.2
2015	Broncos	25	508	0	20.3
2016	Patriots	40	771	0	19.3
Average		68.6	1518.2	0.2	22.1

337

Team Penalties

Year	Team	Penalties	Per Game	Yardage	Per Game	1st D by PEN	Per Game
1994	49ers	109	6.8	890	55.6	30	1.9
1995	Cowboys	90	5.6	695	43.4	28	1.8
1996	Packers	92	5.8	714	44.6	23	1.4
1997	Broncos	116	7.3	1006	62.9	30	1.9
1998	Broncos	115	7.2	1023	63.9	26	1.6
1999	Rams	113	7.1	889	55.6	26	1.6
2000	Ravens	95	5.9	730	45.6	16	1
2001	Patriots	92	5.8	802	50.1	28	1.8
2002	Bucs	103	6.4	789	49.3	25	1.6
2003	Patriots	111	6.9	998	62.4	26	1.6
2004	Patriots	101	6.3	822	51.4	31	1.9
2005	Steelers	99	6.2	876	54.8	33	2.1
2006	Colts	86	5.4	718	44.9	23	1.4
2007	Giants	77	4.8	652	40.8	35	2.2
2008	Steelers	95	5.9	812	50.8	18	1.1
2009	Saints	89	5.6	787	49.2	18	1.1
2010	Packers	78	4.9	617	38.6	20	1.3
2011	Giants	94	5.9	795	49.7	31	1.9
2012	Ravens	121	7.6	1127	70.4	34	2.1
2013	Seahawks	128	8	1183	73.9	31	1.9
2014	Patriots	120	7.5	1080	67.5	37	2.3
2015	Broncos	115	7.2	1063	66.4	28	1.8
2016	Patriots	93	5.8	819	51.2	39	2.4
	Average	101.4	6.3	864.7	54	27.7	1.7

Super Bowl Champions Opponent's Penalties

Year	Team	Penalties	Per Game	Yardage	Per Game	1st D by PEN	Per Game
1994	49ers	108	6.8	912	57	21	1.3
1995	Cowboys	112	7	913	57.1	25	1.6
1996	Packers	107	6.7	797	49.8	23	1.4
1997	Broncos	130	8.1	1118	69.9	30	1.9
1998	Broncos	113	7.1	865	54.1	20	1.3
1999	Rams	114	7.1	1007	62.9	21	1.3
2000	Ravens	84	5.3	535	33.4	22	1.4
2001	Patriots	93	5.8	839	52.4	33	2.1
2002	Bucs	93	5.8	749	46.8	26	1.6
2003	Patriots	107	6.7	845	52.8	25	1.6
2004	Patriots	118	7.4	1014	63.4	30	1.9
2005	Steelers	120	7.5	1031	64.4	21	1.3
2006	Colts	86	5.4	667	41.7	25	1.6
2007	Giants	118	7.4	874	54.6	20	1.3
2008	Steelers	91	5.7	801	50.1	18	1.1
2009	Saints	86	5.4	717	44.8	24	1.5
2010	Packers	98	6.1	758	47.4	25	1.6
2011	Giants	110	6.9	933	58.3	25	1.6
2012	Ravens	107	6.7	929	58.1	34	2.1
2013	Seahawks	98	6.1	879	54.9	43	2.7
2014	Patriots	92	5.8	752	47	45	2.8
2015	Broncos	104	6.5	773	48.3	46	2.9
2016	Patriots	113	7.1	930	58.1	23	1.4
	Average	104.4	6.5	853.8	53.4	27.2	1.7

Super Bowl Penalty Difference (Champions Penalties - Opponent's Penalties)

Year	Team	Penalties	Per Game	Yardage	Per Game	1st D by PEN	Per Game
1994	49ers	1	0.1	-22	-1.4	9	0.6
1995	Cowboys	-22	-1.4	-218	-13.6	3	0.2
1996	Packers	-15	-0.9	-83	-5.2	0	0
1997	Broncos	-14	-0.9	-112	-7	0	0
1998	Broncos	2	0.1	158	9.9	6	0.4
1999	Rams	-1	-0.1	-118	-7.4	5	0.3
2000	Ravens	11	0.7	195	12.2	-6	-0.4
2001	Patriots	-1	-0.1	-37	-2.3	-5	-0.3
2002	Bucs	10	0.6	40	2.5	-1	-0.1
2003	Patriots	4	0.3	153	9.6	1	0.1
2004	Patriots	-17	-1.1	-192	-12	1	0.1
2005	Steelers	-21	-1.3	-155	-9.7	12	0.8
2006	Colts	0	0	51	3.2	-2	-0.1
2007	Giants	-41	-2.6	-222	-13.9	15	0.9
2008	Steelers	4	0.3	11	0.7	0	0
2009	Saints	3	0.2	70	4.4	-6	-0.4
2010	Packers	-20	-1.3	-141	-8.8	-5	-0.3
2011	Giants	-16	-1	-138	-8.6	6	0.4
2012	Ravens	14	0.9	198	12.4	0	0
2013	Seahawks	30	1.9	304	19	-12	-0.8
2014	Patriots	28	1.8	328	20.5	-8	-0.5
2015	Broncos	11	0.7	290	18.1	-18	-1.1
2016	Patriots	-20	-1.3	-111	-6.9	16	1
	Average	-3	-0.2	10.8	0.7	0.5	0

Super Bowl Starting Quarterback Season Stats

Year	Team	Player	G	GS	W	L	Cmp	Att	Cmp %	Yds	TD	INT	Yds/G	Yds/Cmp	Yds/Att
1994	SF	Steve Young	16	16	13	3	324	461	70.30%	3969	35	10	248.1	12.3	8.6
1995	DAL	Troy Aikman	16	16	12	4	280	432	64.80%	3304	16	7	206.5	11.8	7.6
1996	GB	Brett Favre	16	16	13	3	325	543	59.90%	3899	39	13	243.7	12	7.2
1997	DEN	John Elway	16	16	12	4	280	502	55.80%	3635	27	11	227.2	13	7.2
1998	DEN	John Elway	13	12	10	2	210	356	59.00%	2806	22	10	215.8	13.4	7.9
1999	STL	Kurt Warner	16	16	13	3	325	499	65.10%	4353	41	13	272.1	13.4	8.7
2000	BAL	Trent Dilfer	11	8	7	1	134	226	59.30%	1502	12	11	136.5	11.2	6.6
2001	NE	Tom Brady	15	14	11	3	264	413	63.90%	2843	18	12	189.5	10.8	6.9
2002	TB	Brad Johnson	13	13	10	3	281	451	62.30%	3049	22	6	234.5	10.9	6.8
2003	NE	Tom Brady	16	16	14	2	317	527	60.20%	3620	23	12	226.3	11.4	6.9
2004	NE	Tom Brady	16	16	14	2	288	474	60.80%	3692	28	14	230.8	12.8	7.8
2005	PIT	Ben Roethlisberger	12	12	9	3	168	268	62.70%	2385	17	9	198.8	14.2	8.9
2006	IND	Peyton Manning	16	16	12	4	362	557	65.00%	4397	31	9	274.8	12.1	7.9
2007	NYG	Eli Manning	16	16	10	6	297	529	56.10%	3336	23	20	208.5	11.2	6.3
2008	PIT	Ben Roethlisberger	16	16	12	4	281	469	59.90%	3301	17	15	206.3	11.7	7
2009	NO	Drew Brees	15	15	13	2	363	514	70.60%	4388	34	11	292.5	12.1	8.5
2010	GB	Aaron Rodgers	15	15	10	5	312	475	65.70%	3922	28	11	261.5	12.6	8.3
2011	NYG	Eli Manning	16	16	9	7	359	589	61.00%	4933	29	16	308.3	13.7	8.4
2012	BAL	Joe Flacco	16	16	10	6	317	531	59.70%	3817	22	10	238.6	12	7.2
2013	SEA	Russell Wilson	16	16	13	3	257	407	63.10%	3357	26	9	209.8	13.1	8.2
2014	NE	Tom Brady	16	16	12	4	373	582	64.10%	4109	33	9	256.8	11	7.1
2015	DEN	Peyton Manning	10	9	7	2	198	331	59.80%	2249	9	17	224.9	11.4	6.8
2016	NE	Tom Brady	12	12	11	1	291	432	67.40%	3554	28	2	296.2	12.2	8.2
Averages			14.8	14.5	11.2	3.3	287.2	459.5	62.50%	3496.5	25.2	11.2	235.1	12.2	7.6

Leading Rushers on Super Bowl Champions - Rushing Stats

Year	Team	Player	Position	Carries	Rush Yds	Yds/Rush	Rush TDs
1994	SF	Ricky Watters	RB	239	877	3.7	6
1995	DAL	Emmitt Smith	RB	377	1773	4.7	25
1996	GB	Edgar Bennett	RB	222	899	4	2
1997	DEN	Terrell Davis	RB	369	1750	4.7	15
1998	DEN	Terrell Davis	RB	392	2008	5.1	21
1999	STL	Marshall Faulk	RB	253	1381	5.5	7
2000	BAL	Jamal Lewis	RB	309	1364	4.4	6
2001	NE	Antowain Smith	RB	287	1157	4	12
2002	TB	Michael Pittman	RB	204	718	3.5	1
2003	NE	Antowain Smith	RB	182	642	3.5	3
2004	NE	Corey Dillon	RB	345	1635	4.7	12
2005	PIT	Willie Parker	RB	255	1202	4.7	4
2006	IND	Joseph Addai	RB	226	1081	4.8	7
2007	NYG	Brandon Jacobs	RB	202	1009	5	4
2008	PIT	Willie Parker	RB	210	791	3.8	5
2009	NO	Pierre Thomas	RB	147	793	5.4	6
2010	GB	Brandon Jackson	RB	190	703	3.7	3
2011	NYG	Ahmad Bradshaw	RB	171	659	3.9	9
2012	BAL	Ray Rice	RB	257	1143	4.4	9
2013	SEA	Marshawn Lynch	RB	301	1257	4.2	12
2014	NE	Jonas Gray	RB	89	412	4.6	5
2015	DEN	Ronnie Hillman	RB	207	863	4.2	7
2016	NE	LeGarrette Blount	RB	299	1161	3.9	18
1994-2016				249.3	1099	4.4	8.7

Leading Rushers on Super Bowl Champions - Receiving Stats and Total Yards

Year	Team	Player	Rec	Targets	Catch Rate	Rec Yds	Yds/Rec	Tds/Target	Rec TDs	Total Yds	Total TDs
1994	SF	Ricky Watters	66	88	75.00%	719	10.9	8.2	5	1596	11
1995	DAL	Emmitt Smith	62	78	79.49%	375	6	4.8	0	2148	25
1996	GB	Edgar Bennett	31	39	79.49%	176	5.7	4.5	1	1075	3
1997	DEN	Terrell Davis	42	58	72.41%	287	6.8	4.9	0	2037	15
1998	DEN	Terrell Davis	25	38	65.79%	217	8.7	5.7	2	2225	23
1999	STL	Marshall Faulk	87	103	84.47%	1048	12	10.2	5	2429	12
2000	BAL	Jamal Lewis	27	36	75.00%	296	11	8.2	0	1660	6
2001	NE	Antowain Smith	19	28	67.86%	192	10.1	6.9	1	1349	13
2002	TB	Michael Pittman	59	86	68.60%	477	8.1	5.5	0	1195	1
2003	NE	Antowain Smith	14	16	87.50%	92	6.6	5.8	0	734	3
2004	NE	Corey Dillon	15	21	71.43%	103	6.9	4.9	1	1738	13
2005	PIT	Willie Parker	18	24	75.00%	218	12.1	9.1	1	1420	5
2006	IND	Joseph Addai	40	50	80.00%	325	8.1	6.5	1	1406	8
2007	NYG	Brandon Jacobs	23	38	60.53%	174	7.6	4.6	2	1183	6
2008	PIT	Willie Parker	3	10	30.00%	13	4.3	1.3	0	804	5
2009	NO	Pierre Thomas	39	45	86.67%	302	7.7	6.7	2	1095	8
2010	GB	Brandon Jackson	43	50	86.00%	342	8	6.8	1	1045	4
2011	NYG	Ahmad Bradshaw	34	44	77.27%	267	7.9	6.1	2	926	11
2012	BAL	Ray Rice	61	83	73.49%	478	7.8	5.8	1	1621	10
2013	SEA	Marshawn Lynch	36	44	81.82%	316	8.8	7.2	2	1573	14
2014	NE	Jonas Gray	1	3	33.33%	7	7	2.3	0	419	5
2015	DEN	Ronnie Hillman	24	35	68.57%	111	4.6	3.2	0	974	7
2016	NE	LeGarrette Blount	7	8	87.50%	38	5.4	4.8	0	1199	18
1994-2016			33.7	44.6	72.49%	285.8	8.2	6	1.2	1384.8	9.8

Second Leading Rusher on Super Bowl Champions - Rushing Stats

Year	Team	Player	Position	Carries	Rush Yds	Yds/Rush	Rush TDs
1994	SF	William Floyd	FB	87	305	3.5	6
1995	DAL	Sherman Williams	RB	48	205	4.3	1
1996	GB	Dorsey Levens	RB	121	566	4.7	5
1997	DEN	Vaughn Hebron	RB	49	222	4.5	1
1998	DEN	Derek Loville	RB	53	161	3	2
1999	STL	Robert Holcombe	FB/RB	78	294	3.8	4
2000	BAL	Priest Holmes	RB	137	588	4.3	2
2001	NE	Kevin Faulk	RB	41	169	4.1	1
2002	TB	Mike Alstott	FB/RB	146	548	3.8	5
2003	NE	Kevin Faulk	RB/FB	178	638	3.6	0
2004	NE	Kevin Faulk	RB	54	255	4.7	2
2005	PIT	Jerome Bettis	RB	110	368	3.3	9
2006	IND	Dominic Rhodes	RB	187	641	3.4	5
2007	NYG	Derrick Ward	RB	125	602	4.8	3
2008	PIT	Mewelde Moore	RB	140	588	4.2	5
2009	NO	Mike Bell	RB	172	654	3.8	5
2010	GB	Aaron Rodgers	QB	64	356	5.6	4
2011	NYG	Brandon Jacobs	RB	152	571	3.8	7
2012	BAL	Bernard Pierce	RB	108	532	4.9	1
2013	SEA	Russell Wilson	QB	96	539	5.6	1
2014	NE	Shane Vereen	RB	96	391	4.1	2
2015	DEN	CJ Anderson	RB	152	720	4.7	5
2016	NE	Dion Lewis	RB	64	283	4.4	0
1994-2016		No QBs on REC		106.9	443.3	4.2	3.3

Second Leading Rusher on Super Bowl Champions - Receiving Stats and Total Yards

Year	Team	Player	Rec	Targets	Catch Rate	Rec Yds	Yds/Rec	Yds/Target	Rec TDs	Total Yds	Total TDs
1994	SF	William Floyd	19	26	73.08%	145	7.6	5.6	0	450	6
1995	DAL	Sherman Williams	3	3	100.00%	28	9.3	9.3	0	233	1
1996	GB	Dorsey Levens	31	33	93.94%	226	7.3	6.8	5	792	10
1997	DEN	Vaughn Hebron	3	5	60.00%	36	12	7.2	0	258	1
1998	DEN	Derek Loville	2	2	100.00%	29	14.5	14.5	0	190	2
1999	STL	Robert Holcombe	14	27	51.85%	163	11.6	6	1	457	5
2000	BAL	Priest Holmes	32	46	69.57%	221	6.9	4.8	0	809	2
2001	NE	Kevin Faulk	30	36	83.33%	189	6.3	5.3	2	358	3
2002	TB	Mike Alstott	35	48	72.92%	242	6.9	5	2	790	7
2003	NE	Kevin Faulk	48	67	71.64%	440	9.2	6.6	0	1078	0
2004	NE	Kevin Faulk	26	30	86.67%	248	9.5	8.3	1	503	3
2005	PIT	Jerome Bettis	4	4	100.00%	40	10	10	0	408	9
2006	IND	Dominic Rhodes	36	47	76.60%	251	7	5.3	0	892	5
2007	NYG	Derrick Ward	26	40	65.00%	179	6.9	4.5	1	781	4
2008	PIT	Mewelde Moore	40	53	75.47%	320	8	6	1	908	6
2009	NO	Mike Bell	4	4	100.00%	12	3	3	0	666	5
2010	GB	Aaron Rodgers	0	0	0.00%	0	0	0	0	356	4
2011	NYG	Brandon Jacobs	15	23	65.22%	128	8.5	5.6	1	699	8
2012	BAL	Bernard Pierce	7	11	63.64%	47	6.7	4.3	0	579	1
2013	SEA	Russell Wilson	0	0	0.00%	0	0	0	0	539	1
2014	NE	Shane Vereen	52	77	67.53%	447	8.6	5.8	3	838	5
2015	DEN	CJ Anderson	25	36	69.44%	183	7.3	5.1	0	903	5
2016	NE	Dion Lewis	17	24	70.83%	94	5.5	3.9	0	377	0
1994-2016	No QBs on REC		22.3	30.6	0.8	174.7	8.2	6.3	0.8	617.6	4.2

345

Third Leading Rusher on Super Bowl Champions - Rushing Stats

Year	Team	Player	Position	Carries	Rush Yds	Yds/Rush	Rush TDs
1994	SF	Steve Young	QB	58	293	5.1	7
1995	DAL	Daryl Johnston	FB	25	111	4.4	2
1996	GB	Brett Favre	QB	49	136	2.8	2
1997	DEN	John Elway	QB	50	218	4.4	1
1998	DEN	Bubby Brister	QB	19	102	5.4	1
1999	STL	Justin Watson	RB	47	179	3.8	0
2000	BAL	Trent Dilfer	QB	20	75	3.8	0
2001	NE	Marc Edwards	FB/WR	51	141	2.8	1
2002	TB	Aaron Stecker	RB	28	174	6.2	0
2003	NE	Mike Cloud	RB	27	118	4.4	5
2004	NE	Patrick Pass	FB	39	141	3.6	0
2005	PIT	Verron Haynes	RB	74	274	3.7	3
2006	IND	Peyton Manning	QB	23	36	1.6	4
2007	NYG	Reuben Droughns	RB	85	275	3.2	6
2008	PIT	Ben Roethlisberger	QB	34	101	3	2
2009	NO	Reggie Bush	RB	70	390	5.6	5
2010	GB	John Kuhn	FB/RB	84	281	3.3	4
2011	NYG	Danny Ware	RB	46	163	3.5	0
2012	BAL	Tyrod Taylor	QB	14	73	5.2	1
2013	SEA	Robert Turbin	RB	77	264	3.4	0
2014	NE	Stevan Ridley	RB	94	340	3.6	2
2015	DEN	Brock Osweiler	QB	21	61	2.9	1
2016	NE	James White	RB	39	166	4.3	0
1994-2016	No QBs on REC			46.7	178.8	3.9	2

Third Leading Rusher on Super Bowl Champions – Receiving Stats and Total Yards

Year	Team	Player	Rec	Targets	Catch Rate	Rec Yds	Yds/Rec	Yds/Target	Rec TDs	Total Yards	Total TDs
1994	SF	Steve Young	0	0	0.00%	0	0	0	0	293	7
1995	DAL	Daryl Johnston	30	46	65.20%	248	8.3	5.4	1	359	3
1996	GB	Brett Favre	0	0	0.00%	0	0	0	0	136	2
1997	DEN	John Elway	0	0	0.00%	0	0	0	0	218	1
1998	DEN	Bubby Brister	0	0	0.00%	0	0	0	0	102	1
1999	STL	Justin Watson	5	0	0.00%	0	0	0	0	179	0
2000	BAL	Trent Dilfer	1	1	100.00%	-1	-1	-1	0	74	0
2001	NE	Marc Edwards	25	39	64.10%	166	6.6	4.3	2	307	3
2002	TB	Aaron Stecker	13	16	81.30%	69	5.3	4.3	0	243	0
2003	NE	Mike Cloud	1	2	50.00%	8	8	4	0	126	5
2004	NE	Patrick Pass	28	32	87.50%	215	7.7	6.7	0	356	0
2005	PIT	Verron Haynes	11	17	64.70%	113	10.3	6.6	0	387	3
2006	IND	Peyton Manning	0	0	0.00%	0	0	0	0	36	4
2007	NYG	Reuben Droughns	7	15	46.70%	49	7	3.3	0	324	6
2008	PIT	Ben Roethlisberger	1	1	100.00%	-7	-7	-7	0	94	2
2009	NO	Reggie Bush	47	68	69.10%	335	7.1	4.9	3	725	8
2010	GB	John Kuhn	15	18	83.30%	97	6.5	5.4	2	378	6
2011	NYG	Danny Ware	27	37	73.00%	170	6.3	4.6	0	333	0
2012	BAL	Tyrod Taylor	0	0	0.00%	0	0	0	0	73	1
2013	SEA	Robert Turbin	8	12	66.70%	60	7.5	5	0	324	0
2014	NE	Stevan Ridley	4	5	80.00%	20	5	4	0	360	2
2015	DEN	Brock Osweiler	0	0	0.00%	0	0	0	0	61	1
2016	NE	James White	60	86	69.80%	551	9.2	6.4	5	717	5
1994-2016		No QBs on REC	20.1	28.1	64.40%	150.1	6.8	4.6	0.9	365.6	2.9

347

Leading Receivers on Super Bowl Champions

Year	Team	Player	Position	Rec	Targets	Catch Rate	Rec Yds	Yds/Rec	Yds/Target	Rec TDs
1994	SF	Jerry Rice	WR	112	151	74.20%	1499	13.4	9.9	13
1995	DAL	Michael Irvin	WR	111	165	67.30%	1603	14.4	9.7	10
1996	GB	Antonio Freeman	WR	56	107	52.30%	933	16.7	8.7	9
1997	DEN	Rod Smith	WR	70	131	53.40%	1180	16.9	9	12
1998	DEN	Rod Smith	WR	86	139	61.90%	1222	14.2	8.8	6
1999	STL	Isaac Bruce	WR	77	120	64.20%	1165	15.1	9.7	12
2000	BAL	Shannon Sharpe	TE	67	105	63.80%	810	12.1	7.7	5
2001	NE	Troy Brown	WR	101	142	71.10%	1199	11.9	8.4	5
2002	TB	Keyshawn Johnson	WR	76	142	53.50%	1088	14.3	7.7	5
2003	NE	Deion Branch	WR	57	104	54.80%	803	14.1	7.7	3
2004	NE	David Givens	WR	56	106	52.80%	874	15.6	8.2	3
2005	PIT	Hines Ward	WR	69	114	60.50%	975	14.1	8.6	11
2006	IND	Marvin Harrison	WR	95	148	64.20%	1366	14.4	9.2	12
2007	NYG	Plaxico Burress	WR	70	141	49.60%	1025	14.6	7.3	12
2008	PIT	Hines Ward	WR	81	124	65.30%	1043	12.9	8.4	7
2009	NO	Marques Colston	WR	70	107	65.40%	1074	15.3	10	9
2010	GB	Greg Jennings	WR	76	125	60.80%	1265	16.6	10.1	12
2011	NYG	Victor Cruz	WR	82	131	62.60%	1536	18.7	11.7	9
2012	BAL	Anquan Boldin	WR	65	112	58.00%	921	14.2	8.2	4
2013	SEA	Golden Tate	WR	64	99	64.60%	898	14	9.1	5
2014	NE	Rob Gronkowski	TE	82	131	62.60%	1124	13.7	8.6	12
2015	DEN	Demaryius Thomas	WR	105	177	59.30%	1304	12.4	7.4	6
2016	NE	Julian Edelman	WR	98	159	61.60%	1106	11.3	7	3
1994-2016				79.4	129.6	61.00%	1131	14.4	8.7	8

Second Leading Receiver on Super Bowl Champions

Year	Team	Player	Position	Rec	Targets	Catch Rate	Rec Yds	Yds/Rec	Yds/Target	Rec TDs
1994	SF	Ricky Watters	RB	66	88	75.00%	719	10.9	8.2	5
1995	DAL	Jay Novacek	TE	62	90	68.90%	705	11.4	7.8	5
1996	GB	Don Beebe	WR	39	76	51.30%	699	17.9	9.2	4
1997	DEN	Shannon Sharpe	TE	72	114	63.20%	1107	15.4	9.7	3
1998	DEN	Ed McCaffrey	WR	64	99	64.60%	1053	16.5	10.6	10
1999	STL	Marshall Faulk	RB	87	103	84.50%	1048	12	10.2	5
2000	BAL	Qadry Ismail	WR	49	95	51.60%	655	13.4	6.9	5
2001	NE	David Patten	WR	51	94	54.30%	749	14.7	8	4
2002	TB	Kennan McCardell	WR	61	101	60.40%	670	11	6.6	6
2003	NE	David Givens	WR	34	54	63.00%	510	15	9.4	6
2004	NE	David Patton	WR	44	94	46.80%	800	18.2	8.5	7
2005	PIT	Antwaan Randle El	WR	35	69	50.70%	558	15.9	8.1	1
2006	IND	Reggie Wayne	WR	86	137	62.80%	1310	15.2	9.6	9
2007	NYG	Amani Toomer	WR	59	105	56.20%	760	12.9	7.2	3
2008	PIT	Santonio Holmes	WR	55	114	48.20%	821	14.9	7.2	5
2009	NO	Devery Henderson	WR	51	83	61.40%	804	15.8	9.7	2
2010	GB	James Jones	WR	50	87	57.50%	679	13.6	7.8	5
2011	NYG	Hakeem Nicks	WR	76	133	57.10%	1192	15.7	9	7
2012	BAL	Torrey Smith	WR	49	110	44.50%	855	17.4	7.8	8
2013	SEA	Doug Baldwin	WR	50	72	69.40%	778	15.6	10.8	5
2014	NE	Julian Edelman	WR	92	134	68.70%	972	10.6	7.3	4
2015	DEN	Emmanuel Sanders	WR	76	136	55.90%	1135	14.9	8.3	6
2016	NE	Martellus Bennett	TE	55	73	75.30%	701	12.7	9.6	7
1994-2016				59.3	98.3	60.50%	838.3	14.4	8.6	5.3

Third Leading Receiver on Super Bowl Champions

Year	Team	Player	Position	Rec	Targets	Catch Rate	Rec Yds	Yds/Rec	Yds/Target	Rec TDs
1994	SF	Brent Jones	TE	49	72	68.10%	670	13.7	9.3	9
1995	DAL	Kevin Williams	WR	38	67	56.70%	613	16.1	9.1	2
1996	GB	Keith Jackson	TE	40	63	63.50%	505	12.6	8	10
1997	DEN	Ed McCaffrey	WR	45	85	52.90%	590	13.1	6.9	8
1998	DEN	Shannon Sharpe	TE	64	107	59.80%	768	12	7.2	10
1999	STL	Torry Holt	WR	52	97	53.60%	788	15.2	8.1	6
2000	BAL	Jamal Lewis	RB	27	36	75.00%	296	11	8.2	0
2001	NE	Terry Glenn	WR	14	24	58.30%	204	14.6	8.5	1
2002	TB	Michael Pittman	RB	59	86	68.60%	477	8.1	5.5	0
2003	NE	Troy Brown	WR	40	60	66.70%	472	11.8	7.9	4
2004	NE	Deion Branch	WR	35	51	68.60%	454	13	8.9	4
2005	PIT	Heath Miller	TE	39	52	75.00%	459	11.8	8.8	6
2006	IND	Ben Utecht	RB/TE	37	53	69.80%	377	10.2	7.1	0
2007	NYG	Jeremy Shockey	TE	57	93	61.30%	619	10.9	6.7	3
2008	PIT	Nate Washington	WR	40	78	51.30%	631	15.8	8.1	3
2009	NO	Robert Meachem	WR	45	64	70.30%	722	16	11.3	9
2010	GB	Jordy Nelson	WR	45	64	70.30%	582	12.9	9.1	2
2011	NYG	Jake Ballard	TE	38	61	62.30%	604	15.9	9.9	4
2012	BAL	Dennis Pitta	TE	61	94	64.90%	669	11	7.1	7
2013	SEA	Zach Miller	TE	33	56	58.90%	387	11.7	6.9	5
2014	NE	Brandon LaFell	WR	74	119	62.20%	953	12.9	8	7
2015	DEN	Owen Daniels	TE	46	77	59.70%	517	11.2	6.7	3
2016	NE	Chris Hogan	WR	38	58	65.50%	680	17.9	11.7	4
1994-2016				44.2	70.3	63.60%	566.8	13	8.2	4.7

Fourth Leading Receivers on Super Bowl Champions

Year	Team	Player	Position	Rec	Targets	Catch Rate	Rec Yds	Yds/Rec	Yds/Target	Rec TDs
1994	SF	John Taylor	WR	41	64	64.10%	531	13	8.3	5
1995	DAL	Emmitt Smith	RB	62	78	79.50%	375	6	4.8	0
1996	GB	Mark Chmura	TE	28	48	58.30%	370	13.2	7.7	0
1997	DEN	Terrell Davis	RB	42	58	72.40%	287	6.8	4.9	0
1998	DEN	Terrell Davis	RB	25	38	65.80%	217	8.7	5.7	2
1999	STL	Az-Zahir Hakim	WR	36	56	64.30%	677	18.8	12.1	8
2000	BAL	Travis Taylor	WR	28	54	51.90%	276	9.9	5.1	3
2001	NE	Antowain Smith	RB	19	28	67.90%	192	10.1	6.9	1
2002	TB	Joe Jurevicius	WR	37	52	71.20%	423	11.4	8.1	4
2003	NE	Kevin Faulk	RB	48	67	71.60%	440	9.2	6.6	0
2004	NE	Daniel Graham	TE	30	48	62.50%	364	12.1	7.6	7
2005	PIT	Cedrick Wilson	WR	26	53	49.10%	451	17.3	8.5	0
2006	IND	Dallas Clark	TE	30	57	52.60%	367	12.2	6.4	4
2007	NYG	Sinorice Moss	WR	21	37	56.80%	225	10.7	6.1	0
2008	PIT	Heath Miller	TE	48	66	72.70%	514	10.7	7.8	3
2009	NO	Jeremy Shockey	TE	48	67	71.60%	569	11.9	8.5	3
2010	GB	Donald Driver	WR	51	85	60.00%	565	11.1	6.6	4
2011	NYG	Mario Manningham	WR	39	77	50.60%	523	13.4	6.8	4
2012	BAL	Ray Rice	RB	61	83	73.50%	478	7.8	5.8	1
2013	SEA	Jermaine Kearse	WR	22	38	57.90%	346	15.7	9.1	4
2014	NE	Shane Vereen	RB	52	77	67.50%	447	8.6	5.8	3
2015	DEN	Jordan Norwood	WR	22	32	68.80%	207	9.4	6.5	0
2016	NE	James White	RB	60	86	69.80%	551	9.2	6.4	5
1994-2016				38.1	58.7	64.40%	408.5	11.2	7	2.7

351

Fifth Leading Receivers on Super Bowl Champions

Year	Team	Player	Position	Rec	Targets	Catch Rate	Rec Yds	Yds/Rec	Yds/Target	Rec TDs
1994	SF	Nate Singleton	WR	21	28	75.00%	294	14	10.5	2
1995	DAL	Daryl Johnston	FB	30	46	65.20%	248	8.3	5.4	1
1996	GB	Robert Brooks	WR	23	41	56.10%	344	15	8.4	4
1997	DEN	Willie Green	WR	19	43	44.20%	240	12.6	5.6	2
1998	DEN	Willie Green	WR	16	25	64.00%	194	12.1	7.8	1
1999	STL	Ricky Proehl	WR	33	49	67.30%	349	10.6	7.1	0
2000	BAL	Priest Holmes	RB	32	46	69.60%	221	6.9	4.8	0
2001	NE	Kevin Faulk	RB	30	36	83.30%	189	6.3	5.3	2
2002	TB	Ken Dilger	TE	34	48	70.80%	329	9.7	6.9	2
2003	NE	Daniel Graham	TE	38	63	60.30%	409	10.8	6.5	4
2004	NE	Kevin Faulk	RB	26	30	86.70%	248	9.5	8.3	1
2005	PIT	Willie Parker	RB	18	24	75.00%	218	12.1	9.1	1
2006	IND	Joseph Addai	RB	40	50	80.00%	325	8.1	6.5	1
2007	NYG	Derrick Ward	RB	26	40	65.00%	179	6.9	4.5	1
2008	PIT	Mewelde Moore	RB	40	53	75.50%	320	8	6	1
2009	NO	David Thomas	FB/TE	35	48	72.90%	356	10.2	7.4	1
2010	GB	Brandon Jackson	RB	43	50	86.00%	342	8	6.8	1
2011	NYG	Ahmad Bradshaw	RB	34	44	77.30%	267	7.9	6.1	2
2012	BAL	Jacoby Jones	WR	30	55	54.50%	406	13.5	7.4	1
2013	SEA	Marshawn Lynch	RB	36	44	81.80%	316	8.8	7.2	2
2014	NE	Tim Wright	TE	26	33	78.80%	259	10	7.8	6
2015	DEN	Bennie Fowler	WR	16	25	64.00%	203	12.7	8.1	0
2016	NE	Rob Gronkowski	TE	25	38	65.80%	540	21.6	14.2	3
1994-2016				29.2	41.7	70.40%	295.5	10.6	7.3	1.7

Offensive Playoff Stats

Year	Team	Total Pts	/Gm	1st Ds	/Gm	Total Yds	/Gm	Pass Yds	/Gm	Rush Yds	/Gm	Turnovers	/Gm
1994	SF	131	43.7	74	24.7	1079	359.7	656	218.7	423	141	2	0.7
1995	DAL	95	31.7	63	21	1070	356.7	692	230.7	378	126	1	0.3
1996	GB	100	33.3	53	17.7	1012	337.3	557	185.7	455	151.7	3	1
1997	DEN	111	27.8	88	22	1430	357.5	682	170.5	748	187	8	2
1998	DEN	95	31.7	60	20	1212	404	663	221	549	183	1	0.3
1999	STL	83	27.7	63	21	1150	383.3	1039	346.3	111	37	6	2
2000	BAL	95	23.8	44	11	900	225	508	127	392	98	2	0.5
2001	NE	60	20	52	17.3	891	297	623	207.7	268	89.3	1	0.3
2002	TB	106	35.3	60	20	1002	334	682	227.3	320	106.7	4	1.3
2003	NE	73	24.3	67	22.3	1127	375.7	792	264	335	111.7	4	1.3
2004	NE	85	28.3	60	20	978	326	530	176.7	448	149.3	1	0.3
2005	PIT	107	26.8	74	18.5	1338	334.5	811	202.8	527	131.8	4	1
2006	IND	105	26.3	99	24.8	1581	395.3	977	244.3	604	151	9	2.3
2007	NYG	85	21.3	73	18.3	1222	305.5	807	201.8	415	103.8	2	0.5
2008	PIT	85	28.3	53	17.7	909	303	634	211.3	275	91.7	2	0.7
2009	NO	107	35.7	62	20.7	1007	335.7	717	239	290	96.7	1	0.3
2010	GB	121	30.3	86	21.5	1445	361.3	1041	260.3	404	101	5	1.3
2011	NYG	102	25.5	84	21	1610	402.5	1144	286	466	116.5	1	0.3
2012	BAL	124	31	85	21.3	1641	410.3	1102	275.5	539	134.8	4	1
2013	SEA	89	29.7	44	14.7	926	308.7	502	167.3	424	141.3	1	0.3
2014	NE	108	36	82	27.3	1196	398.7	948	316	248	82.7	4	1.3
2015	DEN	67	22.3	42	14	762	254	464	154.7	298	99.3	3	1
2016	NE	104	34.7	83	27.7	1354	451.3	1095	365	259	86.3	5	1.7
	Avg	97.3	29.4	67.4	20.2	1167	348.6	768.1	230.4	399	118.1	3.2	0.9

Defensive Playoff Stats

Year	Team	Total Pts	/Gm	1st Ds	/Gm	Total Yds	/Gm	Pass Yds	/Gm	Rush Yds	/Gm	Takeaways	/Gm
1994	SF	69	23	69	23	1052	350.7	847	282.3	205	68.3	10	3.3
1995	DAL	53	17.7	55	18.3	865	288.3	640	213.3	225	75	6	2
1996	GB	48	16	40	13.3	704	234.7	548	182.7	156	52	12	4
1997	DEN	72	18	76	19	1244	311	861	215.3	383	95.8	9	2.3
1998	DEN	32	10.7	53	17.7	959	319.7	800	266.7	159	53	13	4.3
1999	STL	59	19.7	66	22	1045	348.3	722	240.7	323	107.7	5	1.7
2000	BAL	23	5.8	55	13.8	837	209.3	579	144.8	258	64.5	12	3
2001	NE	47	15.7	63	21	963	321	738	246	225	75	7	2.3
2002	TB	37	12.3	45	15	809	269.7	648	216	161	53.7	13	4.3
2003	NE	57	19	54	18	977	325.7	703	234.3	274	91.3	7	2.3
2004	NE	51	17	61	20.3	1033	344.3	779	259.7	254	84.7	11	3.7
2005	PIT	62	15.5	70	17.5	1336	334	960	240	376	94	7	1.8
2006	IND	65	16.3	48	12	954	238.5	623	155.8	331	82.8	13	3.3
2007	NYG	65	16.3	78	19.5	1145	286.3	849	212.3	296	74	7	1.8
2008	PIT	61	20.3	51	17	895	298.3	774	258	121	40.3	8	2.7
2009	NO	59	19.7	69	23	1266	422	901	300.3	365	121.7	8	2.7
2010	GB	76	19	69	17.3	1234	308.5	899	224.8	335	83.8	11	2.8
2011	NYG	56	14	75	18.8	1312	328	868	217	444	111	7	1.8
2012	BAL	88	22	106	26.5	1713	428.3	1146	286.5	567	141.8	10	2.5
2013	SEA	40	13.3	59	19.7	1023	341	727	242.3	296	98.7	8	2.7
2014	NE	62	20.7	65	21.7	1033	344.3	652	217.3	381	127	6	2
2015	DEN	44	14.7	57	19	1047	349	800	266.7	247	82.3	7	2.3
2016	NE	61	20.3	53	17.7	1014	338	751	250.3	263	87.7	6	2
Avg		56	16.8	62.5	18.7	1063.5	319.1	774.6	233.6	288.9	85.5	8.8	2.7

Super Bowl Quarterback Playoff Stats

Year	Team	Player	Cmp	Att	Cmp%	Yds	YPA	Yds/G	TD	INT	Carries	Rush Yds	YPC	YPG	R TDs
1994	SF	Steve Young	53	87	60.9%	623	7.2	207.7	9	0	20	128	6.4	42.7	2
1995	DAL	Troy Aikman	53	80	66.3%	717	9	239	4	1	8	6	0.8	2	0
1996	GB	Brett Favre	44	71	62.0%	617	8.7	205.7	5	1	14	35	2.5	11.7	1
1997	DEN	John Elway	56	96	58.3%	726	7.6	181.5	3	2	9	25	2.8	6.3	1
1998	DEN	John Elway	45	86	52.3%	691	8	230.3	3	1	9	34	3.8	11.3	1
1999	STL	Kurt Warner	77	121	63.6%	1063	8.8	354.3	8	4	6	3	0.5	1	0
2000	BAL	Trent Dilfer	35	73	47.9%	590	8.1	147.5	3	1	13	7	0.5	1.8	0
2001	NE	Tom Brady	60	97	61.9%	572	5.9	190.7	1	1	8	22	2.8	7.3	1
2002	TB	Brad Johnson	53	98	54.1%	670	6.8	223.3	5	3	8	13	1.6	4.3	0
2003	NE	Tom Brady	75	126	59.5%	792	6.3	264	5	2	12	18	1.5	6	0
2004	NE	Tom Brady	55	81	67.9%	587	7.2	195.7	5	0	7	3	0.4	1	1
2005	PIT	Ben Roethlisberger	58	93	62.4%	803	8.6	200.8	7	3	19	37	1.9	9.3	2
2006	IND	Peyton Manning	97	153	63.4%	1034	6.8	258.5	3	7	8	3	0.4	0.8	1
2007	NYG	Eli Manning	72	119	60.5%	854	7.2	213.5	6	1	8	10	1.3	2.5	0
2008	PIT	Ben Roethlisberger	54	89	60.7%	692	7.8	230.7	3	1	5	0	0	0	0
2009	NO	Drew Brees	72	102	70.6%	732	7.2	244	8	0	5	-4	-0.8	-1.3	0
2010	GB	Aaron Rodgers	90	132	68.2%	1094	8.3	273.5	9	2	14	54	3.9	13.5	2
2011	NYG	Eli Manning	106	163	65.0%	1219	7.5	304.8	9	1	8	20	2.5	5	0
2012	BAL	Joe Flacco	73	126	57.9%	1140	9	285	11	0	8	16	2	4	0
2013	SEA	Russell Wilson	43	68	63.2%	524	7.7	174.7	3	0	11	42	3.8	14	0
2014	NE	Tom Brady	93	135	68.9%	921	6.8	307	10	4	11	10	0.9	3.3	1
2015	DEN	Peyton Manning	51	92	55.4%	539	5.9	179.7	2	1	5	10	2	3.3	0
2016	NE	Tom Brady	93	142	65.5%	1137	8	379	7	3	9	13	1.4	4.3	0
		Averages	65.6	105.7	61.6%	797.3	7.6	238.7	5.6	1.7	9.8	22	1.9	6.7	0.6
		1994-2008	59.1	98	60.1%	735.4	7.6	222.9	4.7	1.9	10.3	22.9	1.8	7.2	0.7
		2009-2016	77.6	120	64.3%	913.3	7.5	268.4	7.4	1.4	8.9	20.1	2	5.8	0.4

Playoff Turnover Ratio

Year	Team	Turnovers	Takeaways	Turnover Ratio
1994	SF	2	10	8
1995	DAL	1	6	5
1996	GB	3	12	9
1997	DEN	8	9	1
1998	DEN	1	13	12
1999	STL	6	5	-1
2000	BAL	2	12	10
2001	NE	1	7	6
2002	TB	4	13	9
2003	NE	4	7	3
2004	NE	1	11	10
2005	PIT	4	7	3
2006	IND	9	13	4
2007	NYG	2	7	5
2008	PIT	2	8	6
2009	NO	1	8	7
2010	GB	5	11	6
2011	NYG	1	7	6
2012	BAL	4	10	6
2013	SEA	1	8	7
2014	NE	4	6	2
2015	DEN	3	7	4
2016	NE	5	6	1
	Total	74	203	129
	Average	3.2	8.8	5.6

Works Cited

Chapter 1

1. Vensel, Matt. "A Few Thoughts on Yesterday's Anquan Boldin Trade." *Baltimoresun.com*, 12 Mar. 2013, www.baltimoresun.com/sports/baltimore-sports-blog/bal-sports-blitz-ravens-anquan-boldin-trade-20130312-story.html.
2. Fitzgerald, Jason. "Sam Bradford Contract Details." *Over the Cap*, overthecap.com/player/sam-bradford/1349/.
3. Pirsig, Robert M. "Chapter 18." *Zen and the Art of Motorcycle Maintenance*, Harper Collins, 1974, pp. 283–283.
4. Holiday, Ryan. *Ego Is the Enemy*. Portfolio, 2016.
5. Add chapter (and page if applicable) for Belichick reference
6. Keri, Jonah. *The Extra 2%: How Wall Street Strategies Took a Major League Baseball Team from Worst to First*. Ballantine Books, 2011.
7. Find Page
8. Fleming, David. "Why Paul DePodesta Is Bringing Moneyball to the Browns." *ESPN*, ESPN Internet Ventures, 11 Apr. 2016, www.espn.com/nfl/story/_/id/15159159/why-paul-depodesta-bringing-moneyball-browns.
9. Reiter, Ben. "Astro-Matic Baseball." *Sports Illustrated Longform*, 30 June 2014, www.si.com/longform/astros/index.html.
10. Klemko, Robert. "How NFL Quarterbacks Are Made." *SI.com*, 11 May 2016, www.si.com/0mmqb/2016/05/11/nfl-draft-quarterbacks-how-modern-qbs-are-made-jared-goff-carson-wentz.
11. Pirsig, Robert M. "Chapter 6." *Zen and the Art of Motorcycle Maintenance*, Harper Collins, 1974, pp. 85–86.

Chapter 2

1. Pirsig, Robert M. "Lila: An Inquiry Into Morals." *Lila: An Inquiry Into Morals*, Alma Books, 2011.
2. Thiel, Peter, and Blake Masters. *Zero to One: Notes on Startups, or How to Build the Future*. Virgin Books, 2015.
3. Gosselin, Rick. "Gosselin: Jimmy Johnson Had SB Wins, Great Draft-Day Skills; Why He's Still a Longshot for HOF." *SportsDay*, 24 Jan. 2015,

sportsday.dallasnews.com/dallas-cowboys/rickgosselin/2015/01/24/gosselin-jimmy-johnson-had-sb-wins-great-draft-day-skills-why-he-s-still-a-longshot-for-hof.

4. Vrentas, Jenny. "On The Hunt For Greatness." *SI.com*, 6 Nov. 2015, www.si.com/mmqb/2015/11/05/mmqb-talking-football-coaches-fired-jed-hughes-nfl-headhunter.

5. "Great GMs Are Made, Not Born." *Korn Ferry*, 10 Sept. 2015, www.kornferry.com/institute/great-gms-are-made-not-born?reports-and-insights.

6. Holiday, Ryan. *Ego Is the Enemy*. Portfolio, 2016.

Chapter 3

1. Jenkins, Sally. *The Real All Americans*. Anchor, 2008.

2. Benedict, Jeff, and Armen Keteyian. *The System: The Glory and Scandal of Big Time College Football*. Doubleday, 2013.

3. "Assessing Risk and Living Without a Rope – Lessons from Alex Honnold." Created by Tim Ferriss, performance by Alex Honnold, season The Tim Ferriss Show, 17 May 2016.

4. Lavin, James. *Management Secrets of the New England Patriots*. Pointer Press, 2005.

5. La Canfora, Jason, and Nunyo Demasio. "Team's Cap May Come to a Head." *The Washington Post*, WP Company, 18 July 2004, www.washingtonpost.com/wp-dyn/articles/A58013-2004Jul17.html.

6. Bechta, Jack. "Are NFL Scouting Departments Underfunded?" *National Football Post*, 12 Apr. 2011, www.nationalfootballpost.com/are-nfl-scouting-departments-underfunded/.

7. Brandt, Andrew. "While They Squabble, the Billions Pour In." *SI.com*, 30 July 2015, www.si.com/mmqb/2015/07/29/tom-brady-appeal-packers-financial-report-nfl-prosperity.

8. "The NFL Draft: Introducing the next Wave of NFL Superstars." *NFL Operations*, operations.nfl.com/the-players/the-nfl-draft/.

9. Hickey, Mike. "Painstaking Task of Finding Right Players for Jets to Pick." *The New York Times*, The New York Times, 23 Apr. 1983, www.nytimes.com/1983/04/24/sports/painstaking-task-of-finding-right-players-for-jets-to-pick.html.

10. Mink, Ryan. "The Caw: Why Ravens Scouts Find Gems ." *BaltimoreRavens.com*, 8 May 2013, www.baltimoreravens.com/news/article-1/The-Caw-Why-Ravens-Scouts-Find-Gems/b96ab6a6-6a10-4f64-868c-9edb638379ae.

11. "Draft Pick Trade Value Chart." *Pro-Football-Reference.com*, www.pro-football-reference.com/draft/draft_trade_value.htm.

12. McManamon, Pat. "Carson Wentz Trade Gave Browns Nine Players, Two More Future Picks."*ESPN*, ESPN Internet Ventures, 30 Apr. 2017, www.espn.com/blog/cleveland-browns/post/_/id/22138/carson-wentz-trade-gave-browns-nine-players-and-future-first-and-second-round-picks.

13. Fitzgerald, Jason. "Thoughts on the Cleveland Browns." *Over the Cap*, 25 Oct. 2017, overthecap.com/thoughts-cleveland-browns/.

Chapter 4

1. Keri, Jonah. *The Extra 2%: How Wall Street Strategies Took a Major League Baseball Team from Worst to First*. Ballantine Books, 2011.

2. "Packers Sign Rodgers through '14; Deal Worth More than $66M, Source Says." *ESPN*, ESPN Internet Ventures, 2 Nov. 2008, www.espn.com/nfl/news/story?id=3675543.

3. Breer, Albert. "What Went Wrong in Washington." *SI.com*, 16 Mar. 2017, www.si.com/mmqb/2017/03/16/washington-redskins-nfl-dysfunction-scot-mccloughan-dan-snyder-bruce-allen.

4. Holley, Michael. *Belichick and Brady: Two Men, the Patriots, and How They Revolutionized Football*. Hachette Books, 2016.

5. Schatz, Aaron. *Football Outsiders Almanac 2016*. Football Outsiders, 2016.

6. Holley, Michael. *Belichick and Brady: Two Men, the Patriots, and How They Revolutionized Football*. Hachette Books, 2016.

7. Kirby, Alex, and Bill Belichick. *The Big Book of Belichick: His Thoughts on Strategy, Fundamentals & History*. CreateSpace Independent Publishing Platform, 2016.

8. Fitzgerald, Jason. "Explaining Free Agent and Contract Terms." *Over the Cap*, 11 Feb. 2016, overthecap.com/explaining-free-agent-and-contract-terms/.

9. Holley, Michael. *Belichick and Brady: Two Men, the Patriots, and How They Revolutionized Football*. Hachette Books, 2016.

Chapter 5

1. Schatz, Aaron. *Football Outsiders Almanac 2016*. Football Outsiders, 2016.

2. Bedard, Greg. "Memorial Day and Football." *SI*.com, 24 May 2015, www.si.com/2015/05/24/memorial-day-nfl-veterans-tom-braady-deflategate.

3. Fitzgerald, Jason. "Thoughts on the Matt Stafford $135 Million Contract." *Over the Cap*, 29 Aug. 2017, overthecap.com/thoughts-matt-stafford-135-million-contract/.

4. Drummond, Rick. "Arrival of the PFF Signature Stats!" *Arrival of the PFF*

Signature Stats! | PFF News & Analysis | Pro Football Focus, 15 Aug. 2011, www.profootballfocus.com/news/arrival-of-the-pff-signature-stats.

5. Barnwell, Bill. "NFL Quality of Play Isn't Worse (but Colin Kaepernick Might Make It Better)."*ESPN*, ESPN Internet Ventures, 18 Sept. 2017, www.espn.com/nfl/story/_/page/Barnwellx170918/nfl-quality-play-worse-2017-colin-kaepernick-make-better.

6. Klemko, Robert. "How NFL Quarterbacks Are Made." *SI.com*, 11 May 2016, www.si.com/0mmqb/2016/05/11/nfl-draft-quarterbacks-how-modern-qbs-are-made-jared-goff-carson-wentz.

7. Korte, Nick. "2016 Cap And Roster Texture Overview." *Over the Cap*, 6 Sept. 2016, overthecap.com/2016-cap-roster-texture-overview/.

8. Monson, Sam. "Why Eagles DE Brandon Graham Is Underrated." *Pro Football Focus*, 7 Feb. 2017, www.profootballfocus.com/news/pro-why-eagles-de-brandon-graham-is-underrated.

9. Renck, Troy E. "Brock Osweiler Agrees to Four-Year Deal with Houston Texans." *The Denver Post*, The Denver Post, 14 Apr. 2016, www.denverpost.com/2016/03/09/brock-osweiler-agrees-to-four-year-deal-with-houston-texans/.

Chapter 6

1. Schatz, Aaron. *Football Outsiders Almanac 2016*. Football Outsiders, 2016.

2. Armstrong, Jim. "2016 Offensive Drive Stats." *Football Outsiders*, 2 Jan. 2017, www.footballoutsiders.com/stats/drivestatsoff2016.

3. Stuart, Chase. "Le'Veon Bell Is The Most Dominant Player In The NFL." *FiveThirtyEight*, 15 Dec. 2016, fivethirtyeight.com/features/leveon-bell-is-the-most-dominant-player-in-the-nfl/.

4. "PFF Elite with NFL Signature Stats; Breakaway Percentage." *PFF Elite Subscription*, Pro Football Focus, www.profootballfocus.com/nfl/elite/stats/running-back/breakaway-percent.

5. Clark, Kevin. "The Near-Perfect Football Team." *The Ringer*, 7 Aug. 2017, www.theringer.com/nfl/2017/8/7/16107814/2007-new-england-patriots-tom-brady-randy-moss-wes-welker.

6. "PFF Elite with NFL Signature Stats; Wide Receiver Rating." *PFF Elite Subscription*, Pro Football Focus, www.profootballfocus.com/nfl/elite/stats/wide-receiver/rating#tools.

Chapter 7

1. Tucker, Ross. "Measuring Beyond Girth." *SI.com*, 6 Mar. 2014,

www.si.com/2014/03/06/nfl-offensive-linemen-grades.

2. Schatz, Aaron. "NFL's Best, Worst O-Lines: Where Do Cowboys and Seahawks Rank?"*ABC News*, ABC News Network, 15 Dec. 2016, abcnews.go.com/Sports/nfls-best-worst-lines-cowboys-seahawks-rank/story?id=44212949.

3. Joyner, KC, and Jim McCormick. "Week 2 Start or Sit: Answering Your Fantasy Football Lineup Questions." *ESPN*, ESPN Internet Ventures, 17 Sept. 2016, www.espn.in/fantasy/football/story/_/id/17572066/fantasy-football-start-sit-advice-espn-experts-nfl-week-2.

4. Gonzalez, Alden. "Numbers Say Todd Gurley Missed Holes in 2016." *ESPN*, ESPN Internet Ventures, 22 June 2017, www.espn.com/blog/nflnation/post/_/id/239607/numbers-say-todd-gurley-missed-holes-in-2016.

5. Joyner, KC. "Chat with KC Joyner." *ESPN*, ESPN Internet Ventures, www.espn.com/sportsnation/chat/_/id/39408/football-scientist-kc-joyner.

6. Miller, Matt. "A Scout's Guide to Grading Offensive Linemen." *Bleacher Report*, 22 Feb. 2012, bleacherreport.com/articles/1076624-a-scouts-guide-to-grading-offensive-linemen.

7. Dalek, Brian. "The Evolution of the Football Player." *Men's Health*, 26 Nov. 2013, www.menshealth.com/fitness/the-evolution-of-the-football-player.

8. Thorne, Brandon. "Under the Microscope: Ali Marpet." *Inside The Pylon*, 19 Dec. 2016, insidethepylon.com/nfl/2016/12/19/microscope-ali-marpet/.

9. Dubin, Jared. "Tom Brady Is NFL's Quickest Draw and It's Paying off for the 3-0 Patriots."*CBSSports.com*, 28 Sept. 2015, www.cbssports.com/nfl/news/tom-brady-is-nfls-quickest-draw-and-its-paying-off-for-the-3-0-patriots/.

10. Chief, Western. "What Stats Tells Us about the Draft by Round." *Arrowhead Pride*, 20 Feb. 2015, www.arrowheadpride.com/2015/2/20/8072877/what-the-statistics-tell-us-about-the-draft-by-round.

Chapter 8

1. Dubin, Jared. "Here's Why the Nickel Defense Is the New Base Defense in the NFL."*CBSSports.com*, 4 Apr. 2016, www.cbssports.com/nfl/news/heres-why-the-nickel-defense-is-the-new-base-defense-in-the-nfl/.

2. Farrar, Doug. "NFL1000: Where Does Jabrill Peppers Fit in the NFL?" *Bleacher Report*, Bleacher Report, 12 Apr. 2017, bleacherreport.com/articles/2701019-nfl1000-where-does-jabrill-peppers-fit-in-the-nfl.

3. Keri, Jonah. *The Extra 2%: How Wall Street Strategies Took a Major League Baseball Team from Worst to First*. Ballantine Books, 2011.

4. Monson, Sam. "Ranking the NFL's 15 Best Edge Rushers in the 2016

Season." *Ranking the NFL's 15 Best Edge Rushers in the 2016 Season*, 10 Feb. 2017, www.profootballfocus.com/news/pro-ranking-the-nfls-15-best-pass-rushers-in-the-2016-season.

5. Curran, Tom E. "Patriots Still Reaping Rewards from Seymour Deal." *NBC Sports Boston*, 27 Apr. 2015, www.nbcsports.com/boston/new-england-patriots/patriots-still-reaping-rewards-seymour-deal.

6. Elsayed, Khaled. "Defensive Signature Stats." *Defensive Signature Stats*, 6 Jan. 2012, www.profootballfocus.com/news/defensive-signature-stats.

7. Rodak, Mike. "How Losing Stephon Gilmore Helped Bills Build a Winning Secondary." *ESPN*, ESPN Internet Ventures, 4 Oct. 2017, www.espn.com/blog/afceast/post/_/id/85084/how-losing-stephon-gilmore-helped-bills-build-a-winning-secondary.

8. Monson, Sam. "What Makes Damon Harrison the League's Best Run-Stuffer." *Pro Football Focus*, 26 Jan. 2017, www.profootballfocus.com/news/pro-what-makes-damon-harrison-the-leagues-best-run-stuffer.

9. Monson, Sam. "PFF's Award for Best Run Defender: Damon Harrison No. 1." *Pro Football Focus*, 13 Jan. 2016, www.profootballfocus.com/news/pro-pff-awards-2015-ted-washington-award.

10. Mays, Robert. "Give Devin McCourty His Due." *The Ringer*, 13 Jan. 2017, www.theringer.com/2017/1/13/16038134/devin-mccourty-new-england-patriots-nfl-playoffs-5064233dd534.

11. "PFF Elite with NFL Signature Stats; Linebackers." *Pro Football Focus* , www.profootballfocus.com/nfl/elite/stats/linebacker/run-stop-percent#tools.

Chapter 9

1. Schatz, Aaron. *Football Outsiders Almanac 2016*. Football Outsiders, 2016.

2. Gasper, Christopher L. "Three Good Reasons Why the Patriots Win the Close Ones."*BostonGlobe.com*, The Boston Globe, 18 Nov. 2015, www.bostonglobe.com/sports/2015/11/18/gasper/w1NUX9lpY7ofI476QzA5PM/story.html.

3. Monson, Sam. "Ranking All 32 NFL Offensive Lines This Season." *Pro Football Focus*, Pro Football Focus, 11 Jan. 2017, www.profootballfocus.com/news/pro-ranking-all-32-nfl-offensive-lines-this-season.

4. Gosselin, Rick. "Rick Gosselin's 2016 NFL Special Teams Rankings: See How High Cowboys Jumped, Which NFC East Team's No. 1 in the League." *SportsDay*, The Dallas Morning News, 15 Feb. 2017, sportsday.dallasnews.com/dallas-cowboys/cowboys/2017/02/15/rick-gosselins-2016-nfl-special-teams-rankings-see-high-cowboys-jumped-nfc-east-teams-1-league.

5. Jones, Johnathan. "Why NFL Playoff Teams Need to Kneel for the Touchback Whenever Possible." *SI.com*, Sports Illustrated, 5 Jan. 2017, www.si.com/nfl/2017/01/06/nfl-playoffs-2017-touchback-rule-change-impact.

6. Ballard, Kurt. "Even With Rule Changes, Touchbacks Have Yet To Increase." *The Harvard Sports Analysis Collective*, 21 Sept. 2016, harvardsportsanalysis.org/2016/09/even-with-rule-changes-touchbacks-have-yet-to-increase/.

7. Klemko, Robert. "The Unfair Catch: How NFL Return Men Became an Endangered Species."*SI.com*, Sports Illustrated, 15 Dec. 2016, www.si.com/mmqb/2016/12/15/nfl-kick-punt-returns-have-become-endangered-species.

8. McGuinness, Gordon. "The Best Special Teamers in the NFL in 2016." *Pro Football Focus*, Pro Football Focus, 12 Jan. 2017, www.profootballfocus.com/news/pro-the-best-special-teamers-in-the-nfl-in-2016.

9. Kirby, Alex, and Bill Belichick. *The Big Book of Belichick: His Thoughts on Strategy, Fundamentals & History*. CreateSpace Independent Publishing Platform, 2016.

10. Seifert, Kevin. "Sam Koch Has Changed the Punting Game -- and Almost No One Noticed."*ESPN*, ESPN Internet Ventures, 15 Dec. 2015, www.espn.com/blog/nflnation/post/_/id/191948/sam-koch-has-changed-the-punting-game-and-almost-no-one-noticed.

11. Wagner, James. "How to Kick Australian." *The Wall Street Journal*, Dow Jones & Company, 29 Aug. 2008, www.wsj.com/articles/SB121997626577982327.

12. Brown, Chris B. *The Essential Smart Football*. CreateSpace, 2012.

13. Pattani, Alok. "Expected Points and EPA Explained." *ESPN*, ESPN Internet Ventures, 15 Sept. 2012, www.espn.com/nfl/story/_/id/8379024/nfl-explaining-expected-points-metric.

14. Zodda, Chuck. "The Case for Britton Colquitt as Super Bowl MVP." *Inside The Pylon*, 16 Feb. 2016, insidethepylon.com/film-study/film-study-nfl/special-teams-film-study-nfl/2016/02/16/the-case-for-britton-colquitt-as-super-bowl-mvp/.

15. Cosentino, Dom. "Johnny Hekker Is The Punter Every Punter Wants To Be." *Deadspin*, Deadspin.com, 9 Dec. 2016, deadspin.com/johnny-hekker-is-the-punter-every-punter-wants-to-be-1789931094.

16. Gagnon, Brad. "Why Johnny Hekker Goes to the Pro Bowl as the Most Dominant Punter Ever." *The Guardian*, Guardian News and Media, 25 Jan. 2017, www.theguardian.com/sport/2017/jan/25/johnny-hekker-rams-pro-bowl-punter-nfl.

17. Kirby, Alex. *The Big Book of Saban: The Philosophy, Strategy & Leadership Style of Nick Saban*. CreateSpace Independent Publishing Platform, 2016.

1. La Canfora, Jason, and Nunyo Demasio. "Team's Cap May Come to a Head." *The Washington Post*, WP Company, 18 July 2004, www.washingtonpost.com/wp-dyn/articles/A58013-2004Jul17.html.

2. Fitzgerald, Jason, and Vijay Natarajan. *Crunching Numbers: An Inside Look at the Salary Cap and Negotiating Player Contracts*. Self Published, 2016.

3. Volin, Ben. "Now More than Ever, We Realize NFL Owners Won." *BostonGlobe.com*, The Boston Globe, 21 July 2013, www.bostonglobe.com/sports/2013/07/20/nfl-owners-destroyed-players-cba-negotiations/ia3c1ydpS16H5FhFEiviHP/story.html.

4. Fitzgerald, Jason. "Drafting Decisions and the Salary Cap 2016." *Over the Cap*, 22 Apr. 2016, overthecap.com/drafting-decisions-salary-cap-2016/.

5. One.Cool.Customer. "2010-2015 NFL Drafts: Team-By-Team Draft Success In First Three Rounds." *Blogging The Boys*, SB Nation, 2 Mar. 2016, www.bloggingtheboys.com/2016/3/2/11145156/2010-2015-nfl-drafts-team-by-team-draft-success-in-first-three-rounds.

6. Brandt, Andrew. "The Fine Print of NFL Rookie Contracts." *SI.com*, Sports Illustrated, 16 May 2017, www.si.com/mmqb/2017/05/16/nfl-rookie-contracts-fine-print.

7. Fitzgerald, Jason. "Drafting Decisions and the Salary Cap 2016 - Page 2." *Over the Cap*, 22 Apr. 2016, overthecap.com/drafting-decisions-salary-cap-2016/2/.

8. Gaines, Cork, and Mike Nudelman. "Why the NCAA May Eventually Be Forced to Pay Some Student Athletes, in One Chart." *Business Insider*, Business Insider, 24 Nov. 2017, www.businessinsider.com/college-football-player-value-2017-11.

9. Beaton, Andrew. "How Much Is Your College Football Team Worth?" *The Wall Street Journal*, Dow Jones & Company, 21 Sept. 2017, www.wsj.com/articles/how-much-is-your-college-football-team-worth-1506000030.

10. Klemko, Robert. "Lousy Football? Blame Newly Re-Elected DeMaurice Smith and the NFLPA." *SI.com*, Sports Illustrated, 21 Sept. 2017, www.si.com/2017/09/20/demaurice-smith-reelected-bad-football.

11. Chief, Western. "What Stats Tells Us about the Draft by Round." *Arrowhead Pride*, 20 Feb. 2015, www.arrowheadpride.com/2015/2/20/8072877/what-the-statistics-tell-us-about-the-draft-by-round.

Zack Moore is a former college football player at the University of Rhode Island where he majored in communications and minored in business. He received his MBA from Rutgers Business School and has written for Over The Cap since 2014. He is the first person to start writing about percentage of the salary cap, which is the only way to understand and analyze salary cap data across years. He is also an NFLPA Certified Player Agent. Zack's research has appeared on various platforms including Sports Illustrated, Bleacher Report, USA Today, and the NFL Network. He has also met with NFL teams to discuss the data and theories in this book.

Author Bio

50443919R10201